METACONTENT

META
CONTENT

The intellectual substrates for sense-making

ASHKAN TASHVIR

Best-selling author of BEING, HUMAN BEING

engenesis

First published 2024 by Engenesis Publications

Copyright © Ashkan Tashvir 2024

Ashkan Tashvir asserts the moral right to be identified
as the author of *METACONTENT* and all associated products.

ISBN 978-1-922433-16-9 Paperback (Australian Print)
ISBN 978-1-922433-17-6 Hardcover (POD)
ISBN 978-1-922433-18-3 Paperback (POD)
ISBN 978-1-922433-19-0 EPUB
ISBN 978-1-922433-20-6 Audio book

publications.engenesis.com

A catalogue record for this
book is available from the
National Library of Australia

NATIONAL
LIBRARY
OF AUSTRALIA

Edited by Phaedra Pym – awaywithwords.net.au

Cover design by Odette Abrenica

Book design and production by Eric and Thymen Hoek – exlibris.com.au

This book is dedicated to the dreamers and outliers
who challenge the status quo, the ones who dare
to dance on the edge of what is known and deemed possible;
to the truth-seekers who carve clarity from the shadows;
to those who have the courage to make 'The Invisible' visible
and see through the darkness of uncertainties
to turn the improbable into possibilities;
and to those whose integrity and magnanimity
make life more bearable and worth living.

Acknowledgements

The path less travelled is often fraught with thorns. But it is also where the wildflowers of innovation bloom. This journey, steeped in the trials of authenticity, was not one of conformity. Like a lone wolf howling at the indifferent moon, this book stands against the tide of convention.

In the silent hours, where shadows dance with the dawn, this work was birthed from the furnace of passion and dedication and crafted from the raw threads of perseverance. To those who walked beside me, both seen and unseen, your presence was the lantern guiding my way through the labyrinth of thought.

To the steadfast few who gave their time, strength and spirit to support me in this endeavour with grace and gratitude, your vulnerability, sincerity, polished being and courteous goodwill illuminated the darkest moments. Your willingness to challenge and critique fuelled forward motion. Please know your contributions have not gone unnoticed. Your unwavering support was the bedrock upon which this work now stands.

To those who offered subtle acknowledgements and even those who remained silent or opposed, know that your presence, or lack thereof, and resistance also played a role in this journey. Like a bird soaring higher against the wind, these challenges served to strengthen my resolve and propel this work forward.

In the solitude of my journey, I found the company of my beloved dogs and pipes to be a source of quiet contemplation and contentment, serene companions in this creative process.

Ultimately, this rich tapestry of thought was woven through the dance of challenge and creativity. May it serve as a beacon for those who seek not just to understand but to transcend.

Foreword

I am honoured to have been asked by Ashkan to write the foreword for *Metacontent*, an important new work about making sense of the world. This is my second foreword for Ashkan, after writing one for his initial work *BEING*.[1]

Sense making matters to each of us

Throughout the ages, across all cultures, making sense of the world has been a quintessential human endeavour. Sense-making led to an overall accumulation of human wisdom and knowledge that we've used to build a civilisation of societal and technological advancement. This advancement makes a profound difference to the lives we have today and the way we live them. To emphasise this impact, the world we were born into – that we habitually take for granted – is undeniably better than the suffering of the Dark Ages. However, today, the loss of our sense of the world has become an existential threat, and the descent into a dystopian abyss is closer than we imagine.

For each of us, the effectiveness of our sense-making of the world affects our outcomes in life through the choices we make and our performance in the activities we undertake. We are driven to make sense of the world at a primal level. Our very survival depends upon the accuracy and completeness of the understanding we develop in our worldview. This is the consequence of us 'being-in-the-world',

---

1   Tashvir, A. 2021. *BEING – The source of power.* Engenesis Publications: Sydney.

where making sense of our parents, partner, siblings, children, work and colleagues are all super important to us. Our worldview has a significant impact on our experience of life. Contrast the impact of having the grounding of satisfaction in ourselves with a lingering sense of dissatisfaction.

In our quest to make sense of the world over time, scholars, artists, scientists, medics, mathematicians, sports champions and performers – to name but a few – have made many significant contributions. If we take the time to look, we see these in fields such as philosophy, religion, science, the arts, sports and anthropology. Yet acquiring understanding, wisdom and knowledge from these critical sources is daunting, time-consuming and requires considerable research skills. Authoring this book was demanding. Ashkan connects this existing source work with his critical thinking, capacity for analysis and insight, extending this sense-making contribution to humankind in the 21st century.

Chapters 1—8 of the book provide a guide of the distilled essence of the most critical insights and advances in understanding, making accumulated human wisdom and knowledge more accessible. This is serious work requiring critical thinking to reach your own understanding of the world. For those interested in delving deeper, Ashkan references source material throughout the book to enable you to undertake directed research of your own where your curiosity or interest has been piqued.

The science of consciousness – structure and emergence

Making sense of the world is an integral part of consciousness studies, and this book shares the forefront of thought leadership in the field of the Science of Consciousness. Furthermore, in Chapter 9, Ashkan reveals and explores a nested model of seven layers: perspectives from which to examine oneself and the world. This work is practical and an example of an applied science aimed at providing individuals with the ability to develop a deeper understanding of the world and the life they live.

It is not surprising that Ashkan's assertions about making sense of the world align with the foundational ideas of 'structure' and 'emergence' used by several thought leaders in the Science of Consciousness. This is an encouraging validation of his nested structure approach.

From 2004 to the present, Giulio Tononi[2] and, later, Christof Koch[3] developed The Integrated Information Theory of Consciousness in which consciousness is identical to a certain kind of information, the realisation of which requires physical – not merely functional – integration and which can be measured mathematically. Taking the work of Kock and Tononi further, Max Tegmark[4], a leading physicist, proposes that mathematical structure alone – the presence of nested layers – is sufficient for consciousness to arise.

From anatomical and physiological perspectives, Material Scientist Anirban Bandyopadhyay[5] has discovered nested anatomical structures in the brain that interact both by classical and quantum means. He proposes that these structures may support theories of Quantum Consciousness.

I believe that this work on consciousness and Ashkan's work on sense-making are attuned to the same fundamental patterns of nature and reality. As Ashkan points out in this work, as he probes the bounds of human knowledge, emergence from complexity runs contrary to the approach of reductionist science of the 1950s and 1960s.

---

2   Giulio Tononi is Professor at the University of Wisconsin School of Medicine and Public Health. A reference work: *BMC Neuroscience, An information integration theory of consciousness,* 02 November 2004.

3   Christof Koch is an acclaimed neuroscientist at the Allen Institute and Chief Scientist at the Tiny Blue Dot Foundation. A reference work: MIT Press, *The Feeling of Life Itself,* September 24, 2019.

4   Max Tegmark is Professor of Physics at MIT. A reference work: Cornell University, *Consciousness as a State of Matter,* January 6th, 2014.

5   Anirban Bandyopadhyay PhD is a Senior Scientist, The National Institute for Materials Science Tsukuba, Japan. A reference work: *Emotion, Cognition and Silent Communication: Unsolved Mysteries,* 2024.

Being, performance, theory and practice

Chapter 10 describes how, in order to understand human performance, the Nested Theory of Sense-making model was used to create the Being Framework, including its ontological model. Chapter 11 offers the practical means and examples of how to apply the Nested Theory in the context of your life.

This work is unusual in that our being, performance and the theory and practice of this work are treated as parts of a whole. The effective learning and application of this work leads to a strong relationship with reality. This process is a performance challenge; how well we do depends on our being. At the same time, without a strong relationship with reality, we are weak in some fundamental ways of being. For instance, we are not able to be responsible in a world we fail to understand sufficiently, and it is easy to be inauthentic from delusion or ignorance when we lack accurate sense-making.

On the author

Ashkan authored this work because making sense of the world is foundational for each of us as it greatly impacts how we experience and live life. He has deeply explored this realm of knowledge and understanding for more than a decade. He recognised the challenge to human beings of sense-making and developing a broad and accurate understanding of the world and has observed and experienced different ways people struggle to understand the world in collaborative ventures aimed at impacting people's performance in work and life.

It takes an exceptional human being to tackle a work of this kind and fulfil the purpose of making our civilisation's accumulated wisdom, knowledge and understanding available to a wide audience. Over the last few years, I've had a number of long heart-to-heart chats with Ashkan that have allowed me to delve deeply into a broad spectrum of topics encompassing our life experiences, people and the world. From these talks, I found that Ashkan's drive, passion and desire to empower others is not an accident. He has lived a life of intense challenges that the vast majority of us can't even imagine. For this reason, I asked Ashkan for permission to share a few personal details of his life experience.

Ashkan has experienced the harsh side of human beings and encountered real-world consequences few of us ever face. Before settling in Australia, he faced severe repercussions simply for his poetic works. During his compulsory military service, he witnessed unimaginable horrors, including the death by suicide of some of his peers. From those moments, he chose to value life for all people – what Aristotle points to as developing one's sense of honour – rather than be permanently scarred by the insanity and brutality that life can throw at us. Instead of being crushed by such adversity, he gained perspective on how we can choose responsibility for ourselves and the world simply because we are here.

Character, virtue, and mastery are crucial in developing and applying sense-making to make a meaningful impact in the world. Without mastery, one's vulnerability – and thus power – is limited, as the journey of acquiring mastery can be translated across different fields. Ashkan's response to life's circumstances has shaped him into the impressive individual he is today. He has developed character, honour and virtue in a manner reminiscent of the Greek philosopher Aristotle's teachings. Through years of immersion, hard work, courage, persistence and pushing his limits, Ashkan has honed his sense-making skills and understanding, achieving mastery in various domains. For instance, he is an accomplished martial artist with extensive training and practice in Aikido – a defensive martial art focused on redirecting an opponent's energy using throws and joint locks, which emphasises peaceful conflict resolution – and Karate Kyokushin – a full-contact style of stand-up fighting rooted in a philosophy of self-improvement, discipline and hard training.

Ashkan's scholarly pursuits have also led him to develop a profound reverence for and knowledge of humanity's greatest philosophers and thinkers from Western, Asian, Persian and faith-based traditions.

This multi-dimensional cultural understanding, which he brings to his work on sense-making, reflects his broad perspective and inclusivity.

As someone who has led an extraordinary life on the edge, where very few travel and where real power can be found, Ashkan has a wealth of knowledge and experience to share. I encourage you to read what he has to say about making sense of the world and everything in it.

My message to you, the reader

This book covers a vast body of humanity's intellectual heritage. Yet its most significant benefits come from practice, that is, when you apply the Nested Theory of Sense-making in your life, as you live it, in the world. For this reason, it is important that you approach reading the book by concurrently looking at your own experiences and how the Nested Theory could be applied in your everyday life to provide a deeper understanding that will strengthen your relationship with reality. This, in turn, will allow you to harness your courage to open up opportunities to discover the type of power that alters the world.

The intellectual approach to this work is likely to hit a mental pain barrier. For instance, this phenomenon occurs when studying pure mathematics or consequential philosophers, such as Ludwig Wittgenstein, who 'torture' language to communicate the depths of wisdom and understanding they discovered in their work. This mental pain comes from physically building new neural pathways – rewiring layers in the frontal cortex of your brain to eventually be able to process reality in a more complete, accurate and, thus, more complex way. It is a journey that takes time.

Another reason to apply the work is the nature of human existence itself, for the world continuously unfolds and changes, and our being in the world also alters. We are never done with making sense of it all and finding meaning.

This book demonstrates the folly of looking for answers to life's quandaries to be spoon-fed to us, collecting a set of recipes, tips and formulas for success or seeking silver bullets to fix our insufficiencies in the face of the world – in the manner of a consumable product that will magically leave us enlightened and successful.

Ultimately, the value you gain as a reader of this book is proportional to how you look at your sense-making and your being in your own life – telling the truth to yourself about your life exactly as you live it and, importantly, sharing your insights with others in dialogue AND noticing what arises.

I wish you a life full of satisfaction and fulfilment as you take on the work in this book and find and unleash your power through your unique contribution to the world and its future.

About John Lowe

John co-designed the initial versions of the Being Profile. He has an extensive study and research background in pure mathematics, logic, philosophy and the history and philosophy of science.

He is a complex systems thinker, designer and developer who has developed and used these disciplines for several decades in a number of professions, including software engineering-architecture-design and corporate strategy as an executive and consultant. During this time, he lived and worked in Australia, Asia, Europe and the US.

John was appointed by the Australian Regulator as an independent financial markets expert and was the primary author of three mandatory technical market readiness reviews for new options and equity exchanges that opened in Australia. He was a key member of the teams that created the world's first fully electronic national equity markets. Subsequently, he was head-hunted to design, code and deploy the original trading engine of the Swiss Stock Exchange in Zürich.

John was also a strategist/analyst on an external team that provided advice on the buy/sell decision and post-acquisition strategy for the world's leading, New York-based private equity acquirer of niche leading technology firms.

As an executive, John was a research and development VP for a famous global technology firm, living in Silicon Valley for a year, and an IT strategist for a leading independent Australian fund and wealth manager.

Preface

In the whirlwind of our ever-evolving world, I've often found myself contemplating the underlying facets of our reality and the deeper layers of our existence. The rapid advancements in technology, the shifting paradigms in social and professional spheres, and the relentless pursuit of progress have prompted me to reflect on what truly underpins our understanding of reality. This book was born out of that contemplation. It sowed the seed to explore the fundamental intellectual foundation – or what I refer to as 'metacontent' – that shapes our perceptions, decisions, behaviours and actions and, therefore, impacts our lives and the lives of others through the sense-making process.

Metacontent is a novel word I came up with to represent the intellectual substrates for making sense of any content through a structured meta-analysis, much like metaphysics is the inquiry into the core concepts that underlie human thought and experience and the relationships between them. While a meta-analysis is a well-established method for synthesising research findings, a metacontent analysis goes further by synthesising knowledge within a domain to create a more accurate understanding. This approach leverages the structured model introduced in this book to delve into the deeper layers of meaning. Essentially, a metacontent analysis is a structured meta-analysis of a phenomenon or subject designed to provide a comprehensive and nuanced synthesis of knowledge. Tapping into metacontent supports us to interpret any given content – literally anything – shaping our understanding and influencing our decisions and actions. This can range from personal matters, like choosing a life partner or a career path, to bringing up children, running a business and electing a leader. It enables us to navigate complex ideas, make informed decisions and act effectively.

Each of us has existing metacontent, formed by the accumulation of personal narratives, interpretations of events, experiences, conceptions and learned knowledge. Our existing personal metacontent, which more well-established dominant metacontents can explicitly or implicitly influence, creates a layered foundation that influences how we understand things and interact with the world. For instance, it is not uncommon for a renowned scientist to attempt to read religious scripture, tapping into the scientific metacontent they are very familiar with. This approach shows an apparent lack of understanding or unwillingness to engage in narrative analysis, dialectics[6] or the interpretation of literary works. Conversely, a person deeply involved in the interpretation or literal reading of religious scripture or various forms of art may neglect to consider scientific metacontent.

A mismatch between content and metacontent can lead to an inability to make sense of the content involved or misconceptions about it. This concept extends beyond textual content. I use the term 'content' in a much broader sense than its conventional use. For me – and how I use the word in this book – human beings, animals, our pets, the plants in our garden, the foods we eat and everything around us are examples of content. The way we relate to, act upon, interact with or consume these contents leads to the decisions we make and the actions we take. These, in turn, shape our conceptions and behaviour, ultimately affecting the fulfilment of our intentions and our overall quality of life. From an individual perspective, the aggregation of such decisions, behaviours and actions may be conventionally referred to as 'lifestyle'. Collectively, these patterns form our culture or traditions.

---

6   Dialectics is a method of reasoning and argument that involves the exchange of logical arguments and counterarguments to explore and uncover the truth.

The key is to become intentionally aware of the fact that a layered foundation (metacontent) is currently guiding our sense-making processes and interactions with all aspects of existence. The good news is that since metacontent is a mental construct, it can be deconstructed and reconstructed, enabling us to critically examine and question our existing opinions, beliefs and knowledge and reconstruct more authentically aware mental constructs. Why does this matter? Take a moment to briefly consider the world we live in and the path that brought us here.

We live in an era marked by super-advanced technologies and psychologically engineered advertisements and marketing techniques that fabricate needs and demands, while fake news, predatory lending schemes, exploitative subscription services and fraudulent investment opportunities proliferate. We are bombarded with the fast-paced creation of manufactured content overlaying an already complex existing reality. The lines between public servants and private citizens have become paradoxical. Many 'public servants' are anything but public, and their true intentions are often unclear. With constant surveillance, breaches of privacy and the erosion of the notion of a private citizen, the ideals of liberalism – defining our independent relationship from the state and corporations – are being challenged.

Media, which should provide facts for us to form opinions, often push the agendas of their funders, leaving us to decipher the facts from manufactured views and propaganda. We face regimes that mandate participation in elections under the guise of freedom and democracy, with penalties for non-compliance. At the same time, other states beg their citizens to participate voluntarily and are branded dictatorships. Is it any wonder we live in perpetual confusion and deceit?

There was a time when the value of human beings was tightly attached to our manual labour output. In other words, we perceived that our value was closely linked to our physical abilities. At the start of the Industrial Revolution, many workers no doubt felt threatened that they were about to be replaced by machines. After all, surely the strength and capability of a human labourer was no match for the might and power of a machine! However, what was perceived as a devastating threat became the vast opportunities we see today. For example, the heavy burden of lifting has predominantly been outsourced to forklifts and other machinery, creating the luxury for human beings to tap into different dimensions of our being – our consciousness, intellect, cognition and computation abilities. Initially feared by the masses, the Industrial Revolution freed up our time and energy to focus on abstract concepts. We started building civilisations differently and coming up with innovative constructs and institutions to significantly improve the quality of our lives. This is an example of why we should not fear or avoid what we don't know and understand – including scientific and technological advancements – but acknowledge, welcome and appreciate them. However, that does not mean we should resign ourselves to take everything at face value without deeper analysis.

There was also a time when a 'computer' was an occupation and job title. Human computers were commonplace at organisations like NASA. They specialised in applied mathematics and would spend their days solving algebraic equations on paper. Then, when the first IBM devices came onto the scene, people began referring to them as 'computers'. Naturally, the human computers were threatened by these new machine computers as they could see how much more efficient they were. Unlike humans, these machines never needed to rest. And they could achieve what human computers could in a fraction of the time with far fewer errors while also being scalable. Much like the Industrial Revolution, the Digital Age gave rise to new opportunities and professions, including computer programmers, developers and analysts, to name just a few. Once again, outsourcing some of the work created the luxury for human beings to tap into other dimensions of our consciousness.

For decades, computer programmers, myself included, dreamed about transforming devices that could only comprehend binary code (0s and 1s) into entities capable of understanding a more human-like language. Since the 1980s, attempts have been made to minimise or eradicate 'coding' from computer programming. While not all attempts were entirely successful, the advent of advanced artificial intelligence (AI) suggests we may soon communicate with computers in plain language, instructing them to develop software to minimise traditional coding and transform them into more than mere computing devices. Some significant progress has already been made here with Natural Language-Oriented Programming.[7]

So, history has shown us that there is no need to be entirely threatened by scientific and technological advancements as long as we humans continue to have the upper hand. To remain in charge, we need effective sense-making and ontological and ethical frameworks that require philosophers, scientists, economists and policymakers to work hand in hand with citizens for the greater good of humanity. This collaboration would allow us to safely and ethically tap into the vast opportunities these advancements bring and prevent us from falling prey to our own creations.

Besides leveraging technological advancements, I also find it crucial to challenge the radical interpretations of humanism and its legacies, which continue to dominate the metacontent of our era. Historically, during the Dark Ages and the emergence of the humanism movement in Europe, there was a significant shift as people sought to set aside the Divine and spiritual aspects due to the atrocities committed in their name. René Descartes' famous saying, 'I think, therefore I am', catalysed the Renaissance and Enlightenment eras, placing human beings at the centre of the universe and fostering a sense of pride in our achievements. While cognitive science and scientific thinking led to the Renaissance, the Industrial Revolution and technological advancements like the internet, e-commerce and AI, these constructs and institutions now face significant challenges.

Thinkers from various fields are critiquing these purely humanistic approaches. For instance, in his book *Freefall: America, Free*

---

7   Beheshti, A. 2024. *Natural Language-Oriented Programming (NLOP): Towards Democratizing Software Creation.* 2024 IEEE International Conference on Software Services Engineering (SSE), Shenzhen, China, July 7—13, 2024. Available at: https://doi.org/10.48550/arXiv.2406.05409 [Accessed 6 July 2024].

Markets, and the Sinking of the World Economy[8], Joseph Stiglitz, an economist from Columbia University, discusses the collapse not just of individual economies but of the entire modern economic system. Various critics and experts are today challenging the authenticity and relevance of constructs and institutions such as capitalism, politics, democracy, human rights, universities, the medical system, equality and marriage. My focus in this body of work is not on the constructs and institutions created by us human beings but on the bedrock – the intellectual substrates or metacontent – on which they have been built and how to not only make sense of them but also how to authentically reconstruct them so they may better serve us.

The most effective and financially prosperous people of the future will be those who not only comprehend technology and leverage it effectively but are also proficient communicators, can interpret human experiences and narratives effectively and have the ability and foresight to engage in multidisciplinary collaborations. They must also possess a profound practical understanding of human beings' fundamental nature and essence, including our vulnerabilities and inauthenticities. This involves delving into what I call 'The Invisible' – things that sit within the realm of the unknown – and identifying opportunities by compassionately seeking out the challenges and burning pains of a group of people (the market). Once the needs have been identified, crafting and communicating a compelling vision is essential to align individuals with diverse yet complementary qualities and expertise with the vision because they know they will never be able to achieve it alone. They must also cultivate a strong workplace culture by establishing a shared mental model while tapping into each team member's uniqueness to foster creativity and innovation. They need to create authentic branding and position it to generate trust. All of this ultimately creates an unfair competitive advantage, and the road to achieving it relies on authentically and sincerely tapping into the metacontent of the various matters in question.

---

8   Stiglitz, J.E. 2010. *Freefall: America, Free Markets, and the Sinking of the World Economy.* New York: W.W. Norton & Company.

Developing an authentic and congruent conception of matters by tapping into the underlying multi-layered metacontent – the intellectual substrates for sense-making – is the antidote to the deception, inauthenticities and confusion we all grapple with daily, and that makes us even more vulnerable than we already are to life's challenges and unknowns. By being acutely aware of the deceptions from all angles and the severe consequences of the resulting dysfunction, manipulation, coercion, tyranny, oppression, suffering and systematic ruin of lives and families, we can challenge our modern ignorance and enslavement. Instead of adopting the typical approach of blame and finger-pointing, the power lies within us all to begin the process of change with ourselves. Furthermore, solving human problems and minimising unnecessary suffering not only relies on the systematic deconstruction and reconstruction of the underlying metacontent but also on the integrity of individuals.[9] Ultimately, we – as individuals – are the ones who form groups, design systems, implement and follow them and allow them to influence our lives. Consider how much AI – technology designed by humans – has already impacted us in such a short timeframe.

My personal journey in writing this book was driven by a passion for knowledge and a commitment to helping others achieve clarity and fulfilment by supporting people to make better sense of the content in existence and then reconstruct their existing metacontent with greater authentic awareness. I have witnessed firsthand how a deeper understanding of our cognitive frameworks can transform our approach to personal and professional challenges. Whether navigating the complexities of human relationships, mastering a craft, excelling in a career or business or making sense of domestic and global matters, the principles of metacontent and sense-making are universally applicable.

Ultimately, this book is designed to help you navigate the complexity of reality, the world and everything in it, including yourself and others, with clarity and purpose. May this book inspire you to delve

---

9   Tashvir, A. 2021. *BEING – The source of power.* Engenesis Publications: Sydney.

deeper into your own understanding and enrich your experience of life, ultimately achieving what Aristotle referred to as 'Eudaimonia' or flourishing.

Introduction

I magine standing at the edge of an ancient labyrinth. The walls are tall and intricate, casting long shadows under the setting sun. This labyrinth, like the world around us, is filled with countless pathways and hidden corners, each representing a different aspect of our reality. As you take your first step into the maze, you carry a simple map drawn from your personal experiences, assumptions and knowledge – your existing intellectual substrate or metacontent. But as you venture deeper, you realise that the map alone is insufficient. To truly navigate the labyrinth, you need more than just a basic outline; you need to illuminate the pathways, understand their complexities and make sense of the stories behind each turn. The question is, how?

Consider a more tangible example. Let's say you are interested in carpentry. To learn this craft, you need to understand the fundamental laws of physics and geometry, accompanied by a grasp of basic mathematics. It is also imperative to know about wood's intrinsic properties, such as its hardness, texture and natural colour. Understanding various wood types and their specific applications is also essential. This involves learning about wood's essence, nature or quiddity – also referred to as 'whatness' – and tapping into the existing literature and tradition about carpenters' experiences with wood throughout history. Neglecting to undertake this depth of learning would confine you to your own limited knowledge, hindering your progress through a lack of awareness. Additionally, misconceptions about wood could arise, emphasising the need to gradually build your conception of wood and how it works over time. This journey involves reading, attending courses, reading online studies and gaining hands-on experience through internships under the guidance of seasoned carpenters to develop a base level of competency.

As a carpenter, you also need knowledge about various other elements, from different types of nails and hammers to technologically advanced machinery. So, beyond understanding the whatness of wood and all things related to carpentry, there's a parallel need to construct an authentic mental model of how carpentry tools function, shifting the focus to functionality and working towards enhanced efficacy in application. By putting all your insights into action, tracking progress, learning and refining, you gradually transition from being incompetent to competent, then proficient and ultimately reach mastery. Over time, you might develop your own unique style, techniques, processes and tools. There is even the potential to expand the carpentry tradition, setting new standards and inspiring future generations in the trade.

Now imagine you want to become a practising physician. This pursuit requires you to delve into the fundamentals of biology before tapping into human anatomy and exploring the 11 systems within the human body to learn the intricacies of each constituent part and comprehend the whatness of the entire human body. Following this, there's a parallel need to construct an authentic mental model focusing on the functionality of each part within the broader context of physiology. Once you've developed a conception of the individual parts and their collective system, including how they work – striving for as accurate an understanding as possible – and established a solid sense of what constitutes their health, particularly in the state of homeostasis, the next phase involves delving into pathology and diseases in order to come to a diagnosis and treatment. Only then can you reach a level of proficiency and knowledge that enables you to treat patients. Eventually, you may decide to specialise within a specific domain of medicine.

Whether you aspire to be a carpenter, a physician, or whatever you wish to become or do with your life, the approach to learning and deepening your conception of the content and its practical application is essentially the same. It's about making sense of and understanding the whatness of things, starting from general to specific, and how they work: their functionality. This approach is not limited to specific fields or skills; it's a universal principle that applies to absolutely anything you choose to do in life, from activities like gardening, fishing, hunting and cooking to pursuits like sports, nutrition, parenting and relationships.

How often do you wonder about the validity or efficacy of something you've heard about and rely on a search engine like Google to give you the answer? Most people conducting an online search won't scroll beyond the first page of results, and many only consider the response at the top of the page! For instance, let's say you want to know if drinking green tea helps with weight loss. Hypothetically, a search might deliver 10 different studies where researchers have investigated this question. Some studies conclude that it does help, some say it doesn't, and others are inconclusive. In a meta-analysis, which is designed to investigate research findings and provide a higher level of evidence by synthesising knowledge extracted from individual studies, you would combine all the data from these 10 studies and analyse it as a whole. By considering a larger set of data rather than relying on the results of just one study, you can identify overall trends and achieve a clearer picture of the effectiveness of green tea for weight loss. But what if you wanted to go deeper than basing your decisions on the combination of those 10 studies alone? Although a meta-analysis considers multiple studies to provide a more comprehensive understanding of the content in question, it does not offer the detail and structure provided by the Nested Theory of Sense-making, an original concept I developed that provides a structured approach for navigating life's complexities and transforming our analysis and decision-making abilities. This multi-layered holistic method is introduced for the first time in this book.

In simple terms, metacontent is the underlying framework of ideas, experiences, perceptions, narratives, mental models, knowledge and paradigms within a specific domain that helps us shape how we make sense of, comprehend and interact with the world. By adopting the structured and readily contextualised and applied approach introduced and explained in this book to access and deconstruct metacontent, we can gain deeper, more holistic and nuanced insights into whatever we are examining. Then, through a process of reconstruction, we can make more informed, authentic decisions about the matter in question.

Beyond what you want to achieve in life, simply being in the world requires you to map out the metacontent of anything and everything you are dealing with if you aim to live a well-informed and fulfilling life. The question is, can you study the whatness and functionality of everything purely scientifically and methodically? This book delves deeply into this question.

Metacontent is not just for individuals; it's equally relevant to societal and global matters that impact us all. To understand the true impact of our advancements, we must consider the lurking variables – the unseen factors influencing outcomes. For instance, the rise in mass shootings in the US may not be solely attributed to gun access but also to societal changes. By examining the broader context – such as educational systems and societal values – through a metacontent analysis, we gain a deeper understanding of the underlying issues.

Consider how metaphysics and ethics – both often overlooked – influence politics, leadership and societal behaviour. A solid ethical framework built on shared metacontent is essential for a free society. This framework influences our constructs like governments, banks, taxation systems and corporations, highlighting the importance of authenticity and ethical considerations in our decisions.

Many today seek quick fixes and superficial solutions, but true understanding requires a deeper exploration of metacontent. This book combines insights from science and philosophy to provide a comprehensive framework for navigating the complexities of our world, including human beings: ourselves and others.

While some might consider this body of work heavy or intellectually demanding, it is relevant to everyone. The complex nature of the discussion was not intentional but due to the inherently sophisticated nature of life and everything within it. This book encapsulates some of these complexities while providing tangible ways to deconstruct and reconstruct these intricate constructs, institutions and their underlying metacontents to make sense of them with greater accuracy and authentic awareness. The goal was not only to make this book accessible to 'intellectuals' but to anyone who cares about mapping out how things are to make better decisions for themselves and, consequently, live a more well-lived life and potentially make a positive impact beyond themselves. It is a book designed to be studied and read more than once.

I invite you to take a deep breath and step into the labyrinth. Together, we will uncover the keys to sense-making, equipping you with the tools to engage with the world in a more meaningful way.

Contents

CHAPTER 1

Confusion

Confusion stands as humanity's greatest challenge, casting a shadow over our individual and collective understanding of the world and our place within it. From the complexities of global issues like climate change, food security, health and conflict to the intricacies of everyday life, uncertainty, bewilderment and ambiguity abound. Whether we confront these uncertainties head-on or choose to ignore them, their impact on our lives is undeniable. With technologies like Artificial Intelligence (AI) and machine learning advancing at an unprecedented pace and creating additional layers of reality, the need to address and navigate this confusion has never been more urgent. Our confusion will only multiply exponentially if we continue to look the other way. Let's delve into the root causes of this pervasive confusion and explore how we can move forward in an increasingly complex world.

The dominant and most commonly accepted substrate beneath the constructs and institutions we have been building in the last few centuries has been humanism[1] – the fundamental belief that all

---

1   Humanism is a doctrine, attitude or way of life centred on human interests or values. Humanism is a philosophy that stresses the importance of human factors rather than looking at 'divine' or spiritual matters. It is a philosophy that suggests our human intellect is enough for us to create a meaningful and prosperous life.

we have is our intellect and that this is sufficient to discover and identify our needs, including how to build and leverage them, and what is 'good' or 'bad' for us. This interpretation of humanism can be challenged – is our intellect truly enough? An alternative would be to approach humanism in a manner that acknowledges that we have no choice but to rely on our intellect. This perspective recognises the need to surrender to the axiomatic reality[2] that each of us is personally responsible for addressing issues, resolving problems and advancing towards a more integrous life through the means available to us, individually and collectively, as opposed to waiting for someone or something to come to our rescue. In this context, we, as human beings, are responsible for establishing integrity by ensuring that everything is in its rightful place, metaphorically piecing together the puzzle of life into a cohesive and harmonious whole. As renowned French existentialist philosopher Jean-Paul Sartre pointed out, the fact that we are free is 'terrifying'. Freedom has been traditionally seen as an inherently positive phenomenon; we have fought to gain more and more of it, particularly in contemporary history. However, Sartre's assertion brought our attention to the other side of the coin: the heavy burden of needing to make what we hope are appropriate choices as life – often harshly – throws matters our way. Life demands us to make 'right' or effective decisions amidst multiple unknowns, uncertainties and dilemmas.

One of our greatest vulnerabilities as human beings is the limitations to how we receive, sense, perceive and conceive matters. Firstly, we receive sensations through our senses – sight, hearing, touch, taste and smell. The difference between a sense and a sensation is that a sense is something we have that detects things, whereas a sensation is the feeling we experience when one of our senses detects something. Notably, both have limitations. For example, when it comes to sensations, a human being's ability to detect scents through our sense of smell is nowhere near as effective as a dog's. Because dogs have more than 100 million sensory receptor sites and a much larger set of scent

---

2   An axiom is a statement or proposition which is regarded as being established,
     accepted or self-evidently true; that which commends itself as evident.

membranes within their nasal cavity, they can process odoriferous molecules more readily than humans. It's a similar story with sound. Dogs can hear frequencies that humans are unable to access. Our hearing is limited to a frequency range of about 20Hz–20kHz. At times, we also receive abductive revelations – a thought or idea that strikes us from an unknown source – through our intuition. Secondly, we pass whatever we receive via our senses through our perceptual structure. Perception is an active process. It is when our brain selects, organises, identifies, interprets and categorises[3] the information we receive through our senses from environmental stimuli or whatever is presented to us. Sensation and perception are closely related. If we don't have access to all sensations, then there will always be certain matters that aren't passed through the filters of our perceptual structure. The third layer that causes confusion due to its inherent limitations is our conceptual structure or rationality – how we rationalise matters.

Our brain plays a crucial role in processing and integrating the sensory information we receive, shaping our perceptions and conceptions or rational comprehension and influencing how we experience, understand and interact with our surroundings. From a psychological perspective, our brain also categorises the information it receives. In psychology, categorisation involves organising objects, events and abstract entities into cognitive categories to help us organise knowledge. As cognitive agents, we humans develop our semantic understanding of things through categorisation. For instance, in early childhood, we learned about apples as a category rather than as individual entities. Even toddlers recognise an apple as an apple, regardless of its size and colour. Semantics, the study of meaning in language, can be applied to individual words and even entire texts. For instance, the word 'destination' and the phrase 'last

---

3   In psychology and philosophy, a category refers to a broad concept or idea. As human beings, we tend to categorise elements of our environment into various groups or classes, such as 'animal', 'car', 'unicorn', 'truck', etc. that help us understand and interpret the world around us. Research in cognitive psychology explains how we categorise and how these mental representations are formed.

stop' technically share the same meaning. However, semantic analysis reveals subtle differences or 'shades of meaning'. While something may be described as 'big', words like 'large', 'huge', 'gigantic' and 'massive' also relate to something being big but convey varying degrees of 'bigness', offering more specific distinctions.

Due to the inherent limitations of our intuition, sensations and perceptual and conceptual structures, **we don't have direct access to the truth of all matters**, from the simple things to the fundamental and meaningful questions we may have, including many of life's big unknowns. For example, we don't rationally know where we came from or whether or not the soul exists. We don't have a solid consensus around the nature of consciousness. We may wonder whether our psyche or consciousness is limited to brain mechanisms and activities. Is it merely our nervous system that captures snapshots of reality with a high frequency in communication with our senses and enables us to perceive space, matter, ideas and time, or is there more to it? Are all of our memories stored in the physical brain, or are some stored elsewhere? Is there an afterlife, and if so, what would it be like? Or are we doomed to be removed from existence once the body resigns from its physiological duties?

Who am I? Am I merely the aggregate of what I think, feel, say and do – my cognitive abilities – or is there more to me than that? Am I fixed, or am I fluid and mutable? Am I only who I say I am? Is there a fundamental and undeniable solid reality – an axiom to adhere to – when it comes to the totality of my being, or do I have free rein to define myself in whatever way I choose? If the latter is the case, to what degree can I define myself? What is the meaning of my life? Why bother being than not being? Given I have been thrown into this world, what is my role here; what should I do? How do we choose our priorities and values? How do I establish the hierarchy of *my* values – the things to which I attach the greatest significance? Is it me choosing them, or are they set? Do we have free will? What possibilities do I have to sacrifice in favour of others? How should I relate to myself, others, other beings and the content of the world?

What defines my relationship with them? Is there such a thing as 'right' or 'wrong'? If so, how do I determine right from wrong? Are ethical codes universal, absolute and dictated, meaning they hold true regardless of the outcome or consequence (deontological[4])? Or are they relative and arbitrary? Is there a universal ethical framework? Is an ethical framework even needed, and if so, which one is right, or which should I choose?

How should I heal my traumas? What qualities should I develop in myself in the course of my growth? What does growth even mean? What qualities should I seek in others, such as a potential life partner, business partner, employee or friend? How do I fit into society and deal with the already-established power dynamics, code of conduct, social norms, etc.? To what degree should I be nice, kind, forgiving, compassionate, altruistic and benevolent? Should I embrace my troubled parts – the characteristics, attitudes and qualities that I know are not serving me or my intentions, the ones that often get in the way of fulfilling my intentions – or should I leave them alone, escape from them or cover them up?

So many questions and unknowns. Many of these inquiries transcend the realm of scientific problems or endeavours, venturing into the domains of metaphysics, philosophy, ethics and axiology.[5] Consequently, even the most 'reliable' scientific methods of examining physical reality and the material world do not fully equip us to answer them. In his book, *A Philosophical Approach to MOND*[6], author and astrophysicist David Merritt writes in the first chapter, 'The Epistemology of Science', 'Scientific epistemology begins from the idea that the truth of a universal statement, such as a scientific law, can never

---

4   In moral philosophy, deontological ethics or deontology is the normative ethical theory that the morality of an action should be based on whether that action itself is right or wrong under a series of rules and principles, rather than based on the consequences of the action.

5   Axiology is the philosophical study of value. It includes questions about the nature and classification of values and about what kinds of things have value.

6   Merritt, D. 2020. *A Philosophical Approach to MOND: Assessing the Milgromian Research Program in Cosmology* (pp.1—19). Cambridge University Press.

be conclusively proved. No matter how successful a hypothesis has been in the past, it can always turn out to make incorrect predictions when applied in a new situation.'

The intention here is not to downplay the importance of science in any way. On the contrary, science is unquestionably the most reliable way of examining the material world. However, as incredible, marvellous and vital as science is, it does not hold the answers to absolutely everything and may not be the epistemological[7] pathway to answering every possible question we may have, especially when it comes to matters beyond the material reality. Examples include ideas, ethics, morality, values and priorities, such as determining which issues should be prioritised over others and whose suffering is deemed more significant than another's. While we might wish that science could offer clear-cut solutions in every instance, there are times when science alone falls short, even in the most unremarkable, everyday situations.

Consider a simple scenario. You're sitting on the sofa watching a movie late one night and find yourself yearning for potato chips. Knowing there is a packet in the pantry, you grab it. The ingredients are scientifically and legally declared on the packet in accordance with government regulatory authorities. Furthermore, there is vast literature detailing the potential consequences to one's health of consuming some of these ingredients, like preservatives, artificial colours and flavours and high levels of saturated fat, sugar and salt, especially just before going to bed. Despite the wealth of scientific information and knowledge available, deciding whether to indulge in chips tonight isn't purely scientific. It delves into deeper considerations, such as your hierarchy of values, meaning it enters the realm of axiology. Axiology is not a science but a branch of philosophy. It helps us understand what we value in order to make effective decisions and prioritise matters. So, you might ask yourself whether you prioritise

---

7   Epistemology is the branch of philosophy concerned with knowledge. Epistemology is a field that studies the nature, origin and scope of knowledge, epistemic justification, the rationality of belief and various related issues.

the instant gratification of eating chips over your health. If health is your primary concern, can you confidently discern whether having a few chips is a significant matter? Trust and faith come into it, too. Should you trust the information on the back of the chip packet, including details about the oil in which the chips were fried and so on? Should you have faith that the government's regulatory bodies have your best interests in mind? If, despite all the information and knowledge you have access to, you decide to go ahead and eat the chips, you are placing your faith and trust in something beyond science that you won't suffer as a consequence of your decision and action.

As you can see, answering these questions so you can make a decision involves far more than just having access to the scientific information available. Ironically, the fact that you may choose to take the risk and eat the chips *despite* the scientific information and literature available adds to the point being made, which is that this is not a purely science-related problem or decision. While the scientific facts are available to you in this case, the decision-making process is more than just a scientific problem to solve. You have the autonomy and freedom to choose whether or not to prioritise the scientific description and put your faith in it.

While the word 'faith' is often used in religious contexts, it is also defined as 'complete trust or confidence in someone or something'. We all consciously or unconsciously tap into faith daily. More specifically, we do so whenever there is a lack of empirical evidence, or we are deciding on a matter that cannot be empirically investigated. That's because faith is an epistemological approach or way of knowing something, especially concerning matters lacking in scientific evidence and those that aren't scientific questions or problems to solve in the first place. Instead, they demand trust.

Considering there is and always will be a degree of uncertainty in life, as not everything can be quantifiably studied or scientifically proven, we often choose to take a leap of faith when making decisions. For example, we don't scientifically choose to trust a friend or the loyalty of our spouse. A bank manager doesn't rely solely on science to determine whether or not to grant someone a loan. We don't scientifically trust the butcher that they sell quality meat. And we don't scientifically have faith that we won't be attacked by terrorists when we attend large events or gatherings. Ultimately, many decisions we make in life are determined by our hierarchy of values – where we choose to place the greatest value – and what we choose to have faith in.

Many of our decisions in modern societies are also based on a common logical fallacy known as 'Ad Populum', a Latin phrase that loosely means to appeal to the public or popularity. In other words, if enough people believe something is 'right', then it *is* 'right'. An example of how Ad Populum manifests in societies is democracy. Many people relate to democracy as if it means that whatever the majority says yes to or is popular must be good or right. However, not everyone who accepts or puts their faith in democracy as a pragmatic doctrine, despite its known pitfalls, believes that the majority is always 'right' and that we should do the 'wrong' thing even if the majority isn't right. The reason we came up with and adhere to ideas such as democracy, despite knowing its downsides, goes back to the limitations of our perceptual structure. However, we can also attribute it to the limitations of our conceptual structure or rationality. Let's look a little more closely at the distinction between our perceptual and conceptual structures.

As explained earlier, perception is when our brain selects, organises, identifies, interprets and categorises the information we receive through one or more of our five senses. However, we also have established perceptions of various ideas or constructs, such as civil rights, governments, money, gender, commitment, honesty, etc., that our brain has access to. Our established perceptions could result from tapping into the thoughts of philosophers, scientists and opinion makers or concepts developed by ideologues or gurus. They may be influenced by our cultural and geographical heritage, family traditions, what we learned at school, what we see and hear in the news and social media and religious anecdotes. In contrast, to conceive a matter, we tap into our intellect and engage in mental processes such as comparison, analysis, contemplation, reflection, discussion and debate, synthesising various sources or perspectives to (hopefully) reach a consensus.

Conception is often subject to error and flaws. For example, esteemed German philosopher Georg Wilhelm Friedrich Hegel[8] devised the Hegelian dialectic process that shaped how we develop literature in various fields, primarily in academia, debates and rational social discussions. Hegel proposed that in a dialectic, one begins by proposing two seemingly opposing ideas – a thesis (original idea) and an antithesis (another, usually opposing idea) and then merges them to arrive at a synthesis, which is then used to develop new, more complete and refined knowledge. The fact that there can be numerous antitheses for any thesis means that our rational conclusions are inherently NOT the exact truth; there is always a gap.

Renowned German philosopher Immanuel Kant proposed a related argument before Hegel. Prior to Kant, Western philosophers generally believed that truth corresponded to reality, following what is known as the Mirror Theory of Knowledge. Rationalists like Plato and Rene Descartes asserted that the mind mirrors reality as innate ideas. However, Kant proposed a nuanced perspective, arguing that truth is not as straightforward as a mere reflection of reality. According to Kant, truth involves a contribution from the thinking mind; it is not fabricated by the mind, yet it is not a mere reflection either. Truth, Kant argued, depends on both the objective nature of things and the subjective contribution of the thinker – the mind.

To illustrate Kant's point, let's consider an example: while we may assume that what we see is solely determined by external factors, such as the objects in our environment, further examination reveals that our vision largely depends on interpretation. For instance,

---

8   Georg Wilhelm Friedrich Hegel was a German philosopher and one of the most influential figures of German idealism and 19th-century philosophy.

our perception of colour varies depending on factors like lighting conditions. The perceived colour of any object can change depending on the lighting conditions and the wavelengths of light present at different times of the day.

Well before any of the aforementioned Western philosophers, the 12th-century Islamic philosopher Shihab al-Din Suhrawardi[9] addressed this notion of a 'blind spot' in his book *The Red Intellect*. Suhrawardi explained that what appears as red is not actually red; it only looks red to the human perceptual structure due to an interplay of light and darkness. Suhrawardi offered a distinct perspective to mainstream Western philosophers by emphasising that perception is a blend of external reality and internal interpretation. This process of interpretation is inherent in even our simplest interactions with the world, let alone more sophisticated ones, challenging the notion of science as purely 'neutral observation'.

While striving for scientific objectivity is commendable, Suhrawardi and Kant's insights remind us that our conceptualisations of truth are not exact replicas but interpretations that seek to capture facets of reality or a meaning closer to the totality of the truth. Therefore, characterising every scientific concept as a direct match with reality is inaccurate and, hence, inauthentic. Again, none of this falsifies the notion of absolutes in existence, which I often refer to as 'first-layer reality'. It just re-emphasises that we do not have direct and unmediated access to them. However, that doesn't mean we should resign ourselves to succumb to this vulnerability or see it as an excuse to make up and fully indulge in fabricated stories and create constructs not rooted in reality. While we may choose to create constructs and fabricated realities for their usefulness or for our pleasure or entertainment, the moment we fail to discern them from the absolutes, we may be doomed to be confused and be left to wander blindly in our defiance, resistance and inauthenticities.

---

9   Shihab al-Dīn Yahya ibn Habash Suhrawardi was a Persian philosopher and founder of the school of Illuminationism, an important school in Islamic philosophy.

History tells us that we have made numerous mistakes when tapping into our conceptual structure or rationality, such as when we 'rationally' and 'scientifically' concluded that the European race was superior and women were inferior to men! There was also a time when human beings collectively engaged in witch hunts, killing countless women and when people from certain ethnic groups were caged and exhibited like animals in a circus! Even today, human beings continue to engage in the horrific practice of 'ethnic cleansing'. Some of these so-called 'scientific discoveries' or 'rational' beliefs influenced many people's lives despite their falsehood or absurdity and the fact that they are all the result of imaginary realities and made-up narratives. Some use the word of God to justify their cause, decisions and actions; others use science. Either way, it's a form of weaponisation.

Learning from our mistakes in the past has led some of us to develop a level of epistemic humility[10] and no longer arrogantly and overly confidently take every so-called 'scientific discovery' as a rock-solid truth. For example, it was epistemic humility that led Karl Popper[11], a philosopher of science, to discover and propose his Falsification Principle as a way of differentiating science from non-science. The Falsification Principle suggests that for a theory to be considered scientific, it must be able to be tested and conceivably proven false. For instance, the hypothesis that 'all swans are white' can be falsified by observing a black swan. So, while science is to be respected as a way of examining material reality, when it comes to scientific discovery, conclusions can be flawed and should not be taken as equal to absolutes. In other words, scientific knowledge should constantly

---

10   Epistemic humility refers to a posture of scientific observation rooted in the recognition that (a) knowledge of the world is always interpreted, structured and filtered by the observer, and that, as such, (b) scientific pronouncements must be built on the recognition that observation is unable to grasp the world in and of itself.

11   Sir Karl Raimund Popper CH FRS FBA was an Austrian–British philosopher, academic and social commentator. One of the 20th century's most influential philosophers of science, Popper is known for rejecting the classical inductivist views on the scientific method in favour of empirical falsification.

be challenged. This aligns with Popper's assertions regarding the falsifiable[12] nature of theories in that we can be confident about science as a relatively reliable way of knowing in many areas and cases but not entirely satisfied that any scientific knowledge presented is 'the truth' or perfect. It is for this very reason that scientific literature progresses dynamically. On the whole, science has been predominantly effective in acknowledging its mistakes, especially when scientists accept the need to challenge everything and refrain from elevating their discipline to a pedestal, worshipping it or treating it like a cult or fanaticism.

If it were scientifically possible to discern 'right' from 'wrong' in ALL the various aspects of life, then rules would simply be dictated to citizens using the so-called logic: 'just because science says so'. So, it is crucial for us to continually monitor and scrutinise anything that might weaponise science as a means to oppress or steer a course in a desired direction. Doing so completely contradicts the ideas many of us value so dearly, like liberty, independence, freedom, democracy and human dignity. For example, we do not phenomenologically deal with politics and electing leaders based on scientific data and discoveries. Instead – and alarmingly – we allow or make it mandatory for people to vote during an election regardless of how 'right' or 'wrong' a voter's perceptions and conceptions of each candidate and party might be. Consequently, many people vote merely on the basis of how they *feel* towards each party or candidate rather than basing their decision on each party or candidate's stance on the matters that count – critical matters like geopolitics, national security, education, climate change, immigration, housing, welfare, etc. It goes back to the earlier remark on humanism being our most dominant and commonly accepted substrate beneath the constructs and institutions we build. Unfortunately, many of us fail to consider that our decisions have a ripple effect.

---

12   Falsifiability is a deductive standard for evaluating scientific theories and hypotheses, introduced by the philosopher of science Karl Popper in his book *The Logic of Scientific Discovery* (1934). A theory or hypothesis is falsifiable (or refutable) if it can be logically contradicted by an empirical test.

Returning to the idea of democracy, while we acknowledge that a form of fallacy or irrationality underlies it – and any system or construct, for that matter – it remains in place, probably because it appears to be the most pragmatic solution compared to other alternatives. The pragmatic approach also applies to the example of voting. So, the pragmatic approach that we so far seem to have consensus on means many significant decisions are made based on feelings, stories and interpretations rather than facts.

We constantly deal with dilemmas, uncertainty and not-knowings, like when attempting to read the intentions of people we interact with, even the ones we think we know so well, like those we made lifelong commitments with or took an oath in front of friends and family in good faith despite knowing the high marriage failure rates. Can exact science[13] – or anything regarded as meeting the six criteria of science[14] – protect us in every instance we face in life, including reading the intentions of the people we love or those who claim to love us? Can we consistently turn to and rely on science when making any decision? What about the times when we must make a decision on the spot, without the luxury of time to gather the data and deeply understand the facts? Can science support us, then? It is worth noting here that not everything that sits in the realm of rationality – matters that are comprehensible to the human mind through reasoning – fits into the realm of science. While all scientific matters should be rational, not all rational matters can be or are scientific. Is it any wonder we are confused?

Whether voting for who should be our nation's next leader or deciding whether to eat some potato chips, our decisions are rarely based on validated scientific knowledge alone. Instead, we typically make decisions based on a combination of intelligence, feelings, values and intuition. We can't solely rely on science when making decisions

---

13   A science (such as physics, chemistry, or biology) whose laws are capable of accurate quantitative expression.

14   The 6 Criteria of Science are: Consistent, Observable, Natural, Predictable, Testable and Tentative.

because although we can verify the scientific validity and authenticity of some things, we can't with others. That's precisely why we have the word 'intelligence'. Intelligence is the aggregation of the verified and the unverified. We make decisions by adding our feelings, values and intuition to the intelligence equation. In other words, how we relate to various matters, through intelligence combined with feelings, intuition and what we value, determines how we make decisions in most situations. It is inauthentic to think that *all* decisions can be based on validated scientific knowledge alone.

Even if our scientific knowledge is validated and crystal clear – which is inherently impossible given scientific 'fact' is, at best, a high-level probability – we must acknowledge that the limitations of our perceptual and conceptual structures combined with our feelings mean we don't always adhere to the 'facts'. Disregarding food safety practices or exceeding speed limits highlights our tendencies to neglect well-founded probabilities, leading to avoidable suffering, as reflected in existing statistics on food poisoning and motor vehicle accidents. Why does this happen? Because, phenomenologically[15], we are not purely rational beings, despite the assertion of many that we are. Consequently, we often fail to adhere to the facts or rules despite being present to the risks. Confronting this reality can be humbling and may make us feel even more vulnerable, which is perhaps why many might prefer to avert their gaze from or neglect to pay attention to what's happening around them. Ironically, while we refer to ourselves as 'Sapiens', which comes from the Latin word for 'wise' or 'intelligent', we are *not* purely rational beings. We may be intelligent, but wisdom only comes from polishing ourselves over time in terms of how to leverage and utilise our intellect practically. Furthermore, even when we tap into our rationality, there is still no guarantee that it will work in our favour! This is in direct contrast with the way many thinkers portray rationality – a purely positive phenomenon – which, in itself, is inauthentic.

---

15   Phenomenology is the philosophical study of objectivity and reality as subjectively lived and experienced.

Confusion typically arises from the limitations of our intuition, senses, sensations, perceptual structure and rationality or conceptual structure – our ability to conceive matters rationally through mental processes such as comparison, analysis, contemplation, reflection, etc. And when we do tap into our rationality, the outcome may be flawed or have an infected and ineffective logic and reasoning behind it. In addition, even when we rationally know the truth of a matter, we might still override it simply because we wish to or don't like it.

Whether we don't see or know something, we know something but have misconceptions about it, or we don't even know what we don't know, they all sit in the realm of the unknown; let's refer to this as 'The Invisible'. Believing in the existence of this mysterious realm is crucial. It means acknowledging and surrendering to the fact that we don't know everything. This acknowledgement leads us to collaborate, bring complementary people together, organise ourselves in teams, consider other perspectives and adopt a pluralistic approach. However, while the importance of this belief might seem obvious in theory, our actions sometimes tell a different story. Indeed, history has shown us the high costs of ignoring this reality.

The world's highest achievers recognise and believe in The Invisible because they deeply acknowledge that they don't know everything. Rather than acting as if they know it all, they consistently tap into the knowledge and resources of others, read books and academic papers, seek guidance from coaches and advisors, and enlist the expertise of professionals in various fields. This approach involves hiring individuals who excel in diverse areas to lead and contribute to advancing their mission or interests, aligning with what matters most to them. Consider that if you lead an organisation, you have authority over many experts in their fields who likely possess far more in-depth knowledge and experience than you in certain areas. If you fail to acknowledge this, both in theory and action, you and, therefore, also the organisation will be in trouble.

Believing in The Invisible releases us from confusion and serves as the foundation for our discoveries and growth. It recognises that we do not see or know all there is to see or know with accuracy. And yet, even when we do know, we sometimes rebel against our own knowing despite accepting it as the truth, authentic or 'right'. Acknowledging our ignorance and belief in The Invisible gave rise to modern science. That's when we discovered how lenient we had been in accepting unverified and untested descriptions of the material world for so long. This leniency led to our profound respect for science and the scientific way of thinking. Hence, the modern scientific revolution did not begin with the discovery of new pieces of knowledge; it was sparked first and foremost by the realisation and acknowledgement of our ignorance and double ignorance. Furthermore, the *belief* in science and the scientific approach to knowing is, in itself, a belief – a topic we will delve into later in this book. For now, let's explore The Invisible in more depth.

CHAPTER 2

The Invisible

In our daily lives, we routinely pay attention to what is visible to us, individually and collectively, rather than looking into all there is. In other words, we often only see what is immediately accessible. Furthermore, not everything is transparent or provided to us with evidence. We don't know what's going on behind the scenes of the movies we watch or the true intentions of certain pharmaceutical companies; we don't have access to classified government documents; we can't read our intimate partner's mind, and we don't know the intention of the person we are about to add to our team. We often take a leap of faith after considering whatever preliminary evaluations are available to us and trust many people, industries, government bodies and so on with little to no proof. For example, if a vet informs you that your dog requires surgery, you can't be certain whether she has your dog's best interest at heart, despite showing you some test results, or if she cares more about her own financial interests. Trust is a choice. We choose to trust because we perceive the vet to be trustworthy, not because we fully understand the medical condition or her advice. Consequently, we cannot be fully self-aware. It seems we are sheer mysteries, even to ourselves!

The problem is that our inclination towards the visible plays a significant role in our vulnerability to coercion, manipulation, deception and misguidance. We are either genuinely oblivious to the truth or ignorant and negligent when we overlook the invisible aspects that significantly shape our understanding of the world and all the content within existence. Let me explain. As discussed, there is a rock-solid fact about human beings and our perpetual system – we do not see everything within existence. Acknowledging this truth is where acceptance of The Invisible becomes an axiom[16] – a fundamental and undeniable reality that is self-evidently true. Just because it is currently concealed from our view doesn't mean it doesn't exist. Consider that failing to acknowledge the axiomatic nature of The Invisible makes us even more vulnerable and confused.

While we are not entitled to know, life demands us to know. We may think that's unfair, but it is what it is. So, unless we are authentically aware of this, we will suffer, potentially cause others to suffer and have little to no workability and effectiveness in our lives. We would relinquish our autonomy to choose and become victims of circumstances. Consequently, our experience of life would become a burden.

How we are and what happens in the world today has been brilliantly captured in the story of *Pinocchio*. Like its main character, we all come into this world semi-autonomous, and we can redeem ourselves, becoming free of both internal and external forces that get in the way of being ourselves. While, as human beings, we have the highest level of autonomy of all beings on earth, that is a quality to be reclaimed and honoured, not taken for granted. When Geppetto first creates Pinocchio, he is nothing more than a puppet, a piece of wooden handicraft. While the puppet essentially has many elements of a human being – like arms and legs, eyes and lips – it is not autonomous like a human being is. In the scene where Geppetto looks upward to the night sky, symbolically asking the supreme power and ultimate reality (existence) to transform his wooden puppet into a real boy, the angel and symbol of Mother Nature mysteriously transforms Pinocchio into a semi-autonomous being.

---

16   A statement or proposition which is regarded as being established, accepted or self-evidently true; that which commends itself as evident.

Like Pinocchio, we are all semi-autonomous beings until we develop our awareness and polish our being – the way we relate to all content in life and act upon it through our conceptions and behaviour. That's what it takes to claim and redeem our autonomy and freedom. It is autonomy that gives us the greatest potential to be leaders who influence circumstances, fulfil our desires and make life better for ourselves and others. It brings us back to integrity (wholeness), the key to becoming effective. True redemption – the process of redeeming ourselves by claiming back our autonomy and freedom – leads us to be aware, integrous (whole) and effective, which, in turn, leads us to fulfilment and prosperity. If you choose not to be responsible around your awareness – the very first place to start – you are likely to outsource your sanity to others, who, as both the internal and external malevolent forces, may not always have the best intentions.

Belief in The Invisible should form the foundation of any inquiry in the pursuit of knowledge, and science is no exception. More specifically, The Invisible is the basis of scientific, methodical and objective discoveries and the source of our acknowledgement of our vulnerability, epistemic humility and openness. For example, there were times in the evolution of science when microorganisms or molecules were invisible to us, or at least beyond our perception. Furthermore, scientific findings in cosmology consistently support the existence of invisible energy and matter in the universe. In standard cosmological models, the universe comprises three main components: matter, radiation and dark energy. Current estimates suggest that dark energy constitutes approximately 68% of the total energy in the observable universe, dark matter makes up about 26% and ordinary (baryonic) matter accounts for roughly 5%.[17] Examples like this highlight the complex and predominantly unseen nature of the universe and how, over time, technological advancements and knowledge brought these once-invisible (to us) entities into view.

---

17   Brout, D., & Scolnic, D. 2022. *Most precise accounting yet of dark matter and dark energy.* Harvard Gazette.

While believing in The Invisible is necessary, it can also be dangerous for truthseekers. On the one hand, it opens our minds to be willing to learn about what we may not rationally think is possible in our current conception of existence and everything in it. On the other hand, it can make us susceptible to falsely believing in superficial or mythical matters or narratives. Being inauthentic with our conceptions suggests the shadow – our troubled sides – is running the show when engaging with The Invisible. This inauthenticity can manifest in one of two ways. The first is disbelief in The Invisible – when we refuse to acknowledge The Invisible. As a result, we restrict our understanding of matters to the confines of our limited intuitive, sensory, perceptual and conceptual structures. The second is fully succumbing to The Invisible, which can lead to an overly lenient and fickle acceptance of unrealistic concepts.

Consider the nature of intuition, for example. When someone claims to receive abductive revelations, like voices or apparitions that don't have a clear origin or root source, or a thought suddenly strikes them seemingly out of nowhere, are these signs of a psychiatric dysfunction? Or are they rare abilities and gifts that can give that person access to matters beyond rationality and normal cognition? How one interprets what is known as a 'calling' – a persistent urge that doesn't leave you alone – raises intriguing questions and may encourage you to pursue something like an idea. For instance, how should an artist interpret their inspirations? How should a thinker interpret an abductive revelation and articulate it to others? Are the experiences of religious individuals or people of 'faith' who claim to receive revelations and talk to God in prayers true or false? Is a monk in a temple glimpsing the 'eternal realm', uniting with the core of existence or a different dimension to our consciousness or psyche? Or are they being delusional?

The broader inquiry extends to whether our individualistic conscious thinking, feeling and experiencing exist in isolation or if there's a collective higher intelligence and consciousness accessible to all. While, traditionally, we know that a significant part of The Invisible still resides within the realms of scientific and methodical studies, other parts defy the familiar, tangible and concrete realms of these 'objective' inquiries, opening up a spectrum of questions that span the mysterious and the unexplored (The Invisible). The intention is not to seek answers to all these sophisticated multidimensional questions in this book. However, the essence of this conversation lies in acknowledging our individual experiences and the subjectivity that accompanies them – we experience what we experience. The question is: does an objective reality underpin the intricate web of meanings, ideas, concepts, constructs, perceptions and conceptions that we encounter?

The experiences of people like mystics, monks, people of 'faith', artists, and visionaries are personal and often transcend the boundaries of conventional language and reason. When shared with others, the responsibility lies in articulating and translating these experiences into words and narratives while being fully transparent about whether or not there is or can be empirical validity of certain aspects and acknowledging that some parts may reside in realms beyond empirical scrutiny. Recognising the arational nature of certain matters – those not governed by logical reasoning and existing outside the realm of comprehensible reason – is essential.

The recognition that not everything can be fully expressed through reason, logic and language gave rise to the arts. Throughout history, eminent thinkers and philosophers like Rumi, Carl Jung, Friedrich Nietzsche, Martin Heidegger and Fyodor Dostoevsky, to name just a few, turned to writing poetry and stories rich in metaphors and symbolism to convey intricate, multidimensional ideas. Engaging with narratives and rhetoric by no means implies a lack of understanding of reason, logic or direct language by these individuals. On the contrary, they were well aware of the limitations of such approaches, and some wrote other eminent bodies of work, including fully-fledged rational arguments and philosophy. However, they also chose to express themselves through poetry and other forms of literature.

Indeed, many profound insights have been conveyed through poetry and other forms of creative expression. Poetry, for instance, is both rational and irrational – that's what makes it poetry. Resulting from emotions recollected in 'tranquillity' – a calm mental state – poetry captures moments of personal perception encountering simple truths or conveying experiences. Such exploration of phenomena and experiences falls within the realm of phenomenology, a branch of philosophy rather than an exact science, given its focus on emotions, feelings and subjective experiences. In contemporary times, qualitative studies serve as a means to gain insight. However, opinions vary on whether these studies belong to the realm of science or social science – an issue we will delve into further in a later chapter of this book.

The point is, not every valuable idea or concept needs to conform logically. Consider Carl Jung, for example. Despite his significant contributions to psychology, many universities still hesitate to give his work 'scientific' credibility, typically confining discussions of his theories to psychology faculties. Indeed, many radically disqualify his entire body of work, which not only voids its value but considers it 'pseudoscience' – not an exact science – inherently giving it a negative connotation. Karl Popper, who mainly focused on the philosophy of science, had a similar argument regarding Sigmund Freud, known as one of the 20th century's most influential thinkers. Popper claimed that Freud's theories were not falsifiable and, therefore, pseudoscience. We will examine the distinction between exact science, non-science and pseudoscience in Chapter 5: Science. Again, consider that not all content needs to be scientific to hold value.

Not all ideas that fit within the realm of rational thought meet the six standard criteria of science and need to be subject to empirical scrutiny. This includes philosophical ideations and discussions around ethics or constructs like human rights and democracy. In essence, not every rational argument needs to be scientifically validated; it simply requires clear and compelling reasoning. Conversely, anything deemed scientific should inherently be rational.

In fact, scientific arguments not only must be rational but also need to have evidence to support them. However, the idea that everything must adhere to scientific standards to possess value contributes to our individual and collective confusion. The reality is many things in life simply are as they are; they don't necessarily follow a particular pattern or logic – they're not rational. Recognising this reality leads to accepting The Invisible as a foundational and unquestionable truth and acknowledges that its existence is not negated by its current invisibility to us. Ignoring this axiomatic truth would only leave us even more vulnerable and confused than we already are. In the following chapter, The Fabric of Knowing, we examine how we come to know and understand matters, including how we perceive and conceive or rationalise content, in more detail.

CHAPTER 3

The Fabric of Knowing

Traditionally, education is meant to support us from an early age in gradually developing our conceptions of various fragments of reality and ensuring they are as authentic as possible and congruent with the latest advancements in knowledge. Why is this important? Because life brings us matters to deal with. It brings us challenges, dilemmas, adversities and traumas. As beings with a relatively high level of autonomy, we are capable of responding to and being the primary cause of any matter in our life, regardless of the source. But if we are not equipped to handle them and respond appropriately, we will be crushed under their weight. Our physical, emotional and mental survival and growth are tightly dependent on our knowledge and valid understanding or *authentic awareness* of ourselves as human beings and the world and its content.

Consider how an orangutan cares for her offspring in the first six to seven years. She knows her baby needs to learn not only about herself but also the world around her in the context of what is relevant to her. The mother teaches her baby to distinguish between edible and poisonous plants and leave the latter alone. She also supports her in learning how to relate to rain, storms, heat and cold and developing a mental model of how to climb trees and swing from branch to branch to retrieve fruit and young leaves. All this knowledge is passed down to ensure her offspring can live her orangutan life confidently and gracefully. The baby instinctively knows that she not only needs to learn to perform each function for her survival but also that existence demands her to become more and more knowledgeable about and effective at this thing called life.

Like the orangutan, we are vulnerable from the moment we are born and must learn over time how to deal with whatever life throws at us. Even when we no longer need our parents and teachers to guide us, we remain vulnerable to illness, diseases, natural disasters, our angry neighbour, our cheating partner, our 'unfair' boss, our unreliable team member, and the list goes on. Furthermore, our vulnerability is not limited to external forces. We are even more vulnerable to the self within, to internal forces like temptation – even a relatively minor one like potato chips – impulses and desires. In truth, we are the ones who get in our own way most of the time. Consider that our inherent vulnerability is that we are flawed in our rationality. Evidently, we humans have made multiple 'rational' mistakes throughout the course of history and continue to do so.

As vulnerable beings, it makes sense that we convey fear and anxiety – not as inherently negative phenomena but as signals prompting concern about our vulnerabilities and perceived danger. Embracing these moods allows us to stay vigilant, contemplate potential scenarios and proactively prepare ourselves so that we can avoid the pitfalls of being reactive when life presents challenges. Care – a self-generating mood or attunement that influences how we disclose and express ourselves in life – becomes pivotal in this context. Vulnerability, anxiety and fear accompany this experience, urging us to tap into authentic and congruent knowledge by leveraging our intellect, rationality and the wisdom passed down in the form of knowledge, infrastructure, tools and resources from those who navigated similar challenges before us. We reveal ourselves through these primal moods or states of mind as we engage with life. The healthier our relationship with these states, the more effectively we can amplify our self-expression. In contrast, the unhealthier our relationship with them, the more likely it is that we will suppress all or some of what we have to express and limit the matters we expose ourselves to in life. Confronting our fears, anxiety and vulnerabilities is driven by care. Care marks the beginning of our quest for knowing and seeking authentic awareness so that we can make effective decisions amidst all the confusion, dilemmas and uncertainties, ultimately contributing to the overall integrity of our lives and enhancing the probability of fulfilling our intentions.

Nature or nurture?

Some tap into the doctrine that we are who and how we are from birth based on factors such as our astrological sign and personality type and that nothing can change that. They may label themselves 'extroverted' or 'introverted' or try to deceive themselves and others using self-selected descriptive labels and adjectives. They tell themselves and others, 'That's just the way I am' as an excuse for their behaviour. Some might even 'discover' their identity later in life. With so many labels and categories designed to make ourselves known to ourselves (self-image) and others (persona), is it any wonder that some people choose to *become* the label or category simply because it's there? Ironically, the more we explain ourselves to ourselves and others, the less meaningful it becomes.

Others tap into the doctrine that there is no nature to human beings whatsoever and that everything is mutable. They believe we don't discover but *define* ourselves, forging what – as opposed to who – we want to be or become till we gradually create the persona we so desperately want to convey to the world. If you hang onto this belief that everything is a construct or mutable, you essentially regard your identity as fluid, as though it's a liquid that can be transformed into any form you choose as part of a science experiment. No matter what you choose to identify as, deep down, this communicates as if you think you have absolute control over the 'whatness', 'howness' and wholeness (integrity) of your being. Whatness refers to the essence or intrinsic qualities that define what something fundamentally is, while howness refers to the manner or method by which something operates or functions.

There is no inference of 'rightness' or 'wrongness' with choosing or adopting a particular pathway in life. That's the beauty of expressing our unique being – sometimes referred to as the soul. We align ourselves with certain political, religious, spiritual or societal ideologies. Indeed, self-discovery is crucial in the process of becoming our future self and being constantly present to our current state of being. We are all in a constant state of becoming. How we relate to the content of the world and our conception of our core self evolves over time.

Notably, categorisation and segregation can lead to separation and division instead of unity. For example, in a political sense, if a ruling political party or regime favours certain groups of people and lets others be marginalised, as is the case in many of the world's nations, that leads to segregation, suppression, polarised societies – with certain groups being treated as first-class citizens while other groups are ignored – and many other issues beyond the scope of this book. Consider that we all identify as *human beings* first and foremost. Some may perceive this as an implicit assumption or consider it obvious. However, deliberately and consciously identifying as a human being and then acknowledging that we possess distinct preferences due to our freedom and autonomy alters how we engage with fellow human beings. Interpreting preferences as 'differences', leads to an 'us versus them' conversation. Such categorisation serves as the root of many unpleasant experiences we undergo as human beings, including sexism, racism, marginalisation and so forth. This is not to imply that there are absolutely no distinctions, such as those between genders, but it hinges on where you direct your intentional consciousness or attention.

Whether you tap into the first doctrine that every layer of your being is fixed and that it is up to you to discover the label, category or adjective that best describes you, or you believe there is no core self and that everything about you as an individual is fluid and mutable, you are encouraged to be open to an alternative view. Consider that you are your soul or unique being. And given that the soul or unique being is mysterious and arational, meaning it can't fully be understood or analysed by reason and logic, it is something to be discovered over time. How? By being constantly in dialogue with your consciousness – more on this later. For now, and in this context, consider that your psyche encompasses your consciousness and your soul or unique being.

We all have more immediate access to our conscious mind because it is the part of ourselves that can be cognitively studied. It is a tool given to us to direct our attention to what we want to and can learn about. The question is: to what extent can we have a conscious understanding of matters and the material world (science), phenomena, ideas, concepts, constructs and philosophies? The answer is that it depends on how well we acknowledge the limitations of our intuition, senses, sensations and perceptual and conceptual structures and how open we are to getting to know and comprehend matters.

Categories of knowing

More than two millennia ago, Aristotle introduced a categorisation of knowledge, dividing human understanding into three categories: episteme (scientific knowledge), techne (skills and crafts) and phronesis (ethical wisdom and virtue). More specifically, techne relates to the mastery of tools and techniques to produce something, while episteme aims to uncover the laws of nature and immutable facts, even if their comprehension might be limited. Meanwhile, phronesis is concerned with ethical discernment. It involves weighing competing values and making decisions when answers are not absolute or multiple options exist. Farmers designing irrigation systems and software engineers implementing an agile process operate within the techne category. Astronomers exploring the rotational patterns of galaxies operate within the epistemic category.

And those faced with having to decide on how to allocate limited resources, such as policymakers, regularly navigate the realm of phronesis.

The term 'epistemology' comes from the Greek word 'episteme', which Aristotle and other ancient philosophers used to refer to specific, theoretical knowledge. While Aristotle categorised knowledge as episteme, techne and phronesis, the field of epistemology focuses on the nature, scope and origin of knowledge in general, not just scientific knowledge. Epistemology evolved into a branch of philosophy in its own right, one that is concerned with the theory of knowledge and explores the nature, sources, limitations and validity of knowledge and belief. Epistemology addresses questions such as: What is knowledge? How is it acquired? What do people know? How do we know what we know? It examines the means and extent to which knowledge and understanding are possible in various fields of study. An example of an epistemological conversation or topic is the debate over the nature of scientific knowledge. Can scientific theories provide accurate descriptions of the world, or are they merely useful tools for predicting phenomena?

Working out what things are and how they work is a fact of life. From the get-go, life demands us to know about matters not provided as part of an onboarding process on induction day. The moment we were thrown into 'existence', there was no instruction manual to guide us on the steps to living happily ever after. And even if there was, would we follow them? Most of us don't even follow the instruction manual that comes with electrical devices, choosing to entertain ourselves – and those watching – by working it out on our own, even if it takes four times as long! Eventually, we all discover – or stumble upon – the limitations to our intuition, senses, sensations and perceptual and conceptual structures, sometimes the hard way, because we either lack visibility regarding what lies within and beyond us or choose to look the other way. Now that we know why we should care about embarking on a continual quest for knowing and seeking authentic awareness, let's explore the different ways we can know or comprehend matters, regardless of which Aristotelian category of knowledge they fall into.

Consider that there is a set of categories when it comes to knowing:

1. **There are things we know that we know well.** For example, I know how to read and write, I know how to speak French, I know how to get a job at a restaurant and serve as a wait-person. It's when you know something with a high degree of accuracy and clarity and act upon this knowledge. If you were diabetic and authentically aware of the dangers of consuming sugary and starchy carbohydrates, you would prioritise healthy eating and monitoring and managing your blood sugar levels.

2. **There are things we know we don't know but can learn about if we choose.** For example, you know you don't know how to speak Spanish but could join an in-person or online course to learn how to if you wish. You know how to wait tables in a restaurant but not how to own and manage a restaurant. However, if owning and running your own restaurant was your ambition, you could learn how to by reading, listening to podcasts, watching videos, attending courses and tapping into the knowledge of experienced business tutors, mentors, advisors, coaches and restaurateurs.

3. **There are things we don't know we don't know ('double ignorance').** Imagine if you were ignorant about your lack of knowledge about the nature of money and how currency works, leaving you incapable of making effective financial decisions and confused about why you are not in a good financial position. But then a friend or mentor might bring the gap in your understanding to your attention, leading you to undertake some learning to bridge the gap. As an amateur in any field, there will always be blind spots.

4. **There are things we know but have misconceptions about.** Let's say your understanding of electricity is incongruent

with how it works. If you were to work with it, ignorantly averting your gaze from your inauthentic knowledge about its potential dangers, you would be jeopardising your life. In this case, you could be open and vulnerable about your inauthentic awareness and leave electrical work to the experts or undertake the necessary study to become an electrician. Or you may think you know how to attract customers to your newly opened restaurant. However, after months of trying different ways or insisting on how you think it should work, you might get humbled and realise your way isn't working, indicating your misconceptions about marketing and generating new business.

5. **There are things we know with a high degree of accuracy and clarity but deliberately ignore, neglect or rebel against that knowledge.** As a result of this negligence, we don't act upon the knowledge. Here is where 'The Invisible' has been made visible, yet we either dare or choose not to surrender to it. Instead, we behave and act in a manner contradictory to what we know to be true. Referring to the diabetes example, despite being fully aware of the health risks, you would ignore them and eat whatever you choose without doing the necessary checks and measures because it gives you instant gratification.

Consider that the fifth category is the most dangerous for us individually and collectively. Take an example that occurs all too often – witnessing what we consider an injustice but choosing to avert our gaze and remain silent because it feels like the safer option. Despite knowing our silence empowers the alleged oppressor and further victimises the oppressed, often we say and do nothing anyway. Therefore, not only do the limitations of our intuition, senses, sensations and perceptual and conceptual structures cause problems, but our lack of vulnerability (openness) or values misalignment often exacerbates them. Knowingly violating our self-selected values despite recognising that something is amiss reflects a lack of self-control or responsiveness and compromises our integrity (wholeness) and the integrity of our lives.

So, there are things we know well and have a relatively authentic awareness of and things we don't know. Furthermore, when it comes to the things we don't know, we are either aware of our ignorance or oblivious to it. For those areas where we are aware of our ignorance, we have an opportunity to prioritise learning about them so we can fill in the gaps and grow. Yet, when certain aspects remain in our blind spot and we are oblivious to our lack of knowledge, we risk getting stuck in an endless, recursive loop – a rat race from which we struggle to escape – especially if we stubbornly refuse to let down our guard and discernibly tap into other people's knowledge and resources.

How do we perceive reality?

Some believe our perception of reality doesn't align with its true form, while others contend it does. This debate has been a cornerstone of philosophical inquiry since the discipline's inception, revolving around whether our experiences truly reflect reality or if we're merely grasping at its fundamental essence. For example, earlier, we shared the views of Hegel, Kant and Suhrawardi on this.

The general consensus is that we don't have direct access to reality. Our understanding stems from our sensory perceptions and the brain's interpretation of these signals, both crucial for constructing our reality. Imagine the brain as being encased in a secluded, quiet chamber – our skull – isolated and oblivious to the external world or bodily states. It relies solely on sensory data from our body, which are mere reflections of external or physical changes, without direct knowledge of these changes. This scenario illustrates the 'Reverse Inference Problem,' where the brain must infer causes from effects. For instance, distinguishing between the sound of a gunshot and a slamming door depends on the brain's inference, which is heavily influenced by past experiences. This inferential process is both reactive and predictive, drawing on historical data to form categories for future reference.

When the brain anticipates future events, it constructs categories based on past similarities. These categories can be based on tangible attributes, like the shape or texture of an apple, or abstract qualities, like its culinary suitability. Unique to the brain, this categorisation allows for the creation of 'social reality' – a collective attribution of function or value to objects independent of their physical properties. Currency serves as a prime example, where society collectively assigns value to otherwise worthless sheets of polymer. This concept extends to the creation of national borders, governmental systems and even the societal roles attributed to individuals, all stemming from collective agreement. Research suggests that many psychological categories are manifestations of social reality, shaped by collective perceptions and cultural agreements.[18]

The notion that our brain is sequestered does not imply confinement. On the contrary, it possesses the remarkable ability to synthesise past experiences into novel creations, a process known as imagination. However, this ability is a double-edged sword – while it enables creativity and foresight, it can also detach us from the present, necessitating a balance between being anchored in reality and exploring beyond it.

The fact that a ripe tomato is red to us is logically flawed. In reality, the object absorbed every colour *except* red when exposed to photons of light. What we see through our sensory ability of sight and perception is what the object rejects, which is the colour red. If we were to examine the surface molecules of the 'red' object, we would see that there is no red. So, objectively, science tells us that the tomato is all colours but red, but our perception tells us it is red because we see what the object rejects from the light it receives.

---

18 Fiske, S. T., Gilbert, D. T., & Lindzey, G. 2010. *Handbook of Social Psychology.* Wiley.
Haslam, S. A., Reicher, S. D., & Platow, M. J. 2011. *The New Psychology of Leadership: Identity, Influence and Power.* Psychology Press.
Hacking, I. 1999. *The Social Construction of What?.* Harvard University Press.

Our tendency to assert that an apple is red simply because we perceive it as such illustrates our self-centric perspective. Similarly, using ourselves as the frame of reference to describe directions, such as left or right, highlights our inherent self-referential thinking. In contrast, some indigenous cultures employ more objective directional references like north, south, east and west, reflecting a worldview that does not position humans as the focal point. Main Character Syndrome (MCS) is a newly coined term that aptly describes individuals who perceive themselves as the central figures in any given situation. People with MCS often believe they are the most significant presence in any room or circumstance. While this inclination toward individualism is prevalent, it reflects a broader human bias towards self-importance. The examples above serve as humbling reminders that our perception often diverges from objective reality. Those who have a healthy relationship with authenticity as a way of being take the time to thoughtfully consider their beliefs and opinions, ensuring they are as congruent as possible with how things actually are. Fortunately, science provides us with tools to access and understand certain aspects of reality. Yet, there remain realms beyond scientific reach, prompting us to contemplate the limitations of our perception and the vastness of the unknown.

As mentioned earlier, Islamic philosopher Suhrawardi metaphorically expresses in his book *The Red Intellect* that when light hits darkness, it appears red. Think of twilight, an aurora or a campfire – the fact that they appear red to us is an illusion. Thanks to science, we now know that visible light is the only light the human eye can perceive. When you look at the sun's visible light, it appears to be colourless, which we call white. Although we can see this light, white isn't considered part of the visible spectrum because white light isn't the light of a single colour but many colours. When we bend light using a prism, we see the colours of the rainbow. Suhrawardi used symbolic language in his book to convey how our intellect can easily lie to us or lead us to have inauthentic, incongruent and illusive perceptions of even the most basic things.

While cognitive studies are actively trying to demystify the intellectual aspects of our consciousness, some radically hypothesise that all there is to our consciousness or psyche is brain activities and the mind. Others strongly assert that there is also a soul – the divine or eternal element that operates in conjunction with our cognitive abilities. From a philosophical perspective, neither of these views can be fully endorsed. Since we cannot be fully clear on this matter – to date, neither cognitive studies nor neuroscience has managed to unravel it in its entirety – consider that a level of our consciousness is far more mysterious than any of us know. Therefore, it should be placed, at least in part, within the realm of arational matters. The bottom line is life demands us to operate and perform. So, it is essential that we at least acknowledge the mysterious nature of our consciousness and be in wonderment of it while continuing to investigate it – at least in part and, wherever possible, methodically – so that we keep developing our authentic conception of it. The latter can be seen as an antidote to our individual and collective confusion, as discussed in Chapter 1. We will explore the mysterious realm of human consciousness in more detail in Chapter 6.

Rationality

'Homo Sapiens' means 'wise human', and, in many ways, we have earned this epithet as a species. We have made significant advancements during our time on the planet so far. We have extended our lifespans, markedly reduced extreme poverty, revolutionised food production through agriculture, industrialised manufacturing processes and advanced technology, among other achievements. However, this characterisation of human beings as solely rational beings is incomplete. While we possess the capacity for reason and rationality, we must recognise that we are also inherently emotional beings. Our consciousness encompasses not only rational thought but also the capacity to experience suffering. This dual nature often leads us to stray from our pursuit of truth. Indeed, at times, it compels us to escape from uncomfortable realities. In other words, we are not only rational beings, but we also have emotions and feelings – the interpretation of our emotions – and, when iterated, our feelings shape our moods or state of mind, which are always in the background no matter what we're doing or who we are with. They can lead to arguments over the most trivial matters and influence our speech, decisions and behaviour.

In conventional understanding, being rational is perceived as diametrically opposed to being emotional, suggesting that emotions carry a negative implication and lack value. Although emotions are often considered irrational in a conventional sense, they are actually quite arational. However, there are disagreements about whether desires and emotions can be evaluated as rational and irrational or arational.[19] Given that our emotions are not systems or robots that follow a clear-cut algorithm, enabling them to be fully understood in a purely rational sense by us human beings, they must be arational. We will examine the difference between rational, irrational and arational in more detail shortly. For now, though, it's worth noting that rationality, as a unitary phenomenon, is commonly seen as sitting on a spectrum from irrational to rational. However, this does not align with the nature of rationality because some matters don't fit neatly anywhere on the spectrum; they are neither rational nor irrational.

When someone accuses another of being 'emotional', it often implies that the person's judgement is influenced by their feelings, suggesting a lack of rationality. This conventional assertion tends to downplay the significance of emotions and invalidate the individual's feelings. From the accuser's perspective, their reasoning may seem logical, albeit potentially flawed. This dynamic is particularly evident in contemporary discussions surrounding sexual consent, where attempts are made to rationalise inherently emotional aspects of human interaction. For instance, there have been proposals for

---

19   Knauff, Markus; Spohn, Wolfgang (14 December 2021). *Psychological and Philosophical Frameworks of Rationality – A Systematic Introduction.* In Knauff, Markus; Spohn, Wolfgang (eds.). *The Handbook of Rationality.* MIT Press. ISBN 978-0-262-04507-0. Archived from the original on 30 December 2023. Retrieved 14 August 2022.

overly rationalised approaches to consent, including the development of software applications designed to track and document consent in intimate encounters. Notably, in Australia, New South Wales Police Commissioner Mick Fuller proposed a sexual consent app be introduced in the state, sparking debates on technology, consent and intimacy. The app digitally and chronologically records mutual consent to address concerns about sexual assault. However, critics express concerns about the potential misuse and commodification of intimacy. This example highlights the challenge of balancing technology for safety without diminishing human connection. While acknowledging the importance of consent, it raises questions about the feasibility of imposing rationality on inherently emotional experiences. Such efforts risk diminishing the spontaneity and authenticity of human relationships, potentially altering the dynamics of romance and interpersonal connections.

In contrast to how being emotional is often perceived, stoicism, or maintaining a calm exterior without expressing emotions, is often considered admirable. However, concealing emotions does not negate their existence. Underlying emotions and feelings can still subtly influence speech, decisions and behaviour, even when one is putting on a brave face. Emotions are not merely sensations to be suppressed through radical stoicism; they are real, tangible and, to a large extent, measurable. Feelings arise from how we interpret our emotions and the significance we attribute to them. While people can readily answer questions about their actions, inquiries about their emotions often leave them at a loss for words. A culture that suppresses emotions, from parenting techniques to law enforcement practices and legislative decision-making, may seem attractive to some, but it risks overlooking the profound impact emotions have on the human experience and on our decision-making processes.

Stoicism points to an unhealthy relationship with vulnerability and is inauthentic. We may wish that a police officer in the line of duty is as stoic on the inside as their persona projects or that a judge is free from emotions when determining the fate of the accused. It would be nice if the HR manager conducting your performance review or the academic panel members assessing and evaluating the progress you have made on your research were utterly objective. There are always more invisible emotions at play than we wish to see on the surface. Moreover, to expect a human being to be completely unbiased is another inauthenticity.

In *A History of Western Philosophy*, author Bertrand Russell writes, 'Stoicism teaches the development of self-control as a means of over-coming destructive emotions; the philosophy holds that becoming a clear and unbiased thinker allows one to understand the universal reason (logos).'[20] Note that this distinction only refers to destructive emotions, not all emotions. This distinction underpins the arguments and perspectives advocated by rationality enthusiasts such as Steven Pinker, Richard Dawkins and Sam Harris, whose influence extends to millions worldwide. The radical enthusiasts of rationality often portray rationality as a purely positive phenomenon. However, while some of our accomplishments through rationality deserve applause, rationality also gave birth to weapons of mass destruction, nano-plastics, justified discrimination, pollutants and various addictive substances. Perhaps these proponents view such adverse outcomes as products of irrationality rather than rationality, perceiving rationality as a definitive and reliable mode of thinking equipped with its own set of tools. This perspective suggests that rationality is one unified discipline in a purely objective sense and is not open to interpretation and perspectives. It also suggests that adherence to rationality ensures solely positive outcomes, a notion that warrants closer examination. It is also worth noting that most of what we individually consider 'mistakes' in retrospect were decisions we once made with confidence, believing them to be rational. This clearly shows that our 'rationality' doesn't always work in our favour, which should be humbling.

We may delve into formal logic, acquire the skill to identify logical fallacies, hone critical thinking abilities, practice analysis and comparison, and even master reflection and contemplation. However,

---

20   Russell, B. 1945. *A History of Western Philosophy* (p.254). Simon & Schuster.

these methods are not immune to misuse; they can be wielded to win arguments solely for the purpose of advancing personal agendas or ideologies. It's rational, from a self-interested perspective, to act in a manner that benefits oneself, even if it means disregarding societal norms or ethical considerations. Consider the 'rational' decision to steal an item when there is no risk of being caught or facing any consequences.

Throughout history, rationality has been employed to justify actions such as land appropriation, colonisation, slavery, sexism and racism. Even within academic research, where access to the same data and control groups is granted, varying conclusions can be drawn based on individual observations and rationalisations, sometimes leading to dramatically contrasting interpretations. Rationality, therefore, does not exist in a realm of absolute purity; our logic and reasoning, like ourselves, are susceptible to flaws, imperfections and biases. Therefore, a human being's rationality cannot be compared with the far more simplistic logic and algorithms we use to instruct computers. This historical misuse of rationality should prompt us to reflect on the potential for our own biases and flaws in our reasoning.

Here's the thing: whatever is comprehensible to human beings is multi-dimensional and must not be oversimplified. If it were oversimplified, it would be inauthentic or incomplete. Yet, for us to more readily comprehend complex concepts and communicate them effectively, we must first simplify them by breaking them down into digestible, communicable chunks. Accepting the necessity of simplification allows us to digest complex matters without becoming overwhelmed. Otherwise, we run the risk of cognitive overload, hindering our ability to appreciate life's richness and intricacies. Furthermore, for creators, inventors or entrepreneurs, navigating through a tremendous amount of unknowns and variables often renders it impractical to pursue a path of complete rationality and meticulous engineering. For example, Apple's 1997 Think Different campaign was launched not long after Steve Jobs returned to the company he founded. It began with the following words from Jobs himself:

'Here's to the crazy ones. The misfits. The rebels. The trouble-makers. The round pegs in the square holes. The ones who see things differently. They're not fond of rules. And they have no respect for the status quo. You can quote them, disagree with them, glorify or vilify them. About the only thing you can't do is ignore them. Because they change things. They push the human race forward. And while some may see them as the crazy ones, we see genius. Because the people who are crazy enough to think they can change the world, are the ones who do.'

The complexity of any entrepreneurial or innovative endeavour can induce a sense of paralysis, hindering progress and stifling innovation. In the words of Elon Musk, 'Running a start-up is like chewing glass and staring into the abyss. After a while, you stop staring, but the glass chewing never ends.' From a philosophical perspective, this analogy extends beyond entrepreneurship to life itself. If you insist on rationalising and engineering every aspect of existence, even the most intimate and arational aspects, fulfilling your intentions may remain elusive.

As you can see, rationality within a social context is not as simplistic as some wish to think. Consider premodern societies, where hunting demanded not only logical planning and strategic thinking but also a reliance on faith in the presence of prey. Hunters had to demonstrate courage, patience and cooperation, acting as integral participants in the hunt.

While we might prefer to view ourselves solely as rational beings, it's crucial to acknowledge our emotional nature and also the role of faith in our lives. Democracy, for instance, operates on the basis of collective sentiment. Citizens cast their votes based not only on reason and knowledge but also on their emotional interpretation of issues.

One perspective often taken by radical enthusiasts of rationality, which I disagree with, is to attribute all positive and constructive progress to rationality while blaming all the dysfunction and negativity in the world on irrationality. It is important to acknowledge that not everything managed through human rationality works consistently in our favour. For instance, many things we either individually or collectively consider mistakes today, such as 'justified discrimination' and the development of plastic microbeads and chemical pesticides, were products of our rationality in the past. Similarly, many creations driven by our rationality and preferences today, like AI and genetic engineering, may not yield only favourable outcomes in the future. Deeply conceiving that 'I cannot fully rely on my rationality' fosters humility, vulnerability and wisdom, rendering you more effective in your decisions. This is not a resignation from rationality but an acknowledgment of its very nature. Therefore, it is wise to understand and relate to your rationality as not an entirely reliable means of knowing, making decisions and taking action. Consequently, while tapping into your rationality is essential, you should always do so with authentic awareness of its limitations and the willingness to consider other perspectives and perceptions. This understanding can empower you to make more informed and balanced decisions, enhancing your overall effectiveness.

Glorifying the concept of pure 'rationality' inherently suggests that rationality is totally objective and that, once learned, provides individuals with a comprehensive means to rationalise everything. This is a fallacy. Although we acknowledge an objective reality when it comes to the absolutes in the world – hence the notion of a universal rationality – everyone has their own version of rationality when it comes to constructs due to their subjective nature. Even if rationality is considered a highly accurate and measurable trait, whose interpretation or explanation of rationality holds as 'the right one'? This is where the terms 'scientific', 'fact', 'truth' and 'objective reality' have sometimes been used and even weaponised to maintain the existing power structure and world order. This aspect has been a focal point in the discussions of several other contemporary philosophers, such as Michel Foucault and Jacques Derrida.

While numerous studies and disciplines delve into rationality, logic and methods to avoid logical fallacies, it's crucial to acknowledge the inherent flaws in human thinking, regardless of one's training. Many of our decisions, whether individual or collective, are heavily influenced by the rationality of the time. While rationality has contributed to advancements such as increased lifespans, technology and efficiency, it has also given rise to destructive forces like nuclear weapons, pollutants and environmental degradation, addictive substances and racism. The aspiration is for rationality to guide us in overcoming these malevolent forces. However, achieving this requires a rationality that collaborates with ethics, science and philosophy rather than existing in isolation. When left unchecked, science and rationality have the potential to both benefit and harm, highlighting the need for them to be integrated into a broader framework that upholds the integrity of our reality.

So, while rationality plays a crucial role in making sense of the world, developing strategies and driving progress, it is essential to recognise its limitations and potential for flaws. Rationality can lead to both constructive advancements and destructive consequences. Rationalists may acknowledge the inherent imperfections in rationality and seek to refine them over time. However, this acknowledgment highlights the dynamic nature of rationality and the fact that there are also diverse opinions and perspectives on the subject. Ironically, what is deemed rational today may be considered irrational tomorrow, and what I consider rational, others might consider irrational. Such disparities can lead to conflict, debate and confusion. On the positive side, disparities lead to pluralistic thinking and intellectual collaboration for true diversity and inclusion. This encourages us to put arrogance and hubris aside and see life through multiple perspectives.

'Conservatives' who staunchly defend the status quo may either be unaware of or intentionally avert their gaze from the reality that they're not allowing everyone to participate in the system they've established. They often justify their actions with arguments about competency hierarchies, believing that by allowing everyone to participate, competency hierarchies will naturally form. On the flip side, those who are deeply frustrated with the status quo may advocate for radical change. They may seek to dismantle existing systems and institutions, even if parts of them are working, believing that an immediate and comprehensive revolution and disruption are necessary for progress. This perspective often stems from the conviction that a more complete theory or vision of society exists, and rebuilding from scratch would result in a vastly improved state of affairs. However, history often demonstrates that such sweeping transformations do not always achieve the desired outcomes. For instance, the French Revolution aimed to completely overhaul the existing monarchy and societal structures to establish liberty, equality and fraternity. However, it led to the Reign of Terror, widespread chaos and eventually, the rise of Napoleon Bonaparte, whose rule diverged significantly from the original revolutionary ideals. This resistance to acknowledging the nature of incremental change and transformation can impede progress and perpetuate cycles of upheaval.

It is important to acknowledge the existence of competency hierarchies. Thanks to the modern world, individuals have multiple avenues to pursue their strengths. If an individual cannot excel in one area, they have the opportunity to find success in another. However, the belief that these hierarchies are naturally occurring and purely based on innate competency is incomplete and inauthentic. Many are human constructs designed by those in power to maintain their advantage. Claiming 'I am just good at it' often ignores the artificial nature of these constructs. Recognising that these hierarchies are designed with specific rules and advantages that benefit certain individuals is essential. Therefore, it is understandable that some people may wish to refrain from participating in a game they never agreed to in the first place.

So, in the realm of rationality, intentions can vary widely. Some intentions may be based on clear and logical reasoning, while others may be driven by instinct, intuition, power or deeply ingrained beliefs. Furthermore, the human capacity for rationality is limited, and individuals may not always make decisions or form intentions in entirely rational ways. Overall, while rationality plays a role in shaping our intentions, it is not the sole determining factor. Our intentions are influenced by a complex interplay of rational, irrational and arational factors, making them a multifaceted aspect of human behaviour.

Our modern arrogance and ignorance threaten to impede our ability to achieve and maintain our integrity, growth, progress and advancement towards the betterment of that which has been gifted to us – life, the possibility of existence or, as Martin Heidegger put it, 'being out there in the world'. The point of this discussion is to highlight the confusion and disparity between what is deemed rational and what isn't. Ultimately, we must avoid weaponising the concept of rationality to uphold the status quo in politics, the economy, power structures, the totality of existing order, social discourse or institutional missions and instead foster inclusivity, diversity and intellectual collaboration.

The difference between rational, irrational and arational matters

The word 'rational' has two opposites: irrational – without the faculty of reason, deprived of reason or logic – and arational. Arational matters sit outside the domain of rational evaluation. The weather is a good example. The weather isn't rational and fully predictable because it doesn't follow a clear, logical flow; hence, we cannot decode it fully. And yet, its nature has a massive impact on us and the entire ecosystem. Non-arational matters, on the other hand, are either rational or irrational depending on whether they fulfil the standards of rationality. For example, beliefs, actions or general policies are rational if there is a 'good reason' for them and irrational otherwise. But who defines what is 'good' or otherwise? The answer is subject to inductive inference[21] and can be open to discussion and debate. For example, concluding that all apples are green based on having only ever observed green apples is an inductive inference. So, what belongs to the domain of rational assessment isn't always straightforward. For

---

21   An inductive inference draws a conclusion about something based on other instances of that thing.

example, disagreements exist about whether desires and emotions can be regarded as rational/irrational or arational, as discussed. In light of the confusion, the word irrational is sometimes inaccurately used when discussing arational matters.

But before we discuss arational matters in more detail, let's dispel a few myths about rationality. Ask any radically 'rational' individual whether or not they believe in progress, and the immediate response of many – if not most – would be: 'I don't believe in progress; as a matter of fact, I don't *believe* in ANYTHING'. It's as if they're allergic to the word 'believe' and choose to relate to it as the opposite of knowing. Just look at the *Oxford English Dictionary*'s definition: 'to accept that (something) is true, especially without proof'. Harvard University psychologist and author Steven Pinker says rationality is 'the ability to think clearly and logically, make informed decisions, and solve problems efficiently'. He has even written an entire book on the subject called *Rationality*.[22] Pinker has openly stated that he doesn't believe in progress as a force of nature in the universe. In a YouTube video introducing the book, he states that he doesn't believe in anything you have to believe in, full stop! The fundamental issue here lies in the misconception or *belief* that rationality is a universally consistent concept, meaning that everyone's rationality leads to the same conclusion when it is founded on 'good' rationality.

Faith is another phenomenon that radical rationalists are typically cognitively biassed towards. For example, British evolutionary biologist and author Richard Dawkins, who regards himself as a rationalist, openly states that he doesn't believe or have faith in anything. However, his books don't just focus on pure, evidence-based science; they are also filled with his beliefs. Ironic, isn't it? It seems there is an unwillingness in some to acknowledge the axiomatic nature of what we've referred to earlier as The Invisible. In other words, there is a tendency to believe that everything invisible to us must be explained through rationality, science and empirical data,

---

22   Pinker, S. 2021. *Rationality: What It Is, Why It Seems Scarce, Why It Matters.* Viking.

with little to no acknowledgment that there are areas where evidence is lacking or may never be accessible and, therefore, we need to take a leap of faith. This perspective overlooks the practicality of faith in trusting our friends, relying on the loyalty of our partners, and so on. Faith, as a mode of understanding, serves a purpose and has its function.

There is no suggestion here that faith is comparable to rationality or evidence-based scientific discoveries in terms of accuracy. It's not about debating the superiority of one over the other. Rather, it's about recognising that there are areas where our knowledge is limited. In such instances, faith may serve as a valuable epistemological approach or way of knowing. Sometimes, placing trust or having faith in something beyond rational understanding can be more effective than facing uncertainty or emptiness. For instance, some individuals experience greater workability mentally, psychologically and physiologically by having faith in an unseen 'God' or higher power. Others may prefer to use an evidence-based substance like prescribed ketamine to help them achieve a similar state of mind and workability. Whether one embraces faith or seeks scientific evidence depends on the circumstances and personal preference. Ultimately, the decision rests with each individual.

Faith is a word that is largely misunderstood and commonly only perceived in a religious context. The *Merriam-Webster Dictionary* defines faith as: 'trust in and loyalty to God; belief in the traditional doctrines of a religion'. However, a more recent entry provides a new distinction: 'A firm belief in something for which there is no proof'. That's the distinction we tap into when we talk about putting our faith in or trusting others, be it our partner, parents, close friends, bank manager, financial adviser, staff, and so on. We also put our faith in science itself.

As mentioned earlier, there is also a tendency to view rationality solely as a positive phenomenon. In other words, rationalists assume that effective decisions result from rationality, while ineffective decisions stem from irrationality or 'mere belief'. However, this perspective oversimplifies the complexities of rationality itself. For instance, consider the scenario where it might be rational for someone to steal something from a friend's house if they are certain there is no evidence pointing to them as the thief. Meanwhile, an individual who, according to our rationalist framework, 'falsely believes' in phenomena like 'God is observing us' refrains from stealing in the same situation. In this context, we see that different rationalities emerge – one justifying the act of stealing and the other following a very different rationality that doesn't. Who is the rational one in this instance? Think of a decision you made in the past that you considered rational at the time but, with the benefit of hindsight and maturity, you now consider a mistake or irrational. To assume our rationality always works in our favour is an irrational and false statement; it's also unrealistic.

We all have the capacity to be more rational in retrospect. But what is rational? And who decides? Step one is to reach a consensus on which perception of rationality we will tap into. However, it's not always that simple. For example, it is not uncommon for a dominant force, like the ruling government, to position something as 'rational' and enforce it, explaining the 'logic' behind their decision. Does that mean anything else is irrational? Consider human rights. Is the general consensus of human rights the only rational one? We build constructs and institutions like human rights on top of an intellectual substrate or bedrock. And while the general consensus may seem quite comprehensible, cohesive and rational to us, others may see it from a radically different perspective and find our understanding irrational. Let's consider another example – dogs as companion animals.

Many local councils, vets and dog breeders in today's modern societies actively promote and encourage people to desex or neuter their dogs. It seems removing the testicles and uterus of male and female dogs, respectively, is considered rational by those authorities. In Australia, for instance, if you wish to keep an 'entire dog', meaning the animal is intact, you are financially penalised because you must pay close to four times the fee to register a desexed dog. Furthermore, you are strongly encouraged to have your dog desexed before it is six months old, despite some scientific evidence suggesting this is not the best time for the dog's health and wellbeing to have it done. Some councils have taken it a step further and made it mandatory for dogs as pets to be desexed, regardless of their owners' views.

Governments typically see the rationale for neutering dogs from a pragmatic perspective – fewer stray dogs to worry about – and vets see it from both an animal health perspective – because some academic literature supports it – and a financial perspective – because they are paid to perform the surgeries. While some dog owners and breeders also perceive the desexing of dogs as rational for practical reasons, others perceive it as entirely irrational. Who is right? Is desexing a rational practice or an irrational, barbaric mutilation of dogs who have no say in the matter? There is no suggestion here that one view is right and the other is wrong. The example simply highlights that rationality is subjective. It is not a unified phenomenon on which all parties can agree. People's logic and pathway of reasoning or rationality can differ, sometimes dramatically. However, this doesn't mean that high-quality reasoning can't be distinguished from flawed and immature reasoning or the use of logical fallacies.

We have the capacity to justify almost anything through our 'rationality,' a concept famously practised by sophists in history. Sophists were itinerant teachers and intellectuals in ancient Greece during the fifth and fourth centuries BCE, specialising in various subjects such as philosophy, rhetoric, music, athletics and mathematics. They taught 'arete,' meaning virtue or excellence, primarily to young statesmen and the nobility. Sophists were skilled in making weaker arguments appear stronger and were known for their ability to argue from any position, which led to accusations of them undermining truth and moral absolutes. However, that does not mean they were irrational. Instead, they held different philosophical views that prioritised the subjective and the pragmatic over the objective and the ideal, which was in stark contrast to the views held by their critics like Socrates, Plato and Aristotle. Their approach to knowledge and truth continues to be a topic of philosophical discussion and debate. The Sophists' legacy lives on in the term 'sophistry', which refers to the use of clever but false arguments, often with the intent to deceive through fallacious reasoning. While there are methods to differentiate between 'good' and 'bad' rationality, there is no foolproof way to determine which form of rationality is absolutely correct and which isn't.

Consider contemporary politics. Political parties employ their own logic and rationality to sway public opinion and secure votes. When advocating for policy changes, each party cites 'scientific papers' and statistics from research centres. Interestingly, these papers often reach polar opposite conclusions, with each political faction presenting a cherry-picked selection of self-serving statistics and rational arguments that align with their agenda. This phenomenon is especially evident in contentious issues such as climate change, abortion, identity politics, taxation, national security and the gender pay gap. Some jokingly suggest, '98 percent of academic papers agree with whoever is funding them.' Naturally, this isn't valid; many scientists and academics maintain ethical integrity, operating within an ethical framework that extends beyond mere rationality. But the fact that people say it underscores the influence of funding sources on research outcomes. It also highlights the necessity for more than scientific methodology alone to ensure the integrity of research outcomes.

Moreover, rationality doesn't always lead us to do the 'right' thing, not only in an ethical sense but also practically. For example, our rationality led us to invent fiat currency to replace gold and silver. Did that 'rational' decision work in our favour? The same question could be asked about the digitisation of currency. Is whatever is considered rational for us and in our best interests equally rational for other nations? Even the powers that waged World War I and II justified the rationality behind their decisions, as did the Nazis with their actions. Most today would agree on the infected logic behind their rationality, adding weight to the point being made here.

As storytelling beings, we love to spin narratives – from the best way to keep dogs as pets to how the government uses the taxes we pay, vaccine mandates and strategies to safeguard our privacy. The only choice we all have is to select the 'best' story, the one that resonates most with us, or we find rational. However, it seems we have become mesmerised by all the narratives we've spun, and many people today are settling into a new form of ignorance. While we might think we know it all, arrogance or hubris – from a purely humanistic perspective – makes us blind to the truth.

This discussion on rationality opens up so many questions. Are we being selective with our data, making us cognitively biassed? Or are we seeing and sharing everything there is to see? For example, if a social scientist identifies as a feminist, would she include specific datasets in her academic research that she anticipates could result in a conclusion that might not favour her beliefs? Or would she prioritise the facts over the ideology she taps into? Is data being used to weaponise science? Is our rationality and reasoning coupled with the progress of scientific discoveries and technological advancements elevating our consciousness or leading us into further confusion and regression? Despite the vast amount of data available on nearly everything, we must acknowledge our limitations in knowing everything. And with a lack of consensus around what is rational and what's not, how are we meant to build authentic awareness of the world and everything in it?

Let's now consider the antithesis of rationality: irrationality and the more mysterious arational matters. Examples of behaviours considered irrational in ordinary discourse include giving in to temptations, going out late despite having to get up early the next morning, eating a lot of sugar and carbohydrates despite being aware of the health risks or believing in horoscopes. Conversely, in intellectual discourse, rationality is usually identified as being guided by reason or following norms of internal coherence. Some of the earlier examples may qualify as rational in an academic sense, depending on the circumstances. Examples of irrationality in this sense include cognitive biases, making arithmetic mistakes and violating the laws of probability theory when assessing the likelihood of future events.

Many discoveries begin with imagination or an abductive revelation. Tuning into someone's thought – 'thought' being a small unit of consciousness – often leads to a hypothesis for research or study, academic or nonacademic. The individual communicating their thoughts, experiences and discoveries must be clear and transparent. Critical thinking and intellectual scepticism are also required to discern the feasibility of the study. Without the latter, phenomena such as pseudoscience, scientism, dogmatism, unrooted ideologies, manufactured religions and cults can arise. In essence, we need to scrutinise our hypotheses, assess their feasibility through methodical approaches, gather empirical data and, if not feasible, be transparent about them. This allows the knowledge being produced to be criticised and intellectually negotiated, ensuring it – or parts of it – sit within the realm of reasoning. Furthermore, when it comes to arational matters, the important thing to be aware of is that we contend with several of them daily and simply accept that they are what and how they are.

Why do we need to be concerned with the arational nature of certain matters? Isn't focusing on rational and irrational matters enough? The answer is no because we are not the ones who created existence, including us human beings and our perceptual and conceptual structures. We humans often have this false expectation that everything must be rational. However, as mentioned, many things in life are not rational in their entirety. But that doesn't necessarily make them irrational, either. The reality is that many aspects, especially those beyond our creation, don't neatly fit into the categories of rational and irrational.

The role of logic in rational inquiry

Now that we have discussed rationality and explored the difference between rational, irrational and arational matters, let's consider the role of logic in any rational inquiry. Firstly, what is logic? Put simply, it is the study of valid reasoning. Logic lies at the heart of human intellect and our quest for understanding. It guides our reasoning and decision-making. More specifically, it provides the structure through which we discern truth from falsehood, make coherent arguments and solve problems systematically. In the realms of rationality and scientific thinking, logic is indispensable. It underpins the methods we employ to examine phenomena, draw conclusions and construct theories that reflect the complexities of the natural world. However, there is an inherently symbiotic relationship between logic and reasoning. Consequently, we require a delicate balance between the two as well as empathy, intuition and ethical considerations to wield logic effectively and avoid logical fallacies. Let's look into this relationship further.

Logic is intrinsically linked to three forms of reasoning: deductive, inductive and abductive. Each serves a unique purpose, as outlined below:

- **Deductive reasoning** is used to derive specific conclusions from general premises. If the premises are accurate and the reasoning is valid, the conclusion must be true. For example, if we know that all men are mortal (premise) and Socrates is a man (premise), we logically deduce that Socrates was mortal (conclusion).

- **Inductive reasoning** uses logic to formulate generalisations based on specific observations. While not as ironclad as deduction, it's crucial for hypothesis formation in science. Observing that the sun rises in the east every day, we inductively reason that it will rise in the east again tomorrow.

- **Abductive reasoning**, also known as inference, uses logic to hypothesise the most likely explanation for a set of observations. For instance, if you observe smoke in the distance, you might hypothesise that there is a fire nearby.

While logic is a powerful tool, its misuse or misunderstanding can lead to logical fallacies. These are errors in reasoning that undermine the validity of an argument. Recognising and avoiding logical fallacies is crucial in all facets of life. For example, the 'ad hominem' fallacy is common in social media and politics. Instead of addressing someone's argument or position, one irrelevantly attacks the person or some aspect of the person making the argument. Such fallacious attacks are sometimes made directly to a group or institutional membership. In scientific research, confirmation bias – the tendency to favour information that confirms existing beliefs – is a logical fallacy that can lead researchers to overlook evidence that contradicts their hypotheses. A few other common examples of logical fallacies include:

- **Straw man fallacy** – Misrepresenting or oversimplifying someone's argument to make it easier to attack or refute. For example, Person A says, 'We should have stricter regulations on industrial pollution.' If Person B then tells others, 'Person A wants to shut down all factories, which would lead to unemployment', they are applying the Straw Man Fallacy to attack and discredit Person A.

- **Appeal to ignorance (Argumentum ad Ignorantiam)** – Claiming something is true because it has not been proven false, or vice versa. For example, 'No one has ever proven that extraterrestrial life doesn't exist, so aliens must be real.'

- **Appeal to tradition** – Arguing that something is good or right because it's an existing practice or has always been done. For example, 'We've always had a meat dish at our family gatherings; we shouldn't change that tradition now.'

- **False dilemma (either/or fallacy)** – Presenting only two options or outcomes when more exist. For example, 'You're either with us or against us.'

- **Bandwagon fallacy (Argumentum ad Populum)** – Assuming something is true or right because many people believe it or do it. For example, 'Everyone I know is buying cryptocurrency; it must be a wise investment.'

- **Slippery slope** – Assuming one action will lead to a series of other actions, resulting in something negative (without sufficient evidence). For example, 'If we allow students to redo this test, next they'll want to retake the entire course.'

- **Circular reasoning (begging the question)** – An argument where the conclusion is included in the premise. For example, 'I'm trustworthy because I always tell the truth.'

- **Hasty generalisation** – Drawing a general conclusion from a small or unrepresentative sample. For example, 'I met two aggressive dogs of breed X; therefore, all dogs of breed X must be aggressive.'

- **After this, therefore because of this (Post Hoc Ergo Propter Hoc)** – Assuming that because one event followed another, the first event caused the second. For example, 'I wore my lucky shoes and won the game, so the shoes must be why I won.'

- **Appeal to authority (Argumentum ad Verecundiam)** – Believing something is true because an authority figure says so, regardless of the evidence. For example, 'The celebrity endorses this health supplement, so it must be effective.'

An overreliance on logic, or its application without consideration of context, can lead to a rigid, dogmatic approach to complex issues. Logic, while a cornerstone of rational thought, is not infallible. It operates within the bounds of its premises, which may not always capture the full spectrum of human experience or the intricacies of the natural world. Furthermore, the weaponisation of logic – using it to dominate, humiliate or belittle others rather than challenge their views – undermines the collaborative, exploratory spirit that drives scientific and philosophical inquiry. It is the opinion that needs to be challenged, not the person voicing it.

In education, logic serves as the backbone, informing every subject from the humanities to the hard sciences. Yet, according to Professor D.Q. McInerny, author of *Being Logical*[23], the subject remains

---

23   McInerny, D.Q. 2005. *Being Logical: A Guide to Good Thinking.* Penguin Random House: Canada.

conspicuously absent from many educational curricula. While the perception of logic as overly technical or complex can be a deterrent to some, oversimplifying it would undermine its depth and do a disservice to its critical role in intellectual discourse. Furthermore, emphasising the 'obvious' within logical instruction is not trivial; it's a deliberate strategy to ensure that fundamental principles are not overlooked due to their seeming simplicity.

In academia, especially in advanced research degrees like PhDs, the critical role of logic is understated in some well-established institutions today. Logic acts as both a science and an art form. It is essential for the integrity of knowledge production and central to clear and effective thinking. Despite its significance in the synthesis of literature, formulation of logical arguments and the rigorous analysis required to reach well-founded conclusions, formal instruction in logic is not typically a compulsory element of research education. This gap highlights a discrepancy in students' academic preparation. Consequently, they are left to navigate complex reasoning without a foundational understanding of logical principles. A more comprehensive engagement with logic across various academic disciplines would enrich the research process, enabling students to navigate the intricacies of their work with greater clarity and sophistication while cultivating a mindset that appreciates the subtleties and complexities of reasoned argumentation. Consider the impact of integrating the study of logic into research programs or projects, where truth-seeking and effective knowledge communication are paramount. And what if advanced degrees emphasised the study of logic in a practical sense? The reliability of the outcomes of academic papers would improve significantly as a result. Unfortunately, ideological constructs sometimes take precedence over the essential tools of thinking and research, such as logic.

Ultimately, it is vital to recognise that being logical is about fostering understanding and advancing knowledge. When balanced with reasoning, empathy, intuition and ethical considerations, logic is a powerful instrument in our quest for understanding. However, it is not a solution for all inquiries. Instead, logic serves as a guide, helping us navigate the complexities of the world with clarity and coherence. Employing logic where appropriate while remaining open to the multifaceted nature of human experience and knowledge ensures that our pursuit of truth is both rigorous and humane. By wielding logic judiciously, avoiding fallacies and acknowledging its limitations, we can harness the true power of logic – not as an end in itself but as a means to enrich our discourse and deepen our insights.

Exploring the multifaceted nature of validity

In our pursuit of understanding and truth, we often gravitate towards methodologies that offer clear, tangible validation, as discussed at length. With its empirical rigour, science serves as our primary compass for navigating the complexities of the physical world. However, the authentication or validation of knowledge encompasses far more than what can be measured and quantified. In different dimensions of our lives – be it in understanding human emotions, moral values, cultural narratives or even personal intuitions – the criteria for validity take on varied forms.

Often, we may not pay sufficient attention to these varied methodologies, especially when they diverge from the scientific. Yet, each dimension of knowledge and each aspect of our lives may require a different lens through which we assess truth and validity. From the logical constructs of philosophy to the rich tapestry of historical analysis, from the intuitive leaps of the creative mind to the pragmatic solutions in business and technology, the ways we validate knowledge are as diverse as the forms of knowledge themselves.

We need alternative epistemological approaches in a world brimming with multiple realities. By expanding our toolkit for understanding and validating different types of knowledge, we enhance our capacity to navigate the world more effectively and empathetically. It also encourages us to acknowledge and respect the multitude of ways that we human beings interpret our experiences and the world around us.

In our quest to understand the world, science provides the framework for deciphering the laws of material reality. Yet, the realm of human experience and understanding extends far beyond the tangible and the quantifiable. Let's consider some of the other ways we come to know and make sense of things.

- **Philosophical reasoning** – Philosophy offers a profound way to understand concepts and ideas that escape empirical measurement. Through logical analysis, argumentation and deductive reasoning, philosophy engages the mind in exploring ethical dilemmas, the nature of beauty and the essence of justice. It teaches us to construct, deconstruct and reconstruct our ideas, examining their foundations and implications.

- **Personal and collective experiences** – Our experiences shape our understanding of social dynamics, cultural norms and individual behaviours. They allow us to perceive patterns and meanings in everyday life, providing a complementary narrative to the statistical and experimental data favoured by scientists.

- **Historical analysis** – History is not just about dates and events; it's a reservoir of human experiences and decisions. By studying historical trends and contexts, we can glean insights into human behaviour, societal changes and the progress of civilisations. Historical analysis also helps us understand the causes and effects of events, offering relevant lessons to current societal challenges.

- **Intuition** – Often overlooked in intellectual or academic discourse, intuition is the internal whisper or inspiration from an unknown source that can sometimes lead to profound insights. It is the unconscious, abductive inference or 'gut feeling' that guides many scientists, artists and thinkers towards breakthroughs. Acknowledging the role of intuition in human knowledge opens a dialogue about the non-linear ways we sometimes arrive at understanding. While intuition is feeling-based rather than the product of conscious reasoning and may not have the reliability, communicability and tangibility of certain more concrete ways of knowing, there are still times when we need to tap into it.

- **Faith** – In the absence of empirical evidence or logical proof, time doesn't stand still; it continues its relentless march, urging us to make decisions and respond swiftly to whatever life brings. In this context, faith refers to trust and confidence in one's beliefs or decisions made without concrete or tangible evidence. When we tap into faith as a way of knowing, we extend beyond ourselves to connect with something bigger than us, whether it be a spiritual belief or a calling from an external, unknown source. Faith provides a sense of confidence and assurance in the absence of concrete evidence, guiding us through uncertainties and aiding in decision-making. Although faith is trust-based rather than the result of conscious reasoning – and like intuition, may lack the reliability, communicability and tangibility of more concrete ways of knowing   there are times when it makes sense to rely on it, particularly when concrete proof is lacking and time is of the essence.

- **Dialogue and reasoning** – The dialectic process is a method of dialogue and reasoning in which contradictory ideas are discussed and reconciled to arrive at a deeper understanding or truth. It is a dynamic process where participants collaboratively examine assumptions, challenge perspectives and refine their viewpoints. Through this interactive engagement, dialogue and reasoning encourage critical thinking and the co-creation of knowledge.

- **Consensus and testimony** – Knowledge is also a social construct influenced by the consensus and testimonies of others. In many areas of knowledge, especially in the humanities and social sciences, consensus helps establish a baseline of what is considered valid or true. Testimony, on the other hand, is crucial in legal, historical and cultural contexts, providing personal insights that are otherwise inaccessible.

- **Pragmatism** – The pragmatic approach evaluates knowledge by its practical applications. If a belief or theory consistently results in successful outcomes, it may be considered valid within those contexts. This approach encourages us to examine the utility of knowledge and its effectiveness in solving real-world problems.

- **Interdisciplinary insights** – In today's complex world, the blending of disciplines often provides more comprehensive answers than any single field could offer. Interdisciplinary research combines methods and insights from various fields to tackle problems that are too complex for a single method of inquiry. This synthesis not only enriches our understanding but also encourages innovation and creativity.

- **The arts** – Capturing truths about the human condition that evade scientific categorisation, the arts offer a unique lens through which to view the world. Through literature, music, painting, poetry and other art forms, we explore and communicate experiences, emotions and insights that other pathways to knowledge can't provide.

Conclusion

In this chapter, we delved into the five categories of knowing, recognising that deliberately ignoring, neglecting or rebelling against what we know to be true poses the greatest threat to us, individually and collectively. We then turned our attention to the complex nature of how we perceive reality, exploring rationality and the nuanced distinctions between rationality, irrationality and the lesser-understood arationality. We also examined the role of logic in rational inquiry, emphasising the importance of logic in pedagogy, education and academia and using logic as a guide rather than weaponising it through logical fallacies. Finally, we discussed the importance of embracing diverse paths to knowledge to equip ourselves with a richer, more nuanced understanding of the world. As we navigate through the complexities of the modern world, it is essential to remain open to the myriad ways of knowing that can inform, enrich and enlighten our journey.

However, amidst these various ways of knowing, there is a crucial missing piece of the puzzle – authentic awareness. Authentic awareness, as explored in the following chapter, involves shaping accurate and congruent conceptions of reality. Moving forward, we must strive to cultivate authentic awareness to navigate our world's complexities with clarity and insight.

CHAPTER 4

Authentic Awareness

Our senses, sensations, perceptions, conceptions and rationality, including logic, are all ways of knowing and gaining a deeper understanding of the world. Combined with our imagination, they are potent forces driving innovation and discovery. However, all have limitations, as discussed, meaning they can result in flawed and incomplete conclusions and outcomes. Choosing the path of authenticity requires us to be present to those limitations and understand that, despite our limitations, life demands us to shape authentic and pragmatic perceptions and conceptions of ourselves, others and matters – the world's content – so that we are equipped to address and respond appropriately to the issues life brings us, regardless of the source. Furthermore, our imagination carries the potential to veer us away from what I term 'authentic awareness'. Alongside the numerous scientific advancements that have reshaped society – achieved by those who dared to believe in the possibilities and explore the unknown – our imagination can also foster falsehoods and deceit, perpetuating confusion and misinformation. Authentic awareness serves as the antidote to this confusion and a beacon of light that guides us through the complexities of individual and collective understanding. Those who are authentically aware are better equipped to navigate life's challenges, make discoveries and understand matters with clarity and integrity.

Some time ago, I introduced the Authenticity Quadrant, described in detail in my book *BEING*[24], as a tool to illuminate the four crucial aspects of self-awareness and refinement necessary to cultivate authenticity.

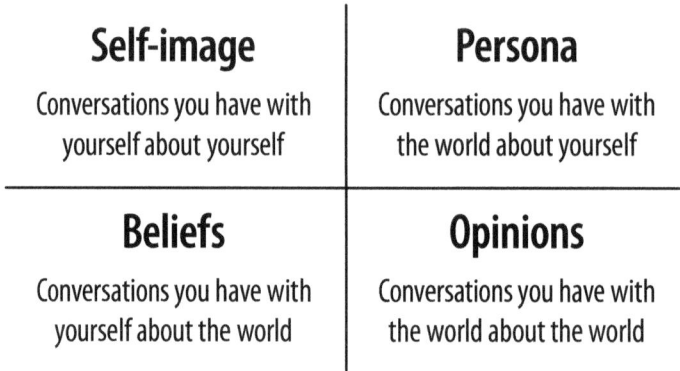

Self-image	**Persona**
Conversations you have with yourself about yourself	Conversations you have with the world about yourself
Beliefs	**Opinions**
Conversations you have with yourself about the world	Conversations you have with the world about the world

Figure 1

The Authenticity Quadrant

As depicted in the Authenticity Quadrant, our relationship with our self-image, persona, beliefs and opinions serves as a gauge of our authenticity. However, authenticity transcends mere self-expression and hinges on how we interpret, perceive and conceive matters – a dimension I refer to as authentic awareness. It also extends to how we choose to interpret, perceive and conceive matters. The latter is the context I refer to when discussing authentic awareness. For instance, if your interactions tend towards excessive positivity, you may lean towards idealism, potentially veering into delusion. Conversely, an inclination towards negativity may breed cynicism, scepticism and pessimism, colouring your outlook with undue negativity. Take, for instance, attitudes towards money and its function in society. If your internal dialogue on finances diverges from reality, it may impede your ability to attain prosperity and wealth. Striving for balanced and authentic beliefs and opinions fosters authentic awareness, enhancing the likelihood of fulfilling your intentions in life.

24   Tashvir, A. 2021. *BEING – The source of power.* Engenesis Publications: Sydney.

As discussed in the previous chapter, the human drive to know and our intrinsic curiosity are inherent aspects of our nature. Our appetite for news and social media exemplifies our inclination to seek information. Moreover, the very nature of life necessitates knowledge. To be effective in fulfilling our intentions, we must engage in the process of knowing. It's an axiomatic law that the more accurately we understand something, the higher the probability of fulfilling our intentions that require those areas of knowledge. This holds true across various domains, from carpentry, teaching and creating a startup to practising law or medicine. However, while we have the capacity for truth-seeking and truth-telling, we are not inherently driven to pursue or uphold the truth at all times. As social beings, we often resort to lies and inauthenticities to fit in, feel proud or superior, maintain social cohesion, avoid upsetting others and evade confronting our vulnerabilities. It requires a conscious effort to maintain our integrity and responsiveness.

Widely regarded as 'the father of Western philosophy', Socrates was said to have famously acknowledged the 'not knowing'. *'Ipse se nihil scire id unum sciat'* (I know that I know nothing) is a saying derived from Plato's account of Socrates: 'For I was conscious that I knew practically nothing'.[25] Many may wish to think that a 'scientific revolution' entails discovering specific pieces of knowledge or methodical ways to examine material reality. However, the re-acknowledgement of the 'not knowing' and the decision not to be satisfied with mythical explanations led to the advancement of science and technology. In other words, it was only when we rediscovered our ignorance and became willing to seek authenticity and congruence with how things are – rather than unquestioningly believing mythological stories and shallow explanations for the material world and nature – that we could give birth to modern science and acknowledge that we don't know everything and are not always right.

---

25   Plato. 1966. Apology. In *Plato in Twelve Volumes,* Vol. 1 translated by Harold North Fowler; Introduction by W.R.M. Lamb. Cambridge, MA, Harvard University Press, London.

Now, recognising our lack of knowledge is not a signal of resignation or succumbing to the darkness of ignorance. It's not us shrugging our shoulders, giving up wanting to know or being powerless. Instead, it's a conscious choice to embrace the reality of how things are, which, in this case, is that, as human beings, we don't – and can't – know everything. Understanding this ontological truth about being human involves recognising our inherent vulnerability and lack of perfection. Surrendering to this reality doesn't hinder our journey towards integrity. Instead, it becomes the foundation for an authentic pursuit of knowledge and understanding. It's an acceptance that perfection, in its true objective sense, is unattainable. But this acknowledgment should not deter us from striving towards authentic awareness, integrity and a deeper comprehension of the world.

As previously mentioned, while authenticity is often understood as being true to oneself – a valid interpretation – a different aspect is being addressed here: the ability to form precise and harmonious understandings of various aspects of reality. It's worth noting that this distinction also encompasses being grounded in realism rather than sentimentality. Consider the following questions. Have you ever been surprised to discover that the reality of a situation you encountered differed from your initial understanding? Have you ever allowed various influences to shape your perception of a situation, including your understanding of yourself, only to realise later that your perception was inaccurate? Have you ever found yourself in a situation where you loosely held a viewpoint, belief or opinion, leading to dysfunction or failure to achieve your desired outcome, such as in building relationships, growing a business or advancing your career? In this context, authenticity refers to how you engage with the realities of life, emphasising your accuracy and thoroughness in discerning what is real and what is not. It also involves your diligence in assessing the validity of the knowledge you encounter and absorb. The word 'authentic' underscores the significance of ensuring the validity of any perception you are considering to shape your awareness or understanding of any matter. This is what is meant by *authentic awareness*.

Now, when it comes to the material world, it's conceivable to develop an accurate conception or authentic awareness of a matter because we can refer to exact science to prove that our conception aligns with reality. For example, we can easily compare our conception of a cat, a dog, a cucumber, an apple, etc., with what and how they are as real entities in nature. As explained earlier, I refer to this as 'first-layer reality'.

It's more complicated, but achievable, to develop a precise and accurate conception of a manufactured construct like currency and the banking and taxation systems. They are part of our shared reality. I refer to this as 'second-layer reality'. However, while we can refer to exact science and nature to develop a congruent conception or authentic awareness of what currency is and how it works, the answers are open to negotiation and debate because we are the ones who created currency. Those who prioritise their financial prosperity and, therefore, want to ensure they are making effective financial decisions would wish to have an authentic awareness of currency and how it works. Someone who has a relatively healthy relationship with authenticity in this sense would put time aside to learn how the currency system works. They would also learn about inflation, how the taxation system works, and the role of central reserve banks in manipulating the cash rate. Realising they don't have as much knowledge and experience as others, despite learning as much as they can on the subject, they would seek the advice of those who do, like financial planners and accountants, in their quest to develop a congruent conception of currency. However, someone who doesn't prioritise their financial prosperity in the same way might be satisfied with their immediate, high-level perception of money or currency and, therefore, might not feel the need to conceive it deeply.

Some may assume that science alone can offer complete clarity about the 'whatness' and 'howness' of the material world or nature, but, in reality, that's not always the case. Take, for example, our relationship with dogs. How individuals choose to relate to a dog goes far beyond what science alone can answer. People may perceive a dog as a cherished family member or a working companion. In some cultures, people may even find the idea of having dogs at home repulsive. Others hold dogs in such high regard that they treat them like children and happily share their beds with them. This raises questions about the authentic or congruent conception of a dog. Now imagine the confusion when it comes to abstract qualities like courage, commitment, assertiveness and freedom!

So, when we talk about content that sits in the first-layer reality, authenticity is when our perception of what and how something is aligns with what and how it is in reality. But it's not as black and white when we seek to develop a conception of matters that are part of the second-layer reality (manufactured constructs). In this case, authenticity extends beyond our individual experiences; it involves collectively negotiating how we relate to something. This has nothing to do with whether or not one agrees with them – that's a matter for discussion beyond the scope of this book. The focus centres on evaluating whether one's conception aligns with the current societal discourse. Given life demands that we know, the pressure is on to come to a consensus on such matters for workability. Congruence or authentic awareness from a pragmatic perspective involves assessing what works and what doesn't. Examples include practical considerations like whether your conception of money aligns with your intentions or if your views on marriage and love contribute to or compromise the integrity of your life. So, pragmatically speaking, authenticity hinges on determining whether your conceptions effectively align with and serve your intentions. You can be as stubborn and insistent as you like in trying to make something go your way, but if your way doesn't align with how things are, it will not deliver the results you seek.

When it comes to the integrity of human beings, knowing about our blind spots is critical, but it's not enough. First, we need to identify our inauthenticities, incongruences, gaps, misplaced parts and the troubled sides of us – or shadows – that are getting in the way of our integrity. Our shadow parts compromise our cohesion and strength and are the source of the disintegration of our being. If your car has a mechanical issue, it will not run efficiently. The same is true for us human beings. However, most of us are unaware of our blind spots or troubled parts because they are invisible to us unless we know where to look and make the time and effort to discover them.

The journey from The Invisible to the visible makes all the difference in developing authentic awareness. It's like when you finally comprehend how money and the banking and taxation systems work, or when you get your head around the dynamics of romance or crack the code of how corporations operate while building your career. During these moments of reception and clarity, you are moving towards a more profound understanding and state of authentic awareness. Similarly, from a metaphysical perspective, our initial naivety and gullibility tend to diminish with maturity and experience, rendering us less susceptible to fraud, scams, betrayal, aggressive competitors, criminals, individuals with psychopathic tendencies, etc. So, while not everything within our existence is visible or apparent to us, recognising The Invisible plays a crucial role in navigating the complexities of life.

It is not an uncommon phenomenon to be constantly in problem-solving mode. However, before attempting to solve any problem, we must discern whether what we perceive as a problem is indeed a problem. Many issues we endeavour to address are facts inherent to the nature of life. Imagine being on board a yacht and continuously blowing into the sail against the ocean's current, expecting the boat to move in the desired direction. To physically blow into a sail is not only ridiculous and inefficient but completely overlooks the fact that it's not you generating the wind or directing the ocean's currents and suggests an implicit arrogance rooted in modern ignorance – a belief that you are the epicentre of the universe, and things should unconditionally go your way. There is no suggestion that you should completely surrender to the ocean and wind. Instead, it emphasises the need to acknowledge forces greater than ourselves and the importance of being authentically aware of them.

To leverage the power of various matters in life, we don't necessarily need an exhaustive understanding of their intricate mechanisms.

The degree of effectiveness we seek in a particular area dictates the depth of knowledge required. While a medical practitioner needs an in-depth understanding of the body's systems, an individual aiming for general health and fitness doesn't require that level of detail. Consider technologies like CCTV, electricity, the internet, the World Wide Web and AI. Unless you are an expert or want to specialise in a certain field, you only need to grasp how to manipulate these tools for your benefit. Context matters.

Authentic and accurate knowledge becomes imperative for maximising benefits, particularly in specialised fields. Yet, the reality of limited time and energy prompts us to establish a hierarchy of values. There are realities in life we need to surrender to, one of which is that we don't have unlimited time, resources and energy. Therefore, not everything can be a top priority. Carefully choosing what takes precedence at any given time is essential. Caring about everything results in caring about nothing. Without defined priorities, nothing holds significance. Learning when and what to sacrifice is an art and science that requires its own exploration, a discussion beyond the scope of this book.

Since becoming an expert in every field is both unattainable and unnecessary, we have organised ourselves into societies, communities and teams where responsibilities and expertise can be distributed, fostering harmony through mutual reliance. Therefore, to assert 'I am an independent person' is not entirely accurate. People commonly use that phrase to infer that they are not reliant on anyone else financially, which can be the case. However, suggesting that we can be totally independent in all aspects of life is inaccurate. We depend on the farmers, the leaders at work, and the list goes on. Economically and emotionally, we are dependent on our interactions with others. Our daily lives are a testament to our interdependence. We tap into others' resources, knowledge and properties, building relationships and partnerships and establishing hierarchies to streamline our collective endeavours. Acknowledging that we can't be masters of everything takes authentic awareness. We depend on each other to navigate the complexities of our shared existence.

Authentication as a philosophical process in the quest for authentic awareness

The term 'authentication' is derived from the Latin word 'Authenticat', meaning 'established as valid'. It traditionally implies the process or action of proving or showing something to be true, genuine or valid. In the realm of knowledge, the process of authentication is crucial, especially in an era abundant with diverse forms of information and varying 'truths'. Let's explore the role of authentication in confirming empirical data's validity and understanding the broader spectrum of human experience and awareness.

With its dedication to exploring the nature of existence, knowledge and values, philosophy provides a critical framework for authentication. Unlike empirical science, which often seeks to validate knowledge through observation and experimentation, philosophical authentication involves examining the logical coherence, epistemological foundations and ethical implications of beliefs and knowledge claims.

Philosophical authentication encourages a deep inquiry into the principles that govern our understanding of truth. It challenges us to question the origins of our beliefs, the structure of our reasoning and the depth of our understanding. This process is vital for developing authentic awareness because it fosters a comprehensive and critical approach to understanding. It compels us to not only accept information based on empirical evidence but also to engage with it critically through reasoning, ethical judgement and philosophical inquiry. This multidimensional scrutiny is particularly essential in areas where empirical methods fall short, such as in dealing with questions of morality, aesthetics and subjective experiences, as discussed in the previous chapter.

Philosophical authentication requirements

- **Logical consistency** – One of the primary methods of authentication in philosophy is scrutinising arguments for logical consistency. This involves assessing whether conclusions follow logically from their premises and checking for contradictions within arguments.

- **Coherence with existing knowledge** – Philosophical authentication also demands that new knowledge claims align with the established body of knowledge. This does not mean that new ideas must always conform to existing beliefs, but they should at least be able to build upon them or engage critically and constructively with them.

- **Epistemological rigour** – This involves examining the sources and methods of knowledge acquisition. It questions the reliability of these methods and the credibility of the sources, providing a thorough vetting of information beyond superficial acceptance.

- **Ethical implications** – In many philosophical frameworks, the validation of knowledge also involves considering its ethical implications. This includes questioning the moral consequences of holding certain beliefs and the impact of disseminating this knowledge to society and individuals.

Conclusion

In summary, while our imagination and creativity have given rise to groundbreaking scientific advancements, they are also prone to generating fanciful ideas and constructs that deviate from authentic awareness. Despite this, our intrinsic hunger for knowledge and curiosity remains steadfast, evident in our engagement with news and social media and our incessant need for information across various domains. In this context, authentic awareness entails shaping accurate and congruent conceptions of reality, with an emphasis on discerning first-layer realities rooted in exact science and metaphysical axioms and navigating second-layer realities – manufactured constructs – through collective negotiation and societal discourse. From a pragmatic perspective, authenticity involves assessing the effectiveness of our conceptions in aligning with intentions across various aspects of our lives, emphasising the importance of congruence between perception and reality as well as context for effective outcomes.

To find answers to life's 'big questions', the ones causing us so much confusion, and in the pursuit of authentic awareness, science is the most reliable way of examining material reality. But how reliable is science, really? Is it fair to put all the burden of knowing and addressing confusion on science alone? Do we have too many expectations of it? For example, we expect liberalism as an apolitical ideology to define our relationship as private citizens and the state, but should that enter the realm of our most intimate relationships in the household? Isn't that taking things out of context?

Remembering the philosophical backdrop of authentication is vital in our pursuit of knowledge. I encourage you to keep this in mind as you read on, particularly in the next chapter's discussion on science. Philosophical authentication ensures that our scientific endeavours are not only technically competent but also philosophically sound and ethically responsible. By integrating these diverse approaches to validation, we aim to cultivate a form of awareness that is both authentic and deeply transformative, influencing how we perceive and interact with the world around us.

CHAPTER 5

Science

W ith its insatiable curiosity and systematic inquiry, science is one of humanity's most profound endeavours. It stands as a testament to our quest for knowledge and is driven by the desire to uncover the underlying truths of the natural world. Through rigorous observation, hypothesising, experimentation and analysis, science seeks to illuminate the mysteries of the universe, empowering us to tackle complex challenges.[26]

It is remarkable to reflect on the tremendous impact that science and the scientific way of thinking have had on our lives. The advancements in medicine, increased life expectancies, improved health and hygiene standards, seamless global travel, technological advancements and the conveniences of the digital age have significantly enhanced our quality of life. However, it's essential to acknowledge that the textbook portrayal of science as an 'objective study' with 'neutral observations' can be misleading. In reality, the complete separation of our subjective, individualistic selves or the collective sense of 'we-ness' is challenging when engaging in scientific pursuits or any endeavour. For example, when general agreement amongst

---

26   Feynman, R.P. 2011. *The Character of Physical Law.* Penguin Books.
Greene, B. 2005. *The Fabric of the Cosmos: Space, Time, and the Texture of Reality.* Penguin Books.

a group of scientists is required, the term 'coming to consensus' is used. And the notion of peer reviews[27] functions as a form of self-regulation by qualified professionals within the relevant field. Its ultimate purpose is to maintain the integrity of science by filtering out invalid or poor-quality articles. Furthermore, although science is undoubtedly a powerful means for understanding the world – more specifically, the material world – it is often glorified beyond what it is capable of to the point where once something is labelled 'scientific', it is inaccurately considered the totality of the truth.

Science can only give us probabilities, not absolute certainties, including medical science, where repeating experiments is challenging due to the complexities and variables involved. Despite this, scientists' probabilities or hypotheses are often presented in scientific journals, academic forums and public discourse as absolute truths, which can be misleading. It's important to recognise that scientific knowledge is a continuous process of refinement and updating based on new and evolving evidence and insights. So, acknowledging that anything scientists convey represents probabilities is crucial for a more accurate and authentic understanding of the content presented.

We've all heard of patients being told by their doctors that they have 'X' months left to live. In reality, no doctor or scientist can predict the exact lifespan of an individual; they can only provide estimates based on statistical averages, visible signs and available medical knowledge. The dynamic nature of health conditions and the influence of various factors make precise predictions challenging. Consider the psychological impact of receiving a prognosis of a drastically reduced lifespan. That could contribute to a self-fulfilling prophecy, affecting a person's mental and emotional state, which, in turn, can influence their overall wellbeing. Dr Deepak Chopra, Indian-American author and professor of internal medicine at the University of Central Florida, also emphasises the importance of patients' beliefs in the healing process, particularly distinguishing between diagnoses and prognoses. He

---

27   A peer review is the evaluation of a piece of work by one or more individuals with similar competencies to those who produced the work.

suggests that while a diagnosis identifies a condition, the prognosis, often based on statistical averages, may not accurately reflect an individual's potential for recovery or progression of a disease. This viewpoint highlights the concept that statistical prognoses do not account for the unique variables and inherent resilience present in each individual.

Traditional approaches to health, characterised by a direct 'problem-solution' model, have shown effectiveness in certain contexts. These approaches typically involve identifying a disease and prescribing a treatment based on objective tests and the probability of effectiveness. For example, the commonly prescribed solution for bacterial infections such as streptococcal throat infections or bacterial pneumonia is antibiotics to directly target and eliminate the bacteria. While this approach has significantly reduced the morbidity associated with bacterial infections, the problem-solution model does not always encompass the full spectrum of factors contributing to health and disease.

The origins of many conditions extend beyond mere biological mechanisms; they are intertwined with our mental processes, senses, perceptions, behaviours, interactions and various other aspects of our daily lives. From the food we consume to our digestion and metabolism, our relationships, emotional experiences, instincts, desires, intentions and memories all play integral roles in our overall wellbeing. These largely subjective components of the human biological organism often avoid strict scientific scrutiny, especially from a natural or exact science perspective. Furthermore, even aspects previously deemed purely objective, such as dietary choices, are now recognised to have subjective nuances, varying significantly from person to person. This complexity calls for a more holistic and personalised approach to health that acknowledges the interplay between the physical, psychological and environmental factors that shape our wellbeing.[28]

---

28   Smith, J. K., & Jones, L. M. 2022. *Beyond Mechanistic Approaches: Embracing Subjectivity in Understanding Disease Origins.* Journal of Holistic Health, 47(3), 215—230.

Dr Ellen Langer, a psychologist and professor at Harvard University, presents compelling critiques of traditional scientific methods. Her research challenges the static nature of scientific truths, emphasising the importance of mindfulness and perspective in shaping human experience. Dr Langer's work underscores the limitations of reductionist thinking – when complex phenomena are analysed and described in terms of their simple or fundamental constituents – and advocates for a more holistic approach to understanding the complexities of life. By encouraging scientists to embrace uncertainty and explore new avenues of inquiry, she has made significant contributions to the field of psychology, prompting a reevaluation of established scientific paradigms.

Science often instils in us a sense of confidence, and sometimes even arrogance. Many fervently believe that science holds the answers to all our questions and concerns or, at the very least, will uncover them in due course. This belief, established more on a bedrock of faith than empirical evidence, advocates a mechanistic approach that, while successful in eradicating diseases like polio, malaria and tuberculosis in various regions, has inadvertently paved the way for contemporary epidemics. Consider the intersection between nosocomial (hospital-acquired) infections introduced by the overuse of antibiotics, which pose greater risks than those contracted naturally, and iatrogenesis – the side effects and risks associated with medical interventions, including adverse drug reactions (ADRs). Both serve as examples of unintended consequences arising from scientific advancements. Alarmingly, if three jumbo jets were to crash every other day, the number of casualties would be similar to those resulting from medical mishaps. This hypothetical scenario highlights the gravity of such oversights. In any other field, such a track record would likely be met with considerable consternation and calls for immediate reform.

The notion that scientists should be confident in their methodologies for uncovering unknowns is valid, particularly within the confines of their respective disciplines. For instance, the exact or natural sciences

– such as physics, biology, chemistry, mathematics, astronomy and statistics – are adept at examining phenomena that can be observed and quantified. These disciplines thrive on empirical data and measurable outcomes, making them well-suited for addressing questions within their domain. However, even in exact sciences like physics, the Uncertainty Principle, formulated by Werner Heisenberg, illustrates inherent limitations in simultaneously measuring certain pairs of physical properties. Fundamental to quantum mechanics, this principle states that one cannot simultaneously know both a particle's position and momentum with arbitrary precision. The more precisely one property is measured, the less precisely the other can be determined.

Psychology, often referred to as a 'social science', delves into subjective processes of observing human behaviour, thought and emotion. It acknowledges the observer's role in shaping the interpretation of data, highlighting the subjective nature of human experience and the complexity of drawing conclusions about human behaviour. However, what about the intentions and biases of the observer and the context within which the observations are made? These grey areas lead to valid questions about the very foundation of how observations are made and the interpretative lens through which data is understood. They also challenge the presumption of 'neutral observation', suggesting that such a stance might be inauthentic or misleading due to inherent biases and societal constructs. Philosophical discussions around the role of the observer in scientific inquiry delve deep into these issues, arguing for a more reflexive approach to understanding the human element in science. This perspective is crucial for appreciating the complexities of knowledge production and the limitations of what can be known through science alone.

The purpose of this chapter is not to undermine the value of science or scientific endeavours in any way. On the contrary, science is remarkable and deserves to be enormously valued. As discussed, when it comes to understanding the material world, including our human anatomy and physiology, science provides the most effective and reliable means to get as close as possible to the absolutes. However, a philosophical concern arises when we falsely assume that science gives us direct access to absolute truths in *all* realms. While any scientific approach may be far more reliable than unscientific stories or narratives, especially in the realm of the material world, it's essential to recognise that it doesn't equate to absolute truth. We may wish it to be the absolute, but the reality is different.

In this chapter, we embark on a journey of discovery to unravel science's essence and characteristics, delving into its methodologies, objectives and evolutionary trajectory. We begin with a definition of science before briefly explaining the tradition of science. Then, we delve into the roles and methodologies of both the exact and natural sciences and the social sciences. We will compare and contrast various traditional research methods, highlighting their applications in academic and professional settings, and introduce research paradigms and their relevance to different scientific disciplines.

This chapter also objectively addresses the criticisms of scientism, the potential ideological elevation of science and the limitations inherent in a purely scientific approach to understanding the world. This includes a discussion on the human elements influencing scientific inquiry, such as perception, consciousness and cognitive biases, and the resulting ethical responsibilities. The chapter aims to provide a balanced view of science, acknowledging its immense contributions while recognising its limitations and the value of non-scientific forms of knowledge. This nuanced perspective encourages a respectful and thoughtful engagement with various forms of understanding existence, promoting a more holistic and inclusive approach to knowledge.

Ultimately, this chapter seeks to define science not merely as a body of knowledge but as a dynamic process driven by curiosity, evidence and rigorous inquiry. By examining its essence and core characteristics, we cast light on the unique ways in which science engages with the natural world, seeking to uncover its underlying truths while remaining open to its limitations.

The overarching objective is to support you in shaping a healthy relationship with science without putting too many expectations on it or succumbing to the forces that might exploit science to advance their own agendas or coerce and manipulate others, a phenomenon not unknown in history.

What is science?

Before delving into and leveraging science as an epistemological way of getting to know the material world better, it is important that we gain an authentic and congruent conception of science itself. So, our exploration begins with a fundamental question: What is science? However, it is important to preface this discussion by recognising that the process of shaping an authentic awareness of what science is doesn't neatly fall within the confines of scientific inquiry. It ventures into the philosophy of science. Questions like: 'What is science?', 'What falls within the realm of science and what doesn't?' and 'What are the limitations of science?' become paramount.

With its systematic methods and institutional framework, science is generally seen as a structured way of gathering knowledge based on observation and experimentation. This process is closely linked to epistemology, the branch of philosophy concerned with the nature and limits of knowledge. Epistemology explores how we come to know what we know and the reliability of different sources of knowledge. Therefore, the philosophy of science serves as an application of epistemological principles, providing a foundation for understanding how scientific knowledge is acquired and evaluated.

In 2009, the Science Council[29] agreed it wanted to be clearer when discussing sound science and science-based policy. Their logic stemmed from the fact that the Council has 'science' in its name and had not previously clarified what this meant. Members also felt that a definition would be useful in developing a better understanding of

---

29   https://sciencecouncil.org

what types of organisations might become members. Furthermore, the inclusion of the advancement of science as a charitable activity in the 2006 Charities Act suggested that a definition would also be useful in that context.

Here is the definition they came up with: 'Science is the pursuit and application of knowledge and understanding of the natural and social world following a systematic methodology based on evidence'.

Philosopher A.C. Grayling was quoted in the March 2009 edition of *The Guardian* as commending the Science Council's definition. In his words, 'Because "science" denotes such a very wide range of activities a definition of it needs to be general; it certainly needs to cover investigation of the social as well as natural worlds; it needs the words "systematic" and "evidence"; and it needs to be simple and short. The definition succeeds in all these respects admirably, and I applaud it therefore.'

I, too, concur – at least in part – with the Science Council's definition. Given science is the most reliable way we have discovered and developed to enable us to get closer to the whatness of the material world, the Council's use of the word 'pursuit' aligns with my view that science is the *pathway* to knowing the material world. More specifically, scientific endeavours are *attempts* to get to know the material world or the absolutes in the world. Unless we acknowledge this, there is no need for science in a traditional sense. But that doesn't mean the totality of these absolutes is fully comprehensible or conceivable to human consciousness. We do not have direct and unmediated access to them.

The limitations of science

We often look to scientific methodologies as a beacon of clarity and objectivity in our pursuit of understanding. However, we must tread carefully when applying these methods to realms beyond the natural sciences, such as the complexities of human experience and societies. While science has proven invaluable in uncovering truths about the physical world, its application to social phenomena can be fraught with challenges and limitations.

Take, for example, the work of Karl Marx, whose theories on society and economics have profoundly influenced many people's understanding of class struggle and historical change. Marx employed rigorous analysis and empirical observation to develop his ideas, yet his approach diverged from traditional scientific methods. His theories were not subjected to controlled experiments or mathematical models but were grounded in historical analysis and dialectical reasoning.[30] While Marx's theories may be considered 'scientific' in their systematic approach and adherence to logical principles, they do not necessarily adhere to the criteria of science in the traditional sense. They are interpretations of social phenomena rather than empirical laws of nature. So, referring to Marx's theories as 'scientific' can lead to confusion about what science is and is not and represents a misuse of the word 'scientific'.

Furthermore, the application of scientific methodologies to the study of human experience and society can give rise to ideologies – sets of beliefs and values that shape our understanding of the world and guide our actions. Marxism, neo-Marxism, feminism, colonialism, identity politics and other ideological movements have emerged from attempts to apply scientific principles to social analysis. While these movements may offer valuable insights and critiques, they are not immune to biases, oversimplifications and ideological agendas.

So, we must exercise caution and critical scrutiny when navigating the intersection of science and the human experience. While scientific inquiry can enrich our understanding of human behaviour and social dynamics, it cannot fully capture the complexity and subjectivity inherent in these realms. We must recognise the limitations of scientific methodologies when applied beyond their traditional domain and remain vigilant against the misuse of the terms 'science'

---

30   Dialectical reasoning occurs when one compares and contrasts solutions to arrive at the truth.

and 'scientific' to lend authority to or feed into the agendas behind unfounded claims or ideologies.

Science and literary interpretation

In the realm of knowledge and understanding, more traditional approaches to science, such as positivism, often fall short when encountering the rich and multifaceted traditions of literary interpretation. Intensely focused on empirical data and evidence, many of these scientists struggle to appreciate the depth and nuance that narratives, rhetoric, symbolism, dialectics and the Jungian tradition of literary interpretation bring to human understanding. However, more modern approaches like interpretivism and constructivism take these matters into consideration.

- **Narrative and Rhetoric:** Literature often conveys truth through stories and narratives, which cannot be fully appreciated through empirical methods alone. Narratives help us explore the human condition, ethical dilemmas and existential questions in ways that raw data cannot.

- **Rhetorical Techniques:** The art of persuasion and effective communication through rhetoric involves subtle nuances, emotional appeals and stylistic choices that transcend logical arguments.

- **Symbolism:** Symbols in literature carry profound meanings that resonate with the collective unconscious and individual psyche. These symbols often represent complex ideas and emotions that defy straightforward scientific analysis. Symbolism is interpreting the symbols within a text to uncover deeper psychological and existential meanings. It is deeply embedded in cultural contexts, requiring an understanding of the historical and societal background that shapes and is shaped by these symbols.

- **Dialectics:** Dialectical thinking – explored in more detail later – involves reconciling contradictory ideas to reach a higher truth and is essential in literary analysis. This process mirrors the complexities of human thought and experience, which cannot be fully captured by empirical data alone. Literature often portrays dynamic conflicts and resolutions, reflecting the dialectical nature of human existence and consciousness.

- **Jungian tradition of literary interpretation:** Based on the theories of Carl Jung, the Jungian tradition of literary interpretation offers a profound example of how deep psychological insights can be drawn from literary works. This approach emphasises exploring the deeper layers of meaning within a text through the lens of archetypes[31], the collective unconscious[32] and individuation.[33] The Jungian approach allows readers to understand literature not just as a cultural artifact but as a window into the human psyche and its universal experiences. It exemplifies how integrating psychological insights with literary analysis can enrich our understanding of both literature and human nature.

If scientists attempt to interpret literature or religious scriptures from a strictly scientific lens, they risk missing the essence of these texts. This narrow approach overlooks the rich metaphors, parables and symbolic language in religious scriptures, which are meant to convey spiritual and moral truths rather than empirical facts. Similarly, reading science fiction through a purely empirical lens ignores the genre's role in exploring ethical implications, societal issues and human creativity.

A well-rounded approach to knowledge must embrace the diverse methods of understanding that different disciplines offer. By

---

31 Archetypes are universal symbols and themes that recur across different cultures and literature, such as the hero, the mother, the shadow and the wise old man.

32 A shared, universal aspect of the unconscious mind that houses these archetypes and is expressed through myths, dreams, and art.

33 The process of personal growth and self-discovery, often reflected in a character's journey within a story.

recognising the value of literary traditions, narratives, rhetoric, symbolism, dialectics and the Jungian tradition of literary interpretation, we enrich our comprehension of the world and our place within it. Failing to do so limits our ability to fully engage with the complexities of human experience and the vast tapestry of meaning that literature provides.

Science as a tradition

On first impression, the notion of tradition might seem incongruous with science. For many, the word conjures up thoughts of old-fashioned and outdated ideologies, doctrines, folklore and even old wives' tales. However, when we perceive tradition as the vast pool of past discoveries and insights handed down from generation to generation, science seamlessly integrates into this broader framework of knowledge production.

Esteemed philosophers of science like Karl Popper and Thomas Kuhn regard science as a tradition in its own right. For example, Ian Hacking's analysis of Thomas Kuhn's *The Structure of Scientific Revolutions*[34] highlights Kuhn's arguments that scientific progress is not a linear path towards an absolute truth but rather a series of shifts in paradigms or frameworks. These shifts occur when anomalies and contradictions within the existing scientific worldview accumulate to the point where the current paradigm can no longer adequately explain or account for them. As a result, scientists must adopt a new paradigm, leading to a revolutionary change in scientific thought.

Hacking's analysis of Kuhn's work suggests that each new paradigm represents an improvement over its predecessor, offering a more accurate and comprehensive understanding of nature. However, it also acknowledges the inherently provisional nature of scientific

---

34   Kuhn. T.S. 1962. *The Structure of Scientific Revolutions.* University of Chicago Press: United States.

knowledge. What may be considered 'true' within one paradigm may be superseded or revised in light of new evidence or insights provided by subsequent paradigms. Overall, Hacking's analysis highlights the dynamic and evolving nature of scientific inquiry, emphasising that progress involves continuous refinement and revision of our understanding of the world rather than a straightforward march towards an ultimate truth.[35]

It is worth noting that the categorisation of scientists into 'typical scientists' and 'revolutionary scientists' is often attributed to Kuhn. In *The Structure of Scientific Revolutions*, Kuhn describes 'typical scientists' as those who work within the established paradigm and 'revolutionary scientists' as those who challenge and change the existing paradigm with new ideas and theories. Popper also categorises scientists into two broad groups; however, his groups differ from Kuhn's. Popper distinguishes them as those who propose theories and those who test them. He refers to the former as speculative scientists or 'conjecturers' and the latter as critical or empirical scientists.

In essence, science and the scientific way of thinking are not separate from tradition but integral components. Through science, we continue to build upon the collective wisdom of our forebears, advancing our understanding and shaping the future. In this context, tradition is far from a relic of the past. Instead, it serves as a repository of collective wisdom accumulated over generations through trial and error, experiences and lessons learned.

The relationship between philosophy and science

In *The Grand Design*[36], Stephen Hawking sensationally proclaimed that 'philosophy is dead'. His assertion may seem perplexing at first glance, especially considering the book he co-wrote with Leonard

---

35   Hacking, I. 2012. Introductory Essay. In T. S. Kuhn, *The Structure of Scientific Revolutions* (4th ed.). University of Chicago Press.

36   Hawking, S. & Mlodinow, L. 2010. *The Grand Design*. Bantam Books.

Mlodinow delves deeply into the philosophy of science and the implications of scientific theories. However, understanding Hawking's perspective requires a closer examination of the context in which he made this statement.

One way of interpreting Hawking's declaration is that it is not an indictment of philosophy as a whole but a reflection of his belief that advances in scientific understanding had superseded traditional philosophical inquiries into the nature of reality. He argued that questions traditionally addressed by philosophy, such as the origins of the universe and the nature of reality, could now be better answered through scientific investigation.

In their book, Hawking and Mlodinow explore the concept of model-dependent realism, which proposes that our perception of reality is shaped by the models or frameworks we use to interpret it. They argue that scientific theories provide the most reliable and accurate models of reality available to us, rendering traditional philosophical speculation obsolete in many respects.

Ironically, despite Hawking's dismissal of philosophy as a means of uncovering fundamental truths about the universe, *The Grand Design* is heavily focused on the philosophy of science. The book grapples with questions of ontology, epistemology and the nature of scientific knowledge, all of which fall squarely within the domain of philosophy.

Consider that philosophy is the antecedent of science. In other words, it preceded and gave birth to science. Metaphysics is the branch of philosophy that deals with the first principle of things, including concepts like being, knowing, substance, cause, identity, time and space. It draws our attention to what can't readily be seen – The Invisible – which is often far more important than what is immediately visible to us.

The role of exact sciences and their contribution

The exact sciences have made a significant contribution to knowledge and society, from our understanding of the natural world to driving technological advancements that have transformed society. In terms of advancements in knowledge, they have given us unparalleled insights through rigorous experimentation and theoretical modelling into the origins of the universe, the mechanisms of evolution and the intricate processes governing life itself.

Technological advancement is another area where the exact sciences have revolutionised our lives. From harnessing electricity and the development of antibiotics to exploring space and decoding the human genome, exact sciences have propelled civilisation forward, enhancing our quality of life and expanding the boundaries of human knowledge.

However, pursuing scientific knowledge in the exact sciences brings ethical implications and societal responsibilities that must be carefully considered. Scientists must navigate the moral dilemmas their discoveries pose, ensuring that their work benefits humanity and minimises harm.[37] For example, medicines come with a list of known side effects. While this list of potential probabilities can be helpful from an awareness perspective, it's important to recognise that they may also cause undue harm. Although the probabilities have undergone rigorous – and hopefully also ethical – testing, it's crucial to acknowledge that they remain probabilities. We cannot assert that *all* side effects, particularly potential long-term ones, have been fully identified, measured and effectively communicated to you as a consumer. So, while we often refer to empirical data, scientific evidence and proof, you, the consumer, along with doctors, pharmaceutical companies, and government and regulatory bodies, are, to a degree, choosing to trust and have faith that these medicines are not only effective for addressing your ailment but are also scientifically effective and safe. This underscores the role of trust and faith in our decision-making process. Although empirical data and scientific evidence enhance the probability of making informed decisions, they don't render the process perfect or error-free. Acknowledging this is

---

37   Caplan, A.L. 2005. *The Ethics of Innovation*. Oxford University Press.
     Resnik, D.B. 2005. *Ethics of Science: An Introduction*. Routledge.

precisely why scientific understanding advances, and many times, these advancements lead to a radical transformation of previous scientific 'facts', ironically rendering the prior 'facts' obsolete.

The rapid pace of technological advancements in fields such as genetics, artificial intelligence and nuclear physics also raises profound ethical questions regarding the use and misuse of scientific knowledge. Examples include the ethical implications of gene editing and the potential negative consequences of artificial intelligence. Therefore, scientists in the exact sciences face complex moral and ethical dilemmas that demand careful consideration. Furthermore, they have a responsibility to not only advance knowledge but also ensure that their discoveries are used for humanity's betterment. This necessitates transparency, accountability and a commitment to ethical conduct in all scientific endeavours. Scientists must actively engage with policymakers, industry leaders and the public to ensure that scientific knowledge is used responsibly and ethically for the benefit of all.

Exact Science vs Social Sciences

The totality of science extends beyond the physical and natural phenomena explored by the exact sciences. We also have social sciences. However, before we compare and contrast the exact sciences with the social sciences, it is worth noting that the word 'science' holds different meanings for different people or schools of thought. For example, some refer to exact science as 'natural science', others refer to all sciences, including social sciences, as 'science'. How the various sciences are prioritised also differs. For instance, positivists might prioritise exact science, while constructivists may favour the social sciences, arguing that our knowledge is merely a reflection of our perceptions, devoid of objectivity. Alternatively, it could be argued that scientists who prioritise authenticity and epistemological humility adopt a flexible approach, selecting their paradigm and methodology based on the specific challenges they encounter. Rather than rigidly and dogmatically adhering to one particular solution or ideology, they assess each field and problem individually, determining which paradigm and approach would be most applicable.

For the purpose of this chapter, let's agree on the terms 'exact science' and 'social science' and on the understanding that while exact sciences like physics, chemistry, astronomy, mathematics, astrophysics and quantum mechanics delve into physical and natural phenomena, social sciences encompass the study of human behaviour, societies and their interactions, including cultural dynamics. Sociology, psychology, anthropology, economics and political science are among the disciplines that constitute the social sciences.

Social sciences seek to understand the complexities of human behaviour, cognition, culture and social structures. They examine how individuals, groups and institutions interact within societies, shaping and being shaped by social, political, economic and cultural factors. In terms of the methodologies employed, both exact sciences and social sciences rely on empirical observation; however, the nature of observation differs. Exact sciences predominantly employ quantitative analysis, utilising mathematical models and statistical techniques to analyse data and test hypotheses, aiming for precision and replicability. In contrast, social sciences often incorporate qualitative analysis, focusing on understanding meanings, contexts and narratives through in-depth data exploration and interpretation. They utilise various research methods, including surveys, interviews, case studies and ethnography[38], to capture the complexities of human behaviour and social phenomena.

Despite methodological differences, both exact and social sciences contribute to our comprehensive understanding of the world, highlighting the interconnectedness of natural laws and human experiences.[39] In other words, they are not mutually exclusive; they

---

38   The scientific description of the customs of individual peoples and cultures.

39   Macionis, J.J. & Plummer, K. 2017. *Sociology: A Global Introduction.* Pearson Education.
      Baron, R.A. & Byrne, D. 2003. *Social Psychology.* Pearson Education.

complement each other. Interdisciplinary approaches that integrate findings from both exact sciences and social sciences offer unique insights into complex phenomena. Let's consider two examples. Understanding the impacts of climate change requires not only knowledge of atmospheric physics but also insights from social sciences on human behaviour, policy-making and economic systems. And addressing public health challenges necessitates not only medical expertise but also insights from social sciences on behaviour change, community dynamics and healthcare delivery systems.

When we synthesise knowledge from multiple disciplines, we gain a more holistic understanding of the world and its intricate systems. So, while exact sciences and social sciences approach the study of the world from different perspectives, they are interconnected and mutually enriching. By embracing their complementary nature, we can develop more nuanced and comprehensive solutions to humanity's complex challenges. In short, we shouldn't consider the two sciences opposing one another but complementing each other because *both* branches contribute to a comprehensive understanding of the world.

Research Methodologies – quantitative, qualitative and mixed-method

Research methodologies serve as guiding frameworks, shaping the way we gather, analyse and interpret data to uncover insights about the world around us. As discussed, the exact sciences and social sciences employ diverse methodologies. These range from quantitative research, which focuses on numerical data and statistical analysis – the predominant type of research employed in the exact sciences – to qualitative research, which delves into human experiences and social phenomena – the primary form of research used in the social sciences. Let's now explore these research methodologies further and introduce a third methodology known as the mixed-methods approach. The latter combines quantitative and qualitative techniques to offer a more holistic perspective, enriching our understanding of complex issues.[40] We will also compare academic and professional research, highlighting the similarities and differences between research conducted in academic settings and research for professional purposes.

Quantitative research measures the tangible aspects of our reality with precision. It operates on the principles of objectivity and numerical data analysis, aiming to quantify phenomena and establish statistical relationships. In exact sciences, quantitative research thrives in controlled laboratory experiments and mathematical modelling, providing concrete evidence to support hypotheses and theories. For instance, in physics, quantitative research might involve measuring the velocity of a moving object or the temperature of a chemical reaction with exact precision. In social sciences, quantitative research enables researchers to analyse large datasets, conduct surveys and perform statistical analyses to understand societal trends, patterns and correlations. For example, in psychology, quantitative research might involve administering standardised questionnaires to measure anxiety levels or conducting experiments to test the effectiveness of therapeutic interventions.

In contrast, qualitative research immerses us in the rich tapestry of human experiences and perspectives. It seeks to understand the nuances, meanings and contexts underlying human behaviour and social phenomena. Qualitative research methods include interviews, focus groups, participant observation and textual analysis, allowing researchers to explore complex social dynamics and uncover deep insights that quantitative methods might overlook. In social sciences, qualitative research offers invaluable insights into the lived experiences, beliefs and values of individuals and communities. It helps researchers explore subjective realities, cultural practices and social norms, shedding light on the intricate fabric of human society.

40   Creswell, J.W. & Creswell, J.D. 2017. *Research Design: Qualitative, Quantitative, and Mixed Methods Approaches.* Sage Publications.
     Denzin, N.K. & Lincoln, Y.S. 2018. *The SAGE Handbook of Qualitative Research.* Sage Publications.

For example, in anthropology, qualitative research might involve ethnographic fieldwork to understand the customs and rituals of a particular cultural group. Qualitative research is not limited to the social sciences. In the exact sciences, it plays a crucial role in complementing quantitative findings by providing contextual understanding and uncovering underlying mechanisms. For instance, in biology, qualitative research might involve observing the behaviours of animals in their natural habitats to understand their social interactions and ecological roles.

Scholars are increasingly embracing a mixed-methods approach because they recognise the strengths and limitations of both quantitative and qualitative research. By integrating quantitative data analysis with qualitative insights, researchers in both exact and social sciences can triangulate findings, validate interpretations and gain a more comprehensive understanding of the matter being studied. This approach provides a more holistic understanding of complex issues, offering a nuanced perspective that transcends the limitations of individual research methods. For example, in neuroscience, researchers often use a mixed methods approach to better understand complex brain functions and behaviours.

Let's say a neuroscience research team has been tasked with a research project to understand the effects of stress on brain function. During the quantitative phase, they might combine neuroimaging techniques to quantitatively measure brain activity in response to stressors and statistical analysis to identify patterns of brain activation associated with stress. Then, in the qualitative phase, the researchers might conduct interviews or surveys with individuals who have experienced varying levels of stress to understand their subjective experiences and qualitatively analyse the data to identify common themes, perceptions and coping mechanisms related to stress. Finally, in the integration phase, findings from both quantitative neuroimaging studies and qualitative interviews can be compared and integrated to provide a comprehensive understanding of the effects of stress on brain function. For example, qualitative data might help explain individual differences in neural responses observed in quantitative neuroimaging studies. In this example, the mixed methods approach allows researchers to not only quantify the neural correlates of stress but also gain insights into the subjective experiences and psychological factors that influence individual responses to stress. This integrated approach can lead to a more holistic understanding of the complex interplay between biological and psychological factors in stress response, which can inform both basic neuroscience research and clinical applications.

Academic research vs professional research

Does research conducted in academic settings differ from research conducted for professional purposes? The answer is that, while research principles remain the same, notable differences exist in their application and objectives. Let's look into those differences.

Firstly, the word 'research' spans a wide range of activities, from understanding consumer behaviour to conducting doctoral-level studies or addressing organisational challenges. It involves a methodical process of involves collecting, analysing and interpreting data to gain deeper insights.

Academic research emphasises rigour and depth, distinguishing it from data-gathering exercises. It is a systematic investigation conducted by scholars to delve into a problem or phenomenon, aiming to uncover facts and offer opinions and solutions. Researchers formulate specific questions to guide their inquiry, employing rigorous scientific methodologies. Academic research typically aligns with established theories, seeking to validate or challenge them, primarily to expand the knowledge about niche subjects within a specific domain.

When it comes to validating research in an academic setting, a rigorous peer review process is standard practice. While the academic peer review is primarily a scientific concept, it also involves ethical considerations. It serves to uphold ethical standards within academic research by ensuring that studies are conducted ethically, with proper consideration for research participants, adherence to research protocols and transparency in reporting findings. In theory, that is precisely what should happen; however, in practice, that isn't always the case.[41]

Professional research, including research and development (R&D) in business and industry, is geared towards real-world problems and improving organisational outcomes and policy. It addresses specific objectives or questions arising from organisational or societal needs, employing methodologies tailored to practical applications. Unlike academic research, professional research tends to be more flexible and pragmatic in its approach and may prioritise applied research methods, collaboration with industry partners and dissemination of findings to stakeholders. Instead of a rigorous peer review process to validate findings, internal reviews by colleagues or supervisors might be conducted. Professional researchers may work within organisations, government agencies or consulting firms, applying research findings to solve specific challenges or improve practices. In R&D processes, the findings are used to invent and produce products, which are tested and prototyped in the market. Therefore, customer reviews and market feedback are an integral part of the validation process beyond internal reviews.

The key variances between academic research and professional research are outlined opposite.

---

41   Furman Shaharabani, Y., & Yarden, A. 2016. *Toward narrowing the theory–practice gap: Characterizing evidence from in-service biology teachers' questions asked during an academic course.* International Journal of STEM Education. Gavin, F. P. 1991. *Theory vs. practice in public personnel administration.* Journal of Public Administration Research and Theory, 1(2), 253—265.

Aspect	Academic Research	Professional Research
Purpose	Advancement of knowledge and theory development	Advancement of one's profession and solving practical problems
Audience	Scholars, students, academia	Practitioners, industry professionals
Funding	Often funded by grants, institutions or foundations	Typically funded by organisations or employers
Focus	Theory-driven, seeking to contribute to scholarly discourse	Application-oriented, addressing specific industry needs
Rigour	Adheres strictly to scientific methodologies	May prioritise practicality over strict scientific methods
Timeframe	Can be long-term with a focus on thorough investigation	Often shorter-term with emphasis on timely results
Dissemination	Published in academic journals, conferences and books	Shared through reports, presentations or internal documents
Peer Review	Rigorous peer review process for validation	May involve internal review by colleagues or supervisors

In summary, academic research is driven by curiosity and the pursuit of new insights, with researchers frequently conducting studies for academic journals or conference presentations. However, professional research is often driven by practical considerations and aims to address real-world problems or inform decision-making in various fields such as business, healthcare or policy. Despite their differences, academic and professional research share common goals to advance knowledge, foster innovation and contribute to societal progress. Both domains benefit from rigorous research methodologies, critical thinking and ethical considerations, ensuring that research findings are reliable, valid and applicable in diverse contexts.

Research paradigms in science

Science is guided by various research paradigms or foundational frameworks, including positivism, post-positivism, interpretivism, constructivism, critical theory and pragmatism. These paradigms shape the philosophical assumptions and methodological approaches of scientific inquiry, influencing how researchers view the world and the questions they pursue. Let's briefly explore the difference between the research paradigms that guide science.

Positivism is grounded in the belief that knowledge is best gained through observable facts and empirical evidence. It stresses objectivity, measurability and the quest for universal laws. Positivist researchers use systematic observation, experimentation and quantitative analysis to discover causal relationships in the natural world.

Post-positivism emerged as a response to positivism. This paradigm acknowledges that absolute objectivity can be challenging to achieve due to researchers' inherent biases and observational constraints. While it still values empirical evidence and systematic inquiry, post-positivism accepts that all observations are fallible and theory-laden. Therefore, it advocates for critical realism and the probabilistic – as opposed to rule-based – nature of knowledge. For example, by respecting, acknowledging and surrendering to the laws – such as the laws of physics – we can tap into various fields like mechanics and mathematics to leverage these laws and redirect our course in a more favourable trajectory. So, while positivists emphasise independence between the researcher and the researched person (or object), post-positivists argue that theories, hypotheses, background knowledge and the values of the researcher can influence what is observed. Nevertheless, they still pursue objectivity in a quest to discover a fraction of the totality of the truth but recognise the likely presence of biases in doing so.

Interpretivism highlights the subjective nature of human experience, emphasising the need to understand the meanings individuals attach to their actions and the world around them. Researchers adopting this approach use qualitative methods to delve into the complexities of human behaviour and social phenomena, appreciating the context and perspective of the participants.

Constructivism suggests that reality is a social construct shaped through human interactions, language and shared meanings. It views knowledge as inherently subjective and context-dependent. Constructivist research focuses on qualitative inquiry to uncover the diverse realities and subjective truths that emerge from social exchanges and cultural contexts.

Critical Theory is focused on critiquing and changing society rather than merely understanding it. This paradigm seeks to identify and challenge power structures, ideologies and inequalities perpetuating social injustices to empower marginalised communities and foster transformative change. The Frankfurt School of Thought significantly contributed to the development of critical theory, intertwining philosophy, social theory and cultural criticism to address the complexities of modern society.

Pragmatism is a paradigm that deliberately avoids the dichotomies often present in other paradigms, such as objectivity vs subjectivity. It is guided by the principle of 'whatever works' in solving practical problems. In politics and economics, pragmatism emphasises practical outcomes and real-world applications of theories and policies, often leading to diverse and adaptive approaches that transcend ideological boundaries.

These research paradigms are not confined to specific disciplines but are applied across both exact and social sciences, albeit with variations in emphasis and methodology. In the exact sciences, positivism and post-positivism often dominate, with an emphasis on empirical observation, experimentation and quantitative analysis to uncover the underlying laws governing natural phenomena. However, elements of interpretivism and constructivism can also be found, particularly in fields such as theoretical physics and systems biology, where researchers grapple with complex systems and emergent properties that defy deterministic explanations.[42]

In the social sciences, interpretivism, constructivism and critical theory play prominent roles, reflecting the subjective nature of human behaviour and the importance of understanding social phenomena within their cultural and historical contexts. Qualitative research methods are commonly employed to explore the intricacies of human experience, societal dynamics and power relations.

The choice of research paradigm has profound implications for research outcomes, influencing the questions asked, methods employed and interpretations made. Each paradigm offers unique insights into the phenomena being studied, highlighting the importance of adopting a pluralistic and multidimensional approach to scientific investigation.[43]

In summary, while Stephen Hawking may have declared philosophy dead in *The Grand Design* because it no longer holds a monopoly on addressing questions about the universe, the discourse within the book he co-wrote with Leonard Mlodinow recognised the enduring importance of philosophical inquiry in guiding and interpreting scientific endeavours. This highlights the symbiotic relationship between science and philosophy, demonstrating how each discipline enriches and informs the other in our quest to understand the mysteries of the cosmos.

The various paradigms that guide science shape the philosophical assumptions and methodological approaches of scientific inquiry. By embracing a diversity of research paradigms and methodologies grounded in philosophy, scientists can engage in multidimensional

---

42   Okasha, S. 2002. *Philosophy of Science: A Very Short Introduction.* Oxford University Press.

43   Guba, E.G. & Lincoln, Y.S. 1994. *Competing Paradigms in Qualitative Research.* In N.K. Denzin & Y.S. Lincoln (Eds.), Handbook of Qualitative Research. Sage Publications.
Kuhn, T.S. 2012. *The Structure of Scientific Revolutions.* University of Chicago Press.

inquiries that capture the complexity and richness of the natural and social worlds.

Deductive, inductive and abductive reasoning

In Chapter 3, we discussed the role of logic in rational inquiry. We learned that logic lies at the heart of human intellect and guides our reasoning and decision-making. We also identified and briefly explored the difference between three forms of reasoning – deductive, inductive and abductive – at a high level and how each serves a unique purpose. Let's now zoom in to compare and contrast how scientists use these forms of reasoning as their approaches to formulate hypotheses, conduct experiments and draw conclusions. In the context of science, each approach has its unique applications and benefits but also limitations, which are essential to acknowledge.

Deductive reasoning: general to specific

Also known as 'top-down logic', deductive reasoning begins with a general hypothesis or theory and tests this against specific instances to confirm its validity. Using Newton's law as an example, deductive reasoning tests broad theories against particular instances, like an apple falling from a tree due to gravity, moving from a general principle to a specific observation. Below is a simple example of how scientists might apply deductive reasoning. It starts with a general principle about living organisms and leads to a specific observation and conclusion about plants.

Premise 1: All living organisms require water to survive.

Premise 2: Plants are living organisms.

Conclusion: Plants require water to survive.

On the positive side, deductive reasoning provides a clear, straightforward pathway from theory to verification, offering strong support for hypotheses when the conclusions are logically derived from the premises. However, if the foundational theory is flawed or too narrow, the deductive conclusions might not accurately reflect reality.

Inductive reasoning: specific to general

Commonly referred to as 'bottom-up logic', inductive reasoning builds general theories from specific observations, similar to piecing together a puzzle where each observation is a piece leading to a broader understanding. For example, observing that the sun rises in the east every morning might lead one to inductively theorise that the sun will always rise in the east. Below is an example of how a scientist might use inductive reasoning to generalise from specific observations to a broader conclusion about the characteristics of a plant species.

Observation: A scientist observes that all observed instances of a certain plant species have green leaves.

Pattern Recognition: After gathering data from multiple observations, the scientist recognises a pattern: all instances of the plant species they've observed have green leaves.

Hypothesis: Based on the observed pattern, the scientist forms a hypothesis that all plants of this species have green leaves.

Prediction: The scientist predicts that if they were to observe another instance of this plant species, it would also have green leaves.

Testing: The scientist collects more data by observing additional instances of the plant species to test the hypothesis and prediction.

Conclusion: If all newly observed instances of the plant species also have green leaves, the scientist may conclude that the hypothesis is supported by the evidence, suggesting that all plants of this species indeed have green leaves.

While inductive reasoning allows for the discovery of new theories based on empirical evidence, making it invaluable for exploring uncharted territories and phenomena, the leap from specific observations to general theories is fraught with uncertainty. The inductive method assumes that future observations will align with past ones, which isn't always the case. It ignores potential lurking variables or exceptions.

Abductive reasoning: let the data speak for itself

Commonly used in Grounded Theory, abductive reasoning starts with neither a hypothesis nor any preconceived notions. Like an artist finding shapes in clouds, this type of reasoning allows patterns, themes and theories to emerge organically from the collected data. Below is a big data analytics example showing how data scientists might infer a plausible explanation (hypothesis) for the observed phenomenon based on available evidence, leading to a testable prediction and further investigation.

Observation: A data scientist notes a sudden spike in the purchase of certain health-related products (e.g., vitamins and supplements) across multiple regions during a specific time period.

Hypothesis: The data scientist hypothesises that a recent public health event (e.g., an outbreak of a viral infection) may have influenced consumer behaviour, leading to the increased purchase of health-related products.

Prediction: Based on this hypothesis, the data scientist predicts that if similar public health events occur in the future, there will be corresponding spikes in the purchase of health-related products.

Testing: To test the prediction, the data scientist:

1. Collects data on public health events, news reports, social media trends and sales data of health-related products over the same period.

2. Performs correlation and regression analyses using big data analytics tools to identify patterns and correlations between public health events and sales spikes.

3. Creates visualisations such as time-series graphs and heatmaps to illustrate the relationship between public health events and the sales of health-related products.

Conclusion: If data analysis reveals a strong correlation between public health events and the increased sales of health-related products, the data scientist may conclude that these events significantly influence consumer purchasing behaviour.

Abductive reasoning is particularly powerful in exploratory research where little is known beforehand. However, this method often raises eyebrows over the accuracy of its conclusions.

In summary, while all three forms of reasoning have benefits, they each introduce a degree of uncertainty and potential for error – particularly the inductive and abductive methods – challenging the notion of absolute accuracy when reasoning is employed in science.

Critique of science, scientism and pseudoscience

While there is no doubt that science has offered and continues to offer invaluable insights into the natural and social worlds, it is not without its limitations and critics. In addition, some elevate science beyond what it is capable of, placing it on a pedestal. The latter is the phenomenon of scientism, an ideology that regards science as the sole judge of truth, overlooking the value of other forms of knowledge. This section offers an objective critique of science, including the limitations of an overly scientific approach to understanding the world, the fact that not all rational arguments are scientific and the dangers of radical scientism. It also explains why distinguishing between legitimate science and pseudoscience is crucial for maintaining the integrity of scientific inquiry and safeguarding against misinformation. Last but not least, we will acknowledge the realms of knowledge outside traditional science and explain why they should not be dismissed as pseudoscience, which has a negative connotation.

When science is elevated to an ideology

Modern science stems from our acknowledgement of our ignorance. Ironically, though, we are also suffering from the phenomena of scientism. Let me explain. Many people consider science the 'be all and end all'. They believe that if something is not backed by science, it's not worth considering. Now, science is, without a doubt, critical to humanity. After all, it gave us vaccines, safe drinking water, air travel and the list goes on. But despite all the incredible contributions science has made, it is not without its problems and critics. For instance, as mentioned earlier, science has given birth to nanoplastics, preservatives, addictive substances, weapons of mass destruction, etc. Some may also argue that we spend too much on science at the expense of the arts, humanities and other disciplines or aspects of life and that science has given us technologies that we would be better off without. People of faith might feel science threatens their faith and belief structure. Many arrogantly assert that Western science is superior to the knowledge or viewpoints of indigenous cultures. These are just a few examples.

The term 'scientific' has acquired a peculiar cachet in modern times. If something is labelled 'scientific', many people will automatically consider it a rock-solid truth. However, if a claim or statement is labelled 'unscientific', those same people will assume it doesn't carry much weight. To many people, scientific conduct is considered rational and praiseworthy, while unscientific conduct is deemed irrational and worthy of contempt, condemnation or being overlooked. The aim here is not to explore why labelling something scientific or unscientific should carry these connotations. Instead, it highlights how modern society holds science and scientists in extremely high regard. Scientists are not only treated as experts but also regularly sought for their opinions on matters of *social* importance. However, like all human beings, scientists make mistakes – sometimes knowingly.

Numerous examples of scientists making accidental and deliberate mistakes have led to the establishment of mechanisms such as ethics committees and peer review processes within academia to minimise these issues. However, simply labelling some of these as 'mistakes' might not capture the full gravity of their impact. It is crucial to recognise that science and scientists often require external scrutiny to accurately identify and address these actions. Consider the following high-profile examples.

John Money and the case of David Reimer: an example of failure on multiple levels

John Money, a psychologist and sexologist, pioneered the study of gender identity. He introduced the concept of gender roles and was a strong proponent of gender reassignment surgery. Money's work significantly influenced the medical treatment of transgender individuals, advocating for the recognition and support of gender identity as distinct from biological sex. However, the following notable and high-profile case highlights the complex and potentially dangerous outcomes of scientific advancements in gender reassignment.

David Reimer was born Bruce Reimer in 1965 in Winnipeg, Manitoba. He underwent a botched circumcision at eight months old, which severely damaged his penis, after which his parents sought the advice of Dr John Money, who was an influential advocate for the theory that gender identity is primarily learned through socialisation. Money recommended that Bruce be raised as a girl, undergo surgery to remove his testes and receive hormone treatments to develop as a female. Bruce was renamed Brenda and raised as a girl without being informed of his medical history until the age of 14.

Money documented the case as a successful example of gender reassignment, supporting his theories on the social construction of gender. However, Brenda experienced significant psychological distress and never identified as female. On eventually being informed of her birth and medical history as a teenager, Brenda decided to transition back to living as a male, undergoing further surgery to reconstruct a male appearance, starting hormone treatments and returning to the name David.

David Reimer's case gained widespread attention through the book *As Nature Made Him: The Boy Who Was Raised as a Girl* by John Colapinto.[44] The book detailed the profound psychological trauma and suffering David experienced as a result of the failed experiment.

---

44   Colapinto, J. 2000. *As Nature Made Him: The Boy Who Was Raised as a Girl.* New York: HarperCollins.

Tragically, David Reimer struggled with depression and other psychological issues throughout his life, and in 2004, at the age of 38, he committed suicide. His story serves as a cautionary tale in discussions surrounding gender identity, medical ethics and the nature versus nurture debate.

Despite the catastrophic outcome of David Reimer's case, John Money's studies have been glorified and are still considered significant contributions to the field of gender identity. His work is often cited as setting the standard for gender transition surgeries and medical treatments for transgender individuals. Money's theories and practices have had a lasting impact on the medical community, influencing protocols and treatments related to gender identity and reassignment surgeries. However, the ethical implications of his methods and the tragic consequences of some of his cases continue to provoke critical examination and debate.

David Reimer's case is a stark example of failure on multiple levels. Firstly, his parents were not fully informed about the potential risks and ethical considerations of the treatment recommended by Dr Money. They relied on the expertise and assurances of a respected medical professional, trusting that his recommendations were in the best interest of their child. Secondly, the medical community failed to adequately protect David Reimer, including those who would have taken the Hippocratic Oath to 'do no harm'. There was an overall lack of critical oversight and ethical review of Money's experimental approach, with the system prioritising experimental outcomes over the wellbeing and autonomy of the patient. Thirdly, the judicial systems and policymakers did not intervene to provide the necessary protections for David Reimer, highlighting a failure in the regulatory and legal oversight mechanisms that are supposed to safeguard individuals from potentially harmful medical practices.

This case represents a significant ethical failure under the guise of scientific advancement. It highlights the importance of ensuring that medical practices are guided by ethical considerations that prioritise individuals' dignity, autonomy and wellbeing. The tragedy of David

Reimer's life serves as a sombre reminder of the consequences when these protections are not upheld.

Alfred Kinsey: the consequences when ethical standards are not rigorously applied

While Alfred Kinsey's work in the mid-20th century was groundbreaking in documenting the diversity of human sexuality, it was also fraught with ethical issues. Kinsey collected data from various subjects, including children and prisoners, under circumstances that have been heavily criticised for lacking ethical oversight and proper consent.

Kinsey's studies of children, in particular, have been condemned for their invasive and harmful nature. He gathered detailed sexual histories from subjects, including accounts of child sexual experiences, which were often recorded without adequate ethical considerations, leading to significant controversy and condemnation. Kinsey's interactions with prisoners have also been scrutinised, including his approach to gathering data through coercion and the capacity of these subjects to give informed consent. Using vulnerable populations in research without appropriate safeguards highlights the potential for harm when ethical standards are not rigorously applied.

The Money and Kinsey examples underscore a crucial lesson: science alone is not inherently valuable. Its worth is realised when coupled with ethical considerations and respect for human dignity. Both examples serve as stark reminders of the critical importance of ethics in scientific inquiry and highlight the need for interdisciplinary collaboration, involving fields such as philosophy, ethics, psychology and law to develop robust ethical frameworks that guide scientific practice.

A case for collaboration

It is not simply that science and scientists can make mistakes; the reality is that competing fields with significantly different interests and areas of focus are necessary to engage in dialectic processes to develop the ethical frameworks within which science and scientists can operate and leverage knowledge effectively. This interdisciplinary cooperation ensures that scientific endeavours are conducted ethically and responsibly.

Humanities and social sciences, particularly philosophy, ethics, axiology, phenomenology, psychology, law and, to a degree, theology, need to collaborate with scientific fields to create comprehensive ethical and pragmatic guidelines. These disciplines bring diverse perspectives and critical thinking skills essential for identifying potential ethical dilemmas and ensuring that scientific progress does not come at the expense of moral and ethical considerations.

Philosophy and ethics contribute to the foundation of moral principles and ethical reasoning, guiding scientists in making decisions that align with societal values. Axiology, the study of values, helps us understand the impact of scientific advancements on human wellbeing and societal norms. Phenomenology, which focuses on the lived experiences of individuals, ensures that human perspectives and experiences are central to ethical considerations. Psychology provides insights into human behaviour and cognition, helping to predict and mitigate potential negative impacts of scientific research. Theology can offer a moral compass based on spiritual and faith-based principles, which can be particularly influential in culturally diverse societies.

This interdisciplinary approach ensures that science is not isolated from the broader context of human values and societal norms. It emphasises the necessity of a collaborative effort in developing ethical frameworks that allow science to advance while safeguarding human dignity and wellbeing. By integrating these diverse fields, we can foster a more holistic and ethical approach to scientific research and application, ensuring that the pursuit of knowledge remains aligned with the fundamental principles of humanity.

Furthermore, the claim that science speaks for itself is disingenuous because science is communicated and interpreted by human beings. It's important to emphasise once again that the aim here is not to critique science itself, but rather to challenge the notion of its perfection and the idealised view of scientific thinking. This discussion inevitably leads us to consider scientism.

Scientism

Scientism is a derogatory term used by some philosophers, including myself, to describe what they see as science worship or an over-reverential attitude towards modern science. The *Merriam-Webster Dictionary* defines it as: '1. Methods and attitudes typical of or attributed to the natural scientist. 2. An exaggerated trust in the efficacy of the methods of natural science applied to all areas of investigation (as in philosophy, the social sciences, and the humanities)'. In contemporary discourse, the term 'scientism' often arises as a critique of the perceived overreach of science into realms beyond its scope. Scientism entails an ideological stance that elevates science to the sole arbiter of truth and knowledge, relegating other forms of inquiry to insignificance. While science undoubtedly offers valuable insights into the natural world, the phenomenon of scientism raises concerns about the potential for science to morph into a dogmatic belief system, dismissing alternative perspectives and diminishing the rich tapestry of human experience.

Radical scientism takes scientism to an extreme, asserting not only the superiority of scientific methods in understanding the natural world but also advocating for the complete exclusion of non-scientific perspectives from discourse or decision-making. An example of radical scientism in the modern era could be seen in the assertion that all aspects of human behaviour and society can be fully explained and understood solely through the lens of neuroscience. This perspective might dismiss the contributions of fields such as psychology, sociology or anthropology.

Given scientism's pejorative connotation, few would explicitly admit to believing in it. However, a growing number of academics and new generations of scientists seem to be implicitly acting upon such beliefs. This fervent belief in the power of science to unravel all the problems of the world, whether related to the inner-self, the environment, material world or outer space, has shaped a narrative that science is the ultimate solution to everything. While science has undoubtedly achieved remarkable success, it hasn't necessarily addressed all facets of human existence. Nor was it designed to.

On the opposite side of the coin from those who espouse scientism are the people who believe that everything is either subjective or intersubjective. They assert that there is no such thing as 'objective reality' and that humans, in particular, are not studiable, especially concerning the realms of the mind. They are also vehemently opposed to measurement and psychometrics. I am referring to those who have been radically influenced by existentialism, constructivism and postmodernism but who have taken it out of its original context.

As mentioned previously, this discussion is not anti-science. On the contrary, science – and what it has brought to our lives – deserves to be revered. This discourse simply opposes the shallow assumption that scientific methods are necessarily applicable to *every* subject. In other words, it rejects the idea that scientific knowledge represents all knowledge, that all rational arguments must be scientific and that science is the *only* way to examine every dimension of reality. Furthermore, consider that scientific revelations are more about acknowledging our ignorance – what we don't know – than acquiring new knowledge. The point is, you cannot eat soup with a fork. While science is marvellous and astounding, it is limited to the questions it can answer. So, let's leverage science where it can maximise the benefit we can gain from it and be open to alternative studies and perspectives on matters beyond science's domain to uncover The Invisible.

Science vs pseudoscience

Distinguishing between legitimate scientific inquiry and pseudosci-entific practices is essential to safeguarding the integrity of science. Legitimate science adheres to rigorous methodologies, peer review and empirical evidence, continually subjecting hypotheses to scrutiny and revision. In contrast, pseudoscience refers to beliefs, practices or theories that claim to be scientific but lack empirical evidence, are not subject to scientific scrutiny or fail to adhere to the scientific method. Those who practise pseudoscience often rely on anecdotal evidence, logical fallacies or flawed reasoning to support their claims and resist critical evaluation.

The rise of pseudoscience poses significant risks, from spreading misinformation to eroding public trust in science and fostering scepticism. An example of pseudoscience in the modern era is the belief in astrology, which suggests that the positions and movements of celestial bodies influence human affairs, personalities and destinies. Despite lacking empirical evidence and scientific support, astrology persists as a popular belief system, with many individuals consulting astrologers for guidance and making life decisions based on astrological predictions. Phrenology, a pseudoscience focused on the study of the shape and size of the cranium as a supposed indication of character and mental abilities, is another example. Scientific studies have consistently shown that phrenological claims are not supported by scientific evidence. In contrast, it might simply be non-science, as described below. Perhaps there are other examples of scientific endeavours we are engaging in today that may be proven incorrect or misguided in the future.

Non-science and its value

As mentioned earlier, not all rational arguments are scientific. Moreover, if someone transparently declares a matter to be rational but non-scientific, that doesn't mean it should be incorrectly labelled as pseudoscience, which has a negative connotation in terms of the intention behind it. Despite the invaluable knowledge and insights we gain from science, it is not the only source of meaningful understanding. Recognising the worth of non-scientific areas of knowledge is crucial for a well-rounded perspective on the world. While science helps us understand nature, it might miss out on subjective experiences, aesthetic insights, ethics and spirituality. Philosophy, art,

literature, spirituality and, most notably, ontology and phenomenology offer different ways to explore human existence, adding depth
to our understanding alongside science.

Approaching science with humility and critical thinking is essential
and involves understanding its limitations and respecting other
forms of inquiry. By embracing a pluralistic view of knowledge and
fostering interdisciplinary dialogue, we can navigate the complexities
of existence more effectively and enrich our collective pursuit of truth
and understanding.

Scientists' ethical and social responsibilities

With great power comes great responsibility, and science, which
is fundamentally a human endeavour, is no exception. Human
cognition, perception and bias can subtly influence every stage of
the scientific process, from formulating hypotheses to interpreting
data. Furthermore, our cognitive limitations, perceptual biases and
subjective interpretations as humans may lead researchers to selec-
tively interpret data that aligns with their preconceived ideas while
dismissing contradictory evidence. This can impact how phenomena
are observed and analysed, potentially leading to a distorted view of
reality.

While some scientists may attempt to portray scientific endeavours
as neutral observations and conclusions, they must recognise the
ethical dilemmas inherent in their work. These dilemmas include
decisions like whether to include certain data sets, remain unbiased
or reconcile personal beliefs with research outcomes. For example,
suppose a feminist researcher's findings don't align with women's
interests. In that case, she has an ethical decision about remaining
unbiased and putting the results forward, despite them not aligning
with her personal beliefs. Consequently, academic research often
undergoes scrutiny by ethics committees to ensure it adherences to
principles such as autonomy, justice, beneficence, non-maleficence,
confidentiality and honesty. Ethical considerations persist throughout
the research process, extending beyond the initial proposal approval

to ongoing decisions at the individual level. So, attempting to divorce ethics from scientific inquiry is inauthentic.

Scientists bear ethical and social responsibilities to ensure that their research serves the collective good and minimises harm. Ethical considerations extend beyond the laboratory or field site to encompass broader societal implications, including environmental impacts, public health consequences and social justice issues. Scientists must navigate ethical dilemmas with integrity and transparency. They also have a duty to engage with the public, policymakers and stakeholders to communicate their findings effectively and responsibly. Ultimately, science's ethical and social responsibility extends beyond the pursuit of knowledge to promoting human wellbeing and advancing a more just and sustainable society.

Scepticism vs cynicism and the role of trust

The distinction between scepticism and cynicism holds significant weight in the pursuit of truth and is rooted in how individuals relate to awareness itself. Generally speaking, a sceptic actively seeks evidence and questions assumptions while acknowledging that not everything sits in the realm of science and can be methodically and empirically evidenced. In contrast, a cynic tends to mistrust everything, perceive the world negatively and be dissatisfied with any evidence provided. The cynic also typically refuses to believe that there are matters that cannot be empirically evidenced.

Sceptics require evidence for any claim and, upon its presentation, carefully evaluate its validity. If the evidence is credible, sceptics – who can distinguish science from non-science and understand that not every rational or valuable discussion must fit within the realm of science – may adjust their viewpoints accordingly. Their approach is reasonable in the pursuit of authentic awareness and knowledge. In contrast, cynics may dismiss any evidence that contradicts their preconceived notions without taking the time to investigate its authenticity. For example, a cynic might criticise the content of a book without having fully read it or judge an individual based on a single statement without understanding the full context or getting to know the person and their points of view. Typically, sceptics are open-minded, while cynics tend to be closed-minded, though exceptions exist. While individuals might transition from cynicism to scepticism, the reverse is far less common. An exception is excessive intellectual scepticism, which can sometimes lead to cynicism, trapping the individual in a recursive loop of perpetual distrust.

Scepticism is a vital quality for any critical thinker and a sign of a healthy relationship with authenticity. It involves questioning perceptions and neither accepting them at face value nor settling for immediate assumptions. Cynicism, on the other hand, signals an unhealthy relationship with authenticity. While sceptics may accept evidence when presented, after careful scrutiny, cynics are unlikely to accept it, even when the evidence is before them. However, there are times when even scepticism fails us, especially when we lack empirical data or evidence in certain realms or we don't yet have access to them. Otherwise, gathering empirical evidence in certain areas might not be possible. With or without empirical data or evidence, life demands that we understand and respond to situations promptly. After all, reality doesn't always afford us the luxury of time or the ability to gather empirical evidence. Those are the times when we must choose to trust, relying on inference and inductive reasoning to make the best choice.

Trust is essential to daily life, whether trusting that our tap water is safe to drink, attending a concert without fear of harm, or entrusting our health to medical professionals. While this doesn't mean we should unquestioningly trust anyone and anything, the reality is that trust is necessary for us to function in society. Despite the potential for betrayal, we trust our colleagues, employers, life partners, employees, business partners and friends, as empirical evidence alone cannot dictate our trust in personal and professional relationships. In short, a level of faith and trust beyond evidence is fundamental to various aspects of life.

Ultimately, we need to know enough to operate effectively in life. There are clear downsides to being a cynic in this regard. Cynical individuals may falsely perceive malicious motives, hindering collaboration and trust. Studies indicate that high levels of cynicism also correlate with adverse health effects, including a threefold increase in dementia risk and higher rates of overall mortality, heart disease and cancer-related deaths. Therefore, cynicism not only hampers mental performance but also jeopardises physical health. Furthermore, from a phenomenological perspective, the life of a cynic would not be a life well-lived.

The role of belief and authentic awareness in science

Even in the realm of science, we need to *believe* that The Invisible exists – that there are things in existence that are invisible to us – before we can look for them. Believing anything else is like arrogantly inferring you are God. However, I acknowledge that the notion of believing is considered a retrograde or backward way of approaching life by many, especially those who assert that a superior alternative to believing is scientific fact-seeking. Ironically, though, science and the scientific way of knowing are constructed upon a solid belief system.

The high-level solution to our individual and collective confusion is clarity or, more specifically, authentic awareness. Developing your conception of various fragments of reality and being concerned that they are as congruent as possible with how things are is a much easier task in the realm of science. For example, understanding how the human body functions involves employing methodical and scientific approaches, delving into fields such as anatomy, physiology and nutrition. Similarly, our comprehension of the ecosystem has progressed through systematic exploration, revealing the roles and interrelationships among its various components. For instance, we have identified the connection between temperature, rainfall, wind and other environmental factors. And discerning between a harmless piece of rope and a venomous snake involves an objective reality; there is an undeniable truism associated with it.

It's a different story when considering something like the impact of sugar on one's body, which varies from person to person to a degree based on their overall health; it has both objective and variable layers to it. While the impact of sugar is studiable at an objective level, it is also variable to a degree in that its effects depend on an individual's overall health. For example, an individual with diabetes should interpret and consume sugar differently from someone without diabetes.

In the realm of ethics or metaphysics, where concepts are not as scientifically tangible, achieving congruence, authenticity and validity presents far more significant challenges. Nobody can ignore these. They are not just exclusive topics for discussion by philosophers; they are relevant to all of us because they are central to our daily lives and decision-making. For example, we all have a perception of concepts like partnership, responsibility, love, compassion, commitment, freedom, empowerment, etc. However, there is no question that these types of concepts lack the clear scientific pathways found in the material world. Unlike tangible entities like dogs, cats, trees and the wind, ethical and metaphysical concepts are nuanced and subjective, making it inaccurate to label one person's perception as 'right' or 'wrong'.

To navigate this complexity, we can gain valuable insights by examining the traditions associated with these concepts, understanding what has historically worked or not, and identifying any missing elements. Taking an Olympic athlete as an example, studying the historical patterns of effective athletes reveals the importance of commitment to daily routines, exercise, diet and training. This historical and phenomenological exploration helps establish what works in a particular domain.

This approach is not limited to sports but extends to various areas, such as the development of civil laws and more. For instance, if your current perception of commitment doesn't align with your intentions or serve your goals, it is advisable to seek alternative perspectives from established traditions or shared experiences. Aligning your perception with those who have successfully fulfilled similar intentions increases the likelihood of success compared to developing an isolated, individualistic view.

In essence, tapping into existing traditions, historical literature and shared knowledge becomes a valuable resource. Rather than relying solely on individual perspectives, leveraging the collective wisdom and experiences of others provides a more robust foundation to navigate the complexities of ethics and metaphysics.

Negotiating the realms of metaphysics or ethics introduces an additional layer of complexity, often entwined with a level of subjectivity. However, despite these domains' relative complexity, there are phenomenological patterns from which we can draw insights. Phenomenological patterns refer to recurring themes observed in human experiences. They include commonalities in perception, cognition and subjective accounts of phenomena like emotions and relationships. For example, anecdotal narratives and historical accounts reveal pathways correlating with specific outcomes. Consider the choice to consistently break commitments, like failing to stick to a diet and exercise regime or not meeting one's promises in a relationship. Such behaviour typically hinders the fulfilment of intentions, from losing weight or maintaining one's health and wellbeing to sustaining partnerships in personal relationships or business endeavours. Given the consequences of an unhealthy relationship with commitment are phenomenologically studiable, they are commonly associated with qualitative research in the humanities or human sciences.

It's a different story when attempting to develop authentic awareness of metaphysical ideas. For instance, the question arises: Why engage in scientific pursuits? The answer lies in tapping into a 'belief structure', a conversation that transcends the realm of science itself and delves into the philosophy of science, a distinct discipline, as well as metaphysics and ethics. The foundation of this field rests on metaphysical axioms: embracing the existence of truth, acknowledging The Invisible, trusting in the comprehensibility of the world to the human intellect – at least some parts of it – and recognising the intrinsic goodness in discovering the truth, the latter being an ethical axiom, not a scientific one. Investigating the mysteries of existence, especially within the material world, is beneficial from an axiological standpoint – what is deemed to be of value. A scientist implicitly expresses a commitment to finding life and all its facets worthwhile, dedicating their life voluntarily to unravelling fragments of the truth and contributing to the production of knowledge. This commitment becomes evident in academic pursuits, such as pursuing a PhD, where individuals engage not merely for personal interest but for the greater good, knowing their discoveries are disseminated through journals and conferences. Therefore, they are contributing to the advancement of our collective and authentic conception of a fragment of reality.

To reiterate, developing authentic awareness in the realm of science requires us to *believe* that a) science exists to uncover truths, b) there is such a thing as 'truth', c) parts of the 'truth' are comprehensible to the human mind, d) the pursuit of knowledge and discovery is inherently 'good' or 'valuable', and e) the notions of 'good' and 'valuable' exist, tapping into axiology and ethics. These are not scientific claims; they are metaphysical and ethical axioms and assertions discussed from a philosophical perspective. Therefore, it is essential to acknowledge that a belief structure forms the foundation or bedrock of any scientific pursuit or endeavour. In other words, an individual must have a foundational belief structure before pursuing scientific work. It is inauthentic and misleading for a scientist to assert complete detachment from beliefs as the substrate or bedrock of their research.

It's important to note that metaphysical and ethical axioms and assertions are not meant to be empirically evidenced initially; gathering empirical data and supporting evidence becomes relevant in later stages of scientific endeavours. One only needs to explore the narrated stories and anecdotes in many religious scriptures to encounter these axioms being discussed and reiterated. Rich in metaphors, these stories have always been susceptible to various interpretations, simultaneously helping and harming humanity and giving rise to fields such as hermeneutics.[45] While it's commonly understood that science and religion, faith, or the idea of the divine sit on opposite ends of the spectrum, there are fundamental aspects that can connect these seemingly disparate paradigms. The history of science is filled with scientists who held beliefs in God, whatever they meant by 'God'. To deny giving God-believing scientists credit for their scientific contributions is not only inauthentic but also disregards the acknowledgment that even those who don't believe in a traditional 'God' may recognise something beyond nature that unifies the various components of existence.

So, as you can see, even the pursuit of knowledge through science – the most objective way of examining the material world – needs a belief structure as its substrate or bedrock to create a solid platform on which all discoveries, constructs, concepts and ideas, theories, theses and discussions, as well as institutions like academia, universities, colleges, research centres and so on (the next layer), can sit. Furthermore, many other constructs and institutions rely on these layers. Examples include governments and corporations, the methodologies we use, the products we consume or interact with, the tools we use and so on. Attacking belief structures or the notion of belief itself – as some scientists do – is akin to pulling the rug from under one's own feet.

Conclusion

Throughout this chapter, we have embarked on a journey to explore the essence of science, its methodologies, paradigms and the human element intertwined within its fabric. We have delved into the significance of science as a systematic endeavour to understand the natural and social worlds, uncovering truths, driving progress and shaping our collective destiny.

---

45   The branch of knowledge that deals with interpretation, especially of the Bible or literary texts.

With its rigorous methodologies and relentless pursuit of evidence-based knowledge, science has immense power to illuminate the mysteries of the universe, address societal challenges and enhance human wellbeing. From the exact sciences' exploration of the fundamental laws governing nature to the social sciences' examination of human behaviour and societies, science offers invaluable insights into the complexities of existence.

However, amidst its triumphs, science also grapples with inherent limitations. The human element introduces biases, perceptual limitations and ethical dilemmas that can influence research outcomes and interpretations. Moreover, the quest for objectivity in science is perpetually challenged by the subjective nature of human experience and the diverse perspectives inherent in scientific inquiry.

Looking ahead, the future of scientific inquiry holds both promise and challenges. Interdisciplinary approaches that transcend traditional disciplinary boundaries are poised to revolutionise our understanding of complex phenomena and address pressing global issues. By fostering collaboration across disciplines, from the natural and social sciences to the humanities and arts, we can harness the collective wisdom of diverse perspectives to tackle the multifaceted challenges facing humanity.

Moreover, the ongoing evolution of scientific methodologies and ethics demands vigilant reflection and adaptation. As scientific inquiry becomes increasingly intertwined with technological advancements and societal transformations, scientists must navigate ethical considerations with integrity, transparency and a commitment to the common good.

So, while science offers unparalleled opportunities for understanding and improving the world, it is not without its limitations and challenges. As long as we acknowledge this, embrace interdisciplinary collaboration and uphold ethical integrity, we can chart a course towards a future where science serves as a beacon of enlightenment and a catalyst for positive change.

CHAPTER 6

Consciousness

In our exploration of authentic awareness and the nature of knowing, it becomes evident that intentional consciousness plays a crucial role. Consciousness – being aware of and able to think about one's own existence, thoughts and environment – is fundamental to making sense of the world. However, my intention is to avoid diving too deeply into the sheer mystery of all consciousness. Instead, I intend to briefly explore several major theories of consciousness before focusing more intently on theories that link consciousness to human suffering.

The meaning of consciousness has baffled human beings for aeons and continues to intrigue philosophers, scientists and spiritual leaders alike. Defining consciousness remains one of the greatest mysteries of existence. Could it be an arational matter that is impossible to define? Or does a concrete distinction emerge when we consider it from various perspectives, such as the one highlighted above? To discover the answer, we must explore the essence of consciousness from multiple angles. As we delve deeper into this subject, the synergy between the exact sciences like neurophysiology[46] and

---

46   Neurophysiology involves the study of the nervous system's functions through direct measurement of neural activity, often using techniques like single-cell recording and electrophysiology.

neurochemistry[47], neuroscience[48], social sciences like psychology and philosophy, and humanities disciplines like ontology and phenomenology becomes increasingly indispensable. Let's begin with science.

Science and consciousness

Various scientific theories attempt to define consciousness. Some 'scientific' studies dare to treat the notion of consciousness as a neutral observer of the world. Some radical scientists even assert that we only need to understand consciousness through exact science, diminishing its inherent subjectivity and other perspectives. In reality, consciousness is the only thing in existence that involves suffering, the exact opposite of neutral observation. It has been one of the primary focal points of care and attention for many contemporary philosophers, particularly existentialists and postmodernists, in the last three centuries. While observation strives to impartially capture the current reality, at the core of any experience of suffering lies the rejection of that very reality. Consider that consciousness is the *capacity* to suffer. This perspective highlights its profound political and ethical implications. Ethics, politics, law, AI, abortion, animal rights and more all fall into the realm of consciousness. Let's explore this mysterious subject, as it is critical to acknowledge it in the context of everything discussed in this book.

From a scientific perspective, the study of consciousness is interdisciplinary, spanning neurobiology, cognitive psychology and quantum

---

47   Neurochemistry is the study of chemicals, including neurotransmitters and other molecules, involved in brain function. This field uses precise analytical techniques to measure and analyse the chemical composition and processes within the brain.

48   Neuroscience is not typically classified as an exact science in the same way as disciplines like physics or chemistry. It is a multidisciplinary field that combines aspects of biology, psychology, medicine and other sciences to study the nervous system. While neuroscience employs rigorous scientific methods and quantitative analysis, the complexity and variability of biological systems, especially the human brain, make it less precise and predictable than the exact sciences.

physics. Put simply, in the realm of science, consciousness encompasses the study of the brain and nervous system and specifically pertains to the quality or state of being aware of an external object or something within oneself. In terms of brain function, we exert direct influence over certain processes while lacking control over others. For instance, while some bodily functions, such as heart rate and breathing, operate primarily beyond conscious control, others, like touch and taste, fall within our direct experience and influence. The act of touching one's wrist or chest to feel the heartbeat exemplifies this division; the heartbeat itself is not consciously perceived, yet the sensation of touch is vividly present in our awareness. Even responses to stimuli we don't consciously perceive involve intricate neurological mechanisms, such as rapid protective reflexes. Despite these processes occurring without conscious awareness, sensory impulses reaching the cerebral cortex, such as touch, pain, hearing and taste, are consciously perceived, highlighting our ability to influence some aspects of our conscious experience while others remain beyond our direct control.

The scope of consciousness extends beyond mere physiological functions. While understanding the brain's workings is crucial, and neuroscience has made significant strides in mapping the brain's activity related to conscious experience, the subjective nature of consciousness remains elusive. The 'hard problem' of consciousness, a term coined by philosopher David Chalmers, addresses the question of why and how physical processes in the brain give rise to subjective experiences. Other factors, such as psychological, social, political, economic, ethical, philosophical and spiritual aspects, also contribute to our understanding of consciousness.

Philosophy and consciousness

Philosophers have debated the nature and origins of consciousness for centuries, exploring questions such as the relationship between mind and body, the existence of free will and the nature of reality. From a philosophical perspective, consciousness refers to the subjective experience of being aware of oneself and one's surroundings. It encompasses the ability to perceive, think, feel and experience sensations, emotions and thoughts. Consciousness is often considered a fundamental aspect of human existence and is central to philosophical inquiries into the nature of existence, knowledge and reality. Thinkers like Descartes, who proclaimed 'Cogito, ergo sum' (I think, therefore I am), highlighted the existence of the self-aware mind.

Ancient philosophical traditions, such as those in the *Vedas* and *Upanishads*[49], also ponder the nature of consciousness, suggesting it as the ultimate reality and the essence of the universe. Islamic philosophy places a significant emphasis on consciousness, intertwining it with concepts of self-awareness and the nature of being. Notable thinkers like Mulla Sadra and Shihab al-Din Suhrawardi have explored these ideas deeply, proposing models that delve into the layers of self-awareness and the profound relationship between knowledge and existence. Their works suggest that understanding consciousness in Islamic thought requires engaging with both philosophical and mystical dimensions, where consciousness extends beyond mere cognition to encompass a broader existential and spiritual reality.

Exploring the metaphysical and philosophical dimensions of consciousness through theological scriptures offers yet another perspective, distinct from conventional religious practice. The intricate descriptions of consciousness found in these texts invite deep theological and philosophical inquiry. However, it's crucial to recognise that they are open to interpretation and that an array of interpretations exists. Spiritual traditions across the world view consciousness as a fundamental aspect of existence. For example, in Buddhism, consciousness is one of the five aggregates that constitute

---

49   The *Vedas* and *Upanishads* are ancient Indian texts central to Hindu philosophy. The *Vedas*, composed between 1500 and 500 BCE, are a collection of hymns, rituals and chants, considered the oldest scriptures of Hinduism. The *Upanishads*, written between 800 and 400 BCE, are philosophical texts that explore the nature of reality and the self, forming the theoretical basis for much of Hindu thought.

the 'self', while in Advaita Vedanta[50], it is the unchanging reality behind the changing phenomenal world. In the biblical context, the concept of Logos, as introduced in the Gospel of John[51], signifies more than just 'word' or 'reason'. It is considered synonymous with God, linking it directly to the notion of consciousness at a divine level.

From political and ethical perspectives, consciousness is intricately tied to the potential for suffering, as explored in the next section. Every perspective adds depth to the rich tapestry of this mysterious phenomenon. Let's now briefly examine some of the more prominent philosophical theories and perspectives on consciousness.

Dualism

While the conversation about dualism has existed for a long time, it is most prominently associated with René Descartes. Dualism proposes that the mind and body are distinct entities. Descartes argued that the mind is non-physical and exists independently of the body, which is a physical entity.[52] This theory suggests that mental phenomena cannot be fully explained by physical processes alone, pointing to a more profound, intangible essence of consciousness that transcends the material realm.

Materialism

Materialism, also known as physicalism, argues that consciousness arises entirely from physical processes within the brain. Neuroscientists and philosophers like Patricia Churchland assert that all mental states and experiences result from neural activity.[53] This theory

---

50 Advaita Vedanta is a philosophical school within Hinduism that emphasises non-dualism, asserting that the true nature of the self (atman) is identical with the ultimate reality (Brahman).

51 The Gospel of John, often simply called John, is one of the four canonical gospels in the New Testament of the Christian Bible, traditionally attributed to John the Apostle.

52 Descartes, R. 1641. *Meditations on First Philosophy.*

53 Churchland, P. S. 1986. *Neurophilosophy: Toward a Unified Science of the Mind-Brain.*

proposes that with advanced neuroscience, we will eventually be able to map and understand the brain processes that generate conscious experience.

Functionalism

Functionalism suggests that mental states are defined by their functional roles rather than their physical makeup. According to this theory, consciousness is the result of complex information processing systems. Functionalists like Hilary Putnam argue that mental states can be realised in multiple ways, not just by human brains but potentially by artificial intelligence, emphasising the flexibility and universality of conscious experiences.[54]

Integrated Information Theory (IIT)

Introduced by Giulio Tononi, IIT proposes that consciousness arises from integrated information. The theory suggests that the more integrated and differentiated the information a system processes, the higher its level of consciousness.[55] This perspective has significant implications for understanding both biological consciousness and potential machine consciousness, such as that associated with AI.

Global Workspace Theory (GWT)

Developed by Bernard Baars, GWT describes consciousness as a global workspace where information is shared and integrated across different cognitive processes. This theory likens consciousness to a stage in a theatre, where various cognitive processes act as audience members observing the information presented on stage. This model helps explain how disparate neural processes contribute to a unified conscious experience.[56]

---

54   Putnam, H. 1967. *Psychological Predicates.*

55   Tononi, G. 2004. *An information integration theory of consciousness. BMC Neuroscience*, 5(1), 42.

56   Baars, B. J. 1988. *A Cognitive Theory of Consciousness.*

Panpsychism

Panpsychism is the view that consciousness is a fundamental and ubiquitous feature of the universe. According to this theory, all matter has some form of consciousness, and human consciousness arises from the combination of simpler forms of consciousness. David Chalmers and others have explored this idea, proposing that consciousness might be an intrinsic aspect of reality, present even at the smallest scales.[57]

Higher-Order Theories

Higher-order theories propose that consciousness arises when a mental state is the object of another mental state. For instance, being aware of a thought or sensation involves having a higher-order thought about that mental state. This meta-cognitive approach suggests that self-awareness and reflective thinking are crucial components of consciousness.[58]

Representational Theories

Representational Theories assert that consciousness is a matter of having mental representations of the world. These theories focus on the content of mental states and how they represent external reality. There are multiple theories within the broader category, with each theory offering a different perspective or approach to understanding how our conscious experiences can be explained in terms of representations. Michael Tye and others argue that the qualitative aspects of consciousness can be explained through the representational content of mental states.[59]

---

57   Chalmers, D. J. 1996. *The Conscious Mind: In Search of a Fundamental Theory.*

58   Rosenthal, D. M. 2005. *Consciousness and Mind.*

59   Tye, M. 1995. *Ten Problems of Consciousness: A Representational Theory of the Phenomenal Mind.*

Quantum Theories of Consciousness

The origin of Quantum Theories of Consciousness, as associated with physicists Werner Heisenberg and Niels Bohr, is linked to the Copenhagen Interpretation of Quantum Mechanics[60], the first general attempt to understand the world of atoms using quantum mechanics. This interpretation highlights the connection between reality and the observation of quantum mechanics, suggesting that reality only exists as we observe or measure it. Often referred to as a philosophical physicist, Bohr extended this idea to imply that our intent and observation create reality rather than merely measuring what already exists. More broadly, Quantum Theories of Consciousness suggest that consciousness is related to quantum processes in the brain. Proponents like Roger Penrose argue that quantum mechanics can explain the non-deterministic and non-local properties of conscious experience.[61] Although controversial, these theories propose a fundamental link between consciousness and the fabric of the universe.

Enactive and Embodied Theories

Enactive and Embodied Theories argue that consciousness arises from the interaction between an organism and its environment. According to these theories, cognitive processes are deeply rooted in the body's interactions with the world. Francisco Varela and colleagues emphasise that consciousness cannot be separated from the physical and social contexts in which it emerges.[62]

Development Theory

Development Theory explores the idea that human consciousness evolves through various stages of development. This theory suggests

---

60   Heisenberg, W., & Bohr, N. 1958. *The Copenhagen Interpretation.* University Press.

61   Penrose, R. 1994. *Shadows of the Mind: A Search for the Missing Science of Consciousness.* Oxford: Oxford University Press.

62   Varela, F. J., Thompson, E., & Rosch, E. 1991. *The Embodied Mind: Cognitive Science and Human Experience.* Cambridge, MA: MIT Press.

that consciousness is not a static trait but one that can progress through different levels of complexity and understanding. Influential thinkers such as Jean Piaget and Ken Wilber have contributed to this perspective, proposing models where individuals move from egocentric to more integrated and holistic stages of awareness. At each stage, there is an expansion in the way individuals perceive and interact with the world, integrating more sophisticated cognitive, emotional and moral capacities. Development Theory proposes that as consciousness develops, individuals are capable of greater empathy, ethical reasoning and understanding of the interconnectedness of all life. This framework provides a basis for examining personal and collective growth, emphasising the potential for higher levels of consciousness that can lead to more enlightened and compassionate ways of being.

For example, Ken Wilbur's Integral Theory[63] incorporates aspects of spiral dynamics as a framework for understanding human development and consciousness evolution aligned with development theories. Initially developed by Clare W. Graves and popularised by Don Beck and Christopher Cowan, Spiral Dynamics proposes a series of stages or levels of human development. These stages are characterised by different value systems and worldviews, ranging from survival-focused and egocentric to more complex and inclusive perspectives. Wilber's integration of Spiral Dynamics within his Integral Theory emphasises the holistic nature of human growth, where individuals and societies evolve through these stages in a spiral-like progression toward greater integration and higher consciousness.[64]

Islamic philosophy and consciousness

Islamic philosophy has also contributed significantly to understanding consciousness, particularly through concepts such as

---

63   Integral Theory is a comprehensive framework that seeks to integrate insights from various disciplines – including science, philosophy and spirituality – to provide a holistic understanding of human development and consciousness.

64   Wilber, K. 2000. *Integral Psychology: Consciousness, Spirit, Psychology, Therapy.* Boston: Shambhala Publications.

universal intellect ('Aql al-Kul') and the unity of being or existence. These ideas suggest a profound interconnectedness and a higher order of knowledge transcending individual consciousness.

Universal intellect, most notably in the works of thinkers like Avicenna (Ibn Sina) and Suhrawardi, refers to an overarching source of wisdom and knowledge that informs and sustains all individual intellects. This concept emphasises a collective, divine consciousness that encompasses and transcends individual human minds.

The concept of unity of being ('Wahdat al-Wujud') was articulated by Sufi mystics like Ibn Arabi. It proposes that all existence is fundamentally one. According to this view, the multiplicity of the world is an illusion and everything is a manifestation of a single underlying reality. This perspective suggests a deep interconnectedness and unity in all aspects of existence, including consciousness.

Universal intellect and unity of being align with the idea that consciousness is not just an individual phenomenon but part of a larger, interconnected reality. They offer a perspective that integrates spirituality and metaphysics into the understanding of consciousness, adding another layer of depth to the discussion.

In conclusion, while the theories from both Western and Eastern philosophers provide valuable insights into the nature of consciousness, they also highlight the challenges of fully demystifying this phenomenon scientifically. Understanding consciousness requires us to navigate both its scientific and subjective dimensions, known as 'qualia', which are inherently personal and extremely difficult to measure objectively. For example, seeing the colour red or feeling pain is a subjective experience that cannot be entirely captured by physical explanations.

While various theories offer frameworks for exploring consciousness, the deeply personal nature of conscious experience and its connection to human suffering highlights the limitations of purely scientific approaches. An example is illustrated in the excerpt below from Chapter 2: Existence and Being of my book *BEING*. It offers a small snapshot of my interpretation of the meaning of existence as the coming together of all quantised parts of the universe, which was inspired by the work of Islamic philosophers like Mulla Sadra. By integrating insights from various perspectives – the primary objective of the metacontent discourse and Nested Theory of Sense-making – we can develop a more holistic understanding of consciousness and its profound impact on our lives.

> Existence is the Ultimate Reality, the supreme power. It is the lawmaker and ruler. Our opinions and perceptions are irrelevant in its presence. Existence is the coming together of all quantised parts of the universe.[65] Everything we know is restricted to the knowledge of the parts that have appeared in ways that our limited human brain can comprehend.[66]

Intelligent Design and consciousness

Intelligent Design (ID) is a modern concept that emerged in the late 20th century, primarily in the United States, as a response to evolutionary theory. ID advocates argue that certain features of the universe and living organisms are best explained by an 'intelligent cause' rather than undirected processes like natural selection. By suggesting that the complexity and order found in biological systems point to a 'designer', ID positions itself squarely within the science-theology debate. However, its scientific credibility is widely debated and it is often criticised for lacking empirical support.

The concept of ID is related to consciousness because it proposes that the complexity of conscious experience points to an intelligent cause, resonating with dualistic theories that suggest the mind and body are distinct entities. When we compare ancient philosophy on consciousness with the modern notion of ID, some fascinating points

---

65   This phrase does not only refer to materialistic or naturalistic components within existence but also encompasses abstract, metaphysical and conceptual aspects of existence.

66   Tashvir, Λ. 2021. *BEING – The source of power.* Engenesis Publications: Sydney.

of comparison emerge. For example, like ID, Islamic philosophy's universal intellect ('Aql al-Kul'), as touched on earlier, proposes that the complexity and order of the universe are not mere products of chance but are guided by a higher intelligence. However, they emerge from vastly different traditions and serve distinct purposes.

While both universal intellect and ID attribute the universe's order and complexity to an intelligent source, their contexts and implications differ significantly. Universal intellect is part of a philosophical and theological framework aimed at understanding reality and the divine through a metaphysical lens. In contrast, ID is positioned within contemporary scientific discourse, challenging naturalistic explanations for the origins of life.

So, while universal intellect reflects the philosophical and metaphysical pursuits of mediaeval Islamic scholars and ID represents a modern attempt to reconcile scientific observations with the notion of an intelligent creator, both share similarities. By examining these concepts, we can appreciate how different cultures and eras have grappled with the profound questions of consciousness and the universe's order and complexity.

Consciousness and suffering

One of the most profound aspects of consciousness is its link to suffering. For us humans, being aware of our own existence and the inevitability of suffering creates a unique existential burden. This awareness can lead to anxiety, fear and emotional pain. The existential philosopher Søren Kierkegaard referred to this as the 'dizziness of freedom', where the realisation of our own freedom and responsibility can lead to existential angst. Buddhist philosophy also addresses the nature of human suffering, known as 'dukkha', and emphasises that suffering arises from attachment and desire.

As sentient or conscious beings, human beings – and other living creatures – have the capacity to suffer. We experience joy, fear, anger, sorrow and pain, distinguishing us from inanimate objects like tables and cars, which do not suffer and, therefore, lack consciousness. In a social and ethical context, when our vehicle incurs damage, our concern often transcends the material harm; it's the emotional distress it causes us as the owner that truly affects us. This sentiment extends to symbols like our national flag, which, despite being nothing more than a piece of decorated fabric, evokes profound feelings in some due to what it represents, such as our nation's identity, history, struggles and collective endurance. This concept of consciousness underlies the democratic principle that everyone, regardless of how 'right' or 'wrong' their understanding or motive, has a voice in decision-making. Modern-day authorities derive their legitimacy not from gods or even the laws of nature, but from understanding and addressing the sentiments of the people they serve. Consequently, the authority becomes vested in the collective consciousness, emphasising the subjective experience over objective truths.

Some naively think it doesn't matter whether we obey the 'divine commandments', as we don't know if they are true; they enter the realm of interpretation and pass through our rationality filter. Religious zealots may contest the potential emotional impact of actions, introducing a complex interplay of feelings. For instance, the status of a deceased political leader may evoke contrasting emotions – some may feel hurt, while others take pride in their history. This raises the challenging question of how we weigh and measure feelings and suffering against one another. Is one person's suffering more significant than another's? Our innate ability to suffer gives us a moral compass, necessitating ethical considerations and empathetic negotiations to determine whose feelings should take priority.

Consider a scenario where two individuals, Lisa and Tom, apply for the same position. Lisa is a single mother struggling to make ends meet, while Tom is a recent college graduate who still lives with his parents and has no financial responsibilities. Both candidates are equally qualified for the job, but the hiring manager can only choose one. In this situation, the hiring manager's decision will inevitably prioritise one person's feelings over the other. If Lisa was selected, she would feel relief and gratitude, while Tom may experience disappointment. Conversely, if Tom was chosen, Lisa may feel disheartened and concerned about how she would look after her family, while Tom would feel elated. This example illustrates how our innate consciousness and ability to suffer necessitates ethical considerations in decision-making processes.

The impracticality of addressing all concerns also has broader implications. It leads to inevitable conflicts across various societal domains, from politics to religion and cultural norms. Imagine a town facing a budget shortfall and needing to allocate funds for public services; however, the priorities of residents and the councillors that represent them conflict between education, healthcare and road infrastructure. With limited resources, the council must make a tough decision, leading to inevitable suffering for those who miss out.

Now, consider the complex ethical dimensions surrounding a highly sensitive subject like abortion. Is an embryo or foetus a conscious entity? Can an embryo or foetus feel pain? Does it suffer? At what level of consciousness does a being become susceptible to suffering, transitioning from an object to a sentient being? Does the significance of the foetus lie solely in whether or not its existence or non-existence causes suffering for the pregnant woman? If so, that is akin to caring about a stolen car, not because the vehicle suffers but because the owner suffers.

When extending this inquiry to animals, another moral dilemma emerges. Is the suffering of our beloved pet dog or cat more significant than that of a cow, sheep or rat? If so, why? The ethical status of animals is a subject of great contention, particularly in sectors such as the meat industry or research laboratories. Scientific evidence reveals that animals possess neuroanatomical, neurochemical and neurophysiological substrates of conscious states, along with a capacity to demonstrate intentional behaviour. Acknowledging this, the New Zealand Parliament passed the Animal Welfare Amendment Act 2015, recognising animals as conscious beings and emphasising the need for their proper welfare in all contexts, including animal husbandry and slaughter. Notably, similar considerations have been present in various indigenous cultures and religious and ethical codes for thousands of years, addressing the ethical treatment of animals, especially in the context of how they are slaughtered for human consumption and other uses.

All of this raises more questions. For instance, are our perceptions of animal consciousness congruent with what it really is? Do animals have the same level of consciousness as humans, and if they do, what are the ethical implications of that? Consider the diverse attitudes towards dogs across cultures: some view them as unclean, while others integrate them fully into family life. Such disparities often have little to do with dogs' intrinsic nature or value but reflect the *meaning* we assign to them. This is evident in the way we treat pets with care yet make decisions like neutering them without a second thought or, in stark contrast, subject wild dogs to cruel fates.

Our actions towards pets reveal that our concern is not solely for their wellbeing but for the significance we attribute to them, underscoring the complexity of human attachment and ethical considerations in our interactions with other sentient beings. The fate of numerous sentient beings hinges on our perspectives. As apex predators, we are inherently responsible for our choices, hence the need for ethics and morality. While science aids our comprehension, should we unquestionably surrender to the latest scientific discoveries, given the many mistakes made in the name of science over time? Just because we can doesn't mean we should. Are these issues purely scientific, or do they delve into ethical domains?

Scientists frequently step forward, claiming to have resolved the mystery of consciousness. But are their claims genuine? This is an area that warrants extreme caution. For example, Integrated Information Theory purports to answer whether embryos are conscious beings. We must err on the side of caution to prevent the weaponisation of science for ideological purposes. Some undergo non-reversible surgery based on a scientific theory, and certain actions are being criminalised in the name of science that could significantly impact the destiny of humans and other sentient beings. Science and scientific claims don't remain confined to laboratories and research centres; they infiltrate politics, policies, laws, society and popular culture. They weave the fabric of our culture and norms, shaping societal taboos and standards.

Attempts to quantify subjective experiences encounter a fundamental challenge rooted in the inherently subjective nature of feelings. At best, discussions about feelings can aspire to become intersubjective, where shared understandings emerge. Consider the example of personal preferences in music. When individuals share their favourite genres or artists, people's reactions to these preferences are shaped by their own feelings, perspectives and experiences, illustrating the subjective nature of interpretation and experience.

Suffering stems from and is exacerbated by inauthenticities: instances where our conception of various fragments of reality is at odds with reality. Additionally, suffering emerges when we refuse to be in a state of surrender in situations that are outside our individualistic preferences or tastes. Consider that our tendency to escape from the truth can be attributed, at least in part, to the uncomfortable nature of certain truths; at times, the truth hurts! For instance, acknowledging our limitations and vulnerability means we're not always able to dictate our priorities. And no matter how powerful we may be, we cannot influence or exert our will onto every aspect of life. We cannot even control every process within our own bodies, let alone all matters in life. Those realisations can be both daunting and humbling. Even when we can't deny or hide from the truth, we rebel and resist instead of surrendering, which ironically leads to even more suffering. We may engage in problem-solving exercises and take pride in our abilities to solve them, but what we may ignore is discerning whether the 'problem' we are solving is, in fact, a problem! Sometimes, our persistent efforts to fix or solve something are completely wasted because we're trying to fix something that is not even a problem; it's just how it is.

A wise and polished individual can ontologically *be with* the way things are and respond appropriately. Failing to recognise this can lead to bitterness and resentment. Without embracing a state of surrender when necessary, your experience of life becomes a burden as opposed to an opportunity; you might be living your life, but not with grace. For instance, attending to parental duties, such as routinely changing a baby's nappy, might not be the most pleasant task, but surrendering to the reality that it is a natural part of life enables one to perform it without resentment. Acknowledging that we are not the sole source of *all* matters in life is critical to maintaining a healthy relationship with autonomy – the knowledge that we can respond to life's challenges. Regardless of the source, our response should ideally aim to influence the matter positively, contributing to the integrity of our lives or, at the very least, minimising potential compromises to it.

Throughout history, we find examples of well-known, so-called intellectuals who harbour bitterness and discontent towards the way things are, a state commonly referred to as 'intellectual resentment'. For example, British actor and comedian Stephen Fry, an outspoken atheist, caused a stir with his comments on the kind of god he doesn't believe in during an interview in 2015. As is his habit, Fry did not hold back: 'How dare you? How dare you create a world to which there is such misery that is not our fault. It's not right; it's utterly, utterly evil. Why should I respect a capricious, mean-minded, stupid God who creates a world that is so full of injustice and pain? That's what I would say.' Resentful statements like this are not unprecedented. They demonstrate a sense of entitlement and a lack of appreciation and open-mindedness towards appreciating that we are not the ones who gave us the opportunity to live.

There is a narrative that life is an unbearable burden, likening it to a disease needing a cure. When an Athenian jury convicted Socrates for failing to obey the gods of the city and corrupting the youth with his philosophical teachings, he serenely accepted his death rather than fight against the outcome. The traditional philosophical view of this story was of Socrates as a martyr for reason and a man who held to his principles. However, Friedrich Nietzsche saw things entirely differently. In his book, *The Gay Science*[67], he writes, 'Whether it was death, or the poison, or piety, or wickedness – something or other loosened [Socrates'] tongue at that moment, and he said : "O Crito, I owe a cock to Asclepios." For him who has ears, this ludicrous and terrible "last word" implies: "O Crito, life is a long sickness!" Is it possible! A man like him, who had lived cheerfully and to all appearance as a soldier – was a pessimist! He had merely put on a good demeanour towards life, and had all along concealed his ultimate judgment, his profoundest sentiment! Socrates, Socrates had suffered from life!'

By invoking Asclepios as the god of medicine, Socrates implicitly called life a disease – and death the cure. The implications here are the reason for the harshest Nietzschean criticism of Socrates: that his philosophy was ultimately one of life-denial. Man as a rational being is incompatible with man as a living being. By associating ourselves with our rational mind, we grow disenchanted with our physical body and its limitations. We grow to distrust our own nature, irrational as it is. For whatever respect he had for Socrates, Nietzsche repudiated this viewpoint.

So profound is the sentiment of life being a burden in some that many other renowned intellectuals are known to have become immersed in the tumultuous ocean of their thoughts, some even opting to detach themselves from existence. Famous Dutch painter Vincent van Gogh struggled with mental illness throughout his life, and his letters often reflect his inner turmoil and feelings of despair. Acclaimed English writer Virginia Woolf grappled with depression and ultimately took her own life. Celebrated American poet and novelist Sylvia Plath battled with depression for much of her life, and her writing often explores themes of existential despair and the struggle to find meaning in a seemingly indifferent universe. Influential German

---

67   Nietzsche named the book *Die Fröhliche Wissenschaft*, which was translated as *The Gay Science*. It was published in 1882, long before the word 'gay' had any connection to homosexuality.

philosopher Friedrich Nietzsche wrote about the concept of 'the eternal recurrence', suggesting that life's suffering and challenges are endlessly repeated, leading some to interpret his philosophy as nihilistic and pessimistic. These are just a few examples of the existential suffering endured by renowned intellectuals.

The notion of enduring severe pain is not universal; individuals may possess extraordinary strength to withstand immense suffering. However, it is essential to acknowledge that even among exceptional individuals, there are instances where the weight of the world's darkness proves overwhelming. Generally speaking, harbouring resentment about circumstances beyond our control lacks wisdom. A wiser approach to intellectual resentment, when no suitable resolution can be found, involves surrendering to the reality of a situation without succumbing to it. Acknowledging what is beyond our direct influence serves as a foundation for innovation, effective problem-solving and creativity. Recognising inherent limitations presents opportunities to devise strategies to navigate around them. For instance, acknowledging the force of gravity led to the development of aircraft.

Life and the possibility of being 'out there in the world' should be seen as a gift. Yet, instead of evoking wonderment, some dare to take it for granted. As receivers of this gift, we should be grateful and care enough to work towards its betterment. To do this, we must first recognise life's inherent value and accept the gift with all its ups and downs, likes and dislikes. We must tap into our rationality, science and technology, philosophy and ethics while keeping the door of spirituality open to minimise the suffering inherent in life. To everything else, we should surrender.

Exploring the profound relationship between suffering, consciousness and growth, several thinkers provide unique insights. Consider the following examples. C.S. Lewis sees pain as a pathway to spiritual awareness, challenging us to align our inner selves with the world's realities. Drawing from his own harrowing experiences, Viktor E. Frankl highlights how finding meaning in suffering can reinforce our identity and purpose. Bessel van der Kolk reveals how trauma shapes our physical being and consciousness, affecting our interactions. Pema Chödrön views suffering as a transformative force, pushing us to embrace life's transient nature. Antonio Damasio and Bhante Henepola Gunaratana delve into the impact of emotional and physical pain on self-awareness and how mindfulness can alter our relationship with suffering. Patrick Wall and Tara Brach emphasise the biological aspects of pain and the liberating power of acceptance and compassion. Each of these thinkers contributes to a nuanced understanding of the interconnection between suffering and consciousness, offering diverse perspectives from scientific, philosophical and spiritual viewpoints.

Building on the insights from the thinkers above, the exploration of consciousness, particularly in relation to the suffering of sentient beings, invites a broader philosophical and ethical inquiry that stretches beyond the empirical confines of neuroscience. As mentioned earlier, while neuroscience has made significant strides in mapping the neural correlates of consciousness and pain perception, it encounters inherent limitations when grappling with the subjective experiences of suffering and the moral implications tied to the consciousness of other sentient beings. The gap between the objective measurements of brain activity and the subjective quality of conscious experience highlights these limitations and points to the necessity of integrating philosophical and ethical considerations into our understanding of consciousness, particularly when contemplating the suffering of sentient beings beyond humans. As you can see, consciousness has a significant influence across various domains. Scholars must be conscious of the potential ramifications of their research and publications. Let's consider a few historical and contemporary examples.

Flawed scientific theories, such as those associating the European race with superiority or pathologising the act of homosexuality, transcend laboratory boundaries. During the time of Winston Churchill, various studies and theories, often rooted in what was considered 'science' at the time, claimed that certain races were superior to others. For example, when asked about the Balfour Declaration[68] and how it could be an injustice to Palestinians, Churchill purportedly said: 'I do not accept that the dog in the manger has an ultimate claim to the manger, even if it has occupied it for a long time. I do not acknowledge this claim. I do not believe that great injustices have been perpetrated against the Native Americans or the indigenous peoples of Australia. I do not believe they have been wronged by the arrival of a stronger, more advanced, or more worldly-wise race taking their place. I do not concede it. I do not believe the Native Americans had the authority to declare, "The American continent belongs to us, and we will not tolerate European settlers." They did not possess that authority, nor did they have the ability to enforce it.'

The Churchill example was part of a broader framework of scientific racism, prominent in the 19th and early 20th centuries. Another example was the Eugenics movement, which advocated for improving human populations through selective breeding. Eugenics was supported by many scientists and intellectuals of the time and had a significant influence on policies and attitudes towards race. Other prominent examples include Craniometry and Phrenology, which attempted to measure intelligence and other traits based on skull size and shape and was used to justify racial hierarchies, and Social Darwinism, a theory that misapplied Charles Darwin's ideas about natural selection to human societies and was used to justify imperialism, colonialism and social inequality. There was even a time not too long ago when certain races or ethnicities were deemed 'less than human' and kept in zoos alongside animals to be observed by those considered 'superior'. These and other questionable studies, theories and practices were eventually discredited as the scientific community recognised the flaws in their methodologies and the ethical implications of their conclusions. Nonetheless, the legacy of these pseudoscientific ideas, allegedly grounded in science, has had

68   The Balfour Declaration was a public statement issued by the British Government in 1917 during the First World War, announcing its support for the establishment of a 'national home for the Jewish people' in Palestine.

a long-lasting impact on social attitudes and policies due, in part, to their influence on the leaders of the time.

More recent history continues to serve as a stark reminder of science's role in promoting racial superiority, leading to atrocities such as colonisation, imperialism and genocide. Certain so-called 'scientific' works, such as those associated with influential figures like John Money and Alfred Kinsey, often blur the lines between genuine scientific inquiry and pseudoscience, as highlighted in the previous chapter. These works can extend beyond academic and scientific circles, exerting influence over politics, social norms, ethics, policymaking and the commercialisation of some industries. In the case of Kinsey and Money, for example, the way their bodies of work contributed to gender ideology sparked controversy and ethical challenges, particularly in how the dissemination of their research findings may contribute to the proliferation of practices such as gender-affirming surgeries and the promotion of hormone blockers, shaping both medical practices and commercial ventures where the construct being manufactured through social science encourages people to change physical reality by surgically altering their body's inherent physiological functions.

All the confusion around consciousness highlights a hefty burden that science alone cannot possibly be expected to shoulder on its own; it couldn't even if it wanted to. Ultimately, constructs are not 'just constructs'; they don't stay within the confines of academic 'ivory towers', university classes, conferences, papers and laboratories. Instead, they infiltrate into the real world – in families and societies. In navigating complexities like these, the scientific community must do everything in its power to steer the ship with diligence and responsibility.

The relationship between consciousness and sense-making

To make sense of our world, meanings and experiences, including consciousness, we require a robust intellectual substrate. This substrate, or metacontent, forms the foundational layers that enable us to process and integrate information meaningfully. The Nested Theory of Sense-making provides a structured approach to dissecting these layers, allowing for a clearer and more authentic comprehension of reality and any content we are attempting to make sense of.

Our exploration of consciousness, especially its connection to suffering, illuminates the core of the human experience. Consciousness allows us to feel, reflect and navigate our existence, deeply influencing how we interpret reality and make sense of our lives. As you can see, consciousness is not merely intellectual; it is fundamental to understanding how we engage with the world, process our experiences and respond to challenges.

This chapter set the stage for delving deeper into the subject of sense-making, beginning in the following chapter with an inquiry into understanding the whatness of things before being introduced to the Nested Theory of Sense-making in Chapter 9. This Nested Theory is a practical tool designed to support you in understanding the deep intellectual substrates that underpin your sense-making processes. Leveraging it helps transcend surface-level interpretations and gain deeper insights into your conscious experiences. Furthermore, by integrating various layers of knowledge and perspectives on a challenging subject like consciousness, you will enhance your ability to understand it, including its impact on you, the people in your life, your community and humanity.

Conclusion

In this chapter, we explored how consciousness is a phenomenon that defies simple categorisation or understanding through the lens of any single discipline. It is multidimensional, encompassing metaphysical, ethical, moral and political dimensions. Consequently, a multidisciplinary approach is essential for unravelling its mysteries and implications, supporting the tough decisions we all need to make in our lives, especially those with legal, moral and ethical implications.

Consciousness extends beyond scientific study alone, intersecting with various disciplines, including psychology, sociology, politics and economics, shaping human experience and societal dynamics. Through the lens of diverse disciplines, we gain a more holistic view of consciousness and its connection to suffering, one that acknowledges the limitations of science and embraces the complexities of every conscious being's experience. By integrating insights from the humanities, philosophy, ethics, and natural and social sciences, alongside advancements in technology and engineering, we can transform scholarly inquiry and our understanding of this mysterious phenomenon.

This integrative approach recognises that understanding consciousness requires collaboration across diverse fields. For example, while neuroscience sheds light on the biological foundations of consciousness, cognitive psychology explores the functions of the mind, and phenomenology emphasises the subjective experience. As we venture into the future of consciousness studies, interdisciplinary collaborations will be essential for both theoretical advancements and practical applications for everything from education, ethics, policy and social justice to climate change, artificial intelligence and mental health. These are just a few examples that highlight the importance of integrating insights from multiple disciplines to address complex societal and global issues and promote the wellbeing of all sentient beings.

Exploring consciousness before delving into the topic of sense-making was crucial because it has provided the foundation for understanding how we experience and interpret reality, directly impacting our sense-making processes. Without this discussion, we would lack the context to appreciate the depth and complexity of our cognitive and emotional responses. The metacontent discourse and Nested Theory of Sense-making empower us to deconstruct and reconstruct our understanding in a more nuanced and holistic manner. By embracing a holistic and interdisciplinary perspective, we can navigate the intricate terrain of consciousness more effectively, enriching our understanding of ourselves, others and the world around us.

CHAPTER 7

Whatness and Quiddity

W hen investigating what something is – its essence, nature, quiddity or whatness – we know we can turn to science as the most reliable method if it is part of nature or our material reality. However, relying solely on understanding the whatness of a matter from a scientific perspective is insufficient for us to deeply make sense of it and develop our conception of it to the extent where we can make sound decisions and take effective actions in the context of our lives. Let me explain.

Consider the whatness of a seemingly simple manufactured object like an axe. Through scientific analysis, we can deconstruct it, identifying and studying its constituent parts, such as the blade and handle, each with distinct qualities and characteristics. Science can tell us that the blade is constructed from stainless steel and the handle is crafted from hardwood. Science can also break it down further and specify the constituent parts of the stainless steel and hardwood, such as the qualities and characteristics of the type of stainless steel and hardwood used to craft the blade and handle. For example, it can tell us how walnut wood performs compared to rosewood and the difference between 304 and 316 stainless steel.

Yet, beyond these measurable factors lies a deeper essence that gives rise to new and emerging properties. For starters, there is its functionality, which is beyond the simple aggregation of the whatness of every constituent part. Most people seeking to buy an axe care more about its functionality than what it is made of. More specifically, they want to know that the material it is constructed from will effectively serve its function. How well will it perform the task for which it is needed? Others may care more about the axe's aesthetic qualities. So, in evaluating an axe's whatness, individuals may prioritise performance, aesthetics or even how they feel about it. For example, some might even 'feel more comfortable' using one type of axe over another. In another example, if someone inherits an axe from their grandfather, a carpenter, who used it to build a cottage on the family ranch, the axe might hold deep sentimental value for them beyond the properties of its constituent parts, functionality or performance. So, simply labelling an axe as nothing more than a tool for chopping wood that is typically constructed from iron with a steel edge and a wooden handle massively reduces the totality of its whatness to its functionality.

Now consider human beings. When examining our whatness through a purely scientific lens, we are reduced to mere collections of cells. But we are so much more than that. Beyond physical beings, we are rational, conscious, emotional entities with the capacity to think, communicate, create and store memories, feel and suffer. A purely scientific approach neglects these aspects. The fact that groups of cells can give rise to such qualities should fill us all with awe and wonder.

The quest to understand and make sense of the whatness of things has long intrigued philosophers and scientists alike. To address our individual and collective confusion and develop authentic awareness, it is beneficial to delve into the historical narratives and various schools of philosophy that have shaped our understanding of ontology and the whatness of matters and ideas. By examining how different philosophical traditions have approached these fundamental questions throughout history, we can better appreciate the complexities of human thought and the evolution of our conceptions of reality. This chapter delves into the history and multifaceted approaches to studying the inherent and subjective whatness of things. It will shed light on how they laid the groundwork for the metacontent discourse and Nested Theory of Sense-making and provide the context for their development and application.

Understanding the whatness of matters: a philosophical inquiry

Throughout history, philosophers have grappled with questions about the nature of reality and existence. These inquiries have given rise to diverse schools of thought, each offering unique perspectives on what things are, how they came to be and how they work. By studying these historical narratives, we gain insights into the foundational concepts that underpin our current understanding of the world. This historical perspective is crucial for several reasons.

Firstly, understanding the evolution of philosophical thought provides context for contemporary theories, including those introduced in this book. It helps you see how ideas have developed over time and how they have influenced each other. For instance, the progression from ancient Greek metaphysics to modern existentialism illustrates shifts in focus from abstract principles to individual human experience. Secondly, you can identify strengths and weaknesses in various approaches by comparing different schools of thought. Thirdly, engaging with historical narratives deepens your philosophical understanding and enables you to appreciate different perspectives.

As mentioned, the metacontent discourse and Nested Theory of Sense-making are built on the foundation laid by these historical philosophical inquiries together with the various inquiries into consciousness and leverage insights from various schools of thought. By acknowledging the contributions of different epistemological approaches, the metacontent discourse broadens our understanding of knowledge and its limitations. And the Nested Theory of Sense-making, as explained in detail in Chapter 9, integrates concepts from different ontological traditions, providing a multi-layered approach to understanding reality. For example, the incorporation of cognitive maps and narrative lenses into its multi-layered approach reflects the influence of phenomenology and constructivism, emphasising both the subjective and constructed nature of human experience.

In summary, understanding the philosophy behind the metacontent discourse and the Nested Theory of Sense-making serves to recognise the sources of confusion in your perception of reality, for example, by appreciating the complexities of meaning and truth. Engaging with these philosophical debates also encourages you to question your assumptions, develop your authentic awareness and recognise that science, while powerful, is not infallible and must be understood within its epistemological limits. It helps you appreciate the role of scientific inquiry in uncovering truths about the material world while remaining critical of its limitations. Understanding that science operates within certain boundaries of knowledge allows you to maintain a balanced view of its capabilities and applications.

In addition to demystifying science, the aim here is to demythologise knowledge. This means stripping away the myths and misconceptions surrounding scientific and philosophical knowledge and promoting a more realistic and grounded understanding of science and philosophy and their role in society.

Last but not least, exploring philosophical concepts prepares you to apply the metacontent discourse and Nested Theory of Sense-making in various dimensions of your life. Whether in personal development, leadership, education, healthcare or entrepreneurship – to name just a few examples – by understanding the philosophical roots of these frameworks, you will be in a better position to apply them to real-world situations, improving your ability to make informed and effective decisions. Building on the foundational insights presented here will also enable you to expand this body of knowledge to address specific needs or niche areas.

Let's begin by comparing and contrasting the stance of some of the early and more recent philosophers on examining the whatness of matters. You will discover that there are various schools of thought on what constitutes an entity and how to inquire into that. On the surface, this might seem like a simple subject to unravel. However, as you will see, particularly when it comes to studying sentient beings, it is a subject that continues to fuel fierce discussion and debate.

Platonic philosophy, Aristotelianism and stoicism represent three foundational pillars of ancient thought in the Western world, each offering distinct perspectives on ethics, metaphysics and epistemology. Understanding these perspectives and their interrelations provides deeper insight into the evolution of Western philosophy and the concept of whatness. Later, we will also examine some Eastern philosophy perspectives to provide a more well-rounded view on the subject.

Aristotelianism and stoicism are fundamental intellectual substrates that have profoundly influenced Western thought. While various fields might not fully acknowledge their influence, they have significantly helped shape the economy, politics, law, social constructs and norms, dominant ethical frameworks, policies and the constructs of policymakers and institutions built upon them. Understanding how each philosophical paradigm approaches this concept provides insight into their broader metaphysical, epistemological and ethical frameworks. However, before we examine the perspectives of Aristotle and the stoics on whatness, let's begin our inquiry with Plato.

Plato's Theory of Forms and ontological dualism

Plato asserted that beyond the physical world lies a realm of perfect and immutable forms or ideas, which are the true essences of all entities. He introduced his dialectic method to engage in philosophical inquiry through dialogue. This method involves an iterative process of questioning, where ideas are proposed, scrutinised and refined. His Theory of Forms and ontological dualism[69] greatly influenced Aristotle, who was his student. Although Aristotle dramatically departed from many aspects of Platonic thought, the dialectical method and focus on defining concepts such as virtue and justice carried over into his work. While not directly descended from Platonic thought, stoicism shared Plato's concern for ethical living based on understanding a higher order of truth. However, stoics discarded Plato's metaphysical dualism, focusing instead on a monistic[70] universe governed by divine reason.

Plato often engaged with alternative views, mainly as a result of dialogues with his teacher, Socrates. However, these dialogues typically aimed to dissect and sometimes refute alternative views rather than embrace them or focus on commonalities. Indeed, Plato's dialogues often highlighted differences in thought, particularly between Socratic (or Platonic) ideas and those of the sophists or other contemporaries, to illustrate the superiority of his philosophical positions. Over the centuries that followed, the focus on differences in philosophical thought grew, reflecting the evolution and expansion of philosophical inquiry into various schools of thought.

The Ancient Egyptians and Persians

It is widely believed in the West that Aristotle laid the foundation for the scientific way of thinking. Indeed, the association of the scientific method with Aristotle primarily stems from his systematic approach to empirical observation, classification and logical reasoning. However, scientific and mathematical knowledge development

---

69   Ontological dualism is a philosophical concept that proposes the existence of two fundamentally distinct types of substances or entities in the universe. The most common form of ontological dualism is mind-body dualism, which asserts that there are two distinct substances: the mind (or soul) and the body (or physical matter), which are separate entities with different natures that interact with each other in various ways.

70   Monism attributes oneness or singleness to a concept, such as to existence. A philosophy is monistic if it postulates unity of the origin of all things; all existing things return to a source that is distinct from them.

predates Aristotle and was not confined to the Greeks. Civilisations such as the Egyptians and Persians significantly contributed to fields like geometry and physics long before Aristotle's time.

For example, the ancient Egyptians excelled in geometry, physics and engineering, as evidenced by the precision of the pyramids. They also had sophisticated knowledge of astronomy, using it to create calendars and align structures with celestial bodies, aiding agricultural planning and religious practices. The Persians made significant advancements in mathematics and astronomy. Scholars like Al-Khwarizmi developed algorithms that form the basis of modern computing, and Persian polymaths like Avicenna (Ibn Sina) made substantial contributions to medicine, philosophy and science, writing comprehensive texts that were used for centuries in both the Islamic world and Europe.

While Aristotle emphasised systematic empirical observation and logic, the Egyptians and Persians relied on hands-on experience and advanced knowledge through practical applications. Aristotle's systematic documentation provided a framework for future generations, while much of Egyptian and Persian knowledge was conveyed through practical applications and texts that were not as systematically organised but nonetheless highly influential. Later, the Greeks, including Aristotle, learned from Egyptian, Persian and other even earlier knowledge systems, integrating and expanding upon them.

The Aristotelian philosophical system

Aristotle laid the foundation for what later became known as essentialism. He asserted that whatness – which he referred to as 'essence' – makes a thing itself and not something else; it is the defining set of characteristics that are necessary and sufficient for something to be what it is. The Aristotelian or 'peripatetic'[71] philosophical system emphasises the study of the natural world through empirical observation, logical analysis and categorisation. He covered a wide

---

71   Of or relating to the Greek philosopher Aristotle or his philosophy.

range of subjects, including logic, science, politics and ethics, and categorised the natural world using a method that applies syllogistic logic – a kind of logical argument that applies deductive reasoning to arrive at a conclusion based on two propositions that are asserted or assumed – to reach conclusions. Those conclusions, and those that preceded them, formed the initial foundation for today's methodical advancements, particularly in the exact sciences.

Aristotle believed in the existence of objective truths and sought to understand the whatness of things through careful observation and analysis. From a metaphysical perspective, he proposed that everything in the physical world can be understood as a combination of form (the essence or whatness of a thing) and matter (the physical substance).

Over the centuries that followed, other philosophical concepts surfaced from the Aristotelian philosophical system, which, together with the teachings from other ancient civilisations, served as a substrate for subsequent philosophical schools of thought. In Aristotle's framework, substances are the foundational entities in the metaphysical structure of reality. A substance is a combination of form (essence) and matter (the substrate that takes on forms). The essence/form of a substance dictates its nature and its capabilities.

Stoic philosophy

Founded in Athens by Zeno of Citium in the early 3rd century BC, stoic philosophy, or stoicism, is also concerned with nature and defining characteristics. However, unlike Aristotle, the stoics approached the concept of essence through its integration of logic, ethics and physics, underpinned by the belief in a rationally ordered universe governed by divine reason (Logos). They emphasise the importance of rational ethics and acceptance of fate, advocating for indifference to external circumstances like pain or pleasure, which are seen as neither inherently good nor bad, and a life of self-control, resilience and detachment from materialism in pursuit of virtue and a life in harmony with the Logos.

Stoicism asserts that each thing's essential nature is best understood by considering how it conforms to its natural purpose – what a thing is meant to do or be according to its rational design. For example, the whatness of a knife – if we focus solely on its functionality – is to cut. Similarly, for humans, stoics argue that our whatness involves rationality and the community-oriented nature of human beings. Consequently, they urge individuals to act in accordance with reason and for the common good.

A crucial aspect of stoic philosophy is the assertion that the true essence or whatness of a human being is not determined by external circumstances but by their ability to live according to virtue and reason. For stoics, living in accordance with one's essence means accepting one's role in the universe and fulfilling it with grace and integrity. This involves practising the four cardinal virtues of stoicism: wisdom, courage, justice and temperance. By embodying these virtues, stoics believe that a person aligns themselves with the rational structure of the universe, achieving eudaimonia – a state of flourishing or good-spiritedness. This view contrasts sharply with other philosophical traditions that may emphasise empirical categorisation, existential choice or social constructs as the basis for understanding whatness.

The evolution of Platonic, Aristotelian and stoic perspectives on whatness

Plato's emphasis on ideal forms and universal truths, Aristotle's empirical methods and the stoic's doctrine of ethical rationalism collectively deepen our understanding of philosophical principles – including the whatness of matters – and their practical applications in life.

Aristotelianism proposes that whatness is determined by form and is intrinsic to the categorisation of all entities. It is more static, focusing on what properties a thing must have to be what it is. In contrast, stoicism regards whatness as a dynamic aspect of the rational order of the universe. It is less about intrinsic properties and more about the role and function derived from divine reason or Logos. While Aristotle relied heavily on empirical observation and logical categorisation to determine whatness, believing in direct engagement with the physical world to understand the form and, therefore, the whatness of substances, stoics adopt a more theoretical approach to understanding matters. For them, knowledge of whatness is more about understanding universal laws than empirical investigation. Both systems ultimately aim to guide individuals toward a fulfilling life through understanding and living in accordance with their whatness.

In light of Plato and Aristotle's significant contributions to Western thought, let's now delve deeper into the pros and cons of their work. For example, while Aristotle's work is often praised for its empirical rigour and systematic nature, Plato's contributions offered unique insights and methodologies that have distinct advantages in various philosophical contexts. Let's look into some of those advantages, beginning with his emphasis on ideal forms and universal truths.

As mentioned, Plato's Theory of Forms proposed that there are perfect and immutable forms or ideas beyond the physical realm, which represent the true essence of all things. This approach offered a foundation for discussing ethical and moral ideals without being confined by the practical limitations of the physical world and the words that are created by human beings to refer to various parts of reality, whether material or abstract. It allowed philosophers and thinkers to explore concepts like justice, beauty and equality in their ideal forms, potentially leading to higher ethical standards and aspirations.

Many centuries later, German philosopher Ludwig Klages introduced a concept called 'logocentrism'. The term describes the tendency in Western science and philosophy to view words and language as a key manifestation of external reality. Logocentrism places 'Logos' (reason) at a higher epistemological level, suggesting that it accurately depicts an original, fundamental entity and, therefore, represents universal truth. Under logocentrism, Logos was considered the perfect depiction of the Platonic ideal, which was not confined to words with all their varied meanings and understandings. Klages' concept of logocentrism or universal truth would later be challenged by poststructuralist philosopher Jacques Derrida.

Returning to Aristotle, there is no question that his contributions to philosophy and science were immense. In particular, his role in establishing a rigorous, systematic approach to thinking, empirical observation and logical categorisation made it possible to build a cohesive understanding of various natural phenomena, building a foundation that would profoundly influence scientific thought and shape scientific methodologies. However, Aristotle's methodologies were limited when it came to addressing more subjective, interpretative realms such as narrative, rhetoric and personal experiences – areas that would much later become central to existential and phenomenological philosophy and which are both key to developing a more comprehensive picture of the whatness of conscious beings, including human beings. Although Aristotle did discuss ethics and elements of human behaviour, his approach often attempted to apply objective reasoning to these highly subjective phenomena that were inherently challenging to categorise.

While Aristotelianism dominated for centuries, its limitations eventually became more apparent with the rise of the existentialist philosophers in the late 19th and early 20th centuries, who argued that individual experience, subjective reality and personal choice are central to understanding human existence. Philosophers like Søren Kierkegaard, Friedrich Nietzsche and Martin Heidegger emphasised the importance of individual perspective, which Aristotle either missed or deemed irrelevant based on his systematic and categorical approaches. This shift highlighted the need for new fields of study that were capable of considering the complexities of human behaviour and social structures, leading to the development of social sciences like psychology and sociology, as well as philosophical branches like phenomenology. These disciplines focus more on understanding human experience from a subjective viewpoint, exploring how individuals perceive and construct their realities, which diverges significantly from the more objective, naturalistic methodologies that Aristotle developed.

Aristotle's influence remains profound in the realms of ethics and axiology (the study of values) to this day. His ethical theories, particularly virtue ethics, emphasise the importance of character and virtues in moral philosophy. However, his approach to these areas has been challenged. Due to the contextual and variable nature of today's moral decisions, modern philosophical inquiries often demand a more nuanced understanding of ethical dilemmas and value systems. Contemporary approaches might incorporate elements of deon-tology[72], consequentialism[73] and other ethical frameworks to address the specific contexts and challenges of modern life. Aristotle's more fixed ethical frameworks sometimes struggled to comprehensively accommodate these types of inquiries, which is unsurprising given that subjects like ethics and morality don't sit comfortably within rational and scientific inquiries. The point is, Aristotle did not believe in fixed, universal moral codes in the same way that some later philosophical traditions advocated. Instead, he emphasised virtue ethics, which focuses on the development of 'good' character traits and virtues over strict adherence to a set of prescribed rules.

Aristotle's Virtue Theory comprised two parts: Arete (virtue or excellence) and Hexis (habit or disposition). Arete represents the highest quality a person can achieve. It is the fulfilment of purpose or function, particularly human potential and moral character, and involves the development and practice of virtues such as courage, temperance and wisdom, which, according to Aristotle, lead to a flourishing life or 'Eudaimonia'. Hexis refers to the stable disposition or habit that underpins virtuous actions. It is the cultivated state of

---

72   Deontology is an ethical theory focused on following moral rules or duties. Derived from the Greek word 'Deon' (meaning 'duty'), it proposes that actions are right or wrong based on their adherence to these rules, regardless of consequences.

73   Consequentialism is an ethical theory that judges the rightness or wrongness of actions based on their outcomes or consequences.

character that consistently enables a person to act in accordance with virtue. Aristotle emphasised that virtues are not innate but acquired through habitual practice and deliberate effort. According to his theory, moral virtue is about balancing extremes of excess and deficiency, tailored to the individual and their circumstances. This tells us that for Aristotle, context mattered. So, while some might perceive his arguments as fixed, I beg to differ.

As mentioned earlier, Aristotle also categorised knowledge in a way that illustrated his deep understanding of the different ways human beings engage with the world and make decisions. Those knowledge categories were:

- **Episteme (scientific knowledge)** – Knowledge that is systematic and verifiable, much like what we consider scientific knowledge today. It involves universal truths that can be known through deduction and can be reliably repeated and applied, such as the laws of physics or geometry.

- **Techne (technical skills or art)** – The knowledge or skill involved in making or doing things, focusing on the ability to produce something and often linked to craftsmanship or art. It involves not just knowledge of processes but also the ability to apply that knowledge effectively to create or achieve a practical end.

- **Phronesis (practical wisdom or prudence)** – The ability to make effective judgments and take the right action in varying circumstances. Unlike episteme, which is about universal truths, phronesis is highly contextual and dependent on the specific details of a situation. It's essential for ethical living, as it helps individuals navigate complex moral landscapes and make virtuous decisions that promote human flourishing.

Ultimately, Aristotle's contributions have been instrumental in explaining the material world and objective reality and, consequently, significantly shaped scientific thought. However, his focus on objective analysis reduced the scope of inquiry, particularly in areas such as the study of subjective experiences. Take traditional medical science, for example. Medical doctors often focus solely on the illness itself, disregarding the patient's subjective experience and how their mental state might influence the condition's progression. This oversight neglects the significant impact of subjective experiences on health outcomes. Modern fields like cognitive neuro-epigenetics address this gap by exploring how personal experiences can activate specific genes within our genome. These genes, which may remain dormant, are triggered by experiences, highlighting the intricate relationship between subjective experiences and biological mechanisms. This research emphasises the importance of considering both subjective and objective aspects of human health, fostering a more comprehensive understanding of medical conditions and the broader human condition.

While Aristotle's foundational methodologies are valuable for certain scientific inquiries, they are limited when applied to the complexities of human subjectivity and the interplay between mind and body. Contemporary science and philosophy have since expanded upon Aristotle's approach, emphasising the need for a more holistic understanding that integrates subjective experiences with objective analysis.

In contrast to Aristotelianism, Plato's philosophy, while also systematic, emphasised the concepts of forms and ideals, which are abstract and not strictly empirical. Although Aristotle's objective and systematic ways of looking into the natural world dominated for centuries, they have been critically reevaluated during the last two to three centuries. Notably, aspects of Plato's philosophical approach, which emphasised abstract ideals, have seen a revival in more recent schools of thought. This revival is evident in modern movements that stress subjectivity and the existential aspects of human experience, such as phenomenology and existentialism, which shift the focus from an empirical and strictly rational investigation of reality to a more nuanced exploration of human consciousness and subjective experiences. Their approach aligns more closely with Plato's philosophy than with Aristotle's.

The progression and impact of dialectic methods in philosophy

In ancient Greece, dialectic was a form of dialogue notably used by Socrates in Plato's dialogues. The dialectic approach also emerged in the East after Muslim scholars engaged with philosophical ideas from Greek, Persian and Indian sources. They subsequently integrated dialectical reasoning to address theological questions such as the nature of God, free will and predestination. Known as 'Kalam', the Islamic dialectic process involves structured debates where propositions are affirmed or negated based on rational scrutiny. As a form of intellectual investigation through dialogue involving the exchange of arguments and ideas between individuals with differing views, dialectic methods encourage openness to alternative perspectives to uncover deeper truths through discussion and debate. Because dialectics promotes critical thinking, questioning and reasoning, the method has been influential in educational theories and practices throughout history. It would also greatly influence future philosophers, such as Georg Wilhelm Friedrich Hegel, Karl Marx and Friedrich Engels.

Hegel's Science of Logic in the early 19th century was grounded in a system of dialectics. As touched on earlier, in Hegelian dialectic, the dialectic is a dynamic and progressive process that helps us understand the development of ideas and history through thesis, antithesis and synthesis. According to Hegel, each idea or thesis gives rise to a contradiction or antithesis, and their interaction resolves into a synthesis, which then becomes a new thesis, continuing the process. This method is seen as a way to capture the dynamic and developmental nature of reality.

Karl Marx and Friedrich Engels adapted Hegel's concept into dialectical materialism. For Marx, the dialectic method was grounded in real-world material conditions rather than Hegel's abstract ideas. Marx used this method to analyse the social and economic interactions in history, focusing on the conflicts between different social classes and how they drove societal change. This process was not seen as a purely intellectual exercise but as a description of human societies' real and often conflict-driven development.

Let's compare and contrast Plato's and Hegel's dialectic methods with Aristotle's, highlighting how they impacted subsequent intellectual discourse. As mentioned earlier, Plato introduced his dialectic method as a way of engaging in philosophical inquiry through dialogue. The method involves an iterative process of questioning, where ideas are proposed, scrutinised, and refined to arrive at a deeper understanding of a matter, including more challenging concepts like justice or beauty. His goal was to move beyond opinion and achieve true knowledge or 'episteme'.

Hegel's approach to dialectic inquiry built on the foundations laid by Plato. Opting for a more structured and progressive approach than Plato, Hegel developed the Thesis-Antithesis-Synthesis method, a dialectic that unfolds through a triadic structure where each thesis encounters its antithesis, and their conflict is resolved in a synthesis. This synthesis then becomes the thesis of a new triad, at which point the process continues with the ultimate aim of achieving Absolute Knowledge – a comprehensive understanding that encompasses all aspects of reality and human experience.

Unlike Plato's timeless Theory of Forms, Hegel's dialectic incorporated a historical perspective, viewing the development of ideas and cultural systems as part of the ongoing unfolding of human consciousness and freedom. In other words, Hegel's dialectic was dynamic, reflecting a more complex and fluid understanding of truth and reality, while Plato's was static in that its goal was to uncover eternal, unchanging truths (Forms). So, Plato's method laid the groundwork for systematic philosophical inquiry, while Hegel's adaptation shaped our modern understanding of gaining a comprehensive understanding or authentic awareness of the whatness of things.

Aristotle's approach to understanding reality was fundamentally different from the dialectic methods used by Plato and Hegel due to several key aspects. Firstly, unlike Plato and Hegel's abstract and ideological frameworks, Aristotle's philosophy was grounded in empirical observations and logical deductions. He prioritised concrete evidence and practical insights over theoretical contradictions and syntheses. Secondly, Aristotle's metaphysics focused on substances and their properties, where entities are defined by static forms and material compositions. This contrasted sharply with the dynamic and evolving nature of dialectic processes where thesis and antithesis interact to produce a synthesis. Last but not least, Aristotle developed formal logic and the syllogistic method – a deductive reasoning method based on forming conclusions from two premises that share a common term – to establish clear and coherent arguments, avoiding the inherent contradictions essential in Hegelian dialectics.

The exploration of dialectic methods in both Western and Eastern traditions directly relates to our broader discussion of whatness and ontology. While some would like to think that science and objective studies can provide accurate answers to all our questions and problems, the reality – particularly as it appears to us or how we comprehend it – is far more complex. It is both sentimentalism and inauthentic to believe that every important aspect of our lives can be established scientifically. As a method of examining reality through discussions and dialogue, dialectics fills this gap. Although scientific methods are invaluable for understanding the material world, they fall short when addressing the breadth and complexities of human experience. For example, science cannot fully explain the chemistry between two people, how to build deep, trusting relationships or how to choose a life partner or spouse. The dialectic approach offers a structured way to explore and understand complexities like this.

By engaging in dialogue, we can uncover underlying truths about aspects of reality that are inherently subjective and relational, leading to a higher level of understanding and the ability to identify and resolve contradictions in our thoughts and beliefs. In personal relationships, dialectical discussions can help individuals navigate emotions, understand different perspectives and build mutual under-standing. In the broader social context, the dialectic approach can facilitate more meaningful and inclusive debates on ethical, political and cultural issues. These are just two examples where dialectics are invaluable.

Essentialism and existentialism

Essentialism and existentialism emerged in the 19th and 20th centuries, respectively. Essentialism delves into the innate qualities of entities, exploring their fundamental essence or whatness and asserting that axiomatic laws govern certain entities. This school of thought extended Aristotle's ideas by maintaining that entities possess inherent attributes that define their identity and function. The essentialist perspective emphasises fixed traits that categorise beings in a somewhat rigid framework, highlighting the universal truths about their whatness. While we may not have direct access to these axiomatic laws, their existence is not negated, and we must strive to investigate them as thoroughly as possible to deepen our conception of them. However, the advancement of the exact sciences and technology distracted our attention from other parts of reality and knowledge that don't fit into exact sciences – areas like phenom-enology, humanities, art, theology, dialectics, axiology, ethics, etc.

In contrast, the emergence of existentialism represented a significant departure from earlier philosophical traditions, including essen-tialism and stoic philosophy, particularly in its treatment of human nature and the concept of essence. Existential philosophers like Jean-Paul Sartre, Simone de Beauvoir and Friedrich Nietzsche argued that existence precedes essence. Consequently, they regarded individ-uals as the architects of their own whatness or essence through their choices and actions, emphasising personal freedom and existential authenticity over predetermined nature.

So, while essentialism proposes the existence of essential and immutable qualities or characteristics inherent to objects, entities or concepts that are universal across different contexts, existentialism radically challenges the idea of anything having innate characteristics, particularly human beings, and that everything is subjective and mutable.

As you might imagine, existentialists have much to say in their rejection of the principles of essentialism. For starters, they reject the notion of a predetermined essence or whatness. Essentialist philosophies, such as those seen in Aristotelian thought, typically maintain that everything has a set of characteristics that defines what it fundamentally is. For human beings, this would mean there is a human nature that defines what it is to be human, established prior to and independent of individual existence. Existentialists flip this notion on its head, asserting that existence precedes essence or whatness. They argue that every human being comes into the world not with a predetermined nature or essence but as a blank slate and that their essence or whatness develops over time through their actions, choices and experiences.

Essentialism and existentialism on the dialectic method

Like Aristotelianism, essentialism emphasises the discovery of immutable essences rather than engaging in the transformative and speculative dialectic proposed by Hegel. While essentialists seek to identify and describe the unchanging whatness of things and seek objective discovery through direct observation and logical analysis, the dialectic method – most notably Hegel's version – explores various perspectives and contradictions to ultimately arrive at Absolute Knowledge.

The stark contrast between the two approaches makes it apparent why essentialist philosophers reject the dialectic method. For instance, their preference for empirical data, logical consistency and practical wisdom naturally diverges from the speculative, process-oriented dialectic methods. Furthermore, the static and objective nature of whatness in essentialism does not accommodate the dialectic method's dynamic, question/conflict-driven process.

Now, let's consider the existentialists and their position on the dialectic method. Existentialists don't use dialectic methods in the traditional, structured way or as prominently as other philosophies, such as Marxism or Hegelianism. That's because their way of thinking emphasises individual freedom, choice and subjective experience. However, dialectics can still be relevant in existential thought, particularly in how existentialists explore the tension and conflict within an individual's experience. More specifically, in existentialism, dialectics can be seen as the internal conflict and negotiation between different facets of existence. This includes the struggle between authenticity and inauthenticity, freedom and responsibility, and existence and essence. Take the battle between authenticity and inauthenticity, a key theme in existentialism, particularly in the works of Sartre and Heidegger. In this struggle, individuals must navigate between societal expectations (the inauthentic existence) and their genuine desires or personal identity (authentic existence). And when it comes to freedom and responsibility, existentialists argue that individuals are fundamentally free and must take responsibility for this freedom. Yet, this freedom also leads to anguish, as making choices involves taking responsibility for one's own existence without definitive guidance from traditional moral or societal frameworks.

While existentialists generally do not formalise their thoughts into a structured dialectical method as Hegel did, they engage deeply with the dynamics of opposing forces within the human condition. The dialectical process in existentialism is more about the unfolding and understanding of these existential tensions rather than resolving them in a synthesis, which is more characteristic of Hegelian dialectic.

Postmodern and poststructural philosophy

Postmodern and poststructural philosophy began to emerge in the 20th century, building upon and critiquing various aspects of existentialism and profoundly impacting our understanding of the whatness of things and ideas by challenging traditional notions of fixed meanings and objective realities. Both are movements characterised by scepticism towards grand narratives or universal truths, a theme that aligns with existentialist ideas.

Several poststructuralist philosophers questioned the existence of a universal essence or whatness, each bringing unique perspectives to the discourse. A notable example was Jacques Derrida, who – as mentioned earlier – challenged Ludwig Klages' concept of logocentrism or universal truth. Known as the founder of deconstruction, a way of critiquing literary and philosophical texts as well as political institutions, Derrida was also known for his work with language, text and meaning. He argued that believing in the Logos as the ultimate reference for understanding reality is fundamentally flawed because it assumes a fixed meaning or truth. Derrida challenged this notion by suggesting that meaning is not fixed but constantly deferred through the play of language, a process he described as 'différance'. His critique disrupted the logocentric idea of a stable, original essence that language supposedly captures, thereby questioning the foundational principles of Western metaphysics that regard speech and rationality as the most accurate conveyors of truth.

Other key figures in poststructuralism, such as Michel Foucault, Roland Barthes, Jean-François Lyotard, Gilles Deleuze, Julia Kristeva and many others, also emphasised that meanings are not fixed, but fluid and contingent. They challenged the notion of absolute truths and highlighted the role of discourse and context in shaping our understanding of the world.

Postmodernists and poststructuralists offered subtly different takes on existential themes, particularly regarding subjectivity, freedom and the nature of truth and meaning. They argued that what we consider the whatness of things is constructed through social and linguistic frameworks, not inherent traits. The perspective shifts the focus from seeking absolute truths to understanding the fluid and contextual nature of reality. In this way, postmodernism enriches our exploration of whatness in both abstract and concrete terms. This school of thought also promotes a view of identities as fluid and ever-changing, influenced by cultural and societal shifts.

While I share the postmodern view that 'all we know is a construct of the mind', I do not conclude that 'all there *is* is a construct of the mind'. I agree with the presupposition but not the conclusion. The fact that we do not have unmediated access to the truth of matters should not justify thinking there is no truth at all. This distinction is crucial; acknowledging the limitations of our access to truth does not negate the existence of truth itself. We must strive to understand reality while recognising the constraints of our perception and cognition. Just because we don't know something doesn't mean it does not exist. When it comes to science and the material world, meanings can be fixed. However, as human beings, we don't always have unmitigated access to those fixed meanings or truths due to the limitations of our conceptual structure and immediate consciousness – the parts to which we have access.

To highlight the key differences between existentialism and both postmodernism and poststructuralism, existentialism suggests that an individual is fundamentally free and responsible for defining themselves and their essence, while postmodern and poststructuralist thinkers took their ideas to the extreme, arguing that human beings have no essence at all. They challenged the notion of a coherent, autonomous subject. For example, Foucault argued that rather than being a stable source of free actions and decisions, the postmodern subject is fragmented and constituted by language, power relations and historical context. So, while existentialism focuses on individual freedom and responsibility, postmodernism and poststructuralism expand the discussion to include how power and knowledge systems shape identities and realities, potentially creating and limiting the possibilities for individual and collective action.

With their scepticism of universal truths and emphasis on relativity and fragmentation, postmodernism and poststructuralism offer a unique lens through which to view and challenge Platonic, Aristotelian and dialectic philosophies. Poststructuralists like Jean-François Lyotard argued against overarching, universal narratives that claim to describe all of reality, directly opposing the dialectic methods aimed at uncovering or developing unified truths. Similarly, Foucault's analysis of knowledge as a form of power critiques the idea of philosophical or historical inevitabilities, suggesting instead that all knowledge systems are contingent and shaped by specific power relations. So, in contrast to Hegel's evolving thesis-antithesis-synthesis model aimed at achieving an ultimate consensus, postmodernism and poststructuralism emphasise that truth is always relative and context-dependent, rejecting the notion of a final, absolute state of knowledge. They embrace fragmentation, celebrating the coexistence of diverse and often contradictory viewpoints.

It is intriguing to note the areas of convergence between Aristotle's empirical realism and postmodern epistemological scepticism. Both Aristotelian philosophers and the postmodernists share a common appreciation for the empirical and the concrete over the abstract. In Aristotelianism, knowledge emerges from sensory experience and the categorisation of the observable world, a viewpoint that aligns with the postmodern rejection of abstract universals. Furthermore, Aristotle's emphasis on context resonates with the postmodern preference for local over global narratives and practical knowledge over universal theories, creating a sense of continuity and connection in philosophical thought.

Postmodernism has been subject to significant criticism, particularly from those who view its principles as challenging traditional values and scientific objectivity. Their critique generally focuses on the following aspects of postmodern thought:

- **Relativism about truth** – Postmodernism is often associated with the idea that truth is relative, contingent on historical or social contexts rather than absolute and universal. This perspective challenges the foundational notions of objective truth that many fields, including science, rely on. Critics argue that this undermines the basis for widespread agreement on important issues and erodes the authority of science and rational debate.

- **Rejection of grand narratives** – The postmodern scepticism of 'grand narratives' – stories or theories that attempt to provide a comprehensive explanation of historical experience or knowledge – is seen by critics as a denial of any unified history or shared purpose. This can be perceived as a threat to the cohesion and stability of society, which often depends on shared beliefs and values.

- **Focus on power and language** – Postmodern theorists often argue that knowledge and truth are constructed through language and are tools of power that dominant groups use to control discourse. Their emphasis on the power dynamics of language and the idea that all knowledge is socially constructed is often refuted by critics who believe in objective standards and merit-based systems.

- **Impact on identity and politics** – Postmodernism has influenced contemporary discussions on identity, particularly around race, gender and sexuality. It often promotes a view that identities are socially constructed and fluid, leading to support for movements like critical race theory and gender studies. Critics argue that this focus on identity can divide society into competing groups rather than encourage unity.

- **Cultural pessimism and criticism** – Postmodernism often critically assesses Western culture and its historical narratives, pointing out inconsistencies, biases and injustices. Some see this critical stance as unnecessarily negative, focusing on deconstruction rather than offering constructive solutions or affirming Western civilisation's achievements.

Many critics find these elements of postmodern thought threatening because they appear to dismantle frameworks like empirical science, rationality and traditional cultural norms that, in their view, form the foundation of successful societies. They also argue that postmodernism can lead to nihilism and moral relativism, weakening society's moral and rational foundations.

However, in their critiques, there are also potential blind spots or areas where their analysis may not fully capture the complexity or value of postmodern thought. Some of these blind spots include:

- **Oversimplification** – Postmodernism is a diverse, multi-faceted intellectual movement encompassing a wide range of theories and perspectives. Critics sometimes treat it as an inflexible and uniformly negative philosophy. This oversimplification can overlook the diversity within postmodern thought and the fact that many postmodern theorists have nuanced views that do not entirely reject notions of truth or scientific rationality but question these concepts.

- **Failure to acknowledge constructive aspects** – While postmodernism is often criticised for its deconstructive tendencies, it also offers various constructive elements that can lead to greater awareness of overlooked or marginalised perspectives. For example, by questioning established narratives and exposing the role of power in the construction of knowledge, postmodernism can enhance critical thinking and encourage a more inclusive consideration of diverse voices and experiences.

- **Equating postmodernism with moral relativism** – Critics often compare postmodern scepticism of universal truths with a rejection of any moral or ethical standard. However, many postmodern thinkers do not advocate for absolute moral relativism. Instead, they suggest that historical and cultural contexts influence our understanding of ethics, which can lead to more adaptable and context-sensitive approaches to morality.

- **Misunderstanding the role of identity politics** – Critique sometimes extends to dismissing identity politics as merely divisive. However, postmodern influences on identity politics can help highlight structural inequalities and power imbalances that might not be adequately addressed by more traditional approaches.

- **Neglecting the benefits of challenging grand narratives**
  – While critics see the rejection of grand narratives as a source of cultural fragmentation, it can also be viewed as an opportunity to challenge authoritarianism and dogmatism, which is essential in a democratic society.

- **Underestimating the value of diverse perspectives in science and knowledge** – Critics ignore or fail to recognise that postmodernism's emphasis on the social construction of knowledge can enrich scientific inquiry by demonstrating how biases can affect even the most 'objective' sciences.

By focusing on the potential negatives, critics may miss these more constructive dimensions of postmodern thought. Acknowledging these aspects doesn't mean critics need to embrace postmodernism. However, greater awareness of the blind spots or misunderstandings could lead to a more balanced conception of its contributions to contemporary intellectual discourse.

This discussion highlights the importance of understanding post-modern thought's nuanced contributions to the whatness of things and ideas. While postmodernism critiques the notion of fixed meanings, it also encourages a deeper exploration of how these meanings are constructed. This balanced view is essential for a comprehensive understanding of ontology and the nature of reality.

Perennial philosophy

Perennial philosophy takes on board various perspectives from the other schools of thought but adds to them by also suggesting the existence of a shared, universal truth underlying all the world's religions and spiritual traditions. This concept has been embraced and discussed by philosophers, theologians and spiritual thinkers throughout history, including Aldous Huxley, who first introduced this school of thought in his book, *The Perennial Philosophy*.[74] Put simply, perennial philosophers suggest that many religious traditions

---

74   Huxley, A. 1945. *The Perennial Philosophy*. Harper & Brothers.

in the world, despite their surface differences, point towards the same ultimate truth – that the divine reality is the source and end of all existence. In this way, stoicism and perennial philosophy share similarities in their emphasis on universal logos or rational order. However, stoicism is more focused on ethical living in accordance with nature rather than mystical unity with a divine reality. There is also some alignment between perennial philosophy and Aristotelian philosophy in that the latter provides a systematic metaphysical framework that is somewhat compatible with the perennialist view of a hierarchical universe. But Aristotle's emphasis is more on empirical categorisation and logical analysis than the perennialist's spiritual insight.

In comparing perennial philosophy to existentialism and postmodernism, the differences are more significant. While existentialists maintain that meaning and whatness are created by individuals rather than pre-existing, perennial philosophers suggest that meaning and whatness are universal and pre-determined by the divine reality. Furthermore, although postmodernists argue against universal truths, emphasising cultural and historical context and the instability of meaning, perennial philosophers emphasise a single, unchanging truth and, therefore, directly oppose postmodernists' relativism.

While perennial philosophy often finds itself in contemporary debates about interfaith dialogue and the integration of Eastern and Western traditions, it nonetheless plays an important role in uncovering the whatness of matters. By advocating for universal spiritual truths underlying diverse religious practices, it encourages us to look beyond superficial differences and explore the fundamental nature of reality from a deeper and more holistic perspective.

Eastern philosophy

Every culture in the world has rich traditions of thought. Civilisations in China, India, the Islamic world, Africa, various indigenous traditions and the Americas have made their share of contributions to human knowledge. However, there continues to be a dominant perception that thought and thinking are primarily a 'Western phenomenon'. This view stems from historical superiority, educational influence and cultural representation, as outlined earlier in the chapter in reference to Aristotle and below.

Historically, Western philosophy is grounded in ancient Greek and Roman thought, both extensively studied and revered. It also draws its heritage from significant philosophical developments during the Renaissance and Enlightenment periods. The Scientific Revolution in Europe is credited with shaping modern thinking. And Western colonial powers imposed their intellectual frameworks on colonised regions, overshadowing local traditions and Eurocentrism during the 18th and 19th centuries, further solidifying Western thought as the universal standard.

Educational systems worldwide commonly emphasise Western philosophers and scientists, often neglecting non-Western traditions. Even prestigious Western universities, seen as primary centres of advanced thought, reinforce this perception. Despite some progress, the curriculum in many schools and universities still predominantly highlights figures like Plato, Aristotle, Descartes, Newton and Einstein, while contributions from non-Western thinkers remain underrepresented. This trend extends to academic publications and conferences, where Western scholars are frequently cited and invited to speak, further solidifying the prominence of Western perspectives.

The influence of Western universities on global education standards has perpetuated a Eurocentric view of knowledge and intellectual history. However, there is a growing movement advocating for the decolonisation of the curriculum. A diverse group of scholars and activists are making a compelling case for a more inclusive approach that incorporates a variety of perspectives, aiming to create a more comprehensive understanding of human knowledge and intellectual history.

The broader reach of Western philosophies has also been extended because Western media and literature tend to place more emphasis on Western thinkers, leading to greater visibility and recognition through books, movies and digital content. Combine all this with the global dominance of the English language, and I'm sure you can see why Eastern philosophy tends to be less talked about.

While the impact of Western thought is undeniable, it's equally important to celebrate the contributions of Eastern thinkers. As global awareness of these diverse intellectual traditions grows, the perception of thought as a solely 'Western phenomenon' is being challenged, as highlighted above in relation to global universities. Let's now delve into an example of Eastern philosophy – Islamic philosophy and its unique perspective on whatness or quiddity, inspiring us to explore the richness of non-Western thought.

Islamic philosophy's perspective on whatness

As mentioned, many philosophers have traditionally ignored Eastern philosophy. However, there are some notable examples, such as Henry Corbin, a 20th-century French philosopher, theologian and professor of Iranian studies who was sincerely curious about Eastern philosophy, particularly Islamic philosophy. He and others like him recognised Islamic philosophers' indelible mark on the global philosophical landscape with their ways of thinking. Let's briefly explore their take on the whatness of things.

Islamic philosophers refer to the essential nature or whatness of a thing as 'Mahiyah', the Arabic word for whatness, essence or quiddity. Heavily influenced by the ideas of Aristotle, Islamic philosophical discussion around Mahiyat often revolves around the distinction between the essence of a thing (what it is) and its existence or 'Wujud' (that it is). This distinction was central to the inquiries of prominent Islamic philosophers like Ibn Sina (Avicenna) and Al-Farabi, who were both instrumental in bringing Aristotelian and Neoplatonic ideas into Islamic thought.

There are several schools of thought and interpretations of whatness within Islamic philosophy. Let's consider one of the more prominent examples – illuminationist philosophy or illuminationism – a prominent example of Islamic philosophy. Founded by Suhrawardi in the 12th century, illuminationism has influenced several philosophers over the centuries. Other notable Illuminationist philosophers who contributed to or were influenced by this school of thought include Qutb al-Din Shirazi (1236–1311), Mulla Sadra (c. 1571–1640) and Mir Damad (d. 1631). For example, Mulla Sadra integrated Suhrawardi's emphasis on illumination and light with a strong foundation in existential metaphysics, significantly influencing later Islamic philosophy and Qutb al-Din Shirazi, a disciple of Suhrawardi, helped to bridge Suhrawardi's philosophical insights with practical scientific knowledge.

Renowned for its mystical approach to whatness, this school of thought emphasises intuition over empirical investigation, using the metaphor of light to describe the interconnectivity between the divine and creation. In this view, essence or whatness is illuminated through divine insight, portraying reality as a continuous divine manifestation. Illuminationism holds a unique position in the landscape of philosophical thought around the whatness of matters because it integrates elements of Aristotelianism, Neoplatonism and mystical elements derived from Islamic Sufism. Its approach and existential concerns are distinct from those typically seen in Western existentialism, but no less important.

Illuminationism emphasises the role of intuitive knowledge and illumination as paths to understanding reality and whatness, contrasting with the purely rational or empirical methods favoured in Western philosophy. In this way, it can be seen as a synthesis that bridges rational philosophy and mystical experience. Both perennial philosophy and illuminationism suggest that a universal truth underlies all religious traditions. However, the latter is more structured around a specific metaphysical and epistemological framework that includes Islamic theological principles. In relation to Western existentialism's perspective that human beings first exist and then define their whatness through the choices they make, illuminationism differs markedly. Like the essentialists, it asserts the opposite – that essence or whatness precedes existence. But unlike the essentialists, the illuminationists assert that knowledge of this essence comes through illumination – an intuitive, almost mystical understanding not rooted in empirical or rational investigation.

Religion or philosophy?

Just as we struggle to precisely define 'science' – a challenge tackled by philosophers like Thomas Kuhn and Karl Popper – defining 'religion' is equally complex, if not more so, due to its broader scope and diverse interpretations within societies. When someone mentions 'religion', it is difficult to ascertain whether they are referring to a spiritual experience, an organised cult, a community for social cohesion, an ethical framework, a codified lifestyle manual or a political and economic doctrine, among other possibilities.

For example, Islam is often referred to as a 'codified religion', but it is so much more than that. Islam encompasses a profound depth of philosophical thoughts and ideas rooted in the principles of the Quran and the core tenets of the Abrahamic faith. However, this rich philosophical tradition is frequently overlooked or intentionally ignored by major Western philosophers.

In reality, Islamic philosophy can be seen as an ontological paradigm because it offers a way to relate to existence, construct cognitive maps, adopt narrative lenses, establish ethical frameworks and form perspectives. While religion can present constructive metacontent, it also has the potential to become an ideology or even a cult. Let's briefly define the distinction between these words and terms to ensure we are on the same page.

- **Ideology** is a system of ideas and ideals, especially one that forms the basis of economic or political theory and policy. It often seeks to predefine a purpose or dictate a 'telos' – an ultimate objective or aim – and prescribes an exact way to achieve it.

- A **cult** is a social group defined by its religious, spiritual or philosophical beliefs, often with a charismatic leader. Cults typically demand unwavering loyalty from their members and can become insular and authoritarian. Members are encouraged to outsource their sanity to one or more of the group's leaders.

- **Philosophy** systematically explores fundamental questions about existence, knowledge, values, reason, mind and language. It emphasises clarity and logical rigour, often avoiding predefined ends in favour of open-ended inquiry.

- **Metaphysics** is the branch of philosophy that deals with the first principles of matters/things, including concepts such as being, knowing, identity, time and space.

- **Ontology** is the branch of philosophy that studies the nature of being, existence and reality. It addresses questions of what entities exist and how they can be categorised and related to within a framework of understanding.

It is important to recognise that many self-identified 'perfect representatives of God on Earth' often assert their own beliefs, interpretations and narratives as divine truth. They regard their rhetoric and proposed cognitive maps and mental models about the nature of existence and how things work as representative of 'what God says'. Consequently, their decisions, actions and behaviours are framed as being ordained by God.

Ironically, this directly contradicts the third of the Ten Commandments: 'Thou shalt not take the name of the Lord your God in vain'. While this commandment is often understood to prohibit swearing in God's name, it holds a deeper meaning: do not falsely attribute your words and actions to God. In other words, do not claim divine endorsement for your own ideas or behaviours. This misinterpretation and misuse of divine authority has been the catalyst for many radical and harmful behaviours. By falsely claiming divine backing, some individuals justify actions that are often in direct opposition to the core teachings of their faith. This misrepresentation not only distorts the true message but also leads to severe consequences and destructive behaviours.

Integrating multiple perspectives

Through these varied lenses, we see a spectrum of beliefs about the nature of whatness, from illuminationist and Aristotelian/essentialism's views that define whatness through metaphysical and empirical lenses, respectively, to existentialism's advocacy for a self-determined essence and postmodernism's critique of the very notion of a fixed whatness or essence. Each philosophy offers a distinct narrative about how individuals and societies interpret the fundamental nature of reality. While stoicism, perennialism and Aristotelianism propose a more predetermined or deterministic view of essence based on logical and natural order, existentialism and postmodernism celebrate the role of individual freedom and cultural context in shaping essence.

Take existentialism and essentialism, two vastly contrasting schools of thought. Consider that neither is sufficient in isolation. For example, while the existentialists radically challenge the idea of anything having innate characteristics, particularly human beings, and that everything is subjective and mutable, the essentialists argue the opposite. These two views present a philosophical contrast: existentialism rejects fixed essences, advocating for the fluidity of existence, while essentialism asserts that stable, core qualities underlie all phenomena. There is no argument that we have certain innate qualities – our temperament and capacity for learning languages are two examples. However, focusing solely on human beings' innate qualities ignores the nurture aspect of human development, which is subjective. Consider the physiological fact that certain animals exhibit tears, a trait inherent to their essence. However, attributing human emotions such as sadness to this phenomenon by calling it 'crying' is a projection of meaning onto it that is inaccurate. Similarly, humans also experience tear production for various reasons, but we distinguish this from emotional crying, highlighting the importance of discerning between inherent physiological processes and subjective, emotional attributions. There is a place for both.

Whether through divine illumination, logical categorisation, personal choice or cultural construction, whatness seems to be open to various philosophical interpretations. Although each perspective provides valuable insights within their respective paradigms into the ways in which we might understand the whatness of a matter or being, they all miss something. More specifically, while they all have gems to offer, they are all incomplete in isolation.

Rather than having various schools of thought operating in silos, I advocate for an integrated approach that enables us to tap into whichever philosophy – or combination thereof – is most effective for the task at hand. For example, when designing and constructing an aircraft or a bridge or attempting to understand the neurological functionality of the human brain, the essentialist way of thinking, where precision and foundational understanding are paramount, is the most effective paradigm to tap into. For the more subjective aspects of human beings, including consciousness, which science and essentialism have never been able to define accurately, aspects of existentialism are most relevant, albeit not to the extent that authentic awareness is compromised or individuals are viewed as isolated entities. Other schools of thought from both Eastern and Western philosophies – or parts thereof – are also relevant in different contexts.

In our exploration of Platonic philosophy earlier in this chapter, we discovered that Plato's rejection of various schools of thought and his inclination towards dialectic and subjective exploration of matters differed from Aristotle, who tended to approach everything from the perspective of objective studies. Overall, Plato adopted a more pluralistic approach than many of the philosophers who came after him. He was far ahead of his time in being open to other ways of thinking. Let's now consider how his universal approach could serve as a unifying force to bridge the divide.

Plato as a unifying force

Plato was not only considered a foundational thinker in Western philosophy but also an innovator of dialectic forms who had a profound influence on various other schools of thought, including thought/thinking, politics and the arts. Let's briefly look into how he influenced these ways of thinking.

Plato's work delved deeply into metaphysical themes, such as the nature of the soul, the structure of reality and the relationship between the material and the divine. In this way, his work offers valuable insights for those interested in the philosophical dimensions of spirituality and religion and supports a deeper exploration of existential questions that transcend empirical observation, appealing to those who seek to understand the spiritual aspects of human existence, like the perennial philosophers and the illuminationists. Plato's multi-dimensional approach paved the way for a broader range of perspectives.

Plato also helped shape Western political thought. For example, in *The Republic*[75], Plato outlines his vision for an ideal state ruled by philosopher-kings who govern based on wisdom and insight into the higher realms of the Forms. His idealistic political theory emphasises the role of education and moral leadership in governance and has been influential in discussions about the role of ethics in public life and the importance of moral and intellectual virtues in leadership.

Plato was critical of certain aspects of art in the context of what he perceived to be its negative impact on society. Most notably, in *The Republic* and his discussions on beauty in *The Symposium*[76] – a philosophical text that explores the nature of love and desire through speeches given at a banquet – he offers foundational insights into aesthetics. Despite his scepticism, his discussions on art and beauty have inspired deeper consideration of the aesthetic experience and its impact on the soul and society. His work offers a philosophical basis

---

75   Plato. 2007. *The Republic*. Translated by Desmond Lee. Penguin Classics.
76   Plato. 1994. *The Symposium*. Translated by C. Gill. London: Penguin Classics.

for evaluating art beyond mere pleasure, considering its ethical and educational values.

Plato also had a significant influence on Eastern philosophy, particularly Islamic philosophy. This was mediated primarily through the translations and commentaries of his works that became available in the Islamic world from the eighth century onwards. Neoplatonism, which integrated many Platonic ideas with those of Aristotle and oriental mysticism, had a particularly strong impact on Islamic philosophy. Philosophers like Al-Farabi, Ibn Sina (Avicenna) and Al-Kindi engaged deeply with Neoplatonic interpretations, adapting and integrating them into their philosophical frameworks. For example, Islamic philosophers used Platonic ideals to discuss the nature of Allah, the soul and the universe. Plato's ideas on ethics and the ideal state also resonated with Islamic thinkers. Often referred to as the 'Muslim Plato', Al-Farabi developed his concept of the virtuous city, which was clearly influenced by Plato's philosopher-king model. Furthermore, Plato's emphasis on the importance of dialectical reasoning in achieving knowledge influenced Islamic philosophers' views on knowledge and enlightenment.

As Plato's work encouraged a holistic view of philosophy that includes the observable world and the realms of ideals and ethics, its influence on other schools of thought has been quite profound. Characterised by its focus on universal ideals, his philosophy provided a valuable framework for bridging diverse theological and philosophical schools of thought and served as a unifying force. His approach can help reconcile and synthesise the varied perspectives, promoting a dialogue focused on universal concepts rather than sectarian differences. Others who embraced philosophical synthesis were the Islamic philosophers. Rather than merely adopting Platonic ideas, they synthesised them with Islamic teachings to create coherent systems aligned with their thinking. For example, the Platonic idea of the soul's immortality was used to elaborate on Islamic views of the afterlife.

Integral Theory and Spiral Dynamics

Twentieth-century philosopher Ken Wilber is the most recent example of a thinker who synthesised various schools of thought to produce Integral Theory, a comprehensive framework represented in his All Quadrants All Levels (AQAL) model. Spiral Dynamics, a model originally developed by Don Beck and Chris Cowan based on the work of Clare W. Graves, is used to show developmental stages, which correspond to the 'All Levels' component of AQAL, and is integrated into Wilbur's Integral Theory. Spiral Dynamics, in particular, influenced me in developing the metacontent discourse and Nested Theory of Sense-making.

Integral Theory and Spiral Dynamics incorporate insights from pre-modern, modern and postmodern philosophies, recognising the value of each philosophy's contribution to our collective understanding of the whatness of things. Take Wilbur's Integral Theory Model, for example. Combining Aristotle's empirical focus, Plato and Hegel's dialectical processes and postmodernism's fragmented perspectives, the framework advocates a more holistic and inclusive view of truth and reality that values coherence and integration. Let's now look into Wilbur's Integral Theory and its integrated Spiral Dynamics in more detail, as both are particularly relevant to our exploration of the whatness of matters and ontology.

Integral Theory

Integral Theory ambitiously integrates insights from a wide range of disciplines, including psychology, philosophy, science and religion. The theory proposes that the whatness of any phenomenon can be understood through four primary quadrants, ensuring no perspective is overlooked. It suggests that every perspective or layer adds to the totality of understanding, contributing to a comprehensive, holistic view of reality.

1. **Interior-Individual (Subjective):** Thoughts, emotions and personal consciousness.

2. **Interior-Collective (Intersubjective):** Shared cultural beliefs, values and social norms.

3. **Exterior-Individual (Objective):** Observable behaviours and physical aspects.

4. **Exterior-Collective (Interobjective):** Systems, structures and institutions shaping society.

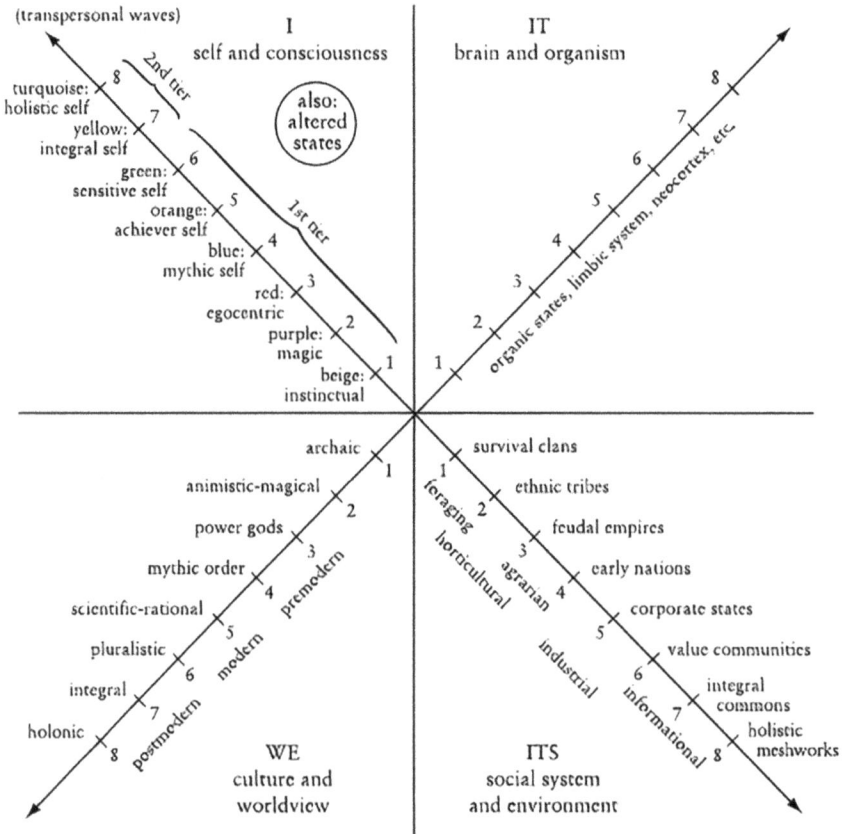

Figure 2

All Quadrants All Levels (AQAL) model[77]

---

77   From *Integral Psychology* book (p.62) and as Fig.3.1 in Ken Wilber's book, *A Theory of Everything.*

Spiral Dynamics

Wilbur's Spiral Dynamics describes the evolution of human consciousness through a series of colour-coded stages, from the lowest to the highest level of evolved human consciousness.

1. **Beige (Survival):** Focus on basic needs and instincts.

2. **Purple (Tribal):** Emphasis on safety, traditions and kinship.

3. **Red (Power):** Driven by ego, power and dominance.

4. **Blue (Order):** Values rules, structure and authority.

5. **Orange (Achievement):** Seeks success, innovation and progress.

6. **Green (Community):** Prioritises equality, empathy and sustainability.

7. **Yellow (Integration):** Recognises interconnections and seeks holistic solutions.

8. **Turquoise (Holistic):** Embraces global consciousness and ecological awareness.

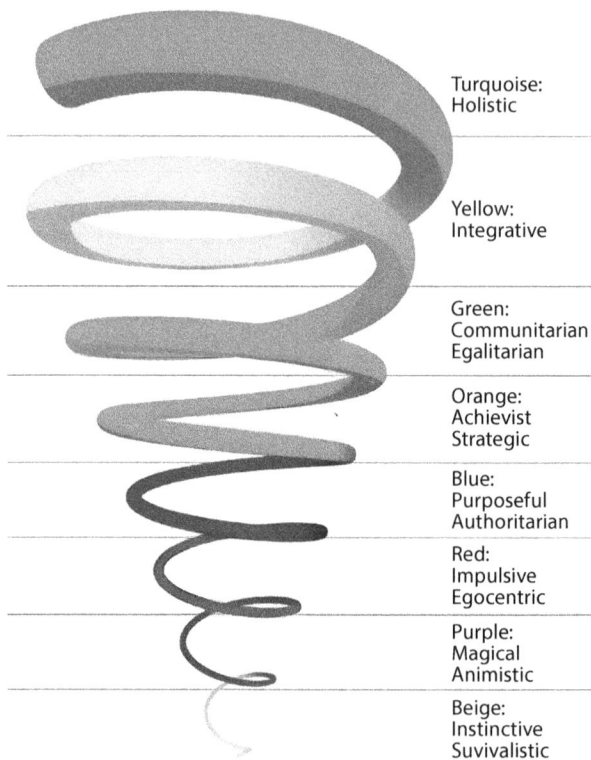

Figure 3

Spiral Dynamics

In Spiral Dynamics, Ken Wilber suggests a fundamentally optimistic view of the evolution of human consciousness, proposing that evolution inherently drives individuals and societies toward greater complexity, integration and higher levels of consciousness. This perspective raises philosophical questions about the nature of evolution and its implications. Are we on a constant upward trajectory for individual and collective thriving, or could the spiral also pull us downward, like a whirlpool leading to regression, disintegration and degeneration? In reality, Wilber does not entirely exclude the possibility of regression. While his model implies a generally positive trajectory, where each stage or level contributes to an upward spiral of development, it acknowledges that individuals or societies can revert to earlier value systems under certain conditions. Factors such as stress, trauma, or cultural shifts may lead to regression.

The dual potential of evolution

On the positive side, Spiral Dynamics describes how evolving consciousness can elevate us to a higher degree of awareness and being. This progression could lead us to transcend our current limitations, enhancing our competency, capability, empowerment, freedom and ethics. This vision aligns with the principle of humanity, moving us toward being both human *and* humane.

However, the other side of this evolutionary potential must be acknowledged. If we let any construct, idea or ideology unduly influence us, it can add to the confusion and lead to gradual or even radical delusion, deception and collective psychosis.[78] This disconnection from reality might cause us to misinterpret what it means to be human and humane, placing ourselves at the centre of the universe and attempting to override first-layer reality.

While the positive trajectory of evolving consciousness is appealing, we cannot ignore the negative potential of digressing and degenerating into what Botticelli depicted in his illustration of Dante's 'Inferno' – human beings spiralling downward into suffering and the depths of a manufactured 'hell'. This descent could be driven by confusion, inauthenticities, hedonism, cynicism, meaninglessness, arrogance, greed and other malevolent forces.

In summary, the overly optimistic and, in part, sentimental view of evolution in Wilber's Spiral Dynamics inspires a hopeful vision of human development and the evolution of consciousness. However, it is essential to remain vigilant about the potential negative trajectories that could arise from misinterpretations and the misuse of these constructs. Balancing this optimism with a critical awareness of the pitfalls ensures a more grounded and realistic approach to understanding our evolution and its impact on the world.

---

78   Collective psychosis is a term I introduced in my book, *BEING* to describe what happens when there is a dissociation with reality on a collective scale. It is the epidemic of madness that occurs when a large proportion of a society loses touch with reality and descends into delusion.

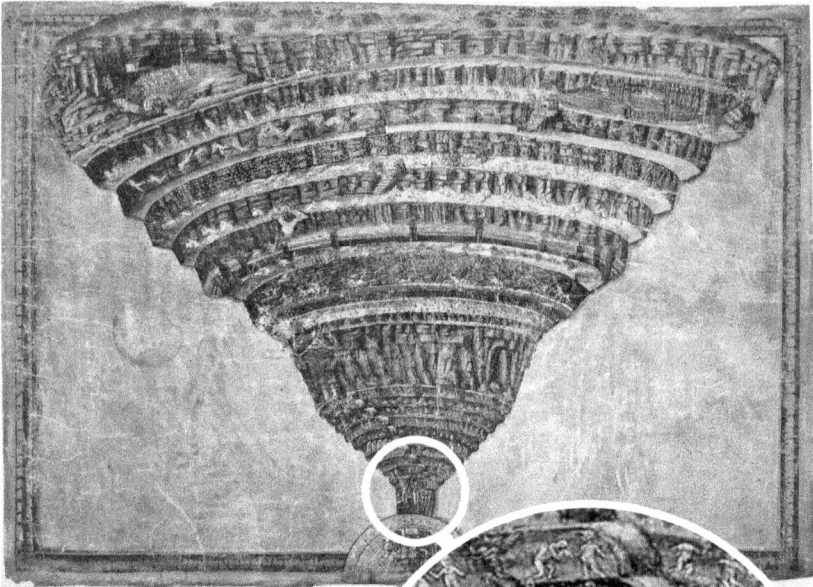

Figure 4

Botticelli's Map of Hell

The gaps and how the metacontent discourse and Nested Theory of Sense-making address them

Wilber's Integral Theory and Spiral Dynamics provide comprehensive frameworks for understanding human development, consciousness and the interplay of different dimensions of reality. Both models have significantly contributed to holistic approaches in philosophy, psychology and spirituality. While they have also greatly influenced me in developing the metacontent discourse and Nested Theory of Sense-making, there are areas where my body of work offers additional insights and addresses gaps within Wilber's work, as outlined below.

Firstly, while Wilber integrates various perspectives, there is less emphasis on the specific epistemological processes individuals use to make sense of these perspectives. The depth of understanding in terms of how knowledge is constructed, perceived and validated could be expanded. The metacontent discourse offers an enhanced epistemological framework by providing a deeper analysis of how individuals construct, validate and refine their knowledge. This involves examining the layers of reality, cognitive maps and narrative lenses in a more detailed and structured manner. By focusing on the processes of sense-making, this approach enhances our understanding of how individuals navigate and integrate different perspectives, which is essential for authentic awareness and personal development.

Secondly, in addressing only broad developmental stages and structures of consciousness, Wilbur's frameworks would benefit from a more granular examination of the cognitive maps and narrative lenses individuals use to interpret and construct their realities. The Nested Theory of Sense-making breaks down the cognitive and narrative structures into detailed layers. This multi-layered approach helps us understand how individuals interpret and respond to their experiences, resulting in a more precise and actionable understanding of ourselves and others.

Thirdly, Spiral Dynamics outlines stages of development, but the interaction between these stages, especially in real-time sense-making processes, is less detailed. They would benefit from an exploration of *how* these layers dynamically interact and influence each other in practical, everyday contexts. The Nested Theory of Sense-making emphasises the dynamic interaction between its layers and considers the ongoing dialogue between content and context, which is crucial for adaptive and responsive decision-making and behaviour. It also provides a structured method for deconstructing and reconstructing sense-making processes, making it relatively simple to apply in everyday life.

Chapter 9 explains the Nested Theory of Sense-making and its relationship with the metacontent discourse in detail. It includes several examples and case studies of how it can be used in practice, using tangible, real-world examples.

Why synthesising various perspectives matters

By exploring the connections between various schools of thought, we enhance our comprehension of how ancient wisdom, modern critique and contemporary holistic theories, like those of Ken Wilber, interact to form a complex, multi-dimensional view of philosophical development. This integrated approach not only honours the contributions of each philosophical tradition but also suggests pathways towards a more unified and comprehensive understanding of human knowledge.

As human beings, we have a relatively high degree of autonomy; we can choose. For example, we can choose to create individual meanings for certain constructs beyond the shared layer of reality that exists in society. While some aspects of identity, like first or last names, are socially constructed, others, such as the passage of time or biological sex, possess inherent meanings beyond our societal frameworks. Take biological sex, for example. It is not assigned but determined at conception, only to be revealed at birth or earlier through the means medical science has made available to us. This recognition prompts a critical examination of societal expectations tied to biological distinctions, highlighting the influence of cultural norms on individual roles and behaviours.

However, it's not so simple when it comes to complex, subjective realms like the development of our consciousness as human beings. In these instances, is building a shared intellectual substrate leading us towards a greater understanding, or is it complicating our thought structures and deepening our collective confusion? In other words, does synthesising various philosophical and scientific perspectives always enable us to progress towards a fuller truth, or does it trap us in complexities that obscure our path to understanding in some cases? The answer is to anchor ourselves in a bedrock founded on authentic awareness.

Ultimately, our discussion circles back to the initial exploration of confusion and the intangible aspects of existence – The Invisible. Our vulnerability lies in our inability to discern such matters due to the limitations of our senses and our conceptual and perceptual structures, as discussed earlier in the book. This highlights the necessity to step outside of the 'philosophical silos' and consider an integrated approach that adopts the most relevant parts of each paradigm to suit the context and the intention behind whatever we are endeavouring to learn more about.

This perspective aligns with the central theme of this chapter, which focuses on understanding the whatness and ontology of things and ideas. By recognising our limitations and embracing an integrated approach, we can better navigate the complexities of reality. The Platonic way of thinking and those influenced by it, including various Islamic philosophers and recent thinkers like Ken Wilber, emphasise the importance of synthesising diverse perspectives. This synthesis helps us appreciate commonalities and alternative viewpoints, enriching our ontological exploration and providing a more holistic understanding of the world.

Conclusion

In this chapter, we compared and contrasted various philosophical paradigms and discovered that, while they all have their merits, they also have gaps when considered in isolation. In adopting a pluralistic approach to understanding the whatness of things, especially human beings and their performance in life, it is imperative to recognise the subjective nature of understanding and the range of perspectives that can exist. For example, perennialism was one of the philosophies we touched on that suggested a common ground. Yet, its interpretation and application can vary significantly across different cultural, social and individual contexts. Critics of this philosophical approach often express concerns about oversimplification and the risk of imposing a homogenous framework onto the rich tapestry of human beliefs and experiences.

I also discussed why we need more than science – as marvellous as it is – to fully comprehend a subject and form a comprehensive understanding that enables us to make informed decisions and take meaningful action. The same is true for philosophy. We can't simply align ourselves with a particular philosophical school of thought and expect it to have all the answers.

The solution is to stop viewing diverse philosophical traditions and scientific methodologies in isolation and, instead, adopt a pluralistic perspective that sees them as contributing layers to our intellectual substrates – or what I refer to as 'metacontent' – which we will unpack fully in Chapter 9. Each approach, with its unique emphasis and methodologies, enriches our understanding and enables a more nuanced exploration of the whatness of matters, including human beings.

The question, is how do we bring them together to create an intellectual substrate that acknowledges The Invisible and our inherent limitations with authentic awareness and enables us to tap into various perspectives when trying to make sense of the world and everything in it?

This book highlights the critical need for interdisciplinary collaboration to establish a more comprehensive understanding of the world. To use an analogy, single-discipline dominance is like growing only one type of agricultural crop. Just as biodiversity strengthens ecosystems, intellectual diversity enhances our understanding and capacity to find solutions to complex problems.

As we have seen in this chapter, there are limitations inherent in every approach when considered in isolation. While the essentialists believe in definite, inherent qualities defining entities, existentialists focus on individual existence and personal meaning-making. It's a constant battle between the search for universal truths and the recognition of individual experiences.

The limitations are amplified when it comes to radical or overly specialised perspectives within various fields. For example, radical scientists advocate for a purely empirical explanation of the world, often discounting the nuanced realities of human experience. Radical theologians may prioritise religious narratives over empirical evidence, leading to conflicts when new scientific discoveries challenge traditional beliefs. Radical social scientists sometimes view all aspects of life as socially constructed, dismissing the biological and physical realities that also influence human existence. Furthermore, radical postmodern thinkers argue that objective truth is unattainable because all knowledge is constructed, encouraging a scepticism that can undermine productive discourse.

For all these reasons, I am advocating for an approach that integrates humanities, theology, philosophy, exact sciences and social sciences. By considering multiple perspectives, we can bridge the divide between these disciplines, reflecting the interconnected systems in nature and human society. While these disciplines may seem radically different on the surface, consider that there are always common grounds and similarities. Even when there are significant differences, there are times when it is best to have them complement each other to enhance our sense-making, develop our consciousness, address unnecessary suffering and progress towards effectiveness and wellbeing, individually and collectively.

Grounded in the study of meaning or 'Minalogy', the metacontent discourse and Nested Theory of Sense-making encourage dialogue and collaboration across all these areas. This enables us to develop robust cognitive and mental models that capture the complexity of human and natural phenomena, which is vital in navigating the complexities of the 21st century. By dismantling the silos of conventional academic and philosophical disciplines and promoting a more holistic exploration of knowledge, the metacontent discourse and Nested Theory of Sense-making not only enhance our understanding of the world and everything in it, including human beings, but also prepare us to tackle the global challenges we face today and the unknown ones of the future. However, before we explore metacontent and the Nested Theory of Sense-making in detail, it's important to understand the tools that enable us to expand the whatness of things into tangible knowledge.

CHAPTER 8

Ontology

Now that we have discussed whatness or essence – the qualities or attributes that make a thing fundamentally what it is – and explored the various philosophical schools of thought on the subject, let's move onto the tools we have at our disposal to expand the whatness of things into tangible, digestible pieces of knowledge.

Whatness, ontic perspectives and ontology all play important roles in philosophical and metaphysical discourse. For example, in existentialism, ontic perspectives focus on the concrete reality of individual existence, emphasising lived experiences. Meanwhile, ontology dives deeper into understanding reality itself, exploring how entities are made up and their connection to 'being'. And whatness, as discussed in the previous chapter, defines the essence of entities, providing crucial insights into discussions about existence and identity within the broader scope of reality. So, while whatness seeks to identify what makes an entity what it is at a fundamental level and is integral to understanding how entities are conceptualised and categorised based on their inherent characteristics, ontic perspectives and ontology address different aspects of existence.

More specifically, an ontic approach focuses on the concrete properties and characteristics of an entity, while ontology is the branch of philosophy concerned with the nature of being and existence. It deals with broader questions about the nature of existence itself and the specific way an entity of a certain kind has its characteristics. So, ontic approaches consider matters from a surface-level perspective, while ontology goes much deeper. It's the difference between identifying and labelling the various parts of the human digestive system (ontic perspective) and conducting an in-depth analysis of how our digestive system works (ontology). Both have a place in expanding whatness into tangible knowledge.

Relevance of ontic perspectives and ontology across various philosophical approaches

Understanding the importance of ontic perspectives and ontology in exploring the whatness of things requires delving into foundational philosophical concepts that transcend specific schools of thought, whether essentialism, existentialism, humanism or Islamic philosophy. In philosophy, ontology is the branch of metaphysics concerned with the nature of being, as opposed to just a field of study examining the nature of existence, and an ontological model is a tool that helps us describe expandable knowledge in the form of a graph or model. In fact, the words 'ontic' and 'ontology' originate from the study of being and existence, with ontology providing a foundational framework that influences how we conceptualise and engage with reality.

Historically, the study of whatness has been central to ontology. According to Aristotle and the essentialists, every entity possesses a set of fixed attributes necessary for its identity and function. His view laid the groundwork for subsequent inquiries into the essential characteristics that define entities. Furthermore, his systematic, more methodical and empirically-based way of thinking also formed the foundation for the scientific way of thinking we know today.

However, it was the existentialists, such as Friedrich Nietzsche and Jean-Paul Sartre, who initiated a profound shift in focus from predefined essences to individual existence and experience. They challenged the notion that essence is a given, arguing that it is constructed through living and experiencing. This transformative perspective was further advanced by poststructuralist and postmodern thinkers, including Michel Foucault and Jacques Derrida. They deconstructed the underlying structures of thought and language that shape our understanding of reality, asserting that meanings and essences are not inherent but products of cultural, historical and linguistic contexts. This questioning of the possibility of accessing a true whatness or essence underscores the fluid and subjective nature of meaning, a stark contrast to the fixed nature of essentialism.

To summarise various philosophical perspectives on ontology, the essentialists use ontology to help define the intrinsic characteristics that make an entity what it fundamentally is, while the existentialists regard ontology as crucial in understanding the existence of the individual and their relationship with the world. They believe ontology allows for a deeper reflection on human freedom, responsibility and the subjective experience, all central to existentialist thought. In Islamic philosophy, ontology plays a significant role in understanding the nature of God, the universe and the essence of human beings, influencing how beings and their purpose are interpreted within a theological framework. This perspective is not dissimilar to that of all Abrahamic faiths. Humanists regard ontology as a critical philosophical foundation that informs our understanding of human nature, dignity and ethical values. Humanism often uses ontological principles to assert the importance of human experiences, rationality and capacities in determining the meaning of human existence, emphasising the value and agency of human beings individually and collectively. As you can see, there are commonalities between the various schools of thought, and ontology has an essential place in all of them. Let's start by considering the perspectives of the Islamic philosophers and the humanists.

Islamic philosophy in the context of ontology and ontic approaches

As mentioned in the previous chapter, Islamic philosophers like Avicenna and Al-Farabi were heavily influenced by the ideas of Aristotle, particularly when discussing the distinction between the whatness of a thing (Mahiyat) and its existence (Wujud). According to Avicenna's metaphysical framework, the whatness of a thing encompasses all its defining features that can be conceived without reference to its existence. For him, understanding the whatness of a thing does not necessarily imply that the thing exists. He asserted that existence was an additional attribute granted by God. From an ontological perspective, Avicenna proposed that Mahiyat (whatness) refers to the properties or attributes that a thing must possess for it to be recognised as a member of a specific category. For example, the Mahiyat of a triangle would be its being a three-sided polygon.

Beyond applying ontology to understand the essence of God, the universe and humanity, Islamic philosophers also use it to shape and guide insight into the purpose and existence of beings in a theological context. The concept of Mahiyat is pivotal in their thought process as it aids in distinguishing between different entities and their metaphysical realities (ontic perspective) before delving deeper (ontology). It also plays a crucial role in theological discussions, where the essence and attributes of God are examined to establish axiomatic laws of existence and to consider the nature of actions and their moral implications based on the essence of those actions.

Humanism and ontology

Humanism centres on the idea that humans have the free will and capacity to shape their own lives and make decisions independently of divine influence or external causes. In this context, humanists use ontology to help define what it means to be human, especially in terms of our cognitive, moral and social capabilities. Ontologically, humanists also argue that, as human beings, we inherently have worth and dignity. Consequently, humanist theories relating to ethics advocate for rights, justice and equality based on those intrinsic qualities.

Unlike Islamic philosophy, where ontology often revolves around the divine and its implications for human existence, humanist ontology focuses strictly on the human being. It explores the potentials and responsibilities of humans as autonomous agents who can reason, empathise and act morally. Humanist ontology has been influential in shaping modern secular ideologies, including secular humanism[79], which specifically rejects religious narrative – and all theology – as the basis of morality and decision-making. Instead, it emphasises scientific understanding, reason and constructed ethics. Overall, in humanism, ontology not only helps articulate a clear vision of what it means to be human but also provides a foundation for discussing how humans should relate to each other, to society and to the environment.

Embracing various perspectives – a notable example

Martin Heidegger, an influential figure in 20th-century philosophy known for his groundbreaking work in ontology and metaphysics alongside his significant contributions to phenomenology, herme-neutics[80] and existentialism, is a notable example of a philosopher who embraced various philosophical perspectives. He did this not only to bridge the divide between science and philosophy but also to integrate the relevant parts of various paradigms to suit a particular context. Heidegger makes a clear distinction between the ontic and the ontological. He maintained that ontic approaches concern the specific characteristics and factual existence of particular entities, while ontological inquiry investigates the nature of being itself – what it means to be. The latter requires a more abstract level of analysis, focusing on fundamental concepts of existence and being. Together,

---

79 Secular humanism emphasises reason, ethics and human fulfilment while ignoring theology of any kind on the assumption that human intellect and feelings reveal all there is to be discovered about human beings.

80 Hermeneutics is the theory and methodology of interpretation, especially the interpretation of biblical texts, wisdom literature and philosophical texts.

his ontic and ontological inquiries aimed to reveal deeper insights into how entities are understood within their broader existential contexts.

Heidegger used the term 'Vorhandenheit' to describe the 'present-at-hand' aspect of beings, focusing on their ontic, factual existence. This contrasts with 'Zuhandenheit' ('ready-to-hand'), relating more to how beings are encountered in everyday use or engagement. His concepts of Vorhandenheit and Zuhandenheit delve into how we perceive and interact with objects in the world. Vorhandenheit reflects an objective stance, where objects are seen as merely present-at-hand, isolated from their use or context. For example, imagine observing sandstone solely as a geological object, focusing on its mineral composition and formation without considering its use. In contrast, Zuhandenheit captures a more involved, practical engagement with objects, recognising them as integral to our daily activities and existence. In this case, the sandstone would be considered in terms of its functionality and aesthetic appeal in construction. These examples highlight Heidegger's distinction between seeing objects as detached versus embedded in human activities and purposes. The first example is ontic and the second is ontological.

Another term commonly used by Heidegger was 'Wesen', which is often translated as essence, nature or whatness. However, in Heidegger's philosophy, Wesen does not simply refer to what a thing is in the traditional sense. Instead, he interprets Wesen as the manner in which something unfolds or comes into being – its 'way of being'. This interpretation aligns with his focus on the process-oriented nature of being, where nature, essence or whatness is seen in terms of becoming and unfolding rather than as a fixed set of characteristics. So, according to Heidegger, while an entity's ontic status tells us about its specific factual existence, its Wesen reveals how these ontic characteristics unfold as part of the entity's way of being. For Heidegger, understanding an entity's Wesen involves looking beyond its mere immediate, tangible aspects to grasp its more profound existential unfolding. While you might think this description of Wesen aligns with ontology, Heidegger argued that traditional ontology often over-looked the dynamic aspect of Wesen, treating essence as something static. His perspective suggests that to truly understand the essence of something, we must consider how it reveals itself in existence over time.

In Heidegger's philosophy – which, unlike other philosophical schools of thought, is challenging to label because of the way it synthesises various perspectives – Heidegger considers concepts like anxiety and care from an ontological perspective, believing these aspects are integral to understanding human existence or, as he calls it, 'Dasein' (being-there). He delves into how these existential conditions reveal the nature of being and our relationship with the world rather than merely describing individual emotional states or psychological condi-tions. For Heidegger, anxiety (Angst) is not merely a psychological state but a fundamental aspect of human existence. He sees anxiety as revealing the underlying uncertainty and groundlessness of human existence, where individuals confront the abyss of nothingness and their own mortality. Instead of viewing anxiety as a negative emotion to be avoided, Heidegger considers it as a gateway to deeper self-awareness and authenticity. In other words, anxiety, according to Heidegger, doesn't only occur at life's darkest moments. It is a mode or state of mind that sits in the background as a way for us to disclose ourselves. Furthermore, to Heidegger, the word anxiety doesn't refer to a visible, surface-level behaviour or an anxiety disorder but is a deep way of responding to life itself.

Similarly, Heidegger's concept of care (Sorge) goes beyond the conven-tional understanding of caregiving. In his ontological framework, care is the fundamental mode of being-in-the-world, encompassing both our concern for ourselves and our concern for the world around us. It involves a holistic engagement with the world, where we are constantly attuned to our own existence and the beings and things with which we interact. Care, for Heidegger, is not just a passive state but an active orientation towards existence, shaping how we relate to ourselves, others and the world.

Let's look at a tangible example to illustrate Heidegger's ontological perspective on anxiety and care. Consider the experience of facing a major life decision, such as choosing a career path. In this situation, you may experience anxiety as you confront the uncertainty of the future and the potential consequences of your decisions and actions. Heidegger would interpret this anxiety not as a sign of weakness but as a profound awareness of the existential freedom and responsibility inherent in decision-making. Furthermore, your care in choosing the right career path extends beyond your own concerns to include considerations of how your choice might impact others, such as your family and society.

These 'moods', as I refer to them, are discussed in detail from an ontological perspective in my book *BEING*.[81] In addition to Heidegger's anxiety, fear and care, I added a fourth mood: vulnerability, due to its significant relevance in the context of human performance, effectiveness and wellbeing.

Ontology, ontic perspectives and consciousness

When it comes to consciousness, the ontic dimension refers to the physical, observable reality of it – the tangible aspects like our brain, physical body and the biochemical processes that underlie our thoughts, emotions and perceptions. This dimension is the domain of empirical science, particularly neuroscience and psychology, which seek to map out the correlations between brain activity and conscious experience. Scientists and researchers in this domain focus on questions like: How do specific brain regions contribute to different aspects of consciousness? What are the neural correlates of conscious awareness? How do chemical neurotransmitters influence our moods and thoughts? The ontic approach is grounded in material reality, aiming to demystify consciousness through measurable and observable phenomena.

---

81   Tashvir, A. 2021. *BEING – The source of power.* Engenesis Publications: Sydney.

In contrast, the ontological dimension of consciousness ventures into its philosophical aspects like the essence or existence of consciousness, raising questions about what it means to be a conscious entity. This dimension explores the subjective, first-person experience of being alive and aware – the phenomenological aspect of consciousness that cannot be fully reduced to physical processes. When it comes to consciousness, ontological inquiries delve into the experience and fundamental qualities of being conscious. They tackle questions like: What is the nature of subjective experience, and can it be fully explained by physical processes? What does it mean to be a self-aware being? How do we understand the experience of consciousness in a way that transcends the physical components of the brain?

The distinction between the ontic and ontological dimensions of consciousness highlights a significant question: Can the subjective experience of consciousness be fully explained by the objective workings of the brain? While the ontic dimension seeks to describe the mechanisms of consciousness, the ontological dimension probes deeper, seeking to understand the essence and meaning of these experiences. There is no question that both have merit. But how do we bridge the divide? The key is to consider a more holistic view of consciousness that respects both the physical reality of the brain and the profound, subjective experience of being. This perspective challenges us to expand our understanding of consciousness, embracing both the empirical and the existential, to gain a fuller appreciation of what it means to be a conscious being in the world.

Ontic and ontological models

Ontic and ontological models are tools that help us articulate and describe expandable knowledge. Ontic models are concerned with tangible specifics, while ontological models delve into broader existential questions. To illustrate the difference, consider a building. An ontic model would focus on the building's specific features: its bricks, windows and structure – its concrete existence. In contrast, an ontological model would explore the concept of 'building-ness': what it means to be a building, how it exists in space and its relationship to other entities, like homes or offices.

Now let's consider the difference between an ontic and ontological model in relation to the study of human qualities. An ontic approach would focus on specific, observable traits such as someone's kindness, impulsiveness or shyness – all tangible expressions and actions. We can clearly see if someone is being shy, for example. A prominent example of an ontic model in psychology is the Five Factor Model of Personality, also known as the 'Big Five' personality traits. This model is widely used in psychology to describe human personality in terms of five broad categories: openness to experience, conscientiousness, extraversion, agreeableness and neuroticism. The Big Five model is ontic in nature because it categorises and measures personality traits based on observable behaviours and self-reported experiences. Psychologists and researchers use various psychometric tools, such as questionnaires and surveys, to assess where an individual falls on each of the five dimensions. This model provides a structured way to understand the complex and varied aspects of human personality in an empirical and quantifiable manner. It is commonly used in research and applied settings, such as clinical psychology and human resources.[82]

In contrast, an ontological perspective of personality traits would delve into the whatness or essence of personality itself: what it means to have a personality, how individual traits combine to form a unique character and the deeper existential implications of personality traits within human existence. More broadly, an ontological model of human characteristics delves into the essence and deeper aspects of being human, often exploring themes of existence, meaning, purpose and self-awareness that transcend empirical measurement. A notable example of an ontological approach to understanding human characteristics is existential psychology, which originates from existential philosophy. Focusing on the human condition as a whole, existential

---

82   McCrae, R. R., & Costa, P. T. 1997. Personality trait structure as a human universal. *American Psychologist*, 52(5), 509—516.

psychology provides an ontological perspective on human characteristics by addressing the deeper, more abstract aspects of human existence like freedom, death, isolation, meaninglessness and authenticity. It does not rely on empirical measures but instead focuses on the subjective, phenomenological experience of being, seeking to understand how individuals come to terms with the very essence of being, how they confront the realities of existence, like the concepts mentioned above, and how they find personal meaning and identity while dealing with life's inherent challenges.[83]

Integrating ontic and ontological perspectives can provide a more comprehensive understanding of human characteristics and aspects of being. By combining the empirical, observable dimensions of personality and behaviour (ontic) with the deeper, existential aspects of human experience (ontological), we can develop a model that addresses both the measurable traits and the subjective experiences of individuals. For example, a comprehensive model of human wellbeing that integrates both ontic and ontological layers would not only assess an individual's emotional and psychological state through observable metrics but also delve into their deeper, more subjective experiences and perceptions of life. An integrated model like this recognises that a person's overall wellbeing is not solely determined by their emotional state or life satisfaction but also by their engagement with deeper existential questions and their ability to find meaning, authenticity, and fulfilment in their lives.

By acknowledging and addressing both the ontic and ontological dimensions of human experience, an integrated model offers a holistic approach to understanding human beings. For example, to create a model that lists surface-level human traits and characteristics like anxiety, care, courage, assertiveness, authenticity, compassion, etc., and examines the relationships between them would generally be considered an ontic model because it focuses on specific, observable traits and their interactions in tangible ways. To transform it into an ontological model, the focus would need to be shifted from specific traits to exploring the essence of what it means to care, be anxious,

---

83   Yalom, I. D. 1980. *Existential Psychotherapy*. Basic Books.

be courageous, be assertive, be authentic, be compassionate, etc. and the interconnectedness between the various qualities. This shift would require an investigation into how these traits contribute to the concept of 'being human' and their role in human existence and identity. An ontological model like this would conceptualise traits not just as individual characteristics, but as integral components that collectively shape what and how we are being.

Ontological models and analytical thinking

You might be wondering at this point if ontological models are relevant in objective domains where analytical thinking is required. Computer science is a good example. Here, ontological models serve as tools for modelling knowledge domains by defining the entities, concepts and their relationships within a specific system. When used in computer science, ontological models help to organise and structure knowledge in a way that supports reasoning about the entities and their relationships. They also allow for the development of expandable knowledge bases by enabling systems to not only store information but also understand and expand upon it through linked data and semantic relationships. This capability is fundamental in fields like AI, where understanding and interacting with complex datasets in a meaningful way is crucial. More specifically, they aid in the comprehension and categorisation of data that AI systems interact with, improving their decision-making and learning processes.

Heidegger was ahead of his time in discussing technology and its relationship to ontology. In *The Question Concerning Technology*[84], he describes the 'Wesen' (whatness) of technology not in terms of various devices and instruments (the ontic view) but as a mode of *revealing* – a way in which reality presents itself and is transformed by human activity. Therefore, Heidegger viewed technology in terms of its way of unfolding in the world, which includes how it transforms both the world and our understanding of being.

---

84   Heidegger, M. 1977. *The Question Concerning Technology*. Garland Publishing.

Another field where ontology has proven invaluable is linguistics, particularly in the study of semantics, the branch of linguistics concerned with meaning. Ontology in linguistics studies the categories of things that exist in the world as they relate to language. It involves understanding how different languages categorise and conceptualise reality through words and structures. For example, some languages have only basic terms for black and white, while others, like English, have a broader spectrum of colours, like pink, teal or magenta. These categories reflect different ontological understandings of colour depending on the culture.

The relationship between ontic reality – how specific instances of entities or phenomena are dealt with in language – and linguistic ontology deeply influences semantic meanings – the meanings that words, phrases and sentences convey in a given context. Semantic meaning in linguistics can be broadly categorised into denotative meanings – the literal, objective meanings of words as directly related to things in the world – and connotative meanings – the subjective associations, feelings, or thoughts that words raise beyond their literal meaning. For example, one denotative meaning of the word 'dog' is a canine animal, while a connotative meaning of the same word might be loyalty or companionship. In semantics, ontic and ontological approaches are crucial for comprehending how meanings are structured and organised in language. For example, a rose is a type or category (ontological) of flower (ontic).

To further clarify the distinction between ontic and ontological models, consider the following tangible examples.

Ontic model examples

The Solar System Model

Most of you would be familiar with the Solar System Model, a model that represents the Sun as the central star with planets, including Earth, orbiting around it. This model is ontic because it depicts the actual arrangement and movements of the sun and planets in space, not just our perception or theories about them. It describes how:

- The Sun is the pivotal point representing the central role it plays in the solar system.
- Planets follow elliptical orbits, reflecting the true motion of the planets.
- Distances vary among planets, leading to differences in their orbital periods.
- Each planet rotates on its axis and revolves around the Sun, affecting day and night cycles and the seasons.
- The planets interact with other celestial bodies like moons, asteroids, and comets

By using this model, which is grounded in empirical observation and scientific understanding, educators and scientists can explain and predict celestial events, making it a practical, real-world application of an ontic model.

The Circulatory System Model

The Circulatory System Model is an ontic model that shows how blood moves through the body, driven by the heart. This model helps explain how the body gets the oxygen and nutrients it needs and removes waste. It is based on real functions and structures within the human body, making it a practical model for understanding how our circulatory system works. The model describes how:

- The heart acts as a pump to move blood through the body.
- Arteries carry oxygen-rich blood away from the heart to the tissues.
- Veins bring oxygen-depleted blood back to the heart.
- Capillaries allow for the exchange of oxygen, nutrients, carbon dioxide and waste products between blood and tissues.

Anatomy

Specifically referring to the study and detailed description of the structures of the body, such as bones, muscles, organs and other tissues, anatomy can be considered an ontic model because it corresponds directly to the observable and tangible elements of the human body. The model depicts:

- Structural relationships – How different parts of the body are connected and interact.

- Physical details – The shapes, sizes and positions of various body parts.

- Functional insights – Understanding these structures helps to grasp how they function, although detailed functional mechanisms more often fall under physiology.

By mapping out where everything in the body is located and how these parts are organised and interact, anatomy provides a foundational ontic model that is used extensively in various fields. It serves as a guide for medical professionals to diagnose diseases, perform surgeries and understand human biology at a fundamental level.

Ontological model examples

Imagine an ontological model of human beings. Rather than depicting the observable and tangible attributes like the ontic models described above do, it would delve deeper, focusing on the fundamental nature and existential categories that define what it means to be human. Such a model would explore concepts such as the essence of human identity, the attributes that constitute a human and the existential relationships between individuals and their environment.

For example, an ontological model focused on human essence (whatness) and existence would consider what fundamentally makes a human being a human. It might explore whether humans are defined by their rationality, consciousness or a combination of physical, mental and emotional characteristics. An ontological model focused on humans as social beings would consider humans as inherently social creatures, whose identities and existences are shaped by interactions with others within cultures and societies. It would include the role of language, social structures and cultural norms in shaping human existence.

Ontological models of human beings have practical implications in areas like ethics, politics, psychology and theology. By defining what it means to be human, such models influence how individuals are treated within legal and moral frameworks, how healthcare is administered and even how societies are structured.

Consider human health and wellbeing. If we can create an ontic model depicting human anatomy, how can we use that as a foundation to create an ontological model for health and wellbeing that considers both mental and physical perspectives? Such a model would consider health and wellbeing holistically rather than simply as a means to avoid or address illness. It would support us to see health as a dynamic and interconnected system, emphasising that caring for one's mental health is as important as maintaining physical health, and that both contribute to a human being's ability to lead a life of effectiveness, wellbeing and fulfilment.

Conclusion

No matter what philosophy, science or school of thought we tap into, it needs to include descriptions of the whatness of things. Whether in philosophical discourse or technological applications, ontic and ontological approaches are indispensable because they provide a structured way to understand and describe the whatness of things across various domains, facilitating deeper insight and more effective knowledge management and application.

Furthermore, whatever meaning we're discussing needs to be describable using either an ontic or ontological model. For example, no software will be created unless people first map out the reality of the problem they intend the software to solve, which requires ontology. While each school of thought might produce a different description of something, they all have one thing in common – the *need* to come up with a description. Ultimately, when it comes to subjective phenomena, no matter what is being studied – from politics and economics to education, healthcare, organisations and consciousness, and regardless of one's intention – ontology matters.

Our exploration of the whatness of things, ontic perspectives and ontology involves tapping into various paradigms to deepen our understanding of matters and make them more congruent or pragmatic, especially manufactured constructs. We learned that in developing authentic awareness of what and how things are, neither science nor philosophy has all the answers. Despite our desire for absolutes, we ultimately rely on our intellect, rationality – with all its perceptual and conceptual limitations – or faith. The essence of being human, with all its complexities and confusion, remains a vast, uncharted territory, inviting us to explore beyond the confines of empirical science. Ultimately, science falls short when it comes to capturing the essence of our subjective experiences.

Also falling short are the various schools of philosophical thought on whatness, ontic approaches and ontology when considered in isolation. While we can turn to ontic and ontological models to expand the whatness of things into tangible pieces of knowledge within a structured framework, it is beneficial to take a step back and consider ways to bridge the divide between philosophy and science. In the following chapter, we delve into my novel approach – the Nested Theory of Sense-making. I developed this ontological model for sense-making not only to bridge the gap between various philosophical approaches and science, each with its diverse yet equally relevant insights, but also to discover, model and map out the ontology or whatness of sense-making in a way that ensures its applicability across various domains.

CHAPTER 9

The Nested Theory of Sense-making

How do we make sense of the world? At a high level, we develop conceptions of matters, meanings and ideas through our intellect. In other words, it is primarily through our intellect and rationality that we come to understand things and their functionality. When we first encounter something new, we start by determining what it is. Next, we consider its functionality or how it works. We then store this new information as a category in our memory to draw on later as needed. However, there is far more to sense-making than identifying what something is and how it works. As we navigate the complexities of the world around us, the notion of sense-making serves as a metaphorical choreographer, guiding our steps. From deciphering our daily interactions to interpreting broader societal and global matters, our ability to make sense of things is fundamental to how we perceive reality, make decisions and take action. But what exactly is sense-making? Sure, we all know what it means at face value. However, understanding the sense-making *process* is like unravelling a rich tapestry woven from diverse threads of perception, thought, feeling and theory.

The previous two chapters explored whatness in considerable depth, including the ontic and ontological tools we use to determine what things are and how they work. However, whatness, while integral to the sense-making process, is only part of the story. To make sense of things, we need to examine the *relationships* between the matter in question and various other related matters. Given our pluralistic landscape, the Nested Theory of Sense-making emerges as a promising framework that encapsulates the multi-dimensional aspects of sense-making. By integrating insights from essentialism, existentialism, poststructuralism, scientific inquiry, phenomenology and epistemology, the Nested Theory of Sense-making proposes that our understanding of whatness is constructed through 'nested' layers of interpretation and meaning-making, both of which are informed by our interactions with the world, linguistic and cultural contexts and subjective experiences. By acknowledging the complexity and interdependence of these layers and the relationships between them, my theory offers a holistic approach to studying whatness that transcends traditional philosophical and scientific boundaries. It encourages us to consider how various factors – from biological and psychological to social and cultural – influence our ability to make sense of things with authentic awareness. By the end of this chapter, you will see how this theory supports us to navigate and interpret the complexities of the world more effectively.

Before we delve more deeply into the Nested Theory of Sense-making, let's zoom out and consider some of the literature behind the notion of sense-making. Over the years, scholars have developed various frameworks to explain this process, each offering unique insights. In studying the literature in detail, I identified multiple gaps, which I will share in this chapter. Understanding the existing schools of thought around sense-making and where they fall short will explain why I felt compelled to develop a novel approach and support your understanding of how my theory reduces confusion, sheds light on The Invisible and encourages authentic awareness. This chapter also explains the difference between content and metacontent, explores the need to consider multiple perspectives and the context when making sense of anything, and provides practical examples of how the theory can be applied in various domains, from business, education, health and relationships to geopolitics and the environment.

Existing sense-making theories – a brief literature review

Sense-making is a complex and multi-dimensional process that people use to understand and navigate the world around them. Several theories have been developed to explain different aspects of this intricate process. Let's briefly look into a few of the more prominent ones and how these theories were either influenced by the views of other philosophers or how they influenced others.

Karl Weick's Sense-making Theory is commonly referred to in organisational studies. Imagine finding yourself in a chaotic situation, unsure of what's happening around you. According to Weick, you start by noticing cues from your environment and grouping them. You then create plausible narratives to explain these cues and act on these narratives. Sense-making, in this view, is not about seeking accuracy but about constructing a story that makes enough sense to move forward. It's a continuous, social process where past experiences shape current interpretations.[85] Weick's theory illuminates the retrospective and social nature of sense-making. This view can also be seen through the lens of philosopher Charles Sanders Peirce's pragmatism[86], which emphasises the role of interpretation and community in the formation of belief and understanding.

Brenda Dervin's Sense-making Methodology is rooted in communication studies and offers a markedly different perspective from Weick's. Dervin's approach treats sense-making as a process of dialogue, where individuals construct and reconstruct narratives to navigate through

---

85   Weick, K. E. 1995. *Sensemaking in Organizations.* Sage Publications.
86   Peirce, C. S. 1931—1958. *Collected Papers of Charles Sanders Peirce.* Harvard University Press.

time, space and the social world. It's about engaging in a conversation with the world (others) to fill in any gaps you might have in your understanding.[87] Philosopher Paul Ricoeur's narrative identity theory resonates with Dervin's approach in its assertion that our identity is shaped by the stories we construct and tell about ourselves.[88]

Russell Ackoff's Data, Information, Knowledge and Wisdom (DIKW) Framework pictures data as raw facts, which are then structured into information. This information, when interpreted and applied in practice, becomes knowledge and, eventually, wisdom, from which we can make informed decisions. Although not exclusively a sense-making theory, Ackoff's framework shows how we can transform raw data into meaningful wisdom through interpretation and application.[89] Ackoff's DIKW framework aligns closely with the epistemological insights of British philosopher Gilbert Ryle, particularly his distinction between 'knowing that' and 'knowing how'.[90]

Gary Klein's Data/Frame Model of Sense-making emphasises the dynamic interaction between data and its frame of reference or our interpretive lens. Imagine you have a frame through which you view a situation. You gather data and fit it into this frame, but as new data comes in, you might need to adjust your frame. With Klein's approach, changes in either the data or the frame of reference can lead to new insights, making the process of sense-making a continuously evolving activity.[91] Klein's Data/Frame model echoes Hans-Georg Gadamer's hermeneutic philosophy, which argues that understanding is always a fusion of horizons between the interpreter and the text.[92]

---

87   Dervin, B. 1983. 'An Overview of Sense-making Research: Concepts, Methods, and Results to Date'. International Communication Association Annual Meeting.

88   Ricoeur, P. 1984. *Time and Narrative (Vol. 1)*. University of Chicago Press.

89   Ackoff, R. L. 1989. 'From Data to Wisdom'. Journal of Applied Systems Analysis, 16, 3—9.

90   Ryle, G. 1949. *The Concept of Mind*. University of Chicago Press.

91   Klein, G., Moon, B., & Hoffman, R. R. 2006. 'Making Sense of Sensemaking 1: Alternative Perspectives'. IEEE Intelligent Systems, 21(4), 70—73. https://doi.org/10.1109/MIS.2006.75

92   Gadamer, H. G. 1960. *Truth and Method*. Sheed & Ward.

Weick, Sutcliffe and Obstfeld's Model of Organisational Sense-making builds on Weick's earlier work, this time focusing exclusively on organisational contexts. This approach is based on shared understandings developed through collective narratives within an organisation. This collaborative process allows members to align their actions and work towards common goals. It's about constructing a shared reality that guides organisational behaviour.[93] Their model can be linked to philosopher Jürgen Habermas's theory of communicative action, which explores how mutual understanding and consensus are achieved through rational communication.[94]

Building on these perspectives, we can further explore how sense-making theories intersect with the ideas of contemporary philosophers like Michel Foucault and Jacques Derrida. Foucault's work on power, knowledge and discourse challenges us to consider how power structures and societal norms influence our understanding of reality. His concept of the 'archaeology of knowledge' delves into the historical and social constructs that shape our perception, aligning with Weick's emphasis on the social nature of sense-making.[95] Similarly, Derrida's philosophical concept of deconstruction urges us to question the inherent assumptions and dualities in our interpretations. Derrida's focus on the fluidity and instability of meaning parallels Brenda Dervin's idea of continually reconstructing narratives to bridge gaps in understanding. His work encourages a deeper examination of the underlying structures that influence how we make sense of the world, highlighting the need for dynamic and adaptable cognitive frameworks.[96]

These theories collectively highlight various ways individuals and groups create meaning from their experiences and align their actions and decisions with their interpreted realities through sense-making.

---

93   Weick, K. E., Sutcliffe, K. M., & Obstfeld, D. 2005. 'Organizing and the Process of Sensemaking'. *Organization Science,* 16(4), 409—421. https://doi.org/10.1287/orsc.1050.0133

94   Habermas, J. 1984. *The Theory of Communicative Action.* Beacon Press.

95   Foucault, M. 1972. *The Archaeology of Knowledge.* Pantheon Books.

96   Derrida, J. 1967. *Of Grammatology.* Johns Hopkins University Press.

They also emphasise the retrospective, social and narrative-driven nature of sense-making and the importance of framing and reframing information due to the dynamic nature of data and its context. However, while each theory has merit, they all fall short of capturing the full complexity of how we understand and navigate the world. More specifically, they all overlook the multifaceted nature of sense-making and that it must encompass both the ontological understanding of *what things are* (whatness) and the epistemological process of *how things work*.

Addressing the gap requires a comprehensive approach that enables us to:

- Understand how we create internal representations of the world to navigate complex environments through cognitive maps and mental models.

- Explore how intentional consciousness or awareness influences the interpretation and understanding of reality through ontology.

- Examine the different narrative lenses through which we interpret our experiences and how these narratives shape our understanding.

- Consider the various angles or perspectives from which we view and analyse matters to understand how this impacts the sense-making process.

- Approach sense-making with epistemic humility by being open, vulnerable and willing to revise our understanding of a matter in light of new information.

- Investigate the epistemological tools and methodologies used to examine reality and their influence on the authenticity, congruence and validity of our mental models.

The Nested Theory of Sense-making is a comprehensive framework that addresses the gaps in the existing literature and, therefore, offers a more holistic and integrated approach to making sense of the world with authentic awareness. Before we explore the Nested Theory in detail, let's examine the difference between content and metacontent a little more closely.

Content vs metacontent

Absolutely everything in existence, from every living thing and every substance and matter to events, ideas, concepts, theories, narratives and more, is content. Content is literally all there is. You, your partner or spouse, every relative and friend, the dog, the cat, the plant, the people at work or in your business and the leaders we vote for all fall into the realm of content.

When we are born, we are 'thrown'[97] into the ocean of existence without having any say in the matter. Like drops of water within the ocean, every one of us matters. The more we grow and develop, the more we interact with and strive to make sense of the content beyond ourselves. At the same time, we are also projecting ourselves as unique beings into that ocean of existence. So not only are we continually interacting with and making sense of the content that's out there, but we are also continually contributing to it. We generate content through our thoughts, speech, decisions, choices, actions and behaviour, and we also consume and interact with others' generated content. Consequently, others will endeavour to make sense of our unique contribution in the form of various content, too. As content-generating and consuming beings, every individual's contribution and self-expression becomes content that expands our shared negotiated reality.

To interact with, deal with, consume and make sense of any content – including ourselves, others and our collective contributions – we need access to far deeper layers and knowledge than what lies on the

---

97 Martin Heidegger's concept of 'thrownness' (Geworfenheit) refers to the condition of being born into a pre-existing world with given contexts and conditions beyond one's control, emphasising the inherently given nature of human existence.

surface. Metacontent supports us in making sense of any content. As you will see in this chapter, it shapes our understanding and influences our decisions and actions concerning the content in question, from choosing a life partner to deciding on a career, starting a business venture or electing a leader, to list just a few examples. Consider metacontent as a multi-layered intellectual substrate that enables us to tap into and gain awareness and understanding of abstract and conceptual knowledge deep below the surface. Each layer contributes to a comprehensive understanding of any matter being examined, allowing us to navigate complex concepts, make informed decisions and take effective action.

As a constructive and open-ended framework, metacontent does not prescribe an ultimate aim or telos. Instead, it provides a framework for individuals to discover their own meaning. In this way, it aligns with analytical philosophy, emphasising personal discovery and critical examination of one's beliefs and knowledge. With this in mind, it is important to recognise that each of us has our own metacontent, shaped by the aggregation of the stories we tell ourselves and our interpretation of events together with our experiences, conceptions, learned knowledge, cognitive maps, mental models and more. This personal metacontent forms a layered substrate that influences how we make sense of things and interact with the world. The key is to become intentionally conscious of this fact – to be aware that a layered substrate (metacontent) is currently guiding our sense-making process and interactions with all aspects of existence. Given metacontent is a mental construct, it can be deconstructed and reconstructed, leaving room for significant opportunities for transformation.

Why did I choose the word 'metacontent' and not 'worldview' in reference to the intellectual substrates for sense-making? While an individual's worldview can significantly shape one's paradigms and mental models, the word 'worldview', which the *Oxford English Dictionary* defines as 'a particular philosophy of life or conception of the world', is too broad and vague for what I am referring to here. For example, the fact that 'worldview' incorporates the word 'world', technically and linguistically restricts it to considering content in the world and being conceptually concerned with material reality. However, many persist in using it to refer to content beyond material reality. Furthermore, while 'worldview' is a broad term encompassing an individual's overall outlook on life, the world and everything in it, 'metacontent' serves a more specific purpose. It refers to the intellectual substrates we use to make sense of any content – within or beyond the world and material reality. It includes distinct layers that provide a structured approach to understanding and interacting with information, allowing for a nuanced analysis of complex concepts.

Although I have introduced the word metacontent in the realm of sense-making, there is existing literature discussing the ideas behind the metacontent discourse. For instance, the Ladder of Inference, introduced by Chris Argyris, illustrates how we select data from the vast amount of information available, make assumptions based on our personal and cultural meanings, and then draw conclusions. Argyris also introduced the concept of Double Loop Learning to emphasise the importance of revising our mental models in addition to incorporating new information.[98] However, the Nested Theory of Sense-making goes far deeper. Think of the Nested Theory of Sense-making as metacontent in a tangible form. It supports us in deconstructing and reconstructing metacontent via its seven layers to access a more authentic and holistic perspective of the content we are examining. It is essential for accurate understanding and effective interaction with all types of content, from the complexities of global politics to the subtleties of personal experiences and relationships, shaping our perceptions, informing our decisions and guiding our actions with more authentic awareness.

Let's say you want to deeply understand the complexities of the situation in the Middle East. This would require more than just reading a few published articles and staying up-to-date with the

---

98   Argyris, C. 1990. *Overcoming Organizational Defenses: Facilitating Organizational Learning.* Boston, MA: Allyn and Bacon.
Argyris, C. 1991. *Teaching Smart People How to Learn.* Harvard Business Review, 69(3), 99—109.

latest news. It would require you to consider multiple metacontent layers. This process, though challenging, is essential for accurate comprehension because misconstrued or incomplete metacontent about the associated content can lead to misconceptions. Simplistic generalisations, such as equating the West with democracy, regarding Muslims as terrorists or viewing the Middle East solely through the lens of conflict, overlook profound and significant truths about the content one is attempting to make sense of. When it comes to matters of extreme importance in the world, such as geopolitics, economics and the environment, misconceptions on a collective scale can lead to detrimental decisions, actions, behaviours and biases. Just be mindful of the contextual variables like cultural, environmental, subjective and intersubjective factors when assessing content via each of the seven layers and their inevitable influence.

On a personal level, tapping into metacontent is crucial for doing anything in life, from setting and achieving goals, establishing and growing a business and building a career to choosing a life partner, bringing up children and gaining expertise in any field. It also enhances our ability to relate to truth and beauty in everyday experiences, such as intimacy with romantic partners, enjoying nature, the arts, parenting and interacting with animals. In short, metacontent matters because it provides the necessary framework for making sense of content and clarifies our confusion. Without it, our understanding is incomplete and inauthentic.

When there is a lack of attention to appropriate metacontent in attempting to make sense of any content, our ability to form an authentic and congruent understanding of it is significantly diminished and often leads us to become biased. This oversight leaves us reliant on surface-level knowledge, ignoring the deeper, more subtle layers crucial for comprehensive understanding and authentic awareness. If fragments of reality remain invisible, our ability to make sense of matters is severely impacted. At times, it might even lead us to resent something or someone for reasons that are actually figments of our imagination.

On a larger scale, two nations can be locked in decades or even centuries of conflict, shedding blood over misconceptions and misunderstandings resulting from the leaders of both nations not considering the bigger picture from a holistic viewpoint by tapping into the appropriate metacontent. A prominent example is the long-standing issues between Iran and the United States. As an Iranian Australian, I have studied the conflict in detail and know that both parties hold numerous misconceived notions about each other, distorting reality to the point where the truth is almost indiscernible. History is filled with examples like this, and the consequences can be devastating. Nations often go to war not merely over resources and territories but because of the narratives we humans create and how we make sense of things. Without accessing every layer of the relevant metacontent, we risk falling into delusion and a state of collective psychosis – a dissociation from reality en masse – with potentially catastrophic results.

Stereotypes, biases and many conflicts stem from neglecting to pay attention to the appropriate metacontent, be it when interacting with content – such as media-generated information – or content we have generated ourselves. Many relationships have been ruined and families separated due to fabricated stories, misunderstandings and ineffective communication. Countless businesses have gone under for the same reasons. The point is, everything is content, including every single one of us. So, doing one's best to develop an authentic and congruent conception of all the content one encounters should matter profoundly to us all. An effective ontological tool to support us in achieving that objective is the Nested Theory of Sense-making.

Contextual variables

In making sense of the world and everything in it, we need to remember that we are not machines but human beings with feelings, beliefs, opinions and biases. Therefore, **context** – which is broken down into **contextual variables** like cultural, environmental, subjective and intersubjective factors in the Nested Theory of Sense-making

– must be considered as it provides situational context and influences every layer in the framework. Understanding these contextual variables and their influence is essential because there is no time in our lives that we exist out of context with whatever is happening around us or what has come before us. Therefore, contextual variables play a huge role in shaping our perceptions, interpretations, decisions and actions. For instance, a person's cultural background and the environment in which they are raised can significantly influence their approach to knowledge and truth. Suppose someone is raised in a culture where religion and faith are seen as legitimate ways of examining reality. In that case, they might be more accepting of anecdotal narratives as truth. This contrasts with someone from a background that highly values empirical evidence and might demand scientific proof, even in personal relationships or when making business decisions.

Consider two individuals making sense of a new business opportunity. If one is from a culture that values empirical evidence above all else, they might be unable to take action unless they first conduct extensive market research and analysis. In contrast, if the other is from a culture that values faith and intuition, they might rely more on personal experience and gut feelings to make decisions. Neither approach is right or wrong; the point is being aware that cultural variables exist across all layers of the metacontent.

Similarly, contextual variables influence different paradigms in the domain of research. A researcher from a positivist tradition might emphasise quantitative data and observable phenomena, while a researcher from an interpretivist tradition might focus on qualitative data and individuals' subjective experiences.

The role of unhealed traumas and childhood experiences also cannot be underestimated. For instance, someone who has experienced significant trauma as a child might have a different sense-making process shaped by their past experiences and psychological state. This can influence their ability to trust others, take risks and interpret data and events.

Consider also the example of trust in a romantic relationship. A person who values empirical evidence might need concrete proof of their partner's fidelity, while someone who values anecdotal narratives might rely more on their partner's verbal reassurances and shared experiences. Recognising these variables ensures that our sense-making process is authentic in that it considers their influence on the outcome.

In other examples, contextual variables such as mental health conditions can significantly impact an individual's sense-making process. For example, anxiety or depression may colour perceptions and interpretations, making it essential to consider these factors in personal interactions and support systems. A person suffering from depression might view a neutral event as unfavourable or in a negative light, affecting their overall outlook on life. In international business, cultural context also plays a critical role. Understanding and respecting cultural differences can prevent miscommunications and foster stronger relationships with global partners and clients. For example, a businessperson negotiating in Japan must understand the cultural importance of politeness and indirect communication to build trust and achieve successful outcomes. Similarly, the state of being assertive may be considered rude or aggressive in some cultures but not in others.

The idea of factoring in contextual variables deeply resonates with Martin Heidegger's concept of 'being there' (In-Der-Welt-Sein). He proposed that our existence is fundamentally situated in a specific context, shaped by the world we inhabit. This context encompasses the dynamic, often intangible factors that influence our perceptions, interactions and understanding. Just as Heidegger emphasises the inseparability of being and the world, the contextual variables permeate all layers of our sense-making process, reminding us that our sense of self and understanding are always interwoven with the cultural, environmental and subjective nuances of our surroundings. These variables create the backdrop against which all other layers of sense-making unfold, highlighting the interconnectedness of our being and the world.

Complexities in sense-making

The complexity of content and its associated metacontent significantly influence how we interpret information, form mental models and make decisions. Therefore, it is another contextual variable we need to consider. To navigate complexities effectively, it is helpful to categorise them.

Dave Snowden's Cynefin Framework[99] is a practical tool that provides a structured approach to categorising content complexity. It neatly divides situations into four main domains: Simple, Complicated, Complex and Chaotic, offering a clear roadmap for sense-making and decision-making.

- **Simple (obvious)** – Clear cause-and-effect relationships that are easily understood. Best practices can be applied directly

  Example: A recipe for baking a cake. Follow the steps as written, and you should achieve the expected result.

- **Complicated** – Requires expert analysis to understand cause-and-effect relationships. Solutions involve good practices based on thorough analysis.

  Example: Diagnosing and fixing a car engine problem. A mechanic's expertise is needed to analyse and resolve the issue.

- **Complex** – Patterns emerge over time through experimentation. Understanding evolves, requiring adaptive and flexible approaches.

  Example: Managing a startup company. Success requires experimenting with different business strategies and adapting based on feedback and market changes.

- **Chaotic** – No clear cause-and-effect relationships. Immediate action is necessary to establish order and make sense of the situation.

---

99   Snowden, D. J., & Boone, M. E. 2007. 'A Leader's Framework for Decision Making'. Harvard Business Review, 85(11), 69—76.

Example: Responding to a natural disaster. Immediate, decisive actions are needed to establish order and provide aid, as there is no clear pattern or predictability.

Integrating the Cynefin Framework into the Nested Theory as another contextual variable allows us to identify whether the content is simple, complicated, complex or chaotic and apply the appropriate strategies accordingly. By recognising the nature of the context and the complexities of the content we are dealing with, along with its corresponding metacontent, we can better tailor our sense-making processes. For instance, straightforward, tried-and-true methods may suffice in a simple context. In contrast, complex situations demand a more iterative and probing approach to uncover emerging patterns.

Whether dealing with straightforward content or complex patterns in cognitive maps, recognising the context helps us apply the right level of analysis, flexibility and action. This integration enhances our ability to interpret and respond effectively across all layers, ultimately leading to more informed and effective decision-making.

The role of language and symbols in shaping our perceptions and refining our narratives

It is important to acknowledge the role of language and symbols in shaping our perception of the world and refining our narratives. Kenneth Burke's concept of the 'terministic screen' provides a profound insight into this phenomenon. A terministic screen is essentially a lens composed of language and symbols that influence how we perceive and interpret various subject areas or domains. Burke emphasises that our choice of words and symbols can direct attention towards certain aspects of reality while obscuring others, consequently shaping our understanding and responses.[100]

For instance, in medical and business contexts, terministic screens can transform how professionals perceive and engage with their

---

100   Burke, K. 1966. *Language as Symbolic Action: Essays on Life, Literature, and Method.* University of California Press.

fields. In their article, 'Rhetoric Unlobotomised: Transformation of Terministic Screens', Dave Logan and Haley Fisher-Wright map out how these screens operate in different domains, highlighting the critical role of rhetoric in professional practice.[101]

John R. Edlund's work in *Teaching Text Rhetorically: Integrating Reading and Writing Instruction* highlights the power of terministic screens in writing and rhetoric. Edlund's examples, such as the impact of labelling groups in political conflicts, illustrate how a single word can reshape our understanding and the broader discourse.[102]

Below are four reasons to consider a terministic screen as a contextual variable:

- **Influence on perception and interpretation:** The specific language and symbols we choose affect how we perceive and interpret information. For example, the terminology used in a scientific study can shape the interpretation of its results, guiding readers towards certain conclusions while potentially obscuring others.

- **Communication and understanding:** The words and symbols employed in communication can affect how different audiences convey and understand information. This can be especially significant in fields like education, healthcare or politics, where clear and precise communication is crucial.

- **Cultural and social context:** The choice of language and symbols is often influenced by cultural and social contexts, making them a crucial variable in understanding how different groups might perceive and react to the same information. For instance, technical jargon might be well understood within a professional community but could be confusing or alienating to the general public.

---

101 Logan, D., & Fisher-Wright, H. 2007. *Rhetoric Unlobotomised: Transformation of Terministic Screens.*

102 Edlund, J. R. 2020. *Teaching Text Rhetorically: Integrating Reading and Writing Instruction.*

- **Behaviour and decision-making:** The language and symbols we use can influence behaviour and decision-making. For example, framing a public health message positively versus negatively can significantly impact public response and compliance.

As we navigate complex personal, societal and global challenges, understanding the terministic screens at play as another contextual variable allows us to critically assess and refine the narratives we construct. By incorporating the Nested Theory of Sense-making, we can further dissect these layers of language and symbols to reveal the metacontent. This process not only enhances our comprehension but also equips us to make more informed and effective decisions.

The Nested Theory of Sense-making – an ontological model

The Nested Theory of Sense-making is essentially an ontological model for making sense of content. In developing the framework, the aim was to discover, model and map out the ontology and whatness of sense-making. The theory considers that sense-making is a multifaceted process that requires a deep understanding of both what things are and how things work while also being aware of the context – or contextual variables, to be more precise – that invariably influence us, such as cultural, environmental, subjective and intersubjective factors.

The theory proposes that everything in existence is content, and to comprehensively and authentically make sense of any piece of content, we need to first access its metacontent – the intellectual substrates for sense-making. The Nested Theory of Sense-making helps us consider the content through the following seven lenses, coupled with contextual variables like culture, environmental, subjective and intersubjective factors that can impact every layer.

1. Initial insight

2. Cognitive map

3. Narratives

4. Mental models

5. Perspectives

6. Domain

7. Paradigms

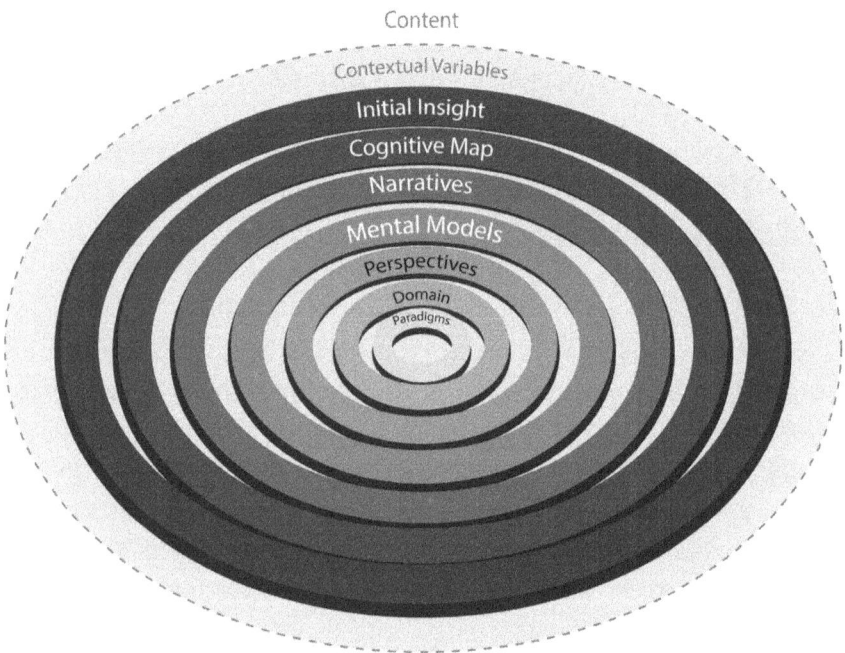

Figure 5a
The Nested Theory of Sense-making

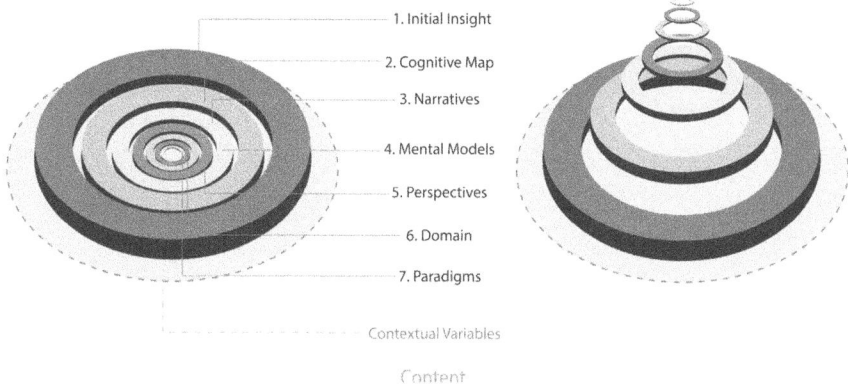

Figure 5b

The Nested Theory of Sense-making

The reason behind the terms selected for each layer will become more apparent once you read the detailed description of each layer. For example, some might wonder why the word 'mindset' wasn't chosen for one of the layers. Mindset refers to an established set of attitudes held by someone and is relevant in the sense-making process. It has, therefore, been incorporated into the framework as the aggregation of three layers – cognitive maps, narratives and, to a lesser degree, mental models.

Just as you can't eat soup with a fork, you need the right tool to understand and make sense of different types of content. The Nested Theory of Sense-making is a tool that supports us in accessing the metacontent or intellectual substrates to make sense of any given content. In this way, it facilitates the process of navigating and interpreting the ever-evolving complexities of our world.

The 7 layers of the Nested Theory of Sense-making

1. Initial insight

When we encounter new information – often referred to as a lightbulb or eureka moment – this initial insight or moment of realisation, where our attention is drawn to a fresh insight on something or a new idea, sparks the sense-making process and a desire to delve deeper to learn more. Any spontaneous idea or intuition that strikes our mind, seemingly out of the blue, is not something we actively generate but rather something we host. This phenomenon is closely related to abductive inference, where we generate the best possible explanation for an unexpected observation.

Picture a scientist strolling in the park when they are suddenly hit by an idea that could revolutionise their research. This 'initial insight' acts as a catalyst, compelling the scientist to delve deeper into the concept, explore its implications and eventually develop a comprehensive understanding of it. This initial spark sets off a chain reaction of thoughts and investigations, leading to significant breakthroughs and innovations. This initial insight, driven by abductive inference, not only sparks curiosity but also fuels the relentless pursuit of knowledge and understanding.

Neuroscience explains these spontaneous insights as follows. When we are relaxed but alert, our Default Mode Network (DMN) is activated, facilitating mind-wandering and spontaneous thought generation. Alpha brain waves, present when we are in this state of mind, help link distant associations, leading to intuitive thoughts. Finally, neurotransmitters like dopamine enhance the feeling associated with those rewarding 'aha' moments, reinforcing the significance of these initial insights and making us hungry to learn more.

2. **Cognitive map**

A cognitive map is a mental representation of our knowledge and understanding of **what things are,** the spatial relationships between objects, as well as our beliefs, opinions, and values. It helps us understand our environment, including how we perceive, organise and interpret new information, by serving as a mental storage system that supports our conception of what things are and how they are linked or related. Imagine arriving in a city you've never visited before. As you orient yourself and begin to navigate through the city, cognitive maps help you remember key landmarks, like a large park or a distinctive building, and understand the city's layout, including the main streets and their connections.

Cognitive maps are also crucial for solving spatial problems, such as finding the shortest route or locating an object in a complex environment, like remembering where you parked your car in a multi-level car park. They integrate past experiences and sensory information, allowing you to predict outcomes, recall and use information effectively and make informed decisions.

Cognitive maps are essentially ontological models because the latter explore the fundamental categories of things that exist and their relationships, aiming to understand what entities exist in the world, how they can be grouped and how they interact with one another.

As they are flexible and adaptable, cognitive maps can be readily updated with new information, helping you adjust to changes in your environment, like learning the layout of a new suburb after moving house or familiarising yourself with a new computer operating system. However, it is important to be aware that cognitive maps are also influenced by one's 'web of perceptions', a term I use to describe how one relates to things. For example, how one person relates to marriage, love, God, etc., might differ markedly from how another relates to it. Contextual variables, such as cultural background, influence our web of perceptions. Consider the following excerpt from *BEING* on the web of perceptions.

> We all perceive things differently because we do not have
> direct access to the truth. Whenever we come across a new
> object, concept or idea, we form a perception of it. We read

about it, we experience it, and so we perceive it in a certain way. It is worth noting that the culture, religion, ideologies, political views, parenting styles, gurus and schools of thinking we follow, or the opinion-makers we admire, have a strong influence over how these perceptions are shaped.

By the time we enter adulthood, we have already shaped our own web of perceptions.

Every node of the web we spin represents a single perception of something, such as: money, confidence, awareness, authenticity, productivity, integrity, love, marriage, employer, race, gender, honour, government, God, police, and so on. Simply put, a perception is a way we think of or get to know something. The same object or the same meaning or concept can be interpreted and understood in different ways by different people. In other words, things can occur to each of us differently. [103]

3. Narratives

Given that we do not have unmediated access to the truth of matters, we observe, interpret and experience things in ways that can radically differ from how others might perceive them. This subjective interpretation means there is always a 'narrative lens' through which we see the world, shaping our understanding and experiences. In other words, the stories we tell ourselves are the personal interpretations and narratives we create to make sense of events or sequences of events. These narratives are strongly influenced by contextual variables like cultural background and beliefs. Nonetheless, they are crucial for connecting disparate events and information into a unified narrative, aiding memory, learning and communication.

The idea that our perceptions and interpretations are subjective and mediated by our experiences has deep roots in philosophy. For example, Immanuel Kant argued that the categories and structures of our mind shape our understanding of the world.

---

103 Tashvir, A. 2021. *BEING – The source of power.* (p 130—131) Engenesis Publications: Sydney.

He asserted that we never directly perceive the 'thing-in-itself'; instead, we experience a mediated version filtered through our cognitive framework. Michel Foucault and Jacques Derrida further explored the idea of interpretation and the role of narratives. Foucault examined how power relations shape our understanding and the narratives we create. He proposed that power and knowledge are intertwined and cannot be separated. Knowledge, he argued, is used to exert power, and power relations affect what is considered knowledge. This concept is central to his analysis of how societies regulate and control individuals through discourses and institutions. Derrida's notion of deconstruction emphasises that texts and narratives have multiple interpretations and that meanings are not fixed but constantly shifting. Martin Heidegger discussed the concept of 'being-in-the-world', highlighting that our existence is always contextual and interpretative. In other words, we don't just exist in an abstract sense but in a specific context. We constantly interpret our experiences and surroundings, shaping our understanding and narrative lens within the given context.

Linguists and phenomenologists also contributed to our understanding of how language and experiences, respectively, help shape our interpretations of the world and, therefore, the narratives we create. Linguists like Ferdinand de Saussure and Noam Chomsky contributed to our understanding of how language shapes our interpretation of the world. Saussure's idea of the signifier and signified illustrates how language constructs our reality, while Chomsky's theory of generative grammar shows how our innate linguistic structures influence our perception and interpretation. Phenomenology, a philosophical movement initiated by Edmund Husserl, focuses on the structures of experience and consciousness. Phenomenologists like Heidegger and Maurice Merleau-Ponty argue that our subjective experiences influence our perceptions and interpretations of the world. This approach emphasises that the way we experience and interpret phenomena is crucial to our understanding of reality. By examining our lived experiences and how we interpret them, phenomenology reveals the deeply personal and variable nature of human sense-making.

Hermeneutics, the theory and methodology of interpretation, especially of religious scriptures, is an interesting example in terms of how it can significantly influence some people's narrative lens. Pioneered by philosophers like Friedrich Schleiermacher[104] and Hans-Georg Gadamer[105], hermeneutics emphasises the importance of context, history and the interpreter's perspective in understanding texts. For example, religious scriptures are often interpreted in various ways depending on the reader's cultural background, historical context and personal beliefs. It explains why stories and verses within sacred texts like the Bible, the Qur'an and the Torah are often interpreted in vastly different ways, leading to personal narrative lenses that can differ greatly from other people's narrative lens of the same text.

Ultimately, the narratives we construct to make sense of the world help us connect events and information, providing coherence and meaning. However, these narratives can vary widely between individuals because they are subjective. Each person's narrative lens influences how they interpret and experience the world, highlighting the importance of recognising and understanding these differences. For example, consider two individuals witnessing the same event, such as a political protest. One might see it as a courageous fight for justice, while the other might view it as a disruptive and dangerous act. Their interpretations are shaped by their personal experiences, beliefs and the narratives they hold. This divergence in interpretation

---

104 Friedrich Schleiermacher was an 18th century German Reformed theologian, philosopher, biblical scholar and the founding father of hermeneutics. His well-known theory is about intuitive interpretation or intuition-based interpretation.

105 Hans-Georg Gadamer was a German philosopher of the continental tradition, best known for his 1960 magnum opus on hermeneutics, *Truth and Method.*

highlights that our narrative lens always mediates our access to the truth.

In intimate relationships, the stories partners tell themselves about their shared experiences are not just static narratives, but dynamic tools that can shape their emotional connection. For instance, a couple who views their challenges as opportunities to grow together will not only strengthen their bond, but also inspire others with their resilience. Conversely, if they see these challenges as insurmountable obstacles, it might create distance. By consciously choosing to rewrite their narratives, they might not only transform their relationship dynamics, but also inspire others to do the same.

In politics, campaigns don't just present policies; they craft compelling narratives to connect with voters. These stories often simplify complex policies into relatable themes. For example, a candidate might frame their economic policy as a story of hardworking families achieving their dream of home ownership. This narrative resonates emotionally with voters, potentially influencing their perceptions and choices.

By understanding the power of narratives, we can become more aware and critical of the narratives we encounter and make more informed decisions. Furthermore, appreciating that others may have different interpretations and narratives can help us engage in more meaningful and respectful dialogues. At the same time, understanding that our personal narratives are constructed and subjective can encourage us to reflect on our biases and work towards a more nuanced and comprehensive understanding of the content we strive to make sense of.

4. **Mental models**

In contrast to cognitive maps that help us understand what things are and the relationships that exist, mental models are frameworks for understanding functionalities or **how things work**. They are essential for problem-solving and decision-making, providing a basis for understanding complex systems and mechanisms. Mental models help us grasp the functionality of systems, objects and processes. For example, they allow us to understand how a car engine works, how parts of the human body function, and how market dynamics operate by simplifying complex concepts and breaking them down into more manageable components.

Imagine a doctor diagnosing a patient. The doctor's mental model of the human body includes knowing how different systems – such as the cardiovascular or respiratory system – function and interact. This model helps the doctor identify symptoms, understand underlying causes and choose the best treatment plan. The doctor's ability to predict how a patient's condition might progress and how different treatments might affect the patient is grounded in their mental model.

In contrast, anatomy can be likened to a cognitive map because it deals with the structural aspects of the body. Just as a cognitive map helps us understand what things are and their relationships, anatomy provides a detailed representation of the physical layout and organisation of the body's parts. It includes the spatial relationships between organs, bones, muscles and other structures, giving us a clear picture of the body's architecture. Indeed, anatomy and physiology serve as powerful analogies for cognitive maps and mental models, highlighting the difference and why they are both integral layers in making sense of things.

Anatomy provides the structural framework, similar to a cognitive map, that helps us understand what things are and how they are related, while physiology offers the functional understanding of how various systems in the body work and interact. Together, they help us navigate and make sense of the complexities of the human body, just as cognitive maps and mental models help us understand and interact with content and the world around us. Doctors studying anatomy learn about the specific locations and relationships of organs and tissues. This anatomical knowledge acts as a cognitive map, guiding their understanding of the body's structure. When they study physiology, they delve into how these organs and tissues function and interact, forming mental models that explain bodily processes and predict responses to various stimuli. Both are equally important. With the physician having a solid and authentic cognitive map and mental model of body parts and their functionality or, more precisely, what 'health' means in the context of the human body, pathology can identify the parts that are not functioning optimally. Combined, they all help with diagnosis and treatment so that the integrity/health of an individual's body can be restored.

Mental models also enable us to predict outcomes and anticipate the behaviour of systems. For instance, predicting how supply and demand changes might affect market prices is rooted in a well-formed mental model. Consider the mental models parents develop for raising children. These models, such as disciplinary techniques, educational approaches and nurturing methods, are the lenses through which they view their interactions with their children. For instance, a parent might believe that praising good behaviour is the best way to encourage it. This mental model shapes how they respond to their child's actions and behaviours, and ultimately, their parenting style. The mental model for parenting extends to 'experts' in the field. For example, in his book *12 Rules for Life*[106], Jordan Peterson, a clinical psychologist, offers radically different advice on how to deal with a disruptive or misbehaving child than Gabor Mate, a physician with a special interest in childhood development. This example highlights how two experts in the same field can have radically disparate views on the same subject matter. Their metacontent, particularly their mental models, leads to these differences.

---

106 Peterson, J. B. 2018. *12 Rules for Life: An Antidote to Chaos.* Random House Canada.

In business, leaders rely on mental models to make strategic decisions. For example, a CEO might use a mental model of competitive analysis to decide how to position their company in the market. This involves understanding how competitors operate, what customers need and how the market is evolving. These mental models help leaders navigate complex business landscapes and make informed decisions.

Mental models are not rigid structures, but flexible frameworks that can be refined with new information and experiences. They guide our actions and decisions, helping us choose appropriate responses to different situations based on our understanding of how things work. This adaptability ensures that our understanding evolves as we gain more knowledge and encounter new scenarios, making mental models a powerful tool for lifelong learning.

5. **Perspectives**

Perspectives are the specific angles or viewpoints from which individuals consider content. They play a crucial role in how we interpret and understand information, with multiple perspectives leading to a more comprehensive understanding.

We can look into matters from many different angles. Where we stand and observe gives us only a part of the totality of a situation. Perspectives should not be confused with perceptions. In this context, perception is how one relates to content, such as an idea or concept. On the other hand, perspectives are the various vantage points from which we can view and analyse these ideas or events. Imagine a soup bowl placed on its side with two people viewing it from opposite sides of the table. If asked whether the bowl is concave or convex, one person will say it's concave while the other will say it's convex. Each person has a different perspective on the same object, and neither is incorrect. However, each person only sees a part of the truth, consciously or unconsciously, which can lead to endless disagreement. Now, consider a third person who responds that it depends on the perspective when asked the same question. This person has opened their mind to the possibility of multiple ways to see something. They understand that to grasp what they observe fully, they must consider different perspectives.

Philosophers and theorists have long acknowledged the importance of perspectives. Hans-Georg Gadamer, a prominent figure in hermeneutics, argued that our historical and cultural horizons always influence our understanding. By engaging with different perspectives, we can expand our horizons and achieve a more nuanced and comprehensive understanding. In cognitive science, the concept of 'perspective-taking' is crucial for empathy and social cognition. Understanding another person's viewpoint allows us to appreciate their experiences and motivations, leading to more effective communication and collaboration. This aligns with the ideas of Martin Buber, who emphasised the importance of genuine dialogue and understanding in human relationships.

Drawing from the literature on Neuro-Linguistic Programming (NLP), it's clear that shifting perspectives is essential for gaining a fuller understanding of any situation. NLP emphasises the importance of putting ourselves in other people's shoes or adopting different perspectives to see more of the totality of a matter. This practice helps us avoid the 'frame theory' trap, where we only see what is made available to us based on our current viewpoint. In any given situation, including our interactions with others, we have the choice to see things from one or more four perspectives: I, Them, Others, Global. I call this the Perspective Quadrant.

- **I** – your perspective as an individual on a given issue or matter. It refers to the perspective you readily have immediate and direct access to. It is the angle from which you see a situation without considering any other angle. Most people stay in this quadrant without seeing things from another person's point of view.

- **Them** – the other individual directly engaged in the matter and their perspective on it. For example, 'Them' could refer to a client, an employer, an employee, your business partner, your life partner or the opposing political party to the one you follow.

- **Others** – anyone else not directly involved in the matter at hand, although they may be impacted by it. They could be other staff or colleagues, the rest of the leadership team or board of directors, extended family members, etc.

- **Global** – a simple, remote overview of the situation. The Global Perspective is a dispassionate, unattached view of the situation and views it as an observer, not a direct participant. It is akin to viewing an event from the other side of the world or a helicopter view.

All four perspectives in the quadrant are valid, though none provide an all-encompassing and overarching view required for effective leadership. That's why I have included a fifth perspective called the Truth-seeker Perspective that encompasses all other perspectives in the quadrant and therefore sits above the Perspective Quadrant to provide a 360-degree view. It describes an individual who seeks the reality or truth of a situation or matter from every conceivable angle, as though they are using a 3D scanner to view it. It is the most comprehensive perspective and provides the ability to see the totality of a matter or situation. To gain this perspective requires us to see things from all four quadrants (I, Them, Others and Global).[107]

I created the Perspective Quadrant, as shown, with human beings as the content to be studied and understood. In developing this model, I was primarily inspired by The Perceptual Positions model created by John Grinder and Judith DeLozier in 1987, which extends the NLP concept of Referential Index.

---

107   Tashvir, A. 2021. *BEING – The source of power.* (p 145—147) Engenesis Publications: Sydney.

Grinder and DeLozier's Referential Index concept involves identifying a sentence's subject, such as 'that', 'they', 'it', 'him' or 'her'. For instance, in the statement 'They are the problem', the Referential Index is 'they'. Building on Grinder and DeLozier's work, Ken Wilber, the founder of Integral Theory and the Integral Institute, identified the four Quadrants – the four integral perspectives of reality – in 1994, even though he had limited knowledge of NLP.

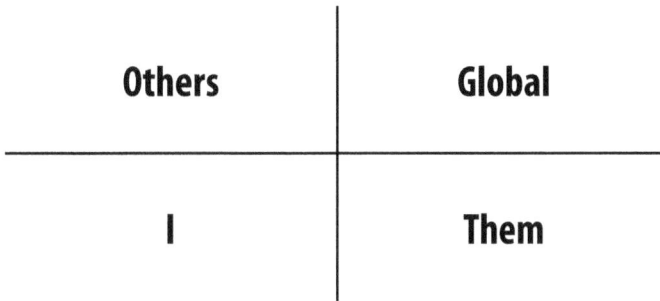

Others	Global
I	Them

Figure 6
The Perspective Quadrant

Adopting multiple perspectives is essential for problem-solving and critical thinking. Just as a detective examines a case from various angles to uncover the truth, we must consider different viewpoints to understand complex issues fully. This approach prevents us from becoming trapped in our biases and assumptions, fostering a more accurate and holistic comprehension of any content studied. For example, consider a business team working on a new project. Each member brings a unique perspective based on their expertise and experience. By combining these perspectives, the team can identify potential challenges, generate innovative solutions and create a more effective strategy.

In conflicts, whether between spouses or nations, understanding the issue from multiple perspectives is crucial. For instance, a mediator in a marital dispute might encourage each partner to see the conflict from the other's viewpoint. This helps both parties understand the broader context of their disagreement and find common ground.

In collaborative projects, team members bring diverse perspectives to the table. This diversity can lead to innovative solutions. For example, in a tech startup, developers, designers and marketers each have unique perspectives on a product. By considering these different angles, the team can create a more well-rounded and successful product.

Considering multiple perspectives is essential for developing a more congruent and comprehensive picture of any content or situation.

6. **Domain**

Domain refers to the constructed framework or 'game' within which we operate, such as law, science, economy, technology, art, pop culture, etc. Understanding the domain we operate within when assessing content is crucial for sense-making, as each domain provides specific context and rules that govern our interactions with and interpretations of the content in question. For example, making sense of content within the domain of science is very different from considering the same content within the domain of poetry or theology.

Recognising the domain helps you align your understanding – or how you relate to the content in question – and interpret the content appropriately. In academic research, the domain dictates the rules and methodologies that guide inquiry. For instance, scientific research follows specific protocols for hypothesis testing and data analysis. Researchers must understand the domain to ensure their work is valid and reliable. In legal systems, the domain provides the framework for interpreting and enforcing laws. Lawyers and judges must navigate this framework to deliver justice.

Without being aware of the domain, some may interpret religious statements about 'laws' as metaphysical laws of existence, such as 'human life is sacred and should be valued', or as physical laws like gravity or civil laws that apply in a judicial system. Even though every interpretation might be correct and offer a different perspective, understanding the domain in which the discussion takes place is essential. Similarly, interpreting a scientific paper requires a different approach than understanding a piece of art or a legal document. Misidentifying the domain can lead to misunderstandings, misjudgments and an inability to make sense of the matters at hand.

To illustrate the importance of considering the domain when attempting to make sense of something, let's look at an example involving climate change. When assessing content about climate change within the domain of science, you are focused on empirical data, measurable effects and logical reasoning. Scientists use methods like data collection, statistical analysis and peer review to understand climate change. For instance, you might analyse temperature records, CO_2 levels and ice core samples to conclude that human activities contribute to a phenomenon commonly referred to as 'global warming'. The context and rules in this domain emphasise empirical evidence.

Now, consider the same topic within the domain of the economy. Here, you are looking at climate change through the lens of its economic impact. You might analyse how climate change affects industries, job markets and global trade. For example, you could assess the costs of natural disasters on economies, the financial benefits of investing in green technologies or the economic policies needed to mitigate climate change effects. The focus is on cost-benefit analyses, economic models and market responses.

Within the theological domain, climate change might be perceived as part of a larger spiritual narrative. Theological discussions might centre on the moral responsibility of humans as Earth's stewards, interpreting climate change as a call to action in line with religious teachings. This domain might employ scriptural references, moral reasoning and spiritual principles to frame the discussion, highlighting the ethical and moral considerations in the theological interpretation of climate change.

By correctly identifying the domain, we can avoid confusion and ensure effective sense-making.

7. **Paradigms**

Once you've established the domain for context, it's important to understand that every domain can be further broken down into paradigms – the specific schools of thought or methodologies within each domain that shape how problems are approached and solved. More specifically, a paradigm is a framework or set of beliefs and practices that guides how we interpret information, conduct research and solve problems within a particular domain. It encompasses the theories, methods and standards that define legitimate work within that field. Understanding the paradigms within a domain is essential for making sense of content, particularly when dealing with complex issues.

For example, in science, various paradigms guide our understanding when making sense of different science-related content. Newtonian Mechanics explains the motion of objects using classical physics. Quantum Mechanics deals with particles at the atomic level. Relativity revolutionised our understanding of space, time and gravity on a cosmic scale. Evolutionary Theory explains the diversity of life through natural selection. Germ Theory identifies microorganisms as the cause of many diseases. The Big Bang Theory describes the origin and evolution of the universe. And the list goes on. These paradigms within the broader domain of science provide specific lenses for scientists to interpret data and conduct research, shaping their methodologies and advancing knowledge.

Consider research as another domain. Here, paradigms include positivism, which focuses on observable, empirical evidence; interpretivism, which helps us understand social phenomena through subjective meanings; pragmatism, which combines quantitative and qualitative methods for practical solutions; constructivism, which asserts that knowledge is constructed through social interactions; and Critical Theory, which uncovers power dynamics and advocates for social change.

Similarly, in law, different paradigms guide legal interpretations. Legal positivism views law as a set of rules from authorities. Natural law is based on moral principles inherent in human nature. Legal realism suggests that law is influenced by social and economic factors. Critical legal studies challenge traditional doctrines and reveal power structures.

Within each domain, paradigms provide the framework for understanding and addressing issues. Additionally, within these paradigms, there are various branches. For example, in law, we have family law, criminal law, commercial law, property law and so on, each focusing on specific legal aspects.

Understanding both the domain and its paradigms helps us interpret information accurately and solve problems effectively. Recognising the branches within a paradigm further refines our approach, ensuring relevant expertise and perspective. So, while the domain gives us the constructed framework within which we operate, paradigms offer specific ways of understanding and solving problems. Identifying these paradigms is crucial for effective sense-making and avoiding misunderstandings.

Construction, deconstruction and reconstruction of content

All knowledge in the world is constructed, and none of us has unmediated access to ultimate reality or 'The Truth'. In other words, all we know is not all there is. While some postmodern philosophers assert that there are no absolutes or truths since 'everything we know is a construct of the mind', there is a fallacy in this reasoning. A more accurate perspective is that there are absolutes – referred to in this book as first-layer reality – but they are not fully accessible or comprehensible to the human mind. The first perspective leads to resignation and the false belief that any interpretation is valid, while the latter keeps us vigilant, acknowledging the existence and importance of absolutes and emphasising the importance of authentic awareness. This distinction is crucial.

Additionally, there is the second-layer reality, or shared reality, which we negotiate through social interaction. While any content that sits within the first-layer reality, like the exact sciences, is immutable and demands our acknowledgment – our opinions on these are irrelevant in the grand scheme of things – the second-layer reality is transformable and negotiable, open to alternative perspectives and interpretations. So, while I align with the postmodern view that 'everything we know is a construct of the mind', I assert that some have taken this view too far by suggesting that 'reality' is a construct. Others may perceive the notion of 'truth' as a conservative or retrograde idea. This may lead them to conclude that everything is mutable, given that we don't have access to the totality of the truth.

Although exact sciences and anything that sits in the realm of first-layer reality demands congruence and authenticity, understanding that all knowledge is constructed necessitates close attention to *how* it is constructed. This is evident in academic scientific research, where the quality of the outcome is judged by the transparency of the research paradigm, its alignment with the research question and the methodologies and methods used. Here, the deconstruction of content, using the Nested Theory of Sense-making as a tool, plays an important role.

I borrowed the term 'deconstruction' from Jacques Derrida. However, it is important to clarify that the way I use this term differs from Derrida's original philosophical context. Derrida used the term to describe a method of critical analysis that seeks to uncover and challenge the underlying assumptions, binaries and hierarchical structures in texts and concepts. In his philosophy, deconstruction involves dismantling these structures to reveal inherent contradictions and ambiguities, demonstrating that meaning is not fixed but fluid and context-dependent. His process of deconstruction aims to show that texts can have multiple interpretations and that the apparent stability of meaning is an illusion. In the context of metacontent and making sense of content in the world, deconstruction refers to the process of untangling and unravelling the complex network of thoughts, beliefs and web of perceptions we have constructed over our lifetimes and that have been compounded by the contextual variables that can impact them. The processes of deconstruction and subsequent reconstruction continue throughout our lifetime. Let me explain why.

As mentioned earlier in this chapter, the metacontent discourse and Nested Theory of Sense-making acknowledge that everyone possesses their own version of metacontent. While the structural components of one's metacontent, such as narrative lenses, perspectives, cognitive maps and mental models, are consistent across individuals, the content within these components varies significantly. This variation is influenced by a person's life experiences, mental conditions, parenting strategies, training in analytical thinking, conception creation, rationality, IQ and other factors. Consequently, each of us has an existing metacontent that functions as an intellectual substrate, providing a layered background platform on which we build our conceptions, cognitive maps, mental models, narratives and, ultimately, our tangible decisions, choices, ideas, preferences and behaviours.

To learn anything new – be it a skill, hobby, language, sport, or when taking on a radically new occupation or starting an entrepreneurial venture, it is essential to alter or expand your metacontent. Think of it as ensuring your foundational metacontent is open and compatible, then expanding it with new elements to support your learning and growth. This is where the processes of deconstruction and reconstruction become critical. Deconstructing your metacontent involves breaking down the cognitive maps, mental models and narratives to identify inaccuracies or limitations. Reconstruction then allows for the reassembly of these components in a more accurate, authentic and effective manner, enhancing your overall understanding and decision-making capabilities. This process promotes a higher degree of awareness at the consciousness level. It supports you in transcending to a higher degree of being, both spiritually and practically. By continuously refining and evolving your metacontent, you can better understand yourself and the world around you, leading to more informed and authentic interactions and decisions. This transformation process is vital for personal growth and developing a more cohesive and effective approach to navigating the complexities of life.

Deconstruction serves several purposes. Untangling complexities helps you clarify how your beliefs, perceptions and understandings were formed and reveals the intricate network of influences you might have received from your parents, culture, the environment and the education system. Furthermore, by deconstructing your thoughts and beliefs, you can identify and rectify any misconceptions and deceptions that have been constructed, whether consciously or unconsciously. It facilitates authenticity by allowing you to dismantle the layers that have contributed to your confusion, enabling you to see clearly and make sense of the world in a way that is congruent with how things actually are. It also facilitates transformation because the deconstruction process allows you to reconstruct your understanding in ways that better serve you, individually and collectively.

The iterative process of continuous deconstruction and reconstruction encourages ongoing transformation because transformation is not something we do once. We are constantly learning and evolving, so transformation is a lifelong journey. So, deconstruction, in the context of sense-making, is the process of untangling and unravelling the complex constructs of our understanding of any piece of content. Doing so can reveal the metacontent for the content in question, allowing us to identify and rectify misconstructed parts. This process of deconstruction does not imply destruction but rather breaking down the construct into more digestible parts for thorough analysis. Let's look into this further.

As discussed in Chapter 5, simply stating that something is 'scientific' does not provide sufficient information to take it as absolute. We need to deconstruct it to understand what that actually means and how that piece of science (a construct) was constructed. Therefore, we need to engage in the deconstruction process. The reconstruction of the constituent parts can lead to either a gradual or a radical reconstruction of the entire initial construct. Why is this important? As discussed in Chapter 1, we often find ourselves in a state of confusion due to our inherent limitations as human beings. To unravel the complexities that cause confusion and suppress our self-expression and active engagement in life, we need to acknowledge that these are constructs in the first place and then deconstruct or break them down into smaller constituent parts so that they become easier to understand. The Nested Theory of Sense-making is a tool that supports us in this deconstruction and reconstruction process.

In summary, the process of deconstruction and reconstruction of any content requires us to:

1. Recognise that all knowledge or content is a construct, accepting that this is the first step in untangling complex ideas.

2. Systematically deconstruct these constructs into their constituent parts, making them more manageable and understandable.

3. Investigate each constituent part using the Nested Theory of Sense-making.

4. Identify the misconstructed parts that need to be transformed or would benefit from alternative perspectives.

5. Reconstruct the identified parts by adopting new, more effective, appropriate and authentic perceptions.

Understanding that all we know has been constructed at one point in time highlights the importance of deconstruction. This process reveals the underlying metacontent, allowing for the identification and reconstruction of misconstructed parts. Let's now look more closely at the process of deconstruction in the context of sense-making and how the Nested Theory of Sense-making supports it.

The deconstruction and reconstruction process

The process of deconstruction involves systematically dismantling the constituent parts of the Nested Theory's seven layers to reveal the misconstructed parts within your existing metacontent relating to any given content.

1. **Initial insight** – Re-examine the spontaneous idea or intuition that initiated your sense-making process. Consider its source and how it influenced your thoughts.

2. **Cognitive map** – Reflect on the origin and influence of your existing perceptions, conceptions, opinions and beliefs about the content in question.

3. **Narratives** – Analyse the personal narratives you have constructed about the content. Evaluate how these stories have shaped your understanding of it and whether they remain valid.

4. **Mental models** – Assess the frameworks you use to understand how things work in relation to the content in question. Determine if these models are still valid or if they need updating.

5. **Perspectives** – Consider the viewpoint from which you are approaching the matter. Explore alternative perspectives that might provide a more comprehensive understanding.

6. **Domain** – Evaluate the constructed frameworks governing the content in question and determine if those frameworks and rules are still relevant.

7. **Paradigms** – Scrutinise the specific paradigms or schools of thought within the domain, identifying whether they still serve you or need reconsidering.

In deconstructing each of the seven layers, it is essential to simultaneously consider the contextual variables, including dynamic elements like time and environmental conditions and the cultural context – how any shared beliefs, values and practices might influence how you make sense of the content within any or all of the layers. By systematically deconstructing these layers, you can untangle the complexities and clarify how you arrived at your current understanding.

The process of deconstruction and reconstruction does not aim to destroy one's constructed reality, although it might lead to a complete metacontent shift in some cases. Instead, it is designed to bring about clarity, congruence and the opportunity for greater authentic awareness and, ultimately, transformation. By dismantling the layers of your constructed reality, you can address misconceptions and continually evolve your understanding of the world. An individual who is committed to continuous deconstruction and reconstruction is inherently committed to transformation. This iterative process allows for ongoing refinement and adaptation of your understanding and beliefs, ensuring you remain relevant and authentic. Through continuous deconstruction and reconstruction, individuals and even entire communities can transform by developing authenticity and integrity in their understanding of and interaction with the world. In this way, new constructs can serve to contribute to the integrity of your life and, potentially, the integrity of humanity.

The dynamic interplay between the seven layers

The seven layers of the Nested Theory of Sense-making are not isolated elements; they are interconnected, each influencing and being influenced by the others. Understanding these interactions is crucial when making sense of any content. Let's explore how some of these layers interact in various dimensions of life, illustrating the nuanced and often subtle ways they shape our understanding, behaviours and decisions.

Initial insight and cognitive map

Imagine you're sitting across from your partner at dinner and you suddenly feel a shift in their mood. This gut feeling, or initial insight, prompts you to ask, 'Is everything okay?' This moment of intuition initiates a deeper exploration into what might be troubling your partner. It might be subtle cues like a change in tone or body language that your conscious mind hasn't yet processed. This initial insight challenges your existing cognitive map – how you perceive your relationship and your partner's emotional state. It might lead you to reassess your perceptions and beliefs about the relationship and how your partner is feeling, leading to authentic awareness and an understanding that is more congruent with how things actually are.

In a professional context, consider an entrepreneur who suddenly has an 'aha' moment while reading an industry report about a new market opportunity. This initial insight is the spark that leads to further research and development. The entrepreneur's cognitive map – comprising their perceptions of the market, customer needs and competitive landscape – evolves to accommodate this new insight, potentially leading to innovative new business strategies and ventures.

Cognitive map and narratives

Our cognitive map shapes the stories we tell ourselves and others. These narratives, in turn, reinforce or alter our cognitive map. For example, in family dynamics, each member has a unique cognitive map shaped by their experiences, beliefs and perceptions. A parent might see strict discipline as a form of love, while a child perceives it as unfair. Recognising this difference can prompt the parent to create new narratives that align better with the child's perspective, fostering a more harmonious relationship.

The collective cognitive map within organisations includes shared beliefs and perceptions about company values, work ethics and goals. This shared understanding shapes the stories employees tell themselves and others about their work environment. For instance, employees might share stories about creative problem-solving and breakthroughs in a company that values innovation, reinforcing the cognitive map that innovation is crucial to success.

Narratives and mental models

The narratives we construct influence our mental models – our understanding of how things work. For instance, a young professional who tells a story about their rapid career advancement might develop a mental model that success comes from hard work and networking. This mental model will guide their future career decisions and actions, reinforcing the narrative of diligence and strategic relationships.

In intimate relationships, the stories partners tell about their shared experiences shape their emotional connection. Positive narratives about overcoming challenges together can strengthen the bond, while negative stories about misunderstandings or conflicts can create distance. By consciously choosing to rewrite their narratives, partners can transform their relationship dynamics and reinforce mental models that promote trust and resilience.

Mental models and perspectives

Mental models influence the perspectives we adopt. Understanding how things work from one perspective can either provide access to or restrict other angles of understanding. For example, a teacher with a mental model that children learn best through hands-on activities will adopt a perspective that values experiential learning. This perspective shapes how they design and implement their lessons, creating a classroom environment that encourages active participation and practical engagement. However, this perspective might restrict the learning of children who are less kinesthetic in their natural or preferred learning style.

In business, leaders rely on mental models to make strategic decisions.

For example, a CEO might use a mental model of competitive analysis to decide how to position their company in the market. This involves understanding how competitors operate, what customers need and how the market is evolving. These mental models help leaders navigate complex business landscapes and make informed decisions, influencing their perspective on market opportunities and threats.

Domain and paradigms

Within each domain, specific paradigms guide thought processes and methodologies. The overarching domain sets the stage for the paradigms that develop within it. For example, in the domain of economics, paradigms such as capitalism and socialism influence policy-making. A government's approach to economic management will differ significantly depending on its adherence to a particular economic paradigm.

In education, paradigms like constructivism and behaviourism shape teaching methods. Educators who follow a constructivist paradigm might focus on student-centred learning, encouraging students to construct knowledge through experience. In contrast, those adhering to behaviourism may emphasise structured curricula and reinforcement techniques. These paradigms influence educational policies, classroom practices and student outcomes, demonstrating the profound impact of paradigms or schools of thought within domains.

The impact of contextual variables on the seven layers

As mentioned, contextual variables, including cultural context, profoundly impact every Nested Theory of Sense-making layer. Let's consider three examples.

Contextual variables and initial insight

Contextual variables create the environment in which initial insights occur. The situational context, including cultural and environmental factors, can spark new ideas and intuitions. For example, an artist living in a culturally rich and diverse neighbourhood might have initial insights inspired by their vibrant surroundings. These insights lead to innovative art that reflects the unique cultural context.

In mental health, contextual variables such as anxiety or depression can significantly impact an individual's sense-making process. These mental states colour perceptions and interpretations, influencing how initial insights are formed and understood. Recognising these contextual influences is essential for providing appropriate support and interventions.

Contextual variables (cultural context) and perspectives

Our cultural context deeply influences our perspectives. Culture provides a lens through which we view the world, impacting our interpretations and viewpoints. In a collectivist culture, individuals might adopt perspectives that emphasise community and group harmony. This cultural context influences how they view personal success and societal roles, shaping their interactions and decisions.

In political campaigns, the cultural context shapes the narratives that resonate with voters. Campaigns craft stories that align with cultural values, using perspectives that reflect shared beliefs and aspirations. These perspectives, in turn, reinforce the cultural context, creating a feedback loop that shapes public opinion and voter behaviour.

Contextual variables (cultural context) and domain

Cultural context shapes the domains within which individuals operate. A culture's values, norms and practices influence the rules and frameworks of specific domains like law, science and art. In a culture that highly values scientific innovation, the domain of science will be robust and well-supported. Researchers in this context are more likely to receive funding and recognition, influencing their work and contributions to the field.

Cultural context also plays a crucial role in shaping legal interpretations and practices in the legal domain. Cultural attitudes towards justice and fairness can influence how laws are applied and enforced.

Lawyers and judges must navigate these cultural nuances to deliver justice effectively, understanding that the domain of law is deeply embedded in cultural values and societal norms.

Comparing and contrasting the metacontent discourse with poststructuralism and postmodernism

The metacontent discourse offers several unique contributions that extend beyond the insights of poststructuralist philosophers and postmodernists. Let's begin with poststructuralism and its comparative limitations.

As a structured framework for sense-making

While poststructuralists like Derrida, Foucault and others critique fixed meanings and highlight the fluidity of knowledge, they fail to provide a structured framework for individuals to navigate and construct their own understanding. In contrast, the metacontent discourse's Nested Theory of Sense-making offers a structured, layered approach – initial insights, cognitive maps, narratives, mental models, perspectives, domains, paradigms within domains and contextual variables – that helps individuals systematically deconstruct and reconstruct their sense-making processes. This practical framework aids in methodically achieving clarity and understanding.

As a way to integrate multiple perspectives into a coherent whole

Poststructuralists emphasise the fragmentation of perspectives and the decentralisation of universal truths but stop short of integrating these perspectives into a coherent whole. The metacontent discourse aligns with the poststructuralist emphasis on multiple perspectives but goes further by integrating these perspectives into a cohesive model. This integration helps construct a holistic understanding of reality, balancing the diversity of viewpoints with the need for coherence.

As a way to become more authentically aware and apply the learnings in practice

Poststructuralism is critical of grand narratives and universal truths but lacks ways to apply the theories in practice. In contrast, the metacontent discourse emphasises the development of authentic awareness and provides a tool – the Nested Theory of Sense-making – for practical application in various domains, such as personal development, leadership and organisational culture. This pragmatic approach ensures that philosophical insights are not just theoretical but actionable.

Postmodernism – aspects of alignment and divergence

Although there are areas of alignment between postmodernism and the metacontent discourse, there are also some divergent aspects. Let's begin with the areas of alignment. Firstly, like the postmodernists, the metacontent discourse questions the existence of fixed, universal truths and, instead, emphasises the constructed nature of knowledge and reality. Secondly, both endeavour to uncover multiple perspectives. More specifically, the metacontent discourse's emphasis on multiple layers and perspectives in the sense-making process aligns with the postmodern focus on the plurality of viewpoints and the rejection of single, authoritative narratives. Thirdly, the metacontent discourse's process of deconstructing existing narratives and mental models to reconstruct more authentic and coherent understandings aligns with postmodern deconstruction techniques.

Moving on to the divergent aspects between the two schools of thought and their approaches, while postmodernism often highlights fragmentation and the lack of coherence, the metacontent discourse aims to provide a structured framework that integrates diverse perspectives into a coherent whole. Like poststructuralism, postmodernism is often critiqued for its lack of practical application. The metacontent discourse addresses this by providing concrete tools and methodologies for personal and organisational development. Lastly, postmodernism can sometimes lean towards a more pessimistic view of the fluidity and instability of meaning. This viewpoint highlights the challenges in finding definitive truths or stable interpretations in a world where meanings are constantly shifting and subject to individual perspectives. For example, those who take pride in their colonial founders may regard them as heroes. However, for others, colonisation can represent racial oppression and injustice. This stark contrast in interpretations can undermine societal cohesion and lead to the categorisation of people. Such polarisation can extend to humanity, where focusing excessively on different interpretations and fluidity prevents us from agreeing on even the basics of communication and interaction, essentially reducing us to a collection of individuals with radically different conceptions of reality.

Imagine if our individual metacontent was so radically different that we would need APIs[108], like computers, just to interact with each other. Picture yourself trying to order a coffee and having to download a 'barista communication app' to ensure your idea of a 'latte' matches the barista's. It would be like living in a world where every conversation required a software update, complete with terms and conditions nobody reads. Instead of simply chatting, we'd spend most of our time ensuring compatibility, like tech support agents in a never-ending conference call. While this example might seem far-fetched, it highlights a genuine risk: without shared understanding, our society could become a patchwork of isolated individuals, each speaking their own incomprehensible language. While acknowledging the fluidity and instability of meaning, the metacontent discourse emphasises the potential for positive evolution and the development of higher consciousness and competency.

In summary, the metacontent discourse builds upon the insights of both poststructuralist and postmodern philosophers by providing a

---

108   An API (Application Programming Interface) is a set of rules that lets different software programs communicate with each other, even if they are written in completely different programming languages. Think of it like a translator that helps two people who speak different languages understand each other.

structured, integrative and practical framework for understanding and navigating the complexities of reality. It bridges the gap between the critique of universal truths and the need for coherent, actionable methodologies, offering a comprehensive approach to individual and collective sense-making that extends beyond theoretical insights.

Transformability vs mutability: navigating the thin line between fact, construct and concept

In comparing and contrasting the metacontent discourse with postmodernism and poststructuralism, we discussed how the metacontent discourse questions the existence of fixed, universal truths or facts and, instead, emphasises the constructed nature of knowledge and reality. But what exactly do we mean by universal truths (facts), and how do they differ from constructs and concepts? Understanding the difference between facts, constructs and concepts is crucial for effective sense-making.

- **Facts** are pieces of information that are empirically verifiable and objectively true within a given context. For example, the statement 'water boils at 100 degrees Celsius at sea level' is a fact that can be repeatedly verified through empirical observation.

- **Constructs** are theoretical ideas developed to explain and organise facts. They are not directly observable but inferred from observable phenomena. For instance, intelligence is a construct because it is not directly measurable. Instead, we use various tests and indicators to infer an individual's level of intelligence.

- **Concepts** are mental representations or ideas that help us understand and categorise our experiences. They are more abstract than constructs and can encompass a wide range of phenomena. For example, the concept of freedom can have different interpretations and meanings depending on the context and perspective. Transformability and mutability are also examples of concepts. They relate to how we perceive and engage with knowledge, facts and constructs. Let's now examine the difference between transformability and mutability.

Transformability versus mutability

Transformability refers to the capacity to deconstruct and reconstruct our understanding of reality. It acknowledges that all we know is constructed by our minds, meaning it can be re-examined, re-evaluated and transformed. This perspective aligns with the metacontent discourse, which emphasises the continuous evolution of one's cognitive maps, mental models, narratives and perspectives.

In contrast, mutability suggests that everything is completely fluid and subject to change. This perspective, which aligns with some aspects of postmodernism, asserts that there are no absolute truths and that all knowledge is perpetually changing, dismissing the importance of objective reality and empirical evidence. If everything is deemed mutable to the point of disregarding the notion of facts, it can lead to relativism, which blurs the line between credible knowledge and opinion. This undermines the foundation of scientific inquiry and the pursuit of objective understanding. For instance, dismissing established scientific consensus on climate change as merely one of many mutable interpretations can hinder effective policy-making and collective action.

Navigating the fine line between transformability and mutability involves recognising the importance of facts while understanding their constructed nature. Facts should not be weaponised or considered absolute. Instead, they should be seen as part of an evolving understanding. Scientific facts derived from empirical evidence are always subject to revision based on new evidence and improved methodologies. This is seen in the progression of scientific knowledge, where previous facts are often re-evaluated and refined. For example, in medicine, what was once considered a fact about the safety and efficacy of a drug can be overturned by new research revealing previously unknown side effects. In astronomy, our understanding of planetary orbits has evolved from the geocentric model to the heliocentric model and further to the understanding provided by general relativity. We also saw the classification of Pluto as a planet change to a dwarf planet. While we can celebrate examples like these as progress, they also illustrate the dynamic and evolving nature of what we consider 'facts'.

Since transformability emphasises that meanings are constructed, they can be deconstructed and reconstructed. This does not mean discarding the notion of truth or facts but approaching them with humility and openness to change. As mentioned in Chapter 5, scientists rely heavily on inductive inferences, even in the exact sciences. So, while the notion of fact is extremely important, it should never be weaponised, as no one has unmediated access to the ultimate truth.

The metacontent discourse and its associated ontological tool, the Nested Theory of Sense-making, promote awareness of the layers of reality and the constructs that shape our understanding. By recognising and deconstructing these layers, individuals can transform their perspectives, interpretations and narratives. This process leads to higher degrees of awareness and intentional consciousness, which, in turn, leads to growth and transformation. In an organisational context, a culture of transformability can lead to more adaptive and innovative environments. Encouraging employees to question assumptions, reframe challenges and embrace continuous learning supports resilience and growth. This approach contrasts with rigid adherence to outdated facts that may stifle innovation and adaptability.

In summary, the contrast between transformability and mutability highlights the importance of a balanced approach to knowledge and sense-making. Transformability offers a pathway to evolve and refine our understanding, whereas extreme mutability risks undermining the foundation of credible knowledge. By integrating these insights into the metacontent discourse and the Nested Theory of Sense-making, a more comprehensive and adaptive approach to human performance and sense-making can be achieved.

Applying the Nested Theory of Sense-making in practice

Now that we have explored the theory in detail, including the interplay between its seven layers and the impact of contextual variables, let's consider a few practical examples and case studies that demonstrate how it can be leveraged and applied in practice within various domains.

Imagine if you were struggling with self-doubt. Using the Nested Theory of Sense-making, you could deconstruct your thoughts and feelings by working through the seven layers to identify your underlying beliefs, perspectives, narratives and contextual influences. You would begin the process by reflecting on the initial insight – let's say it was a negative comment from a peer – before moving on to your cognitive map – a belief that you are not good enough. Considering the 'narratives' layer of the model, you acknowledge that you have told yourself stories about not being good enough. In examining your mental model and perspectives, you realise that your view of yourself as a failure has impacted your mental model of success within the domain (your profession) and the paradigm within the domain (meritocracy). Additionally, you factor in the contextual variables of society's pressure to succeed and your current state of mental health. This deconstruction would support you in identifying which layers need reworking (reconstructing) to adopt a more positive and empowering narrative and transform your relationship with confidence.

Organisations can apply the Nested Theory of Sense-making to enhance their strategic planning and problem-solving processes. For example, when launching a new product, a company can use the model to deconstruct market perceptions, competitor strategies and internal capabilities, ensuring a holistic and informed approach. A tech company developing a new gadget can deconstruct its strategy using the seven layers. The initial insight might be a gap in the market for a user-friendly smart-home device. The cognitive map involves understanding customer needs and preferences. The story could be about how this device simplifies daily routines. Mental models might include usability and integration with existing technologies. To consider various perspectives, they might tap into the viewpoints of designers, engineers, consumers and marketers. The domain is consumer electronics, and the paradigm within the domain is user-centric design. Contextual variables might include current tech trends, consumer behaviour and cultural variables, such as how different cultures use technology.

At a societal level, policymakers and leaders can use the Nested Theory of Sense-making to understand complex social issues. By deconstructing public opinion, historical narratives and cultural contexts, more effective and inclusive policies can be developed to address societal challenges. For example, policymakers can use the model to deconstruct the issue when developing policies to reduce homelessness. Initial insights might come from data on rising homelessness rates. The cognitive map involves understanding the root causes, like unemployment and housing shortages. Stories from affected individuals can provide personal insights. Mental models include understanding how the existing economic and social support systems operate. Perspectives from various stakeholders, including government, NGOs and affected individuals are considered. The domain is social policy, and the paradigms within the domain could be considering the pros and cons between a welfare state and neoliberal approaches. Contextual variables include current economic conditions, the political climate and societal attitudes towards homelessness.

Case studies

Let's now look at three distinctly different hypothetical case studies that demonstrate how we might use the Nested Theory to make sense in various contexts and from different perspectives. The case studies have been randomly selected to showcase how the theory can be leveraged in multiple situations and contexts. As such, you are encouraged to focus objectively on the analysis process without giving undue weight to any hypothetical views presented.

Case study 1: Sense-making in the context of societal conflict

Topic: The trade conflict between the United States and China

The trade conflict between the United States and China offers a fascinating lens through which to explore the Nested Theory of Sense-making. The ontological model provides a robust framework for deconstructing and reconstructing our understanding. By examining the issue through the model's seven layers, we can see how individuals, the general population within each country and external observers make sense of the situation. Let's begin with sense-making of this topic at an individual level.

Making sense of this topic at an individual level

John is an American who works in the manufacturing sector. His journey through the complexities of the trade conflict begins with a sudden increase in job uncertainty due to new tariffs on Chinese goods. This initial insight strikes John unexpectedly as he reads news reports highlighting the impact of these tariffs on the local economy. He feels a wave of anxiety and concern as he realises his livelihood is at stake.

John's cognitive map is shaped by his experiences and beliefs about job security, the economy and global trade. He perceives China as a competitor responsible for the decline in American manufacturing jobs. This perception is reinforced by stories he hears in the media and from his community – narratives that paint a picture of American workers losing out because of China's 'unfair' trade practices.

His mental model of how international trade works is heavily influenced by political rhetoric and media coverage. John believes that tariffs are necessary to protect American jobs and industries from Chinese competition. This mental model shapes his perspective, which is firmly rooted in his role as a worker directly impacted by these trade policies. He sees the conflict primarily through the lens of job security and economic stability.

John adheres to a paradigm that prioritises protectionist policies to safeguard domestic industries. This school of thought influences his support for tariffs and other trade barriers. Additionally, contextual variables such as local economic conditions, the political climate and media representation of the trade conflict further influence John's sense-making process. Furthermore, his cultural context includes a national narrative that emphasises American exceptionalism and economic independence. This context reinforces his belief in the need for protective measures against foreign competition.

Operating within the domain of manufacturing and labour economics, John is guided by the rules and frameworks of this domain, such as supply and demand, labour laws and international trade agreements.

Through this multi-layered analysis, we see that John's understanding of the trade conflict is deeply intertwined with his personal experiences, cultural context and the broader economic environment. This case study illustrates the complex interplay of insights, narratives and contextual factors that shape individual sense-making.

How the general population of the two countries involved might make sense of this topic

The trade conflict's impact extends far beyond individuals like John. The general population in the United States and China also engage in sense-making processes influenced by various factors.

American and Chinese citizens are constantly exposed to media reports and political statements about the trade conflict. These initial insights shape their preliminary understanding and emotional reactions. National narratives and historical experiences influence the cognitive maps of the general populations in both countries. Americans may view China as a rising competitor, while Chinese citizens might see the US as trying to hinder their country's growth.

These cognitive maps give rise to powerful narratives. For example, the story might be about protecting American jobs and standing up to unfair trade practices in the US. However, in China, the narrative might focus on resisting foreign pressure and achieving national pride and economic sovereignty. These narratives simplify complex economic interactions into themes that resonate with the public, reinforcing their cognitive maps.

Mental models develop from these narratives, shaping how people understand the mechanics of international trade. Many Americans might support tariffs to balance trade, while Chinese citizens might see economic policies as a means to strengthen national resilience. Different segments of the population adopt varied perspectives based on their socioeconomic status, profession and political affiliation. In the US, some might prioritise economic nationalism, while others advocate for free trade. In China, perspectives might range from support for the government's stance to concerns about economic stability.

Cultural values and national identity play significant roles in shaping public opinion. In the US, individualism and free-market capitalism might influence views on trade policies. In China, collectivism and national pride could shape the public's response to the conflict. These cultural contexts intertwine with the domains of international economics and geopolitics, guiding public understanding.

Within these domains, different paradigms influence public opinion. In the US, economic paradigms might range from protectionism to neoliberalism. In China, paradigms could include state-led capitalism and economic self-sufficiency. In addition to culture, other contextual variables like economic conditions, political events and media influence further shape how the general population in each country makes sense of the conflict.

This case study demonstrates how the general population of two countries construct their understanding of the trade conflict through a complex interplay of narratives, cultural contexts and economic paradigms. Both personal experiences and broader societal influences shape their sense-making.

How external observers might make sense of this topic

Governments and citizens in other countries also engage in sense-making processes regarding global topics of significance, such as the US/China trade conflict. For example, when governments and policymakers in the European Union receive initial insights from global news coverage and diplomatic communications about the trade conflict, their cognitive maps are generally shaped by their own economic interests and geopolitical positions. Consequently, they would typically view the conflict through the lens of its impact on global trade and their economies.

The stories they tell themselves reflect these perspectives. For example, the EU might frame the trade conflict as challenging global economic stability and testing international trade norms. These narratives influence how the EU might formulate its responses and strategies, guiding its mental models of the potential impacts on global supply chains and international relations.

Different nations have varied perspectives based on their economic and political relationships with the US and China. Some might see the conflict as an opportunity to strengthen their trade positions, while others might be concerned about the ripple effects on global markets. Each nation's cultural context influences these perspectives, shaping their understanding and response to the conflict.

The trade conflict operates within the domains of international relations and global economics. The rules and frameworks of these domains, such as WTO regulations and international trade laws, shape external perspectives. Different paradigms within these domains guide the analysis and response of external observers. Some might emphasise multilateral cooperation and global trade, while others focus on bilateral agreements and economic self-interest.

Other contextual variables, in addition to culture, include regional economic conditions, political alliances and historical relationships with the US and China. These variables influence how external observers make sense of the conflict. For example, countries that are economically dependent on trade with China or the US might have a vested interest in resolving the conflict.

By applying the Nested Theory of Sense-making, we can see how different layers interact to shape the understanding and responses of individuals, the general population and external observers towards the US-China trade conflict. This comprehensive approach reveals the global complexities and nuances of sense-making, highlighting the importance of considering multiple perspectives and contextual factors in understanding and resolving such conflicts.

Case study 2: Sense-making in the context of family dynamics

In the United States, nearly 50% of marriages end in divorce[109], and around 40% of children are born to unmarried parents.[110] These statistics highlight the critical need to better understand family dynamics and relationships. By applying the Nested Theory of Sense-making, we can explore the underlying factors that could influence these dynamics and offer pathways to more harmonious and resilient family structures.

Individual sense-making of family dynamics – a parent's perspective

Sarah is a mother of two who often feels overwhelmed by her children's behaviour. One particularly challenging afternoon, she experiences a pivotal moment of clarity – an initial insight that her usual disciplinary methods are ineffective and that she needs a new approach. This insight doesn't just appear out of nowhere; it's a gut feeling shaped by subtle cues and mounting frustration.

Sarah's cognitive map is shaped by her upbringing, cultural norms and personal experiences. She perceives discipline as essential for

---

109   American Psychological Association.
110   Centers for Disease Control and Prevention.

raising respectful and well-behaved children. This belief system includes ideas about strict rules and consequences, which she inherited from her parents. These deep-seated beliefs form the foundation of her approach to parenting.

The stories Sarah tells herself revolve around her desire to be a good mother and her fear of failing her children. She believes that if she isn't strict, her children will grow up to be irresponsible. These narratives reinforce her cognitive map and guide her actions.

Sarah's mental models of discipline involve clear rules and immediate consequences. She believes that consistency and firmness are key to effective parenting. This mental model shapes her perspective, which is firmly rooted in her role as a parent responsible for shaping her children's future.

Within the domain of child-rearing, Sarah subscribes to a traditional paradigm that emphasises authoritative parenting. This paradigm prioritises structure and discipline as essential components of effective parenting. However, contextual variables such as her stress levels, her relationship with her spouse and external pressures from work and society also play significant roles in her sense-making process. Furthermore, Sarah's cultural context includes societal expectations about parenting and discipline. In her community, respect and obedience are highly valued, reinforcing her approach to discipline.

By examining Sarah's journey through the Nested Theory of Sense-making, we see a complex interplay of beliefs, narratives and contextual influences that shape her approach to parenting. Understanding these layers helps her identify where her strategies may be misaligned with her goals and where adjustments can be made for more effective and empathetic parenting.

Sense-making of family dynamics from the perspective of other family members

Like individuals, families are influenced by societal pressures and media portrayals of the 'ideal family'. These insights shape how family members perceive their roles and responsibilities, often creating a cognitive map based on societal norms and personal experiences.

Family members' cognitive maps are influenced by their backgrounds and experiences. Parents might believe that providing financial support for their children is their most critical role. In contrast, children might prioritise emotional support and quality time. These differing perceptions can lead to conflicts and misunderstandings within the family.

Family members construct narratives that define their identity and values. Their narrative lenses might include themes of hard work, resilience, love and support. However, conflicting narratives can arise, leading to misunderstandings and conflicts. For instance, a parent might justify long working hours by telling a story of sacrifice and dedication, while a child might interpret the same scenario as neglect.

Different family members develop mental models of how a family should function. These models include expectations around communication, conflict resolution and support. Misaligned mental models can lead to frustration and disconnection. For example, one partner might expect open and frequent communication, while the other might prioritise privacy and independence.

Family members bring diverse perspectives based on their roles and experiences. Parents and children often have different viewpoints on issues like discipline, education and freedom. Understanding these multiple perspectives is crucial for encouraging empathy and effective communication.

Family dynamics operate within the broader domain of societal and cultural expectations. The principles and practices within this domain, such as social norms and legal frameworks, guide family interactions and responsibilities. Different paradigms within the domain of family dynamics influence how family members approach issues such as discipline, education and conflict resolution. These paradigms can range from authoritative to permissive parenting styles, each with its own set of beliefs and practices.

Cultural values and norms play a significant role in shaping family dynamics. Cultural context influences attitudes towards gender roles, parenting styles and family responsibilities. For example, in some cultures, extended family involvement is seen as essential, while nuclear family independence is prioritised in others. Other contextual variables, such as financial stability, health, external stressors and social support networks, also significantly impact family dynamics. These variables can either strengthen family bonds or exacerbate existing tensions.

By applying the Nested Theory of Sense-making to family dynamics, we can better understand how these layers interact to shape the overall family environment. This understanding allows families to address conflicts, improve communication and build stronger relationships.

External observers on family dynamics

External observers, such as extended family members, friends and societal institutions, also play a role in shaping family dynamics. These observers bring their own narrative lenses, perspectives and cultural contexts to the conversation.

External observers' cognitive maps are shaped by their experiences and cultural contexts. For example, grandparents might have different expectations for child-rearing based on their generational experiences, while schools might have specific expectations for parental involvement.

External observers contribute to the narratives that families construct about themselves. Positive reinforcement from friends and community members can strengthen family bonds, while criticism can create additional stress. Institutions such as schools, religious organisations and social services might have their own mental models of what constitutes a healthy family environment. These models influence how they interact with and support families.

Different perspectives from external observers can provide valuable insights but also add complexity to family dynamics. For example, a teacher might view family dynamics through the lens of a child's academic performance and behaviour, while a social worker might focus on the overall wellbeing and safety of the child in their home environment.

External observers operate within their respective domains, such as education, social services or community support. The principles and practices within these domains influence how they interact with and perceive family dynamics. Furthermore, various paradigms within each domain guide the actions and recommendations of external observers. For example, a health professional might operate within a paradigm emphasising mental health and emotional wellbeing, influencing their advice to families.

Contextual variables such as community resources, societal attitudes and policy frameworks significantly impact how external observers interact with families. These variables can either support or hinder family wellbeing. Additionally, cultural differences can lead to varied expectations and interpretations of family dynamics. For instance, what is considered appropriate discipline in one culture might be viewed as harsh or lenient in another.

The Nested Theory of Sense-making provides a comprehensive framework for understanding the complexities of family dynamics. By deconstructing and examining each layer, individuals and families can untangle the intricacies of their perceptions, narratives and beliefs, leading to more authentic and informed relationships. This iterative process of deconstruction and reconstruction encourages continuous transformation, empowering families to adapt and thrive in an ever-changing world.

Case study 3: Sense-making in the context of identity

Identity is at the core of how we understand ourselves and interact with the world. Today, issues surrounding identity are more pronounced than ever. The rise of identity politics and tokenism has led to widespread confusion about who we are, both as individuals and as members of society. According to a Pew Research Center study, about 77% of Americans say that gender identity and racial equality are significant issues facing the country today.[111] However, these issues are often oversimplified or misrepresented in public discourse, leading to a lack of authentic awareness and genuine understanding within the general population.

By applying the Nested Theory of Sense-making, we can explore how identity issues are constructed, offering a path toward deeper, more authentic self-awareness and societal cohesion.

Individual sense-making: navigating personal identity

Alex is a young professional grappling with their identity in a multi-cultural urban environment. One day, during a diversity training session at work, Alex experiences a moment of clarity – an initial insight that their feelings of not fitting in stem from deeper issues related to their racial and gender identity. This insight doesn't just appear out of nowhere; for Alex, it's a gut feeling shaped by subtle cues and mounting frustration.

Alex's cognitive map is shaped by their diverse background and experiences. Growing up in a biracial family, Alex has always felt torn between cultural expectations and norms. This cognitive map is further complicated by societal messages about race and gender, which often conflict with their personal experiences. These deep-seated beliefs form the foundation of Alex's identity, influencing how they perceive themselves and their place in the world.

The stories Alex tells themselves revolve around being different and not fully belonging to any single group. These stories are reinforced by experiences of tokenism, where Alex feels they are only recognised

---

111 Pew Research Center. 2022, June 28. Views of gender in the U.S. Retrieved from https://www.pewresearch.org/fact-tank/2022/06/28/views-of-gender-in-the-u-s/ Pew Research Center. 2023, June 23. 5 key findings about LGBTQ+ Americans. Retrieved from https://www.pewresearch.org/fact-tank/2023/06/23/5-key-findings-about-lgbtq-americans/

superficially for their diversity rather than their unique qualities and contributions. The narrative lens Alex has created causes a sense of isolation and confusion.

Alex's mental models of identity are shaped by a variety of influences, including mainstream media and the current trends on college campuses, which often promote fluid and non-binary views on gender and race. On the other hand, more established and traditional perspectives emphasise binary views on these matters. As a young person experiencing an identity crisis – a common challenge – Alex is caught between these conflicting views. This dual influence creates confusion in determining which metacontent to tap into, making it difficult for Alex to integrate all aspects of themselves into a coherent whole. This struggle underscores the complexities of navigating identity in today's diverse cultural landscape.

Operating within the domain of social identity and inclusion, Alex navigates principles and practices related to diversity, equity and inclusion. Within this domain, they encounter paradigms that range from tokenism – where diversity is acknowledged but not deeply valued – to genuine inclusivity, where individual uniqueness is celebrated and integrated into the community.

Contextual variables such as the current political climate, media representation of identities and personal relationships also play a significant role in Alex's sense-making process. Their cultural context includes a workplace that promotes diversity but sometimes falls short of inclusivity. Society's broader cultural debates about identity politics and equality also shape Alex's views and experiences.

Through this multi-layered analysis, we can see that Alex's sense-making process involves a complex interplay of insights, narratives and contextual influences that shape their understanding of identity. By deconstructing these layers, Alex can reconstruct a more authentic and empowered sense of self.

How society might make sense of identity

The general population is continually exposed to media portrayals and political rhetoric about identity. These initial insights shape public perceptions and discussions about identity politics, often simplifying complex issues and creating stereotypes.

Cultural norms, historical contexts and personal experiences influence the general population's cognitive maps. People often develop beliefs about identity based on what they see and hear from influential sources, such as news outlets, social media and community leaders. These beliefs can form a collective understanding of identity that shapes societal attitudes and behaviours.

Society constructs narratives around identity that can either reinforce stereotypes or challenge them. For example, the story that diversity is a strength is often countered by narratives that view it as a source of division. These conflicting narrative lenses can shape public opinion and policy, influencing how people interact with each other and understand their own identities.

Mental models of identity within the general population often rely on fixed categories, such as race, gender and nationality. These models can limit the understanding of identity as a dynamic and evolving construct, leading to oversimplified views and policies that fail to address the breadth and complexities of human experience.

Different segments of the population often hold varied perspectives on identity issues based on their socioeconomic status, cultural background and personal experiences. For example, younger generations might have more fluid views on gender and sexuality than older generations, reflecting broader societal shifts in understanding and acceptance.

Identity politics and social justice movements operate within the broader domain of societal and cultural discourse. This domain includes debates about rights, representation and equality, which guide public understanding and engagement with identity issues.

Different paradigms within the domain of identity politics influence public discourse and policy. For instance, tokenism acknowledges diversity but often fails to address deeper issues of inclusion and equity, while paradigms focusing on intersectionality and systemic change seek to address the root causes of inequality.

Cultural values and societal norms significantly influence public attitudes towards identity. In some cultures, collectivism and communal identity are emphasised, while individualism and personal identity are more prominent in others. These cultural contexts can shape how identity is perceived and discussed, influencing both personal sense-making and collective social policies. Other contextual variables such as economic conditions, political events and media representation also play crucial roles in shaping public opinion on identity issues. For example, economic downturns can exacerbate tensions and lead to scapegoating of marginalised groups, while positive media representation can promote understanding and acceptance.

Adding another layer to this complexity is the confusion between our 'whatness', 'howness' and 'whoness', as discussed in my book *BEING*.[112] In the context of human beings, whatness refers to the common qualities that make us human, such as authenticity, responsibility, compassion, commitment, courage, fear, anxiety and care. These are universal attributes shared by all humans. On the other hand, howness is about how each individual *relates* to these qualities. One person might relate to courage through acts of bravery in public speaking or standing up against injustice, while another might freeze, shut down or withdraw in the face of difficult circumstances when challenged or frightened. The Nested Theory of Sense-making helps to articulate these differences, highlighting the subjective nature of howness.

Whoness is even more complex and often intangible. It represents the unique aggregation of an individual's qualities and characteristics, which can be challenging to define with manufactured labels. This is

---

112   Tashvir, A. 2021. *BEING – The source of power.* Engenesis Publications: Sydney.

where much of today's identity confusion stems from. People often try to clarify their whoness through socially constructed labels, leading to identity crises and the pitfalls of identity politics. For instance, first-layer reality qualities like date of birth or name are clear-cut, while aspects like gender and the associated roles, such as who should be the primary income earner versus who can biologically bear children, blur the lines between biological facts and social constructs. The problem lies in our use of the word 'identity', which we apply to vastly different concepts. For instance, while your birth date is a fixed point in history that cannot be changed, your name, which is assigned to you, can be easily and technically altered. By applying the Nested Theory of Sense-making to the general population, we can better understand how societal attitudes towards identity are constructed and how they can be deconstructed and reconstructed to foster a more inclusive and equitable society.

External observers on identity

External observers, such as international organisations, foreign governments and global media, provide additional perspectives on identity issues within a society. Such insights are often shaped by their cultural contexts and geopolitical interests.

External observers' cognitive maps are influenced by their understanding of global diversity and human rights. For example, an international human rights organisation might view identity issues through the lens of equality and justice, advocating for policies that promote inclusion and protect minority rights. These perspectives help frame the global discourse on identity politics, highlighting both progress and ongoing challenges.

External observers construct narratives about identity issues in other countries based on their observations and interpretations. These stories can either highlight progress and best practices or expose challenges and injustices. For instance, a global media network might report on identity politics in the US, framing it as a struggle for civil rights and social justice, influencing international perceptions and policies.

Institutions such as the United Nations and international NGOs have mental models of identity that emphasise universal human rights and the importance of diversity. These models guide their advocacy and policy recommendations, shaping how they engage with and support various social movements worldwide. For example, the United Nations' 2030 Agenda for Sustainable Development[113] suggests investing billions of dollars to steer the general narrative on these issues for various intentions.

Different nations have varied perspectives on identity issues based on their own experiences and cultural contexts. For example, a European government might view American identity politics through the lens of its own multicultural policies and integration challenges, offering diverse solutions and critiques.

External observers operate within the domain of international relations and global governance. The principles and practices within this domain, such as diplomatic protocols and international treaties, shape their interactions with, and perceptions of, identity politics in other countries. Different paradigms within these domains guide the actions and recommendations of external observers. For example, some might prioritise diplomatic engagement, while others might focus on direct intervention and policy advocacy.

Cultural differences can lead to varied expectations and interpretations of identity issues. For instance, what is considered progressive in one country might be regarded as radical in another. External observers operate within their own cultural contexts, influencing how they perceive and engage with identity issues in other societies. Other contextual variables, such as geopolitical interests, economic relationships and historical ties, also significantly impact how external observers make sense of identity issues. These factors can either support or hinder efforts to promote understanding and cooperation, influencing international relations and global solidarity.

---

113   https://sdgs.un.org/goals

By understanding the sense-making processes of external observers nationally and globally, societies can better navigate international expectations and leverage worldwide support to address identity issues and promote social cohesion on a global scale.

Conclusion

In this chapter, we learned that everything in existence, from living beings and physical matter to events, ideas, concepts, theories and narratives, constitutes content. Content encompasses all that exists, including ourselves, our partners, our partners, friends, colleagues, leaders, dogs, cats, birds, every element in nature and even the abstract.

To effectively interact with, process and understand any content – including ourselves, others and our collective contributions – we need access to deeper layers of understanding below the surface. Metacontent refers to the intellectual substrate that aids in making sense of any content. By offering a more holistic view of the world, metacontent shapes our perceptions, informs our decisions and guides our actions. It is crucial for accurate understanding and effective interaction with all types of content, from the complexities of global politics to the subtleties of personal experiences and relationships.

The Nested Theory of Sense-making is an ontological model that integrates insights from science and philosophy to give us access to the metacontent concerning anything we are trying to understand. It provides a high-level yet accurate structure to minimise vagueness and ambiguity when it comes to making sense of any content. By deconstructing and examining each of its seven layers while also taking into account the prevailing contextual variables, we can untangle the intricacies of our perceptions, narratives and beliefs, leading to more authentic and informed sense-making and supporting us in navigating the complexities of our constructed realities. This iterative process of deconstruction and reconstruction encourages continuous transformation, empowering individuals, groups, communities and societies to adapt and thrive in an ever-changing world.

CHAPTER 10

The Nested Theory and Human Performance

O f all the complex entities in the world, human beings are perhaps the most intricate. In exploring human behaviour and performance throughout history, scientists, philosophers and others have tried to obtain a deeper understanding beyond surface-level observations but struggled to find a way to do so comprehensively. Others have remained fixated on the behavioural aspects, ignoring what's driving those behaviours. Why is it necessary to delve so deeply beneath the surface? Simply put, what human beings say and how we behave – the observable aspects – don't always reveal our true intentions. To uncover what influences our decisions, behaviours and, ultimately, the results we achieve or how we perform, we must look deeper to understand not only our whatness – the qualities we all share with other members of our species – but also our howness – how we relate to and act upon each quality. To only pay attention to the surface-level behaviours is like ignoring what lies beneath the tip of an iceberg or only paying attention to your car's exterior, neglecting all the constituent parts that ensure it runs effectively.

As discussed at length in the previous chapter, the Nested Theory of Sense-making offers a structured approach to making sense of and understanding any content. By deconstructing content and identifying its underlying metacontent, the theory enables us to explore and deepen our conception of the content in question, as seen in the case study examples. Applying the theory in the context of human performance helps us delve beyond surface-level observations of ourselves and others. In this way, the theory supported the mapping out of the metacontent of human performance and effectiveness, which led to the development of the Being Framework and its associated ontological model, assessment tool and transformation methodology. In this chapter, we explore how the Nested Theory of Sense-making has been contextualised in the domain of human performance to create the Being Framework and how it can be applied to enhance human performance.

Integrating the metacontent discourse and the Nested Theory of Sense-making into the Being Framework

As you now know, the Nested Theory of Sense-making is an ontological model that supports us to delve deep beneath the surface to uncover the metacontent or intellectual substrates and build a more complete picture of anything we are studying. Contextualising the metacontent discourse and the Nested Theory in the realm of human performance led to the development of the being discourse and the Being Framework.

What is the Being Framework and how was it developed?

The Being Framework is a dynamic and comprehensive framework that represents a holistic map of the metacontent of human beings within the domain of performance and effectiveness. It enables individuals to navigate the complexities of human performance, encouraging greater self-awareness, awareness of others and overall effectiveness. As a multi-layered paradigm, the framework maps out the metacontent of human performance and effectiveness by identifying the qualities that constitute the overall integrity of one's being. 'Being' is a cluster word encompassing initial insights, thoughts, emotions, feelings, perceptions, conceptions, decisions, choices, actions and behaviours – essentially, one's manner and attitudes combined with decisions and behaviours, reflecting how a human being carries themselves.

The framework was constructed by synthesising insights from philosophy and science and tapping into the metacontent discourse, which gives us access to the intellectual substrates deep below the surface to explore the deeper meanings, assumptions and cognitive frameworks that shape our perceptions and behaviours. Its construction also leveraged the Nested Theory of Sense-making, which provided a structured approach to understand and interpret the complexities of human experience. The framework is essentially a contextualised version of the Nested Theory of Sense-making applied specifically to human performance and effectiveness. It is designed to help individuals and collectives – like teams, organisations and societies – make sense of themselves and others, ultimately enhancing their participation and interaction within the world.

The development of the Being Framework involved a thorough review and deconstruction of major paradigms within human performance. These paradigms were reconstructed to form a more robust and meaningful framework by identifying areas that were not well-constructed. This process was not performed from a specialisation perspective, as is typically the case in academic settings, where you need to dive deeply into highly niche areas that remain unanswered or need more attention to extend the literature of that particular, often very specific niche. Instead, it was undertaken from a philosophical perspective, focusing on the metacontent in intellectual layers proposed by various paradigms in the domain of human performance.

My approach emphasised discovery and articulation of metaphysical – particularly ontological and phenomenological – axioms. While incorporating a level of engineering in synthesising human performance, the focus was far more on these philosophical elements than scientific knowledge, due, in part, to the subjective characteristics of human performance. This comprehensive process facilitated the articulation and reconstruction of the framework's key constructs and core components.

Why did I create a new paradigm? In deconstructing some of the existing dominant paradigms operating within the domain of human performance using the Nested Theory of Sense-making's seven layers, it became increasingly apparent that each ignored the potential to transform holistically and the means to achieve this. For example, Personality Type Theory categorises people into different personality types and assumes that is how they are inherently programmed to be. Similarly, Temperament Theory suggests our temperament is hardwired from birth with little hope for transformation. These approaches treat human beings as fixed objects doomed to be dealing with their shortcomings for life. Some experts even go so far as to suggest that we should learn to just deal with our dysfunctional sides.

Behaviourism is another approach favoured by many that I deconstructed using the structure the Nested Theory provides. Behaviourists primarily focus on individual behaviours or, at best, behavioural patterns and habits. The issue with Behaviourism is that it primarily focuses on observable behaviours and the external stimuli that influence them, often neglecting the internal drivers and mental processes behind those behaviours. Its focus on surface-level stimuli and responses stems from the foundational principles laid out by key figures in behaviourism like J.B. Watson[114], B.F. Skinner[115] and W.M. Baum.[116] Critics argue that behaviourism's focus on surface-level stimuli neglects the deeper psychological and emotional factors driving behaviour, thus providing an incomplete understanding of

114 Watson, J. B. 1913. Psychology as the behaviorist views it. *Psychological Review*, 20(2), 158—177.

115 Skinner, B. F. 1953. *Science and Human Behavior.* New York: Macmillan.

116 Baum, W. M. 2005. *Understanding Behaviorism: Behavior, Culture, and Evolution.* Wiley-Blackwell.

human psychology.[117] It is a psychological approach that encourages us to correct individual dysfunctional behaviours, patterns and habits and prepare our environment to be conducive to this. It also begs the question: who defines which behaviours are acceptable and which are not?

More modern approaches like Cognitive Behavioural Therapy (CBT) focus on uncovering cognitive distortions and limiting beliefs that lead to maladaptive behaviours. While more effective in some cases, CBT's focus on rapid behavioural changes or on individual parts in isolation fails to consider the relationship between various aspects of us. In deconstructing the effectiveness of this method, I found several references critiquing the effectiveness of CBT when it focuses on surface-level stimuli. For example, C.R. Blease discusses the limitations of CBT in addressing deeper, underlying psychological issues in a journal article. The article highlights her concerns about the therapy's tendency to focus on reducing symptoms rather than exploring the root causes of mental health problems.[118] Similarly, R.G.T. Gipps critically examines the philosophical foundations of CBT, arguing that its focus on cognitive restructuring often overlooks the complexity of human psychological experiences and the need for a more holistic approach.[119] Furthermore, there have been documented cases of publication bias in studies supporting CBT, suggesting that the therapy's effectiveness may be overstated, highlighting the need for more comprehensive approaches that address not just symptoms but also underlying psychological conditions.[120]

---

117   Leahey, T. H. 2000. *A History of Psychology: Main Currents in Psychological Thought.* Prentice-Hall.

118   Blease, C. R. 2015. 'Talking more about talking cures: Cognitive behavioural therapy and informed consent'. *Journal of Medical Ethics*, 41(10), 750—755.

119   Gipps, R. G. T. 2013. Cognitive behavior therapy: A philosophical appraisal. In Fulford, K. W. M., Davies, M., Gipps, R. G. T., Graham, G., Sadler, J. Z., Stanghellini, G., & Thornton, T. (Eds.), *The Oxford Handbook of Philosophy and Psychiatry* (pp.485—501). Oxford University Press.

120   Cuijpers, P., Smit, F., Bohlmeijer, E., Hollon, S. D., & Andersson, G. 2010. 'Efficacy of cognitive-behavioural therapy and other psychological treatments for adult depression: Meta-analytic study of publication bias.' *The British Journal of Psychiatry*, 196(3), 173—178.

Some of the approaches touched on here have merit. However, they all miss fundamental requirements that facilitate transformation. That's primarily because, while these and many other disciplines of mainstream modern psychology focus on fixing or refining individual behaviours or, at best, behavioural and cognitive patterns, they ignore the deeper, more subtle, yet far more important qualities driving our behaviours. It is those deeper qualities and drivers of our behaviours that I set out to define and map out through a process of reconstruction, resulting in the novel paradigm explored in this chapter.

The approach with the creation of the Being Framework was to deconstruct the complexity of human beings – in the domain of performance and effectiveness – into smaller, more manageable chunks. The goal was to discover our whatness and howness, while also paying attention to the ontological and phenomenological meanings behind each identified quality, referred to in the framework as 'distinctions'. Once there is clarity on the whatness, individuals and teams can leverage the framework's tools to gain visibility on how they are being (howness), identify their blindspots or shadows and work on restoring or reconstructing their integrity (wholeness) for enhanced performance and effectiveness.

The Being Framework supports us in developing cognitive maps and knowledge graphs of our collective whatness and individual subjective howness. More specifically, it helps us understand what we are (our whatness) within the domain of human performance and effectiveness and the paradigm of leadership, and how we are being (howness) in relation to that whatness. The ontological model facilitates the development of intentional consciousness or awareness regarding these constituent parts, which either contribute to or compromise our overall integrity or the integrity of our being. It also enables us to address these aspects through provided mental models, guiding us through the transformation process. Last but not least, it offers practical tools to measure how we are being, transform and project our unique being – who we were born to be – to the world.

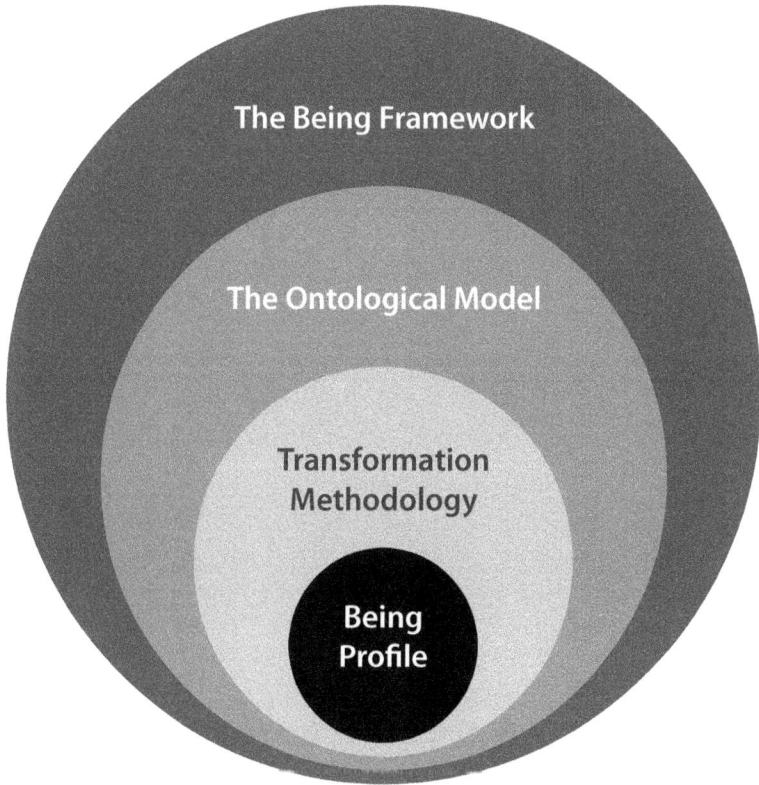

Figure 7

The Being Framework – the model shows a helicopter view
of the paradigm and its core components

The Being Framework Ontological Model – Here is where the 31 qualities of human beings tied to our performance and effectiveness – referred to as 'Aspects of Being' – are mapped out. It gives us the ability to see the qualities of ourselves (how we are being) and others with great clarity and depth, offering a new, more powerful lens through which to see human beings, including ourselves. This newfound awareness can reshape your perceptions and the narratives you've constructed about human behaviour and performance, including the stories you've told yourself and others about yourself.

Transformation Methodology – A practical tool that supports an individual to undergo a process of transformation in an area that is impeding their effectiveness. It involves a series of processes and practical exercises that support you in reconstructing more authentic perceptions, conceptions, opinions, beliefs, mental models and perspectives and working towards a higher degree of awareness and effectiveness in the specific areas you need to polish.

The Being Profile – The core assessment tool associated with the Being Framework and the world's most comprehensive and effective ontological profiling tool for performance, effectiveness and leadership by which all Aspects of Being can be accurately measured.

The philosophy and approach behind the Being Framework is that when your being is relatively polished and you are committed to maintaining its integrity, effective behaviour unfolds. Multiply this on a collective scale, and the benefits will be apparent on a larger scale. Correcting behaviour is like applying a quick fix to a software bug, only addressing the immediate issue on the surface. In contrast, transforming the Aspects of Being – of which there are 31 in the Being Framework – is akin to rewriting the underlying code, ensuring the system's stability and performance at a fundamental level. Just as software occasionally requires updates and maintenance to stay efficient and secure, our various Aspects of Being also need ongoing attention and refinement to achieve and maintain the overall integrity of our being.

From a systematic perspective, behavioural approaches are like checking and refining the data inputs/outputs, cognitive approaches are like software reprogramming, while ontological approaches – like the Being Framework – deeply examine the human operating system. Firmware – essentially the foundational layer of embedded instructions and settings – initialises and manages the basic functions of our human 'hardware' (our physical and biological systems). Just as the firmware is essential for a computer's basic operations before any software (like an OS) can run, our foundational beliefs, instincts and subconscious patterns (our 'human firmware') underlie all our thoughts, behaviours and deeper existential inquiries.

So, while your computer may not appreciate it when you spill coffee on the keyboard, it will still dutifully boot up because the firmware tells it to – just as our deeper, often unnoticed patterns keep us going, even when life gets messy. Metacontent is like the combination of all of these elements: the input/output processes, the software and operating system and the firmware. It's the overarching platform or construct that helps us make sense of ourselves and the world, integrating all levels of our experiences and functions.

The Being Framework Ontological Model

Building on the Nested Theory, the Being Framework Ontological Model was created to make sense of human performance. The structure provided by the theory was instrumental in its development, as you will see shortly. The ontological model offers a structured way to understand how you, as an example of the class 'human being', are being and how you relate to various aspects of life. For instance, everyone has a relationship with qualities like awareness, vulnerability, authenticity, fear, care, courage and commitment. While these attributes are common to all humans, each individual relates to them in their own way. The ontological model outlines these attributes as metadata, and how you relate to each quality is the data. Together, this metadata and data help to extract meaningful insights about you, including the areas – the missing parts or shadows – you need to reconstruct in order to restore integrity (wholeness).

Another way to look at the Being Framework Ontological Model is that it maps out the whatness of human beings in the domain of performance and effectiveness. In other words, it identifies and organises human qualities (Aspects of Being) into a structured framework. The goal in its development was to determine what qualities matter most in contributing to an individual's overall integrity and effectiveness in the context of human performance. In addition to whatness, the model's ontological distinctions support us in considering *how we are being* (howness) or how we, as individuals or teams, relate to and act upon each of the 31 Aspects of Being. The healthier our relationship with each Aspect of Being, the more they contribute to our overall integrity.

The Being Framework Ontological Model, as shown, has been constructed in a four-layered format and designed to allow us to visualise, break down, digest and articulate the qualities we share as human beings and work out how we individually and collectively relate to them. In this way, it offers a powerful lens through which to see human beings, ourselves and others. It is structured in four layers:

1. **Meta Factors** – Awareness, integrity and effectiveness are foundational qualities that shape overall performance. Awareness has an impact on all Aspects of Being, integrity is impacted by our relationship with the Primary Ways of Being and Moods, while all Aspects of Being contribute to our effectiveness.

2. **Moods** – Also referred to as 'states of mind', moods influence one's emotional and mental state. They are the qualities that set the scene, give context to our participation and are at the heart of what drives us deep down. They are also the channels through which we disclose ourselves to the world. The four Moods in the model are fear, anxiety, care and vulnerability. Put simply, the healthier our relationship with these states of mind, the more effectively we disclose ourselves to the world.

3. **Primary Ways of Being** – These distinguish the fundamental ways through which we project the true manifestation of who we are and how we experience ourselves to be in the world. These primal qualities, which include responsibility, commitment, courage and authenticity, impact our behaviour, performance and the subsequent results we produce in life. In other words, they determine the way we contribute to our work, engage in relationships, participate in life and also how we experience and expand on the reality around us. Primary Ways of Being are deep and subtle and, therefore, might not be clearly visible in our behaviours.

4. **Secondary Ways of Being** – These support us in bridging the gap between what lies in the deeper parts of us (Meta Factors, Moods and Primary Ways of Being) and what is presented on the surface. They are readily observable, as we project our Secondary Ways of Being through our decisions, actions and behaviours. They include qualities like confidence, assertiveness, resourcefulness and resilience.

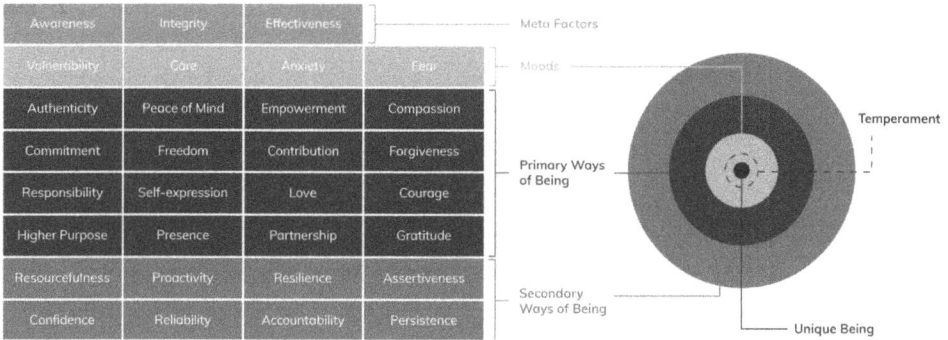

Figure 8

The Being Framework Ontological Model

The nature of the qualities identified in the model resides firmly within the ontological domain. These existential characteristics transcend empirical measurement; they relate to the essence of human existence and experience. For example, courage, fear and anxiety reflect the existential confrontation with life's uncertainties and the inherent vulnerabilities of existence. Care and responsibility involve the recognition of one's interconnectedness with others and the world, acknowledging the impact of one's actions within these relationships. And awareness and presence denote the depth of engagement with the present moment and the capacity to perceive one's existential situation fully. These and other qualities in the ontological model represent the 'being' in human beings, the subjective experience of existence and how individuals navigate their existence, make meaning and relate to themselves, others and the world.

However, while the qualities themselves are ontological, the investigation into the relationships between these dispositions, especially as constructed within the four layers of the model, may introduce ontic elements – observable, measurable aspects of being. If you seek to study or measure how these qualities manifest in behaviour or influence outcomes, you're moving into the ontic domain. For instance, how does someone's commitment (an ontological quality) influence their persistence in tasks (an observable behaviour)? Furthermore, structuring these dispositions into four layers implies a systematic organisation that could be subjected to empirical analysis, which is an ontic approach. Each layer might represent different aspects or manifestations of these qualities, from more internal, personal experiences to outward, observable behaviours.

So, while the fundamental qualities the Being Framework Ontological Model explores are ontological – concerning the essence of human experience and existence – the method by which you might explore their interactions and layered construction can involve ontic elements. Therefore, the model represents a synthesis of ontological depth with ontic qualities such as assertiveness and confidence, offering a comprehensive approach to understanding human beings within the domain of performance and effectiveness. This integration allows for a rich exploration of human dispositions that honours the depth and complexity of human existence while also providing avenues for empirical investigation and practical application.

The role of distinctions in human performance

Do you ever struggle to find the right word to convey a particular meaning? Even philosophers, writers and poets sometimes find themselves limited by words and language. There is a valid reason for this: meanings are beyond words. Words are tools – a means to communicate and describe both transcendent and constructed meanings. However, the way people relate to various words can differ. The word responsibility is a good example. Many people link responsibility with duty and obligation, such as who is responsible for completing a task or project. Alternatively, they might think of it in terms of blame, like identifying who caused a problem or overlooked an error.

From an ontological standpoint, responsibility isn't about either of the aforementioned common definitions, even though they are widely accepted and used. Ontologically, responsibility is about being willing to take charge of your life, irrespective of circumstances or who is at fault, owning your role in any situation, and choosing to take action. Consider the Being Framework's ontological distinction for responsibility.

The Being Framework ontological distinction of responsibility

Responsibility is being the primary cause of the matters in your life, regardless of their source. It is the extent to which you choose to respond rather than react to them. Responsibility is distinguished by how you honour the autonomy that you have as a human being and is considered the power to influence the affairs, outcomes and consequences you are faced with. Responsibility is not about blaming or determining whose fault it is. Instead, it is to intentionally choose, own, cause and bring about outcomes that matter, work and produce results while also being answerable for the impact and consequences.

A healthy relationship with responsibility indicates that you have the power to influence the circumstances you find yourself in and/or cause. Others may consider you capable of appropriately responding to matters, which is a prerequisite to producing and bringing to fruition effective results. You fully accept ownership of both outcomes and consequences and have the capacity to make informed, uncoerced decisions. You are unquestionably the active agent in your life.

An unhealthy relationship with responsibility indicates that you may often be stuck, experience a loss of power, and are a victim of circumstances. You frequently experience being disarmed, as though you have no choice in influencing outcomes and there is an inevitability about your future. You may be inclined to self-sabotage and make repetitive complaints without seeking, putting forward and implementing solutions. You frequently make excuses for your lack of accomplishments while abdicating or avoiding consequences. You may be considered ineffective in consistently fulfilling the promises you make and producing intended results. You are a passive victim in your life. Alternatively, you may live life from the viewpoint of being the sole cause of matters and exert your will onto your surroundings and others or be over-responsible and attempt to control all matters all the time. You may also expect that matters should always go your way.[121]

The anatomy of a distinction

Each of the 31 Aspects of Being has an ontological distinction and is structured uniformly with a distinct anatomy, as illustrated by the example of responsibility and depicted below:

1. The ontological distinction of the term.

2. A description of what a healthy relationship with this Aspect of Being entails.

3. A description of the shadow side of the Aspect of Being, or what an unhealthy relationship with it looks like.

Rather than mere definitions, these 'distinctions' offer vivid depictions of each disposition or quality, highlighting healthy or effective relationships with them. These are termed 'stable dispositions,' derived from qualitative studies. Various forms of 'shadows' – or unhealthy relationships with these Aspects of Being – are also outlined, capturing the 'whatness' or essence shared by all human beings in character and kind. Refer to *BEING*[122] or *Human Being*[123] to read all 31 distinctions.

Notably, the Being Framework also distinguishes between first and second-layer reality, as described earlier in the book. This is a

---

121 Tashvir, A. 2021. *BEING – The source of power.* (p.277). Engenesis Publications: Sydney.

122 Tashvir, A. 2021. *BEING – The source of power.* Engenesis Publications: Sydney.

123 Tashvir, A. 2022. *Human Being – Illuminating the reality beneath the facade.* Engenesis Publications: Sydney.

critical distinction because first-layer reality refers to the absolutes in existence, such as axiomatic laws that are not subject to change or interpretation, while second-layer reality represents the constructed and negotiated aspects of reality shaped by human interactions, cultural norms and individual perceptions. The distinction between these layers helps address the semantic problem where different meanings are overloaded onto the word 'reality', potentially misleading communication. By recognising these layers, the Being Framework aligns with the metacontent discourse and the Nested Theory of Sense-making, providing a clearer understanding of how reality is constructed and perceived.

Beyond quick fixes – embracing holistic transformation

To address dysfunctions, many people favour rapid behavioural changes and quick fixes over deep, meaningful transformation. Studies indicate several reasons for succumbing to the temptation of a quick fix. They include:

1. **Instant gratification** – Quick fixes often provide immediate, tangible results, which can be very appealing as they provide an immediate sense of accomplishment and relief.[124]

2. **Modern society's preference for rapid results** – People today value speed and efficiency, which has resulted in a cultural perception that faster solutions are more desirable than solutions that might take longer but result in more sustainable outcomes.[125]

3. **Less effort and commitment** – Rapid behavioural changes usually require less effort, time and commitment compared

---

124 Baumeister, R. F., & Tierney, J. 2011. *Willpower: Rediscovering the Greatest Human Strength*. Penguin Press.

125 Seligman, M. E. P. 2002. *Authentic Happiness: Using the New Positive Psychology to Realize Your Potential for Lasting Fulfillment*. Free Press.

to deep, meaningful transformations, which can involve prolonged and intensive work.[126]

4. **Perceived effectiveness** – Many people believe that quick fixes are effective because they address the symptoms of problems directly, even if they do not tackle the root causes.[127]

5. **Accessibility** – Quick fixes are often perceived as being more accessible than other options because they are typically heavily marketed as easy solutions that can be integrated into a busy lifestyle, making them more attractive to a broader audience.[128]

6. **Fear of fundamental change** – Deep, meaningful transformation often requires confronting uncomfortable truths and making significant changes, which can be daunting and induce fear. Quick fixes allow people to avoid this discomfort.[129]

As you can see, addressing dysfunctional behaviours quickly and directly, often through behaviouralism, can be tempting. We might focus on changing a single emotion, feeling, thought or behaviour at a time and then wonder why we revert to old habits so quickly. Quick fixes are like only watering the leaves of a tree to support its growth. Anyone who understands horticulture knows that to sustain the health of a whole tree, one must nurture the roots and the surrounding soil, ensuring a balanced and thriving ecosystem.

Extending the horticultural analogy, modern agriculture often aims to mass-produce specific plant species in an industrialised manner, utilising techniques such as monocropping, pesticides and herbicides

---

126   Prochaska, J. O., & DiClemente, C. C. 1983. 'Stages and processes of self-change of smoking: Toward an integrative model of change'. *Journal of Consulting and Clinical Psychology,* 51(3), 390—395.

127   Norcross, J. C. 2011. *Changeology: 5 Steps to Realizing Your Goals and Resolutions.* Simon & Schuster.

128   Fogg, B. J. 2009. *Persuasive Technology: Using Computers to Change What We Think and Do.* Morgan Kaufmann.

129   Kabat-Zinn, J. 1990. *Full Catastrophe Living: Using the Wisdom of Your Body and Mind to Face Stress, Pain, and Illness.* Delta.

to eliminate anything that doesn't fit the desired outcome. While this approach might yield immediate results that are relatively easy to achieve compared to other, more sustainable methods, it disregards the natural laws of ecosystems and biodiversity, ultimately leading to long-term ecological damage due to detrimental side-effects. This analogy reflects our radically humanistic, egocentric and hubristic tendencies to override nature's laws to fit our agenda and highlights the unrealistic expectations we often have about our own personal growth and transformation. No doubt many of us would be thrilled if there were such a thing as a 'correction department' for our emotions, feelings and behaviours – where we could simply file a request to 'fix' whatever seems out of place. But in reality, this 'quick fix' approach only leads to superficial changes and doesn't address the root causes of our issues. So, to expect sustainable transformation through a quick fix is a fallacy. Genuine and sustainable transformation requires a deeper, more integrated approach.

Imagine if you wanted to transform your body shape and get fit. Instead of taking a holistic approach involving changes in diet, sleeping patterns and exercise, you decide to focus solely on specific muscles. For example, let's say you want to lose fat around your belly and think the solution is to do sit-ups. However, a deeper look reveals that full-body aerobic exercise combined with a healthy eating regime is also key to achieving the desired outcome. Even leg workouts can contribute significantly to reducing one's waist size. From a scientific perspective, leg exercises such as squats and lunges engage some of the largest muscle groups in the body. This engagement increases overall metabolism and burns more calories, which helps reduce fat throughout the body, including the belly. While focusing on your legs might seem counterintuitive if your goal is to reduce belly fat, consider it an 'invisible' aspect that can't be ignored. So, it would be wise not to forgo leg days at the gym if your goal is to reduce belly fat, as much as many would prefer to!

The Being Framework draws our attention to the need to begin any process of transformation with awareness and provides the tools, principles and practices to do so. By focusing on the deconstruction and subsequent reconstruction of existing knowledge while encouraging a deeper awareness of our being, the framework offers a comprehensive approach to personal transformation.

Transformation as an iterative process

The Being Framework considers transformation an ongoing, iterative process that involves moving through stages of awareness – reception, perception and conception – followed by application, validation and refinement. For example, an individual working on improving their assertiveness might go through multiple cycles of tracking, learning, refining and executing, receiving feedback and adjusting their approach based on what they learn. *BEING*[130] and *Human Being*[131] explore the process of transformation and the methodology to apply it in detail, using various examples and case studies to make it more tangible.

The role of integrity in transformation

Integrity is a cornerstone of the Being Framework. As discussed earlier, the ontological model encourages the development of awareness of the constituent parts that either contribute to or compromise our overall integrity and supports us in addressing the gaps to restore integrity through the transformation process.

Consider the following Being Framework ontological distinction of this critical Meta Factor.

The Being Framework ontological distinction of integrity

Integrity is the state of being whole, complete, unbroken, sound and in optimal condition. Integrity encompasses all primal Aspects of Being in the same way that the various limbs and organs are

---

130   Tashvir, A. 2021. *BEING – The source of power* (Part 3, Ch 2). Engenesis Publications: Sydney.

131   Tashvir, A. 2022. *Human Being – Illuminating the reality beneath the facade* (Ch 5). Engenesis Publications: Sydney.

the constituent parts of your body. Integrity is the prerequisite to being effective and operating at the optimal level of performance and is fundamental to generating trust and workability. Integrity brings about ease and flow and is considered 'being well', 'well put together' or the wellness of your Being.[132]

A healthy relationship with integrity indicates that you know yourself to be sufficient and mostly experience flow and workability in life. Ease, trust and consistency are present for both you and those around you. You actively address and maintain whatever may impair your integrity, particularly qualities that are diminished, misplaced or require refinement or transformation.

An unhealthy relationship with integrity indicates that you mostly experience frustration and dysfunction, with recurring problems and unresolved issues. There are many areas in your life you feel the need to fix. Others may experience an absence of workability and consistency around you, hence trust and effectiveness are often compromised and brought into question. Alternatively, you may be obsessed with perfection and struggle to be with shortcomings or incompletion. You may avoid pursuing matters unless success is ensured.

Integrity also involves aligning our actions with our values and intentions, exponentially increasing the probability of fulfilling what we care most about. By encouraging a higher degree of overall integrity, individuals can achieve greater ease, flow and workability in their lives. The following depicts, at a high level, how the Being Framework supports individuals in restoring their integrity.

1. **Reception (initial insight) and perception**

   Reception is the initial insight or 'aha' moment of awareness. It's when new information is received. Acknowledging the information as the first step towards transformation requires a degree of openness and vulnerability. Once the new information is received and acknowledged, you objectively study it and verify its validity as part of the perception process. For

---

132   Tashvir, A. 2021. *BEING – The source of power* (p.176). Engenesis Publications: Sydney.

example, you might suddenly realise that procrastination is one of the key reasons you are not hitting your objectives.

2. **Raising your awareness of the misconstrued or incomplete parts**

   The next step towards transformation is becoming aware of where your understanding or awareness is misconstrued or incomplete. The resulting self-awareness allows you to identify areas for growth and development, such as recognising that procrastination is not just a matter of poor time management but also linked to deeper fears and anxieties.

3. **Reconstruction of understanding**

   Reconstruction involves re-evaluating and updating your awareness and understanding of various Aspects of Being. This leads to a more accurate and holistic view of yourself. An example might be learning about the underlying psychological reasons for procrastination and developing strategies to address these root causes.

4. **Iterative process of transformation to restore or contribute to your integrity**

   Engaging in an iterative process of transformation – consistently applying, reflecting and refining – not only enhances your integrity and overall effectiveness but also brings you closer to your desired outcomes. For example, if time management is hampering your integrity, you would continuously practise new time management techniques, reflecting on their effectiveness and making necessary adjustments to improve. This process instils hope and motivation as you see yourself getting closer to your goals with each iteration.

5. **Increased probability of effectiveness and fulfilment**

   As integrity is restored, the likelihood of achieving your intentions increases. This is not a coincidence but a direct result of your actions becoming more aligned with your core values and intentions. For example, as an individual becomes more assertive, vulnerable and authentically true to themselves, their integrity improves and, therefore, they are more likely to be effective and fulfilled in the matters they care about.

Awareness – the foundation for transformation

Examining the metacontent of any matter, including ourselves and others, makes 'The Invisible' visible to us. As mentioned, developing this initial degree of authentic awareness is the starting point of any transformation. Why? Consider that awareness delivers:

- **A foundation for understanding** – Awareness is the first step in understanding both oneself and the environment. It enables individuals to perceive and comprehend their internal states and external surroundings, which is crucial for any further cognitive and emotional processing.[133]

- **Intentionality and direction** – Awareness is inherently intentional and directed. It allows individuals to focus their attention on specific thoughts, emotions and environmental stimuli, which is necessary for meaningful engagement with the world.[134]

- **Self-knowledge and insight** – Being aware of one's own consciousness and the processes that drive it is key to gaining deeper self-knowledge. This self-awareness helps individuals recognise their strengths, weaknesses, motivations and biases, which is essential for personal growth and effective decision-making.[135]

---

133 Brown, K. W., & Ryan, R. M. 2003. 'The benefits of being present: Mindfulness and its role in psychological well-being'. *Journal of Personality and Social Psychology,* 84(4), 822—848.

134 Husserl, E. 1913. *Ideas Pertaining to a Pure Phenomenology and to a Phenomenological Philosophy. Book One: General Introduction to a Pure Phenomenology.* Springer.

135 Duval, S., & Wicklund, R. A. 1972. *A Theory of Objective Self Awareness.* Academic Press.

- **Interpersonal understanding** – Awareness also extends to understanding others and the impact of one's actions on them. This interpersonal awareness is critical for building empathy, improving communication and fostering healthy relationships.[136]

- **An impact on transforming one's performance** – In the context of human performance and effectiveness, awareness allows individuals to monitor and adjust their actions in real-time, leading to improved outcomes. Being aware of one's performance, receiving feedback and making necessary adjustments are crucial for achieving excellence.[137]

Let's now look into the Being Framework's ontological distinction of awareness. As mentioned earlier, the distinction – like all distinctions in the framework – is structured in three layers: a description outlining what is being measured, what a healthy relationship with the distinction looks like and how an unhealthy relationship with it manifests.

The Being Framework ontological distinction of awareness

Awareness is the state of being intentionally conscious of your consciousness. It is how you relate to what you know and understand as well as what you don't know and don't understand. Awareness is always intentional and directed at something. It is to know and understand yourself, others and the world around you, in particular the impact of the world and others on you and the impact you have on the world and others. Awareness is your access to knowing and understanding and is required to fulfil your intentions.

A healthy relationship with awareness indicates that you have a clear understanding of your impact on others and on the world around you. You are not easily misled, coerced and/or manipulated. You are both self-aware and aware of how you are perceived by

---

136 Goleman, D. 1995. *Emotional Intelligence: Why It Can Matter More Than IQ.* Bantam Books.

137 Tashvir, A. 2022. *Human Being – Illuminating the reality beneath the facade.* Engenesis Publications: Sydney.

others. You are attentive, alert and rarely surprised or caught off guard. You can find your way forward despite uncertainty or not knowing, and are available to consider feedback, guidance and critique.

An unhealthy relationship with awareness indicates that you may choose to ignore or be oblivious to matters and the impact you have on others and the world around you and vice versa. You may often be confused and shocked by matters and how others respond to you and blindsided when they fail to live up to your expectations. You may deliberately choose to ignore what there is to see. Alternatively, you may freeze or find it difficult to progress in the face of uncertainty or not knowing as you are compelled to know everything before making decisions or taking action.[138]

Awareness lays a critical foundation for deeper exploration of cognitive processes and frameworks that drive human behaviour and performance. These include:

- **Narratives** – The Being Framework emphasises the power of narratives in shaping our understanding of ourselves and the world. By examining and re-authoring our personal stories, we can identify and transform limiting beliefs and behaviours. For example, an individual who sees themselves as perpetually unlucky can explore and rewrite this narrative, recognising instances of success and resilience in their life.

- **Perspectives and perceptions** – Adopting multiple perspectives allows us to see beyond our initial viewpoints and understand the complexities of our experiences. This broadened perception helps us navigate challenges with greater empathy and insight. For example, in conflict resolution, considering the perspectives of all parties involved can lead to more effective and harmonious solutions.

- **Conceptions and mental models** – Mental models are the cognitive frameworks we use to make sense of the world. The

---

138   Tashvir, A. 2021. *BEING – The source of power* (p.109). Engenesis Publications: Sydney.

Being Framework encourages the continuous refinement of these models to ensure our conceptions align more closely with reality. For example, updating one's mental model about leadership from an autocratic style to a more collaborative approach can enhance team dynamics and performance.

- **Principles and practices** – The framework provides specific principles (conceptions and values) and practices (mental models) that facilitate the iterative process of transformation. This includes mindfulness, reflective practices and proactive learning. For example, regular mindfulness practices can help individuals become more aware of their emotional triggers and respond more thoughtfully and proactively rather than reactively.

Ultimately, the desire to address our behaviours and emotions in a rapid, ad hoc fashion is understandable but insufficient for sustainable transformation. The Being Framework offers a holistic approach that builds a strong foundation, much like ensuring the stability of a building from the ground up. By beginning with awareness, leveraging narratives, perspectives, mental models, principles and practices and engaging in an iterative process of transformation, we can achieve a higher degree of integrity, facilitating effectiveness and fulfilment.

In conclusion, the Being Framework is a comprehensive paradigm grounded in the metacontent discourse and the Nested Theory of Sense-making that supports us in developing a more congruent and authentic conception of the reality of human beings in the scope of performance and effectiveness. Its ontological model component directs our attention to the essence or 'whatness' of human beings in a generic manner, particularly within the domain of human performance and the paradigm of leadership. By revealing and examining our underlying qualities – the ones we all share but relate to differently – the framework enables us to decode and make sense of human beings, ourselves and others and, in so doing, see the reality behind what drives our decisions, behaviours and actions.

Importantly, the Being Framework views human beings as transformable, though not entirely mutable or fluid. Being entirely mutable or fluid suggests you are whatever you say you are as if there is no objective limitation or restriction beyond one's self-created boundaries or social construct. Furthermore, the Being Framework does not conform to rigid categorisations like personality types, nor does it equate human beings to their behaviours alone. Instead, behaviours are seen as consequences of how an individual is being,' how they 'relate to' various qualities such as assertiveness, authenticity, anxiety, courage, commitment, empowerment and responsibility, among others. Importantly, it also provides us with tools – the Being Profile and Transformation Methodology – to measure and transform how we are being for greater and more sustainable effectiveness in our endeavours as we progress through life.

Making sense of human beings: ontological models, cognitive maps and knowledge graphs

As discussed in the previous chapters, we develop and use various tools to structure our understanding and make sense of any content, including human beings. Ontological models provide a foundational framework, cognitive maps personalise this structure with individual knowledge and knowledge graphs integrate these details into a comprehensive, interconnected representation. These tools help us navigate complex information. And what could be more complex than us human beings?

An ontological model is like a blueprint, defining a particular domain's categories, properties and relationships. It outlines what attributes and dispositions entities can have, creating a structured framework for understanding. A cognitive map is an individual's mental representation of their understanding and knowledge about a specific subject and how they relate to it. In this way, it applies the abstract structure of the ontological model to an individual's specific knowledge and experiences. A knowledge graph organises detailed, interconnected data into a graph, incorporating various cognitive maps to show relationships and patterns.

In defining the attributes of a human being, an ontological model might include general attributes like name, age, occupation, personality traits, skills and relationships. We would enter specific details for a particular human being in a cognitive map. For instance, 'Jane Doe, 34, software developer, curious, diligent, introverted, skilled in Java and Python, and has a close friendship with John and a mentorship with Sarah.' It also focuses on intentionality and contextual variables to create greater opportunities for sense-making, thereby facilitating the process of transformation. Then, a knowledge graph would integrate Jane's information with data from many other individuals, creating a network that shows how her attributes and relationships connect to a broader community. It might illustrate how Jane's skills in Java relate to job opportunities or how her relationship with John connects her to a broader social network.

Application in the Being Framework

The Being Framework encourages individuals and collectives to direct their attention to the ontological distinction of each Aspect of Being to examine the 'howness' – how, in a subjective sense, they relate to them. By assessing where they currently reside on the spectrum of stability or health in their relationship with these qualities, individuals can identify growth opportunities for transformation towards healthier, more stable relationships with these Aspects of Being, enhancing their performance in life.

The ontological model, combined with a person's subjective relationship with each quality, leads to a well-formed, studiable cognitive model or map. This process is further facilitated by leveraging the Being Profile, the assessment tool associated with the Being Framework that measures the howness of one's relationships with these Aspects of Being. By using this tool, subjective, human-specific cognitive maps can be created.

Individuals can work with highly trained coaches and practitioners who have rigorously mastered the framework and the tool to further enhance this process. These professionals can help build knowledge graphs, offering more detailed, contextualised and nuanced descriptions of their howness. This collaboration transforms generic ontological insights into personalised cognitive maps and knowledge graphs, providing a deeper understanding of 'how I am being' as an individual.

Are the qualities in the Being Framework's ontological model the only ones that relate to human beings? The simple answer is no. However, the studies leading to the development of the Being Framework identified a generic template consisting of fundamental qualities that matter most when it comes to our performance in life – how we participate in life, engage in projects, build relationships, etc. Each of these fundamental qualities manifests itself in more detailed and specific attributes. For example, how one relates to or perceives authenticity manifests in the more visible surface-level behaviours like honesty or lying. It's the difference between being true to who you know yourself to be and consciously being in pretence or exaggeration. In other words, are you honest and authentic, or are you a hypocrite pretending to be someone you're not? Furthermore, are you authentic in your approach to validating and conceiving various fragments of reality, or are there no solid foundations for your beliefs and opinions and how you choose to examine reality? The latter is another aspect of the distinction of authenticity, as shown.

The Being Framework ontological distinction of authenticity

Authenticity is how you relate to the reality of matters in life. It is the extent to which you are accurate and rigorous in perceiving what is real and what is not. It is also how sensitive and diligent you are to the validity of the knowledge you perceive. Authenticity is paramount for you to carefully consider that your conception of reality – including your beliefs and opinions – is congruent with how things are. When you are being authentic, you are compelled to express your Unique Being – what is there for you to express – while being consistent with who you say you are for others and who you say you are for yourself. It is the congruence or alignment of your self-image – who you know yourself to be – and your persona – who you choose to project to others.

A healthy relationship with authenticity indicates that you take the time to thoughtfully consider your beliefs and opinions, as the validity and accuracy of your conception of matters is important to you. You mostly experience yourself as being true to yourself and others. Others may consider you genuine, distinct and trustworthy, and that your actions are consistent with who and how you are and what you communicate.

An unhealthy relationship with authenticity indicates that there may be no solid foundation for your beliefs and opinions and how you choose to examine reality, and you are often lenient and fickle with how you express your views and the truth. You may consider yourself to be fake or an imposter and often question your own abilities. Others may consider you to be someone who lacks sincerity and often acts inconsistently with who you say you are. You are frequently uncomfortable with being yourself and being with yourself. Alternatively, you may be righteous, opinionated, biased or prejudiced, considering your 'truth' to be the only truth, and may be unwilling to give up being 'right'.[139]

The Being Framework's ontological model is a construct that guides us where to look. The framework in its entirety also offers clear onto-logical distinctions for each of these qualities, as explained earlier, so we are all on the same page. That's not to say it imposes meanings or perceptions, suggesting that all other perceptions and distinctions are wrong. It simply establishes a ground rule and agreement that whenever we use the word 'responsibility' in the context of the Being Framework, for example, we are referring to the ontological meaning of responsibility conveyed in the framework's distinction. So, the ontological model maps out the qualities, and the distinctions depict a tangible picture of how they manifest themselves in our daily lives. After accessing the ontological model of the framework and studying the distinctions, you can create knowledge graphs of yourself or

---

139   Tashvir, A. 2021. *BEING – The source of power* (p.250). Engenesis Publications: Sydney.

another person, as an instance of the class 'human being', with a relatively high degree of accuracy.

Once you have an authentic awareness of how you are being, it is crucial to extend this understanding to how others are being. This is particularly important in the context of our relationships. As social beings, we share our lives with others. Therefore, living with the belief that we only need to focus on ourselves is a misconception. In partnerships and interactions, it's vital to comprehend human beings – to be able to see beyond the surface and value the authentic qualities of each person – from the life partner you plan to choose or the person you are considering for a job, to the leader you are thinking of following or the politician you are about to vote for, to name just a few.

By breaking down the qualities we all share but relate to differently into readily digestible chunks, the Being Framework supports you in developing authentic awareness of our nature or primal qualities as human beings and seeing how you and others are being. Think of it as looking in a mirror – or a lens when looking into others – without rose-coloured glasses to gain an authentic conception of yourself and others.

Why is gaining an authentic conception of us human beings so important? Considering all the confusion and uncertainty, it is vital to appreciate that, at least to some extent, we are studiable, even if not fully objectively. Understanding something is better than understanding nothing. Therefore, if there are ways to identify patterns or methodical approaches to gaining more understanding, we should take them seriously and not take them for granted. This is why gaining an authentic conception of human beings is so important. It allows us to bridge gaps between various disciplines, creating multi-disciplinary collaborations between philosophy and science, ontology, phenomenology, engineering and analytical thinking. Such efforts are crucial for a more comprehensive understanding of human nature and behaviour. Consider the following tangible example, an excerpt from *Human Being*:

> Think of a first date you have been on where your date spends the entire evening working overly hard to portray the best possible image of themselves in the hope of a second date. Imagine if that person managed to maintain that facade and you ended up making a lifelong commitment to them. Eventually, the walls are bound to come down, but what if you are already sharing a life, a mortgage and children by then? Imagine the pain and suffering that would cause. Compare that to a first date where your date was open and honest with you from the start and continued to show you who they really are, warts and all, from that moment forward. This would enable you to decide whether or not you wish to pursue the relationship based on fact, not fiction.[140]

Let's consider an example that highlights why developing an authentic conception of any fragment of reality is essential. If I asked two people what comes to mind when I say 'marriage', they might answer very differently. One might say things like 'heated arguments, constant compromise, limitations and restrictions, obligations, burden', etc. In contrast, the other might convey the opposite sentiments with words like 'love, intimacy, family, warmth, happily-ever-after' and so on. While I am not suggesting either perspective is right or wrong, neither is authentically aligned with the totality of the truth around marriage and how it has evolved as a significant human experience. The first is overly pessimistic, while the second is excessively optimistic. It's clear they both have sentimental views around marriage, but their views are one-sided, incomplete and, in part, unrealistic.

An authentic, congruent or realistic perception of marriage combines both sides. A person with a healthy relationship with authenticity would shape a holistic, relatively comprehensive perception, neither dreamy and romantic nor overly pessimistic and gloomy. If we set our expectations inauthentically, we set ourselves up for disappointment. We may take things for granted and not be present and grateful to the light side or see the dark side so heavily that it frustrates us and prevents us from fully engaging in the relationship. An authentic

---

140 Tashvir, A. 2022. *Human Being - Illuminating the reality beneath the facade.* (Ch 1). Engenesis Publications: Sydney.

conception of a fragment of reality, be it marriage, business, politics or human beings, makes all the difference. Think of how much more effective your decisions and actions would be if you made them with a foundation firmly grounded in reality.

In summary, using the Being Framework Ontological Model as a foundation, cognitive maps help individuals visualise their subjective relationships with various Aspects of Being, while knowledge graphs offer structured, detailed representations of these relationships, facilitating personal growth and transformation. By engaging with these tools, individuals are better equipped to navigate the complexities of their own being, leading to more effective and fulfilling lives. The result is a well-rounded, holistic approach to personal development, grounded in the deep theoretical foundations of the metacontent discourse and the Nested Theory of Sense-making. This integration ensures that individuals can achieve greater awareness, maintain integrity and enhance their effectiveness in all areas of life.

Leveraging the metacontent discourse and the Nested Theory of Sense-making to create the Being Framework

As discussed, the creation of the Being Framework was deeply rooted in the metacontent discourse and the Nested Theory of Sense-making. Their theoretical foundation was essential for understanding and mapping the complexities of human performance and being. Let's examine how they helped shape the highest level Aspects of Being – the Meta Factors of awareness, integrity and effectiveness.

Awareness

The Nested Theory of Sense-making outlines layers of understanding, contributing to a comprehensive and authentic awareness of reality. As shown below, these layers align with the ontology of awareness in the Being Framework and ensure a nuanced understanding of human experiences and behaviours. Notably, awareness has an impact on all Aspects of Being.

- **Web of Perceptions** – The interconnected sensory inputs and interpretations that form our immediate experience.

- **Narrative Lens** – The stories and interpretations that shape our understanding of events and actions.

- **Perspectives** – The angles and viewpoints from which we consider matters

- **Cognitive Map** – The mental representation of our understanding of concepts and their relationships.

All four layers of the ontology of awareness are influenced by contextual variables like our background and past experiences.

Integrity

In the Being Framework, integrity is a cluster Aspect of Being whereby the health of one's relationship with all Moods – the underlying emotional states that influence our perceptions and actions – and Primary Ways of Being – the underlying dispositions that define how we engage with the world – feed into or contribute to it. As mentioned earlier, the better the health of one's relationship with all Moods and Primary Ways of Being, the more complete one's integrity. This holistic approach to integrity ensures that individuals are seen as whole beings whose performance and effectiveness are influenced by their internal consistency and alignment.

Effectiveness

All Aspects of Being contribute to one's effectiveness. When individuals are deeply aware of their perceptions, narratives and perspectives and maintain integrity in their Moods, Primary Ways of Being and Secondary Ways of Being, their performance and effectiveness are significantly enhanced. Consequently, effectiveness represents the tangible results and contributions individuals bring to their interactions and roles.

Mapping out metacontent for human performance

In leveraging the metacontent discourse and the Nested Theory of Sense-making, the Being Framework provides a comprehensive map of human performance. It identifies the intellectual substrates (metacontent) that influence how individuals engage in life, participate in work and interact with others. By deconstructing existing metacontent, the framework identifies areas that need reconstruction or transformation on an individual or collective scale. For instance, if an organisation struggles with low employee engagement, the Being Framework can deconstruct the cognitive maps, mental models and narratives influencing this behaviour. By reconstructing these elements to align with positive engagement strategies, the framework can encourage a more motivated and productive workforce.

Let's now explore how each layer of the Nested Theory of Sense-making has been leveraged to contextualise and develop the constructs and models within the Being Framework. Doing so will give you an insight into how the Nested Theory could be leveraged to create any new ontological model. I encourage you to consider how it could be applied in your endeavours as you read on.

Initial insight: The spark of awareness

The Being Framework was sparked by a moment of awareness and clarity about the dysfunction in the world. This insight emerged from observations of human interactions and challenges, prompting further exploration into what truly constitutes effective and authentic human performance. It was the catalyst for deeper investigation into the intrinsic qualities driving human performance and effectiveness. Below is an excerpt from the preface of my book *BEING*[141] that highlights how an initial insight or ah-ha moment can strike, stir the emotions and inspire us to take action.

> I was wide awake. It was 3.35am and I was as alert as if it was midday. My mind and heart were racing, and the anger and

---

141   Tashvir, A. 2021. *BEING – The source of power*. Engenesis Publications: Sydney.

frustration welling inside me had reached a point where I felt I would burst; I couldn't take it anymore. As I lay there in the dark, I was intensely aware of and present to the misery, dysfunction and unworkability that exists in the world and its devastating impact everywhere. That pivotal moment arose at a time when I was dealing with an enormous amount of inauthenticity and lack of integrity all around me, on every level, from the people I worked with and commercial partners to suppliers, government services, banks, etc., with obstacles on every front.

On a global scale, I, like everyone else, was being bombarded from all sides with news of the gross dysfunctionality in our world, everything from wars to domestic violence, lack of preparedness in the face of natural disasters, fraud, disease, poverty and collective psychosis. I had become so concerned about this widespread and pervasive disregard for reality and the subsequent dangerous and sometimes subtle deception in the world that I couldn't shake it from my mind.

Night after night, I was unable to sleep. It felt as though I was experiencing the suffering in the world within each and every cell of my being. All the old wounds I had managed to heal in the past were rising back to the surface, bringing back memories of the unique collection of experiences I had been through that were so impactful, it was as if they had altered my DNA, the very fabric of my being.

In that moment, I had become so acutely aware that the intensity of my fury, combined with my deep care and compassion for humanity sparked a fire within me that erupted in a raging desire to take action. There was no turning back, no retreat. My path forward was crystal clear and I was suddenly calm. The urge was ignited.

Cognitive map: Shaping perceptions, conceptions, opinions and beliefs

Understanding the cognitive map, which refers to our network of perceptions and conceptions of reality, is a crucial aspect of the Being Framework. This layer maps out how individuals construct their understanding of what things are. By leveraging cognitive maps, the Being Framework successfully identifies how individuals perceive their roles, responsibilities and interactions in various contexts. This understanding allows for the development of tailored strategies to enhance individual and team performance based on their unique cognitive structures.

The cognitive map layer in the Nested Theory of Sense-making considers the origin and congruence of one's perceptions, conceptions, opinions and beliefs about a matter. In relation to the Being Framework, the matter being studied is human beings, ourselves and others. This is where awareness, a Meta Factor, plays the most central role.

In exploring the three Meta Factors of awareness, integrity and effectiveness earlier, we learned that awareness encompasses various elements in its ontological breakdown relating to how we shape our perceptions, conceptions, opinions and beliefs, such as our web of perceptions, narrative lens and perspectives.

Our opinions and beliefs, including our perceptions and conceptions, are largely shaped and influenced by our relationship with awareness – how we relate to knowing and understanding – along with the narratives we construct and the perspectives we adopt. We often fiercely defend these beliefs and opinions, even if they are misaligned with reality or not beneficial to us. Human beings can be so delusional that some live entirely in a world of fantasy. This can make us susceptible to being misled by others or ignorant and negligent about the true state of affairs. Consider the long-term consequences if everyone deliberately ignored global issues that require collective attention or if no one took the initiative to create jobs and support the economy. In the context of the Being Framework, an unhealthy relationship with awareness will prevent you from recognising the obstacles within yourself, others and life situations that hinder you from fulfilling your intentions.

Narratives – the stories we tell ourselves

Each of us views life, our surroundings, people and our experiences through a unique personal narrative or narrative lens. The stories we consistently tell ourselves and others, shaped by this narrative lens, impact our interpretation of events and experiences and eventually form our reality, unless we consciously take the time to deconstruct and reconstruct them. Narratives created about oneself and others significantly shape behaviour and our relationship with others and ourselves. The Being Framework incorporates the narratives layer by supporting individuals to examine and reconsider their existing narratives. It then helps individuals reframe negative or limiting stories into more empowering ones.

The framework emphasises the importance of authenticity in how we relate to different aspects of reality. It requires us to be genuine in our awareness and understanding of various life matters, including the economy, societal issues, politics, family dynamics and relationships. Achieving authentic awareness involves not only how we perceive and present ourselves but also extends to our perceptions of others and the broader issues in the world as reflected in the Authenticity Quadrant in Chapter 4.

Mental Models: Frameworks for understanding

Mental models are frameworks for understanding how things work, including knowledge and beliefs about processes, cause-and-effect relationships and system functionality. In the Nested Theory of Sense-making, mental models form a crucial layer that shapes our perceptions, decisions and actions. By tapping into the metacontent discourse, individuals can articulate and formulate their mental models, making explicit the often implicit frameworks that guide their behaviour. By leveraging the Nested Theory of Sense-making, particularly its emphasis on functionality in real-world contexts, individuals can better understand how their mental models and internal states of being influence their external outcomes.

Mental models are critical for supporting us in identifying and developing effective strategies and solutions within and beyond the Being Framework to restore integrity (wholeness) and fulfil our intentions. By analysing the existing mental models, the framework can identify gaps and misalignments that hinder performance. This analysis allows for the creation of new, more effective mental models that align with our intentions and values.

The framework not only supports us in shaping our own mental models but also offers a comprehensive suite of mental models designed to facilitate understanding and personal development. They include methodologies and tools such as the Being Profile, Transformation Methodology, the Projection Process and the Fulfilment Pyramid. These frameworks offer structured approaches to understanding various Aspects of Being in terms of their functionality and provide practical tools for implementation in real life. For instance, the Being Profile and debrief processes help individuals gain insights into the underlying reasons behind their behaviours and mindsets. Additionally, the framework includes training programs for coaches and practitioners, ensuring there is support and guidance available to help individuals and organisations effectively use these tools. This structured approach highlights the thoughtful consideration behind the creation of these tools, aimed at enabling individuals to fulfil their intentions and achieve their potential. Let's consider an example – the Projection Process.

Human beings are continuous content generators. We project our being through ideas, conceptions, decisions, actions and behaviours. This 'projection process' reflects how we relate to matters and act upon them, creating a constant dialogue between generating content and interacting with content generated by others. In the Being Framework, the Projection Process is a key concept that models how human beings express their being through various aspects, from thoughts and emotions to actions and behaviours. This process is depicted in the Projection Process diagram and is integral to understanding how individuals manifest themselves and their intentions in the world.

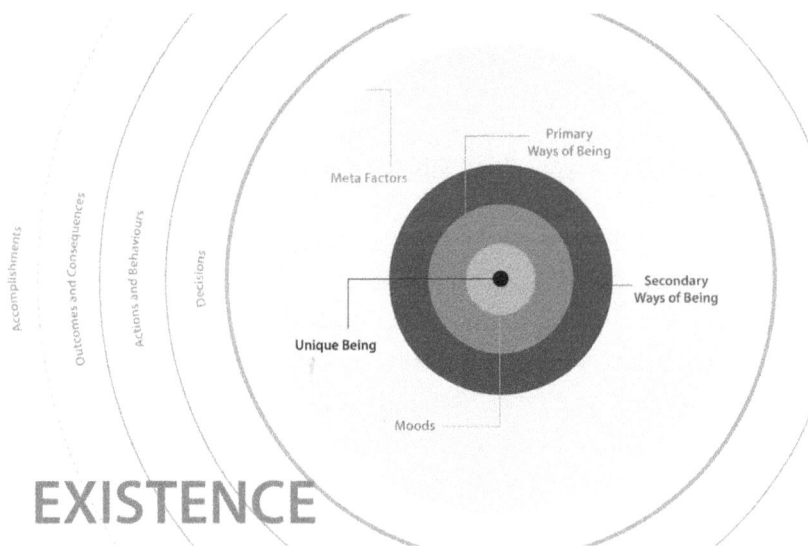

EXISTENCE

Figure 9

The Projection Process

When we are born, we are 'thrown' into the ocean of existence. From that moment on, however, everything we are and whatever we do in life releases another drop of water into that 'ocean', creating a ripple effect, as depicted by the outer circles in the diagram. This is a metaphorical way of articulating that you are constantly expressing yourself, whether or not you are present to that fact, just as a rose expresses itself through its exquisite beauty and scent. This expression of self starts from your Unique Being – what is there for you to express – before passing through your Moods, then your Primary Ways of Being, followed by your Secondary Ways of Being before ultimately being projected as your decisions, actions and behaviours. You could say that your decisions, actions and behaviours are the actualised version of the potential that is within you, waiting to be expressed. Then your decisions, actions and behaviours impact the reality around you. (Excerpt from *Human Being*[142])

The metacontent discourse provides a framework for understanding the deeper layers of human cognition and behaviour. The Projection

---

142   Tashvir, A. 2022. *Human Being – Illuminating the reality beneath the facade* (Ch 1) Engenesis Publications: Sydney.

Process involves projecting these mental models into the world through our actions and behaviours. Understanding and refining these mental models can lead to more effective decision-making and better alignment with one's intentions and goals.

The Being Framework's Transformation Methodology is another example of a mental model. As discussed earlier, it provides a structured approach, as briefly depicted below, to achieving personal and professional transformation by supporting individuals in mapping out the 'howness' or functionality of transformation in the domain of human performance.

Stages of transformation

1. **Awareness**

   - Reception – This is the initial stage where new information is received. It requires openness and vulnerability to allow new information to enter one's consciousness.

   - Perception – In this stage, the information is processed through an 'authentic awareness filter' to verify its validity and acquire objective knowledge.

   - Conception – Here, the information is related to one's life, forming subjective understanding and eventually leading to wisdom.

2. **Application Process**

   - Execution – Acting based on the current conception of a matter.

   - Tracking – Observing and reflecting on decisions, actions and behaviours.

   - Learning – Gaining insights from the outcomes of these actions.

   - Refinement –Tweaking and improving based on what has been learned, leading back to execution.

3. **Effectiveness**
    - Competency – Initial stage of effectiveness, demonstrating basic proficiency.
    - Proficiency – Intermediate stage where skills and understanding are refined.
    - Mastery – Final stage where deep understanding and skill are demonstrated consistently.

Perspectives: Viewing from different angles

Perspectives represent various viewpoints from which matters are approached, shaped by roles, experiences, cultural context and individual differences. The Being Framework encourages considering multiple perspectives to gain a comprehensive understanding of situations, encouraging empathy, collaboration and a deeper appreciation of diverse experiences and insights. The Nested Theory of Sense-making was influential in the development of the Perspective Quadrant, as modelled in the previous chapter. It supports us to consider matters from multiple angles: I (personal perspective), Others (anyone who might be impacted by a decision or action), Them (people directly involved in the matter) and Global (a broader, big-picture perspective).

Domain and paradigm: Narrowing the scope of attention

The Being Framework operates broadly within the domain of human performance and the paradigm of leadership – be it in an organisational context or being the leader of one's own life – providing a structured approach to understanding and enhancing individual and team performance in various contexts. However, it can be leveraged in various domains and paradigms. For example, within the domain of human performance, different paradigms influence how issues are approached and solved. The Being Framework introduces a paradigm shift, focusing on intrinsic qualities driving authentic and sustainable performance, emphasising being – how individuals relate to themselves, others and the world – as the foundation for achieving meaningful results in any domain and paradigm within a domain.

The objective behind the Being Framework has always been to not only make sense of human performance but also to identify patterns and turn them into a reusable framework that is broad enough to be expanded and contextualised in various ways. The domain was intentionally kept broad, focusing on how human beings participate in life and perform, while remaining specific enough to ensure the framework's applicability and practicality.

Contextual variables: overarching influential factors

Contextual variables include dynamic elements such as cultural, environmental, subjective and intersubjective factors. This layer also acknowledges mental and physical health conditions, geographic impacts and other unique factors that might influence an individual's perception and interpretation. The Being Framework acknowledges these variables' potential influence on human performance and how they could impact one's relationship with various Aspects of Being and, ultimately, one's overall integrity and effectiveness.

Reconstruction and deconstruction in the Being Framework

The Being Framework applies the principle of deconstruction to human performance, using the Nested Theory of Sense-making to untangle and clarify complex behaviours and actions and miscon-strued opinions, beliefs and perceptions. Reconstruction occurs through the process of transformation, encouraging us to move from a degree of awareness to a degree of effectiveness, ultimately resulting in mastery and all constituent parts coming together to create a whole, integrous being.

Conclusion

Amidst all of life's complexities, uncertainties and confusion, we acknowledge that life, perhaps unfairly, demands us to be effective and perform. These expectations arise from the fact that we all have intentions we wish to fulfil. A fundamental intention shared by almost everyone is the drive for survival. Now that we are 'out there in the world', we aim to keep being, minimise unnecessary suffering and attain and maintain wellbeing, health, prosperity and peace. We strive to maximise our experiences in life, and many of us genuinely seek to explore how we can contribute beyond our lifespan. Finding meaning in participation, engagement, service and adventure is a common human aspiration, with many also seeking to expand the shared layer of reality by adding to what is already there through art, music, innovation, etc.

Numerous aspects of life extend beyond individual responsibility. They demand alignment, communication, trust-building, influence and leadership. This applies if you are simply focused on meeting basic needs like paying bills, establishing effective communication for personal and professional relationships, building trust and a compelling personal brand, navigating a career, cultivating close relationships with friends and family or nurturing intimacy with significant others. It's equally applicable to activists dedicated to broader causes like human rights, environmental issues, societal concerns, or advocating for minority groups. And it's no different for individuals leading organisations, building enterprises or launching startups. In short, whether you are an ambitious artist, entertainer, entrepreneur, dedicated parent or carer, climbing the corporate ladder, in a profession or anyone with significant intentions, how you are being matters. Effective individuals intentionally identify and bring to their consciousness the matters they can influence and surrender to the parts they know are beyond their control or influence. That's why being – the way you make sense of, relate to and act upon ideas and meanings, your thoughts, feelings and behaviour – is your source of power.

At the start of this book, we discussed confusion and vulnerability, including that one of our greatest vulnerabilities as human beings is the limitations of our perceptual and conceptual structures. We tap into our sensory abilities to perceive what is immediately visible and access our mental processes to develop conceptions of those that are not immediately visible. Consequently, we can't always rely on our perceptions and conceptions and don't always have access to authentic awareness, making our understanding of matters unreliable and making us even more vulnerable to the challenges of life.

With its roots firmly grounded in the metacontent discourse and the Nested Theory of Sense-making, the Being Framework offers a comprehensive structure for understanding and enhancing human performance and effectiveness and ensuring one's being can be the source of true power. By mapping out the metacontent of human beings within the scope of human performance, the framework provides a structured approach to navigating the complexities of our interactions with the world, ourselves and each other. The domain and paradigm is intentionally broad enough for the framework to be contextualised and expanded in various contexts.

While life is undoubtedly filled with challenges, leading many of us to become stuck in our suffering, confusion and misery, it doesn't have to be this way. Someone who is willing to identify their shadow sides or troubled parts and commit to transforming their relationship with those qualities in order to return to wholeness (integrity) is not crushed by the weight of the inevitable challenges in life. They are someone who cannot easily be manipulated, coerced or dominated. They choose to be an active agent in life instead of a passive victim. When things go wrong, they forgive others and themselves and move forward with grace. They can step forward with courage despite the presence of fear and anxiety and willingly let down their guard when they know they are in the wrong. They are open to learning, present to others, meet their commitments, reliable, resourceful, assertive and the list goes on. Their healthy relationship with every aspect of their being makes them integrous human beings.

To sum up, each of us has concerns that hold significance, matters we care about. When we invest care in something or someone, we want to fulfil our intention. Achieving fulfilment necessitates effective decision-making and actions. This effectiveness is contingent on maintaining integrity, which, in turn, requires authentic awareness of the parts (shadows) getting in our way. The more we deviate from integrity or wholeness, the more pronounced the suffering, impacting not only ourselves but also others. The reason behind this is universal, transcending personal narratives, religious affiliations, geographic locations, cultural backgrounds and individual stories. Regardless of these factors, your presence, existence, actions, creations, the authentic expression of your ever-evolving and being-discovered conception of your true self (unique being), and even the things you don't do, all carry significance. How you are being matters.

The development of the Being Framework is a testament to the value of the metacontent discourse and the Nested Theory of Sense-making. By leveraging these foundational theories, the framework provides a structured, integrative approach to enhancing human performance and engagement. It offers practical tools and methodologies for individuals and organisations to transcend their current limitations and achieve higher levels of competency, capability, empowerment and effectiveness. Through this process, the Being Framework not only addresses existing challenges but also paves the way for sustained growth and development.

In uniting various disciplines, the framework also encourages collaboration between science, engineering and philosophy. Furthermore, the infusion of metaphysics, ontology, epistemology, phenomenology, axiology and anecdotal and metaphorical language drawn from stories and the principles of various faiths facilitates effective communication and understanding. The ultimate goal is to create a unified whole that significantly contributes to the integrity and wholeness of humanity.

CHAPTER 11

Contextualisation and Application

In the previous chapter, we delved deeply into how the metaccontent discourse and the Nested Theory of Sense-making were leveraged to create the Being Framework with a specific focus on human performance. In this final chapter, we extend our exploration to a broader application because the Nested Theory of Sense-making is by no means confined to the domain of human performance. Instead, it is a versatile tool that can be contextualised to make sense of absolutely any subject matter by mapping out its metacontent, from day-to-day personal matters we are dealing with to work, business, academic, community, societal and global issues. Consequently, it enables anyone, any group or a combination of groups to deconstruct and then reconstruct increasingly nuanced and detailed ontological maps, constructs and frameworks tailored to their specific areas of interest for greater clarity and effectiveness.

This chapter aims to demonstrate the practical possibilities of applying the Nested Theory across various domains and provide some tangible examples and comprehensive, step-by-step instructions to leverage and apply it across different domains, paradigms, contexts and intentions. The aim is not to map out the complete metacontent of complex systems like education or healthcare. To do so would require a detailed report or potentially an entire book for each scenario! If you'd like to review a deeper exploration of how this framework has been applied to the domain of human performance, read my earlier books: *BEING*[143] and *Human Being*.[144] While the Nested Theory can be applied to make sense of relatively simplistic everyday matters, it can also be used to map out highly convoluted and multifaceted issues, which demand the assessment of multidisciplinary studies and contributions from various experts. So, it is important to be aware that the examples in this chapter are intended to demonstrate the application of the theory only, not convey the detailed investigations they would require if we were to conduct a comprehensive metacontent analysis. Let's begin by considering a few high-level examples to illustrate how the Nested Theory could be applied in practice and the potential benefits.

Imagine a world in which policymakers, educators, politicians, company executives, entrepreneurs, tradespeople, healthcare practitioners and other professionals had access to a structured way of conducting a meta-analysis to deeply examine the cognitive and conceptual layers underpinning all areas under consideration before making decisions and taking action. Although a meta-analysis considers multiple studies to provide a more comprehensive understanding of the content in question, the approach does not offer the detail and structure provided by the multi-layered and more holistic Nested Theory of Sense-making. Consider how much more effective their policies, decisions and outcomes could be if they conducted a metacontent analysis using the Nested Theory rather than limiting their approach to a less structured and detailed meta-analysis. Hypothetically speaking, it could manifest itself as follows:

- **Educators** might design curricula that cater to diverse learning styles by understanding students' cognitive maps

---

143   Tashvir, A. 2021. *BEING – The source of power*. Engenesis Publications: Sydney.
144   Tashvir, A. 2022. *Human Being – Illuminating the reality beneath the facade*. Engenesis Publications: Sydney.

and mental models. For example, by recognising that some students are visual learners while others are auditory or kinesthetic, combined with factoring in contextual variables and other deeper insights revealed in a thorough metacontent analysis, educators could develop lesson plans incorporating various teaching methods to engage all learners effectively. A mathematics teacher, aware of these differences, might use visual aids like graphs and charts for visual learners, interactive activities and hands-on experiments for kinesthetic learners and verbal explanations and discussions for auditory learners. This approach would not only enhance comprehension but also foster a more inclusive and supportive learning environment, ensuring that each student has the opportunity to thrive.

- **Business leaders** might create strategies that align with their teams' intrinsic motivations and authentic ways of being. By understanding team members' underlying motivations and values through a comprehensive metacontent analysis, leaders can foster a work environment that promotes engagement, satisfaction and productivity. For example, they might work collaboratively with team members to shape their 'job description' instead of dictating it to them. This could be initiated and negotiated by mapping out the parts of the metacontent relevant to the jobs that need to be undertaken. Not only would this lead to higher job satisfaction, but it would also result in a team of individuals who both *care about and are effective at*[145] their roles to maximise the benefits to the organisation.

- **Healthcare professionals** might develop holistic treatment plans that consider patients' contextual variables and personal narratives. By integrating medical history, lifestyle, background and personal experiences, healthcare providers

---

145   The Contribution Quadrant: Tashvir, A. 2021. *BEING – The source of power.* (p 424). Engenesis Publications: Sydney.

could create comprehensive treatment plans that address patients' physical, emotional and psychological needs. So, beyond establishing a general treatment layer effective for a broad population, a subjective, individualistic, customised layer could be developed based on the individual's unique metacontent. This layer would include not only the specific combination of their physical health conditions but also factors such as their response to pain and potential discomfort triggers. In other words, this approach would focus on both the illness and the patient, akin to the personalised care often seen in naturopathic treatments. This method would ensure that healthcare decisions are deeply informed by a thorough examination of the cognitive and conceptual layers that influence each patient's overall wellbeing.

- **Policymakers** might craft policies informed by a deeper, more holistic understanding of societal perspectives and domains. For instance, when addressing housing policy, policymakers might conduct more comprehensive and detailed community forums, surveys and focus groups to gather deeply relevant and inclusive insights from a diverse range of residents, including low-income families, seniors and young professionals. This would lead to a more comprehensive and nuanced understanding, enabling them to develop policies that more effectively address people's actual needs, rather than just their perceived needs. Conducting a thorough metacontent analysis by passing all data through the seven layers of the Nested Theory of Sense-making to deeply understand the issues at hand would allow policymakers to develop a more accurate, comprehensive and all-encompassing conception, leading to policies that are actually effective and meet the needs of all constituents.

- **Tradespeople** like carpenters, electricians, plumbers, etc., could significantly enhance their craftsmanship, client satisfaction and business by delving deeper into each client's specific needs and preferences. Although most tradespeople already consider their clients' aesthetic preferences, functional requirements and lifestyle contexts, this often represents only a superficial layer of understanding. To truly customise their solutions, a tradesperson should also consider the deeper layers of metacontent, such as clients' cultural heritage, personal values and long-term aspirations. For instance, recognising the cultural significance of certain design elements or materials to a client could result in a carpenter creating more meaningful solutions. Furthermore, by providing insights into multiple paradigms and perspectives, they can help clients see any gaps in their understanding that they would otherwise miss. Mapping out the metacontent can lead to clients making more appropriate decisions, higher quality work, more referrals and greater professional success for the tradesperson. It could also lead a tradesperson to expand their business and even the entire trade into new areas not previously considered.

As you can imagine, the possibilities are limitless. There is a level of shared metacontent relevant to everyone in any field or aspect of life that can be mapped out in this way. Once we have this foundational understanding, we can delve deeper into the details and gain a nuanced, comprehensive and pluralistic outlook by examining the metacontent via various subcategories, leading to more authentic, congruent and all-encompassing conceptions of the examined content. Consequently, this process can contribute to making more effective decisions and taking actions that are more likely to work and bring benefits. As the Nested Theory of Sense-making provides a structured way of conducting a meta-analysis – transforming it from a meta-analysis into the far more detailed and holistic metacontent analysis – it is a powerful tool for leaders and others to navigate and influence their respective fields in ways others might not have thought of. It also provides the structure to make sense of, deconstruct and transform matters that impact our day-to-day lives, such as intimate relationships, parenting, personal health and fitness, raising animals as pets, gardening – literally anything you can think of.

Depending on your needs from any meta-analysis, you may want to focus on the metacontent of collectives, such as all patients in a healthcare study, or on the metacontent of an individual patient. In social sciences, a clinical psychologist taking a psychoanalytical approach may focus on mapping out one person's metacontent. In contrast, a social scientist might be more interested in mapping out the metacontent of a group of people. Similarly, in the business world, a product manager may be interested in mapping out the metacontent of a larger market – one solution for the benefit of many – whereas a solutions consultant working to solve a specific problem for a particular client would likely be more interested in that individual client's metacontent. With this in mind, let's see how the Nested Theory can be used to map out the metacontent through the lenses of its seven layers. The examples given are based on hypothetical scenarios and are designed to provide a small glimpse into how to leverage the tool to conduct a metacontent analysis of any matter with the intention of delivering more accurate, authentic and comprehensive sense-making outcomes to influence one's decisions and actions.

Example 1: Fasting for health and wellbeing

- **Initial insight:** The belief that intermittent fasting, which includes cycles of eating and not eating, can have significant benefits on one's health and wellbeing by promoting better metabolic health, mental clarity and overall longevity.

- **Cognitive map:** An ontological model that outlines the fasting journey, from the initial decision to fast through to the short-term and long-term effects on the body and mind. This cognitive map identifies key stages and potential challenges individuals might face, such as hunger pangs, social situations involving food and maintaining motivation.

- **Narratives:** Narratives from individuals who have undertaken intermittent fasting to understand personal experiences, challenges and successes provide valuable insights. Qualitative research, including interviews or diaries, can reveal common themes such as increased energy levels, improved mental focus and difficulties during the initial adjustment period.

- **Mental models:** The mental models related to nutrition, the digestive system and gut microbiome and how they work together as well as alternative mental models relating to how the body works and processes energy, and the frameworks that individuals use to understand and implement fasting. For example, in relation to the latter, understanding how people plan their eating windows, manage their calorie intake and address hunger can reveal important cognitive processes and areas for improvement.

- **Perspectives:** The various viewpoints of individuals who fast, healthcare providers who support or oppose fasting and scientific perspectives that both support and rebuke the health benefits of fasting. These perspectives highlight different needs, concerns and evidence that must be considered to provide comprehensive guidance on fasting.

- **Domain:** The specific areas of health and wellbeing being addressed, such as weight management, mental health and/ or metabolic health. Each domain has its own set of best practices and challenges.

- **Paradigms:** The prevailing health theories and practices regarding fasting, such as traditional nutrition advice, holistic health approaches or new scientific findings about the benefits of intermittent fasting. These paradigms shape how fasting is perceived and implemented.

To gain a complete picture, individuals should also consider:

- **The contextual variables as an overarching element that impacts all layers:** The broader environment in which fasting takes place, including cultural attitudes towards fasting and the narratives and perspectives they create, availability of healthy foods, economic factors affecting food choices and individual lifestyle factors such as work schedules and family commitments. These variables impact how fasting is adopted and maintained.

- **The importance of authenticating fasting practices**: Through scientific research, personal experimentation and feedback from healthcare providers, fasting protocols are ensured to be safe, effective and tailored to individual needs. Continuous monitoring of health indicators and adaptation based on personal outcomes and new research findings will enhance the authenticity and effectiveness of fasting practices.

This comprehensive mapping process would not only enable individuals to decide whether or not fasting is an appropriate strategy for them to engage in but also design and implement personalised, effective and sustainable fasting strategies to maximise its benefits in the context of their lives.

Example 2: Romantic relationships

While it may initially seem somewhat far-fetched and overly analytical in the context of romantic relationships, the application of the Nested Theory of Sense-making can empower us to map out the metacontent of a potential new romantic relationship. This understanding enables us to transcend surface-level impressions and delve into the deeper layers of attraction and compatibility, giving us a sense of control and confidence in our romantic pursuits.

- **Initial insight:** Imagine you are single and meet someone new. You feel an immediate attraction. This initial insight is the spark that ignites your interest, leading you to explore what makes this person attractive to you. You realise that your attraction is not just about physical appearance but also about shared values, interests and emotional connections.

- **Cognitive map:** You create a cognitive map that outlines how you and this person interact with each other and relate to various key concepts such as marriage, long-term relationships, commitment, courage, responsibility and love.

This map visualises the journey from initial attraction to a deeper emotional connection, identifying potential challenges like differing expectations or communication barriers. It also reveals individual perceptions and how each party views these concepts. For instance, one might view a long-term relationship through an overly optimistic lens, expecting a fairytale ending, while the other might have a more cautious or even pessimistic view, fearing constant arguments and restrictions. Some may approach romance sentimentally, while others might require empirical evidence and lengthy rounds of testing before they can fully trust. Additionally, some individuals might see a partnership as a lifelong commitment, while others may be more open to going separate ways if things don't work out.

- **Narratives:** The stories that shape your understanding of romantic relationships and interpretation of unfolding events play a significant role, whether from past relationships, cultural influences, experiences with parenting and/or the experiences of loved ones. They provide context and influence how you perceive and engage with romantic partners. Awareness of these narratives can make you more conscious of their influence, guiding you to engage with your romantic partners more consciously and intentionally.

- **Mental models:** The frameworks or mental models you use to understand how romantic relationships work might include beliefs about what makes a relationship successful, such as trust, respect and open communication. For instance, you may believe that regular quality time together is essential for maintaining a solid bond.

- **Perspectives:** The various viewpoints that influence your romantic choices, including your own, your partner's and those of friends and family, are crucial. Understanding and considering these different angles can help you navigate the complexities of romantic relationships with more empathy and consideration, leading to more informed and thoughtful decisions.

- **Domain:** The specific area of romantic love being addressed could be dating, long-term relationships or marriage. Each domain has its unique challenges and dynamics. For example, the domain of dating might focus on getting to know each other, while marriage might emphasise long-term compatibility and shared life goals.

- **Paradigms:** The prevailing theories and practices regarding romantic relationships include various established ways of relating to romance that depend on cultural backgrounds, societal norms and personal beliefs. These paradigms shape how people perceive and approach romantic relationships. For instance, some cultures emphasise arranged marriages, while others prioritise love marriages. Understanding these paradigms provides a broader context for individual romantic choices.

- **Contextual variables:** In the context of a romantic relationship, various contextual variables can significantly impact the dynamics between partners. These include socio-economic status, cultural backgrounds, personal histories and external influences such as family and friends. For example, financial stability or instability can affect relationship decisions and stress levels. Cultural expectations might dictate certain behaviours or attitudes towards relationships and marriage. Recognising these variables helps in understanding the broader context within which the relationship operates and provides insights into potential areas of conflict or harmony.

- **Authentication:** Within the domain of long-term romantic relationships, for example, authentication involves continuously checking the practical applicability and effectiveness of the relationship dynamics in real-life contexts. For instance, both partners can reflect on their interactions and assess whether their approaches to resolving conflicts or expressing love and support are effective. Seeking feedback from a relationship counsellor or through mutual discussions can help validate and adjust their strategies, ensuring that the relationship remains functional and fulfilling. This ongoing process of reflection and adaptation helps maintain the integrity of the relationship and supports its growth and resilience.

Example 3: Education

In education, the Nested Theory of Sense-making can be used to map out the metacontent of curriculum development. Traditionally, curricula are designed based on predefined standards and learning outcomes. However, by applying the Nested Theory of Sense-making, educators can go deeper, examining the cognitive and conceptual layers that underpin student learning.

1. **Initial insight:** The foundational assumption that education should be teacher-centred has been challenged by the idea that learning should instead be student-centred, prioritising individual student needs, interests, and learning styles in the teaching process.

2. **Cognitive map:** An ontological model of how students currently relate to and interact with the content, considering factors such as attention spans, engagement levels and common beliefs, opinions, perceptions and misconceptions. Customer journey mapping is a powerful process and is rarely used for students in the education system. Typically, neither parents nor teachers ask children how they are relating to school and education, let alone specific course content. The cognitive map helps in visualising the journey students take from initial exposure to content mastery and what might hold them back, such as their existing web of perceptions. For example, some students might perceive mathematics as inherently difficult and anxiety-inducing, influenced by past experiences, societal attitudes and possibly parental opinions.

This perception can create a mental barrier that prevents them from engaging fully with the subject, leading to lower attention spans and higher frustration levels during lessons. Others might hold the belief that certain subjects, such as history or literature, are irrelevant to their future careers or daily lives. This belief can stem from a lack of understanding of how these subjects apply to real-world situations or from cultural attitudes that prioritise STEM fields over the humanities. Consequently, this perception can result in disengagement and a lack of motivation to invest effort in these areas.

3. **Narratives:** Narratives that shape students' interpretation of events and motivation include success stories of students overcoming academic challenges that can inspire and guide others, highlighting common obstacles and effective strategies for addressing them. Narratives can encourage them to identify new possibilities they might have thought were impossible before undertaking this metacontent analysis. A thorough analysis of this layer might also reveal deeper narratives at play. For example, it could show that many students no longer believe in the traditional dominant narrative that students need to get better grades, get university admissions and get a degree or professional certificate to find a job and their role in society because of the vast number of graduates today who can't find a suitable job or find it challenging to survive in a changing world. The analysis could reveal that the narrative of success that worked for a while in the 20th century is incongruent with today's realities and challenges.

4. **Mental models:** Uncovering the mental models of teachers, parents and students to reveal shared mental models combined with frameworks for understanding that students use to comprehend complex and other subjects. Systems scientist and senior lecturer Peter Senge emphasises the importance of finding a shared mental model of the reality at hand before jumping into any solutions. In *Schools That*

Learn: A Fifth Discipline Fieldbook for Educators, Parents, and Everyone Who Cares About Education[146], Senge elaborates on this in the context of the education system. He says recognising and aligning these mental models is crucial in improving educational outcomes. Furthermore, in high school learning, it is also beneficial to develop mental models around logical reasoning, not just through implicit learning but with explicit instruction. That's because logical reasoning, identifying logical fallacies and the abuse of language and reasoning are not subjects that are explicitly taught and trained, even at high levels such as PhD programs. Instead, students are expected to implicitly become more logical by interacting with other materials. Consequently, high school students, especially those interested in pursuing research or STEM fields, would benefit from formal courses on logic and reasoning before they enter university. By incorporating these courses alongside traditional subjects, educators can ensure students build a strong foundation in critical thinking and analytical skills, essential for their future academic and professional endeavours. During a metacontent analysis of this layer, educators could also unpack the frameworks for understanding that students who wish to pursue other fields use to comprehend subjects of interest to them.

5. **Perspectives:** The various viewpoints that influence how students engage with the curriculum, ensuring it is inclusive and relevant to a diverse group of students. For example, students' perspectives are shaped by their backgrounds, mental health conditions, neurodiverse traits and preferences, leading them to view certain matters from particular angles. These unique angles influence their overall outlook and engagement with the curriculum. Understanding and integrating these diverse perspectives can create a more inclusive

---

146 Senge, P.M., Cambron-McCabe, N., Lucas, T., Smith, B., Dutton, J. & Kleiner, A. (2000). *Schools That Learn: A Fifth Discipline Fieldbook for Educators, Parents, and Everyone Who Cares About Education.* New York: Doubleday.

and effective learning environment. Using the Perspective Quadrant[147] would also be beneficial here for revealing and analysing various perspectives on student-centred learning: student perspectives, teacher/educator perspectives, the perspectives of families, communities and other stakeholders and the global perspective.

6. **Domain:** The specific area/s of education being addressed, whether it's early childhood education, primary education, secondary education, higher education or more than one of these domains combined. In this particular scenario, the domain is secondary education. Each domain has unique challenges and requirements, but there are times when it is necessary to assess multidisciplinary or multi-domain issues. For example, higher-level matters related to how children and adolescents learn could impact several sectors within the broader domain of education. This layer would also be used to delve deeper than simply defining the domain by age. Ideally, curriculum development should tap into at least four domains, such as students' physical, psychological and social needs, as well as the economic and ecological challenges they face externally. Additionally, teachers could discuss and debate their overarching objective for achieving student-centred learning in the classroom. Is it reaching a certain academic standard, improving student wellbeing or a combination of the two?

7. **Paradigms:** The prevailing educational theories and methodologies, such as constructivism or experiential learning, combined with various pedagogical and research paradigms that might be applicable. These paradigms provide the theoretical foundation for curriculum design and instructional strategies. This layer also prompts us to consider deeper paradigms that can impact how we perceive the education

---

147   Tashvir, A. 2021. *BEING – The source of power* (Ch 1.5). Engenesis Publications: Sydney.

system, such as the nature versus nurture debate, including theories like Blank Slate Theory and Nativism.[148]

In addition to the seven Nested Theory layers outlined above, the following also need to be factored into the analysis:

- **The contextual variables**, including socio-economic factors, cultural background, family dynamics and available resources. These contextual variables influence how students interact with and absorb the curriculum and would also support educators in considering any behavioural factors arising from these contextual variables that might impact student learning.

- **The importance of authenticating curricula design** through feedback from educators, students and external educational experts. This would support education departments in ensuring their curricula are congruent with educational goals and authentic to the student-centred learning experience. Continuous iterations based on feedback and new educational research will enhance the authenticity and effectiveness of each curriculum. While we can leverage scientific methods to some extent in the authentication process, it primarily involves dialectics to reach consensus, which requires taking ethical considerations into account and deeply understanding the preferences of the people involved beyond what statistical data may show. This approach recognises that curriculum design is not an exact science; it involves human elements beyond science and should prioritise both efficiency and the emotional responses and preferences of those it serves.

By mapping out the metacontent underpinning the existing curricula, education departments would be armed with the information required to create more impactful and meaningful student-centred

---

148   Blank Slate Theory – also known as Tabula Rasa – suggests that individuals are born without built-in mental content and all knowledge comes from experience or perception. Nativism proposes that certain skills or abilities are 'native' or hard-wired into the brain at birth.

curricula. Meanwhile, teachers undertaking the process would have the comprehensive information they need to improve the assigned curricula to ensure it effectively and holistically addresses the real needs of their students.

Example 4: Healthcare

In healthcare, the Nested Theory of Sense-making can be utilised to improve patient care by mapping out the metacontent of patient experiences and medical practices. In the following example, patient care is considered as a collective. Remember, like other examples in this chapter, the following is simplified for the purpose of demonstrating the process.

1. **Initial insight:** The fundamental belief that patient-centred care that prioritises the needs, preferences and values of individual patients, in addition to the illness and presenting symptoms, is essential for effective treatment.

2. **Cognitive map:** An ontological model that maps out the patient journey through the healthcare system, from initial consultation to treatment and follow-up. This cognitive map identifies key touchpoints and potential pain points in the patient experience. It also considers the cognitive maps of various systems impacting the patient journey, such as the physiological and operational systems. If any system or aspect is omitted, it will affect the comprehensiveness of the analysis and, consequently, the decisions and output.

3. **Narratives:** To understand patient experiences, fears and expectations, patient narratives provide valuable insights into what they find most important and challenging in their care journey. Qualitative research that includes interviewing a sample of patients might be undertaken to reveal and examine the dominant narratives.

4. **Mental models:** The frameworks that healthcare providers use to diagnose and treat illnesses. Examples include:

- Differential Diagnosis: How doctors systematically rule out potential conditions based on patient symptoms and medical history.

- Treatment Pathways: The step-by-step protocols that clinicians follow for specific conditions, such as diabetes management or post-surgical care.

- Patient Adherence Models: Understanding why patients follow or deviate from prescribed treatments, which can influence the design of more effective patient education and support programs.

- Risk Assessment Models: How healthcare providers evaluate the likelihood of various health outcomes based on patient data and evidence-based guidelines.

5. **Perspectives:** The various perspectives of patients, healthcare providers and family members highlight the different needs and concerns that must be addressed to provide holistic, patient-centred care. Perspectives are critical because they encompass diverse ideas and engage multiple stakeholders in the decision-making process. For example, a patient with chronic pain might prioritise immediate relief. A healthcare provider would focus on evidence-based practices and clinical outcomes to ensure treatments are scientifically validated and effective. A family member would be concerned about the patient's overall wellbeing, including emotional health. Meanwhile, the socioeconomic perspective would highlight the need for tailored support to ensure equitable access and better outcomes. In line with the Perspective Quadrant, the global perspective must also be considered. This perspective goes beyond what patients, families and healthcare providers see, considering patient care from a broader context. For example, it might pose questions like: Is health just the absence of disease? What would optimising patient care mean for communities, societies and humanity? This comprehensive approach ensures that the different needs and concerns

of all stakeholders are addressed, leading to better patient outcomes and a more holistic healthcare system.

6. **Domain:** The specific area of healthcare being addressed encompasses various specialised branches of knowledge. While traditional domains include chronic disease management or acute care, a more integrative approach is essential for patient care. This requires combining different domains, including Western and Eastern health practices, holistic and integrative medicine, nutrition and interdisciplinary approaches, all of which typically operate in silos. Integrative approaches aim to address the disconnect by fostering dialogue and collaboration among the various branches. For example, combining medical treatments with lifestyle and environmental changes for chronic disease management could enhance patient care by considering the full spectrum of influences on health.

7. **Paradigms:** The prevailing medical theories and practices, such as evidence-based medicine or holistic health approaches. These paradigms shape how patient care is delivered and what outcomes are prioritised. There are also deeper paradigms that could be considered here, such as those that consider various ways to consider and deal with pain, longevity and even life and death.

To gain a complete picture, healthcare policymakers and providers would also consider:

- **The contextual variables** such as the prevailing healthcare environment, including cultural beliefs about medicine, economic factors affecting access to care and technological advancements. These variables impact how patient care is delivered and received.

- **The need to authenticate healthcare practices** through patient feedback, clinical trials and peer reviews, ensuring that treatment plans are congruent with the latest medical research and patient needs. Continuous monitoring and adaptation based on patient outcomes and new medical findings will enhance the authenticity and effectiveness of patient care.

This comprehensive mapping process would enable healthcare providers and policymakers to design and implement more empathetic, efficient, effective and holistic patient care strategies.

Example 5: Conflict resolution in a long-term relationship

In a scenario where a husband and wife find themselves entangled in frequent arguments and on the verge of a breakup, despite years of relative stability in their relationship, the Nested Theory of Sensemaking can be instrumental in unravelling the underlying sources of their issues. By working through the layers to systematically explore various aspects of their relationship, they can take significant steps towards resolving conflicts and restoring integrity. Note that this final example includes reconstruction and authentication as iterative processes. Reconstruction and ongoing authentication apply to all scenarios and any content you wish to examine and make sense of with the ultimate intention of transformation and restoring the integrity of your relationship with the content in question.

- **Initial insight:** Both partners recognise that their relationship is in trouble. This realisation prompts them to explore the underlying causes of their conflicts, moving beyond surface-level arguments to understand the deeper issues.

- **Cognitive map:** Together, they create a cognitive map to outline how each partner relates to various significant concepts like conflict, marriage, long-term relationships, commitment, courage, responsibility and love. By highlighting individual perceptions and how each party views these key concepts, the cognitive map allows them to identify potential challenges like differing values, expectations or communication barriers. For example, one partner may view conflict as inherently negative and something to avoid, while the other may see conflict as opportunities for growth. Furthermore, one might see marriage as an unbreakable lifelong commitment, while the other may consider divorce a viable option if conflicts persist.

- **Narratives:** How each partner interprets the unfolding events – the stories they tell themselves about those events – could vary significantly. For example, one partner might view a disagreement as a sign of underlying relationship issues, shaped by past experiences of conflict in their family. In contrast, the other partner might see the same disagreement as a normal and healthy part of communication, influenced by their cultural background that values open and direct dialogue. Gaining visibility on these differing narratives and how they impact the relationship can be extremely beneficial for both parties.

- **Mental models:** Here, each partner unpacks their personal framework for understanding how marriages work. One partner might have entered the marriage with an overly optimistic expectation of achieving 'happily ever after' but now feels disillusioned due to unmet expectations, while the other might have been more pragmatic in their expectations of marriage. One partner may believe in discussing and resolving issues immediately, while the other might prefer to avoid confrontation, hoping issues will resolve on their own.

- **Perceptions:** Differences in how emotional support is perceived and provided can lead to misunderstandings and feelings of neglect. Understanding how each partner recounts conflicts and arguments can reveal underlying emotional triggers and patterns. Similarly, exploring past events where each partner felt hurt or misunderstood, contributing to accumulated resentment, can also be beneficial when examining the metacontent revealed by the perceptions layer. By stepping into each other's shoes, partners can better understand the motivations and fears driving their actions and reactions. Furthermore, the couple might also realise how the perspectives of close family members and friends might have influenced each partner's approach to the relationship.

- **Domain:** The domain in this scenario is intimate relationships within the institution of marriage. This domain focuses on the dynamics of long-term romantic partnerships and the broader context of married life. It includes various aspects such as exploring the emotional, psychological and physical connections between partners and how love, trust, intimacy and companionship can be nurtured and maintained over time. It might also address how different life stages, such as career changes, parenthood, ageing and health issues impact the relationship.

- **Paradigms:** Within the domain of intimate relationships and marriage, there are several established paradigms that provide different frameworks for understanding and building relationships. One of the benefits of exploring various paradigms within this particular domain is to determine the value of leveraging one or more of them, for instance, through coaching or therapeutic support. Examples include Attachment Theory, which focuses on how early attachment experiences with caregivers shape one's expectations and behaviour in adult relationships, and various therapeutic models like Cognitive-Behavioural Therapy (CBT) and Emotionally Focused Therapy (EFT). Some individuals prefer to approach relationships systematically. This might include using relationship assessments, engaging in premarital counselling and consistently seeking feedback to improve the relationship dynamics.

- **Contextual Variables:** Within the domain of intimate relationships and marriage, contextual variables include prevailing socio-economic conditions, the cultural background of one or both parties, mental health, family dynamics and individual life experiences. For example, financial stress, differing cultural expectations, the mental health of each individual in the relationship and the influence of extended family can all impact how conflicts arise and are resolved. Recognising and addressing these contextual variables can provide deeper insights and more tailored strategies for conflict resolution.

- **Reconstruction:** Once the couple has deconstructed each of the layers and identified areas of misunderstanding and radically different constituent parts of their metacontent, the next step is to engage in a structured process to reconstruct their understanding and approach to the relationship. To rebuild common ground, they must acknowledge and understand their differences and reconstruct a shared narrative and mental model that respects both perspectives. This is not a one-off project; transformation never is. It's an iterative process involving continuous dialogue, reflection and adaptation, allowing them to refine their relationship dynamics over time.

- **Authentication:** To ensure the effectiveness of their efforts, the couple must engage in a process of authentication to check the congruence or internal validity of their newly reconstructed understanding within the context of their marriage. This means continuously validating their new approaches and solutions to ensure they work effectively for them. It could involve regular check-ins with each other, seeking feedback from a relationship counsellor or coach, or reflecting on their progress over time. Ensuring that their solutions are practical and work within the unique dynamics of their relationship is key to restoring integrity and building a stronger partnership.

By applying the Nested Theory of Sense-making and engaging in the metacontent discourse, the couple can take a significant leap forward in resolving their conflicts. This approach of deconstruction and subsequent, ongoing reconstruction helps them move beyond surface-level arguments to build a deeper, more integrated understanding of their relationship. Through continuous reconstruction, authentication and mutual sense-making, they can restore the integrity and strength of their partnership, paving the way for a more harmonious future.

As you can see, the Nested Theory of Sense-making is not just for the meta-analysis of large-scale individual and collective matters but also for areas in our day-to-day life that may appear considerably insignificant in the larger scheme of things. At the end of the day, our lives, particularly our experience of life, are the result of the aggregation of all these so-called 'insignificant' or 'small' matters, decisions, emotions, thoughts, actions and behaviours.

Applying the Nested Theory of Sense-making in practice

Now that you have the foundational knowledge of the metacontent discourse and the Nested Theory of Sense-making, you can build upon this foundation to achieve your unique intentions within an area in which you operate and in your day-to-day life. The objective is to illustrate how this philosophically-engineered body of work can be expanded and facilitate the creation of new frameworks and models, even in niche areas and those that might exist some time in the future.

To apply the Nested Theory of Sense-making and map out the metacontent of any content you are examining, follow these detailed steps:

- *Identify the content*

  Determine the specific content or phenomenon you wish to make sense of or address. This could be a problem, a concept or an area of interest. For example, imagine you are a training and development manager identifying the challenge of how to increase participant engagement in online learning for induction training within your organisation and improve their subsequent effectiveness on the job.

- *Initial insight*

  Reflect on the initial insight that sparked your curiosity and inquiry. For example, you suddenly came to realise that new recruits might be disengaged from your organisation's online induction training modules due to a lack of interactive elements. This initial insight can lead to further investigation into how to make online learning more engaging. Begin by pinpointing the foundational assumptions or hypotheses that underpin the content you are exploring. These foundations serve as the starting point for your analysis and provide a base from which all other insights will emerge. For instance, in the context of adult education, the foundational assumption might be the belief that learning should be participant-centred, engaging and interactive. This assumption prioritises the needs, interests and learning styles of participants in the online training process, shaping the way these types of courses are developed and implemented.

- *Map the cognitive landscape*

  Create an ontological model that captures the key elements and relationships within the content. Consider how different components interact and influence each other. This cognitive map serves as a visual and conceptual guide to understanding the intricate connections within the subject matter. For example, in the case of online induction training, a cognitive map might outline the journey of a new recruit, from onboarding to completing the required induction training modules. It might include the support provided during and after the training, the touchpoints, interactions and potential challenges a participant might face, providing a comprehensive overview of their experience.

  In formulating the cognitive map, include current perceptions, conceptions, opinions and beliefs about the content, and identify the contextual variables influencing these perceptions. For example, you might discover that a participant's cultural background and access to technology at home can affect their engagement. Mapping out these variables helps in creating a more inclusive learning environment.

- *Construct the narrative lens*

  Develop the narratives or stories surrounding the content. These stories provide insights into how people experience and interpret the subject matter. By analysing these narratives, you can identify common themes, challenges, areas for improvement and successes that offer valuable context. Additionally, crafting a compelling narrative that highlights the potential of online learning to provide flexible, engaging and personalised adult education that results in effectiveness and efficiency on the job can motivate new recruits as well as senior management and other stakeholders to embrace online learning for delivering the organisation's induction training.

- *Formulate mental models*

  Determine the mental frameworks and conceptual structures that people use to understand the content. These models shape their perceptions, decisions and actions. This involves understanding processes, cause-and-effect relationships and system functionalities. Identifying and refining these mental models can lead to a more accurate and effective understanding of how the content is understood and applied in the real world. For example, creating a mental model of how interactive elements such as quizzes and discussion forums enhance participant engagement can guide the design of future online induction training courses to include more interactive components. Mental models might also include visual aids and teaching strategies used to explain complex concepts. These models help instructional designers convey information in a way that aligns with how participants process and retain knowledge.

- *Consider multiple perspectives*

  Analyse the content from various perspectives to gain a holistic understanding and ensure that the analysis is inclusive and comprehensive. Consider different viewpoints, roles, experiences and cultural contexts. For example, taking into account the perspectives of participants, fellow team members, leaders and other stakeholders in designing online induction training ensures that your platform meets the needs of all concerned. Each group has different needs, concerns, and insights that contribute to a well-rounded understanding of inducting new recruits into the organisation.

- *Define the domain*

  Clearly define the specific area or field you are focusing on to ensure your analysis is targeted, relevant and addresses the unique challenges and opportunities within that domain. This could be a specific field such as law, science, financial services or art. Furthermore, in business, defining whether you are focusing on marketing, operations or finance helps tailor the strategies and interventions to the specific needs of that area. For example, understanding that your domain is operations within the financial services sector will help you identify the most effective ways to design and deliver online induction training to serve that specific domain's requirements.

- *Explore paradigms within the domain*

  Investigate the prevailing theories, methodologies and paradigms that influence the content. Understanding these existing frameworks provides context for your analysis and helps in aligning your approach with established best practices and innovations. In adult education, examining theories like constructivism or experiential learning provides a theoretical foundation for curriculum design and instructional strategies. For example, adopting the constructivist paradigm, which emphasises active learning and student-centred approaches might lead to the development of more engaging and effective online learning experiences.

- *Account for other contextual variables*

  Contextual variables include cultural, social, economic, political and environmental factors that influence the content you are examining. These variables impact perceptions, interpretations and outcomes, so understanding them ensures a comprehensive and relevant analysis. For example, recognising that new recruits in different geographical locations may have varying access to high-speed internet and personal computers would allow you to ensure that all participants have equal opportunities to succeed in online learning by encouraging them to complete the modules at work.

- *Deconstruct, reconstruct and continually authenticate*

  Use the Nested Theory of Sense-making to deconstruct the content into its constituent parts. Analyse how each part contributes to the whole and then reconstruct the content by integrating insights from the analysis to create a more comprehensive understanding, authenticating all new insights and changes as you go. For example, the iterative process of deconstructing the elements of an online induction training course to identify areas for improvement and then reconstructing the course with interactive and engaging content – authenticating its workability and effectiveness ongoingly – can lead to continuous improvement in the quality of your organisation's online education. This will generate additional benefits in engagement, productivity and continuous refinement of your ideas based on feedback and new information.

Extending the application of the Nested-Theory of Sense-making to create new constructs

In the previous chapter, I revealed how I used the metacontent discourse and Nested Theory of Sense-making to create the Being Framework, including its ontological model. To build your own construct or framework using the Nested Theory, follow these steps:

1. **Define your objective:**

   - Clearly state the purpose or goal of your construct. What do you aim to achieve or understand?

   - **Example:** A healthcare professional aiming to create a holistic treatment plan for patients with chronic illnesses.

2. **Leverage the existing metacontent:**

   - Apply the layers of the Nested Theory of Sense-making to gather and organise relevant existing metacontent. This provides a strong foundation for your construct.

   - **Example:** Collecting data on patients' medical histories, backgrounds and personal narratives and experiences. This comprehensive data collection ensures that all relevant factors are considered in achieving your objective of creating a novel, holistic treatment plan for patients living with a chronic illness.

3. **Integrate your new insights:**

   - Synthesise insights from each layer to form a cohesive and comprehensive understanding of people living with a chronic disease. Ensure that all perspectives and contextual variables are considered.

   - **Example:** Integrating insights on patients' lifestyles, mental health and environmental factors to design personalised treatment plans for their chronic health condition. This holistic approach ensures that your treatment plan addresses all aspects of the patient's wellbeing.

4. **Develop the framework:**

   - Create your construct or framework based on the integrated insights. This could be a model, strategy or plan that addresses your objective.

   - **Example:** Developing a holistic healthcare model that includes physical, mental and social wellbeing for patients living with a chronic health condition. This model provides a comprehensive approach to patient care.

5. **Test, authenticate and iterate:**

   - Implement your construct and observe its effectiveness. Gather feedback and refine your framework as needed.

   - **Example:** Testing the holistic healthcare model with a group of patients and making adjustments based on their feedback. This iterative process ensures that the model remains effective and relevant.

6. **Document and share:**

   - Clearly document your process and findings. Share your insights with others to contribute to the broader body of knowledge.

   - **Example:** Publishing a research paper on the effectiveness of your new holistic healthcare model. Sharing your findings can help others adopt and refine the model in their practice.

The relationship between existing and new metacontent

While we have discussed metacontent as something to be mapped out, it's important to recognise that there are established, overarching and often dominant or widely accepted metacontents in the world that influence each other and us in various ways, even though many are still evolving. These come in the form of various schools of thought, faith-based religions and institutional frameworks. For example, consider the existing metacontent proposed by the following:

- **Abrahamic Faith:** All faith-based religions propose their own metacontent. Religions like Christianity, Islam and Judaism offer comprehensive frameworks that cover ethical guidelines, moral imperatives and existential narratives: personal or collective stories that help us make sense of fundamental questions about life, purpose, identity, freedom, mortality and authenticity. These religions provide well-documented and deeply developed metacontent, including cognitive maps, mental models, narratives and perspectives that guide believers' thinking and lifestyles.

- **Liberalism:** As a political and moral philosophy, liberalism encompasses ideas about individual freedom, equality and justice. It proposes a structured metacontent that shapes societal norms and governance practices.

- **Postmodernism:** This philosophical movement challenges traditional narratives and emphasises the role of power, language and social constructs. It provides a critical framework for understanding cultural and intellectual phenomena.

- **Mandate for Leadership 2025 – The Conservative Promise:** This document outlines a vision for conservative governance rooted in traditional values, individual responsibility and limited government. It provides a metacontent that emphasises the importance of preserving cultural heritage, promoting economic freedom and maintaining national security. By advocating for policies that strengthen family structures, uphold religious freedoms and encourage free-market principles, the Mandate for Leadership 2025 offers a comprehensive framework for navigating the complexities of contemporary governance while staying true to foundational conservative ideals. This document, like others, presents a specific worldview and set of principles that shape political discourse and policymaking and offers a perspective that influences contemporary governance and societal structures.

- **2030 Agenda for Sustainable Development:** This United Nations document outlines goals for global development, focusing on sustainability, diversity and inclusion. It offers a comprehensive metacontent that envisions a future where poverty is eradicated and environmental sustainability is achieved.

- **Multiculturalism:** This perspective promotes acknowledging, understanding and appreciating cultural diversity within societies. It offers a metacontent that supports the coexistence of different cultural identities, fostering inclusivity and mutual respect.

- **Globalism:** This framework emphasises the interconnectedness of nations and the importance of global cooperation. It shapes how people view international relations, economic policies and cultural exchanges, promoting a worldview that transcends national boundaries.

- **Scientism:** This ideology elevates scientific knowledge and methods as the ultimate authority on all questions in life, dismissing other forms of understanding as inferior or irrelevant. It provides a metacontent that shapes attitudes toward technology, progress and the nature of reality itself.

- **Hegelian Philosophy:** Hegel's comprehensive philosophical system articulates a framework that integrates all aspects of reality. His dialectical method emphasises the process of thesis-antithesis-synthesis, aiming to reconcile contradictions and provide a holistic understanding of history, culture and consciousness.

- **Feminism:** This social and political movement seeks to address and rectify gender inequalities. It offers a metacontent that challenges traditional, heteronormative gender roles, advocates for women's rights and promotes gender equality.

- **Capitalism:** As an economic system, capitalism focuses on private ownership, free markets and the pursuit of profit. It provides a metacontent that shapes economic policies, business practices and societal values regarding wealth, work and competition.

- **Agenda of the World Economic Forum (WEF):** The WEF promotes global cooperation to address pressing economic and social issues. Its agenda includes themes like sustainable development, technological innovation and inclusive growth, offering a metacontent that influences global policy-making and corporate strategies.

- **Frankfurt School of Thought:** Initially a philosophical movement, this school of thought evolved into an institution that critiques modern society, culture and politics through a blend of Marxism, psychoanalysis and critical theory. It provides a structured metacontent that challenges capitalist ideologies and explores power dynamics and societal change.

Many people adopt these metacontents either explicitly by choice or implicitly by allowing themselves to be influenced by them. As established metacontents, despite the fact that many are still evolving, they exert enormous influence and power over people's thinking and lifestyles.

No content exists in isolation; it always exists in relationship with other content. However, with some content, particularly man-made constructs, it can be challenging to discern its relationship to existing content. This type of content could either be trivial or, conversely, the undiscovered work of some unknown 'genius'. Often, we rank content by the extent to which it has been necessary for other content to come into existence. For example, if we consider every academic book in existence as content, the citations within those books highlight how they have been influenced by prior content. Major studies that have caused significant leaps and disrupted the status quo in their respective fields illustrate this point. Books that have greatly influenced other books hold relevance across various fields in terms of textual content. Similarly, genres of poetry or literature often follow this pattern. This principle also applies in evolutionary theory, where the evolution of cells has manifested in the diversity of all species and beings.

There can be a chronological order to content that reflects on its corresponding metacontent. For instance, existentialism massively influenced postmodernism, and the Enlightenment ideals of reason and individualism significantly shaped the development of modern democratic governance. By understanding these connections, we can appreciate how new content evolves from and interacts with existing content and metacontent, leading to the continuous development of knowledge and ideas.

Some content and their respective metacontent serve as 'A Priori'[149] knowledge for others and certain maxims or axiomatic laws have stood the test of time. Although some may be reluctant to see such contents as transcendental, they can at least be considered transhistorical. For example, the works of Aristotle, the principles of Newtonian physics or the writings of influential philosophers have formed the bedrock for subsequent developments in their respective fields. These foundational elements serve as essential building blocks, enabling the progression and evolution of knowledge across various domains.

It's important to acknowledge that just as all content interacts with and influences other content – even if that interaction is opposition or denial – their corresponding metacontents do as well. Established metacontents proposed by ideologies such as feminism, capitalism, liberalism and others listed earlier are examples of these. Each of these metacontents has its own influence, shaping and being shaped by the evolving landscape of human thought and societal norms. Therefore, if you are attempting to develop a more comprehensive metacontent of the world, it is crucial to at least engage in a high-level synthesis of the preceding metacontents.

Ultimately, to make sense of any existing content and metacontent, including well-documented examples like those shown, we need to

---

149 'A Priori' is a Latin term that means 'from the earlier'. In philosophy, it refers to knowledge that is independent of experience. A Priori knowledge is derived through reasoning and logic, rather than from sensory experience. For example, mathematical truths and logical deductions are often considered A Priori because they can be known to be true without needing to observe the world.

deconstruct and subsequently reconstruct them to arrive at a more nuanced version that gives them meaning in the context of one's life and leaves us with a more comprehensive understanding of such matters. Furthermore, understanding that there are broad, established metacontents and individualised metacontents is crucial for a comprehensive view of how we make sense of the world and our place within it.

Conclusion

As we reach the conclusion of this journey together, I invite you to reflect on the path we've walked. This book is a guide to navigating the intricate web of human understanding and performance. The desire for valid knowledge and authentic awareness in a world full of dilemmas and uncertainties sowed the seeds for this exploration. We discovered that the limitations of our sensory abilities and rationality exacerbate our confusion and vulnerability to life's challenges. And we recognised that science, as incredible as it is, cannot provide all the answers, particularly in terms of gaining a deeper understanding of the more subjective realms like human performance and effectiveness, and shedding light on 'The Invisible'. Authentic awareness is the intentional light that illuminates both what we know and what we have yet to discover. Becoming authentically aware of any content we are exploring is not merely an intellectual exercise but a profound connection to ourselves, others and the world around us.

The Nested Theory of Sense-making provides a robust structure to authentically make sense of anything. By working through its layers, we reveal an authenticated, nuanced and holistic intellectual substrate or metacontent for any matter being examined, from personal issues to work, business, societal and global challenges. Just as it guided the development of the Being Framework, it can also be leveraged to navigate the complexities of life and make informed, effective decisions with potentially transformative outcomes. The examples and step-by-step instructions provided in this chapter serve as a practical guide for applying this theory to various domains with the aim of developing well-constructed metacontent that leads you towards greater authentic awareness, integrity and fulfilment.

In closing, I sincerely hope that this body of knowledge will empower you to create meaningful and sustainable outcomes in your personal and professional lives, contributing to a better understanding of the world and the human experience. Like nurturing a tree, true transformation requires tending to the roots and soil, not just the leaves. It's about fostering an ecosystem where your potential can truly flourish. Ultimately, I hope this book inspires you to make wiser, more coherent decisions that resonate deeply with your values, aspirations and intentions.

Thank you for embarking on this journey with me. May the knowledge and wisdom you've gained here be a source of strength, clarity and inspiration in all your endeavours. I encourage you to carry forward the insights and perspectives we've shared. Let them guide you in your daily interactions, decisions and quest for meaning. By embracing these principles, you are not just enhancing your own life but also contributing to a more thoughtful, understanding and connected world.

With gratitude and hope,

Ashkan Tashvir

References

American Psychological Association. 2020. 'Ethical Principles of Psychologists and Code of Conduct'. APA. Available at: www.apa.org/ethics/code

Aristotle. (no date) *Metaphysics*.

Asimov, I. 1994. *Asimov on Science Fiction*. New York: Doubleday.

Atkins, P. and de Paula, J. 2018. *Atkins' Physical Chemistry*. 11th edn. Oxford: Oxford University Press.

Baars, B.J. 1988. *A Cognitive Theory of Consciousness*. Cambridge: Cambridge University Press.

Baines, J. 2007. *Visual and Written Culture in Ancient Egypt*. Oxford: Oxford University Press.

Bandyopadhyay, A. 2024. *Emotion, Cognition and Silent Communication: Unsolved Mysteries*. Singapore: Springer Nature B.V.

Baron, R.A. and Byrne, D. 2003. *Social Psychology: Understanding Human Interaction*. 10th edn. Boston: Allyn and Bacon.

Baronett, S. 2008. *Logic*. Oxford University Press.

Baum, W. M. 2005. *Understanding Behaviorism: Behavior, Culture, and Evolution*. Wiley-Blackwell.

Baumeister, R.F. and Tierney, J. 2011. *Willpower: Rediscovering the Greatest Human Strength*. New York: Penguin Press.

Beauchamp, T.L. and Childress, J.F. 2013. *Principles of Biomedical Ethics*. 7th edn. Oxford: Oxford University Press.

Beck, D.E. 2002. *The Crucible: Forging South Africa's Future*. Dallas, TX: New Futures Study Group.

Beck, D.E. and Cowan, C.C. 1996. *Spiral Dynamics: Mastering Values, Leadership, and Change*. Malden, MA: Blackwell Publishing.

Behe, M.J. 1996. *Darwin's Black Box: The Biochemical Challenge to Evolution*. New York: Free Press.

Bhaskar, R. 2015. *A Realist Theory of Science*. London: Routledge.

Blaikie, N.W.H. 2010. *Designing Social Research*. 2nd edn. Cambridge: Polity.

Blease, C.R. 2015. 'Talking more about talking cures: Cognitive behavioural therapy and informed consent', *Journal of Medical Ethics*, 41(10), pp. 750-755.

Brach, T. 2003. *Radical Acceptance: Embracing Your Life With the Heart of a Buddha*. New York: Bantam Books.

Brier, B. 2013. 'Ancient Egyptian Science', *The UCLA Encyclopedia of Egyptology*. Available at: escholarship.org/uc/item/4mq8k3z4

Brout, D. and Scolnic, D. 2022. 'Most precise accounting yet of dark matter and dark energy', *Harvard Gazette*, October.

Brown, K.W. and Ryan, R.M. 2003. 'The benefits of being present: Mindfulness and its role in psychological well-being', *Journal of Personality and Social Psychology*, 84(4), pp. 822-848.

Bryman, A. 2016. *Social Research Methods*. 5th edn. Oxford: Oxford University Press.

Burke, K. 1966. *Language as Symbolic Action: Essays on Life, Literature, and Method*. Berkeley: University of California Press.

Burke, K. 1969. *A Rhetoric of Motives*. Berkeley: University of California Press.

Caplan, A.L. 2005. *Am I My Brother's Keeper?: The Ethical Frontiers of Biomedicine*. Bloomington: Indiana University Press.

Caplan, A.L. 2005. *Science and Ethics*. Tuscaloosa: University of Alabama Press.

Capra, F. 1975. *The Tao of Physics: An Exploration of the Parallels Between Modern Physics and Eastern Mysticism*. Berkeley: Shambhala Publications.

Caputo, J.D. 1987. *Radical Hermeneutics: Repetition, Deconstruction, and the Hermeneutic Project*. Bloomington: Indiana University Press.

Caputo, J.D. 1997. *Deconstruction in a Nutshell: A Conversation with Jacques Derrida*. New York: Fordham University Press.

Chalmers, A.F. 1999. *What Is This Thing Called Science?*. 3rd edn. St. Lucia: University of Queensland Press.

Chalmers, D.J. 1996. *The Conscious Mind: In Search of a Fundamental Theory*. New York: Oxford University Press.

Charmaz, K. 2014. *Constructing Grounded Theory*. 2nd edn. London: Sage.

Chödrön, P. 1997. *When Things Fall Apart: Heart Advice for Difficult Times*. Boston: Shambhala Publications.

Chomsky, N. 1957. *Syntactic Structures*. The Hague: Mouton.

Chomsky, N. 1965. *Aspects of the Theory of Syntax*. Cambridge, MA: MIT Press.

Churchland, P.S. 1986. *Neurophilosophy: Toward a Unified Science of the Mind-Brain*. Cambridge, MA: MIT Press.

Cohen, L., Manion, L. and Morrison, K. 2017. *Research Methods in Education*. 8th edn. London: Routledge.

Colapinto, J. 2006. *As Nature Made Him: The Boy Who Was Raised as a Girl*. New York: Harper Perennial.

Creswell, J.W. and Creswell, J.D. 2017. *Research Design: Qualitative, Quantitative, and Mixed Methods Approaches*. 5th edn. Thousand Oaks, CA: Sage Publications.

Creswell, J.W. and Poth, C.N. 2018. *Qualitative Inquiry and Research Design: Choosing Among Five Approaches*. 4th edn. Thousand Oaks, CA: Sage Publications.

Csikszentmihalyi, M. 1990. *Flow: The Psychology of Optimal Experience*. New York: Harper & Row.

Cuijpers, P., Smit, F., Bohlmeijer, E., Hollon, S.D. and Andersson, G. 2010. 'Efficacy of cognitive-behavioural therapy and other psychological treatments for adult depression: Meta-analytic study of publication bias', *The British Journal of Psychiatry*, 196(3), pp. 173-178.

Damasio, A. 2000. *The Feeling of What Happens: Body and Emotion in the Making of Consciousness*. New York: Harcourt.

Deaton, A. 2010. 'Instruments, Randomization, and Learning about Development', *Journal of Economic Literature*, 48(2), pp. 424-455.

Dembski, W.A. 1999. *Intelligent Design: The Bridge Between Science &* *Theology*. Downers Grove, IL: InterVarsity Press.

Dennett, D.C. 1991. *Consciousness Explained*. Boston: Little, Brown and Co.

Denzin, N.K. and Lincoln, Y.S. 2018. *The SAGE Handbook of Qualitative Research*. 5th edn. Thousand Oaks, CA: Sage Publications.

Derrida, J. 1967. *Of Grammatology*. Translated by G.C. Spivak. Baltimore: Johns Hopkins University Press, 1976.

Derrida, J. 1978. *Writing and Difference*. Translated by A. Bass. Chicago: University of Chicago Press.

Derrida, J. 1981. *Positions*. Translated by A. Bass. Chicago: University of Chicago Press.

Derrida, J. 1982. *Margins of Philosophy*. Translated by A. Bass. Chicago: University of Chicago Press.

Descartes, R. 1641. *Meditations on First Philosophy*. Translated by J. Cottingham. Cambridge: Cambridge University Press, 1996.

Dhanani, A. 2002. 'Islamic Astronomy and Mathematics in the Medieval Period', in Selin, H. (ed.) *The Encyclopaedia of the History of Science, Technology, and Medicine in Non-Western Cultures*. 2nd edn. Dordrecht: Springer.

Diamond, M. and Sigmundson, H.K. 1997. 'Sex Reassignment at Birth: Long-term Review and Clinical Implications', *Archives of Pediatrics & Adolescent Medicine*, 151(3), pp. 298-304.

Diener, E., Emmons, R.A., Larsen, R.J. and Griffin, S. 1985. 'The Satisfaction with Life Scale', *Journal of Personality Assessment*, 49(1), pp. 71-75. doi. org/10.1207/s15327752jpa4901_13

Douglas, H. 2009. *Science, Policy, and the Value-Free Ideal*. Pittsburgh: University of Pittsburgh Press.

Dreyfus, H.L. 1991. *Being-in-the-World: A Commentary on Heidegger's Being and Time, Division I*. Cambridge, MA: MIT Press.

Duval, S. and Wicklund, R.A. 1972. *A Theory of Objective Self Awareness*. New York: Academic Press.

Eagle, M.N. and Wolitzky, D.L. 1992. 'Psychoanalytic theories of psychotherapy', in Freedheim, D.K., Freudenberger, H.J., Kessler, J.W., Messer, S.B., Peterson, D.R., Strupp, H.H. and Wachtel, P.L. (eds.) *History of Psychotherapy: A Century of Change*. Washington, DC: American Psychological Association, pp. 109-158.

Edelman, G.M. 2004. *Wider than the Sky: The Phenomenal Gift of Consciousness*. New Haven, CT: Yale University Press.

Edinger, E.F. 1994. *The Eternal Drama: The Inner Meaning of Greek Mythology*. Boston: Shambhala Publications.

Edlund, J.R. 2020. 'Teaching Text Rhetorically: Integrating Reading and Writing Instruction', Teaching Text Rhetorically Available at: textrhet. com/2020/10/14/kenneth-burke-on-terministic-screens

Eliade, M. 1959. *The Sacred and the Profane: The Nature of Religion*. Translated by W.R. Trask. New York: Harcourt, Brace & World.

Eliot, T.S. 1920. *The Sacred Wood: Essays on Poetry and Criticism*. Methuen & Co.

Esbjörn-Hargens, S. and Zimmerman, M.E. 2009. *Integral Ecology: Uniting Multiple Perspectives on the Natural World*. Boston: Integral Books.

Feyerabend, P. 2010. *Against Method*. 4th edn. London: Verso Books.

Feynman, R. 2011. *The Feynman Lectures on Physics*. New Millennium.

Feynman, R.P. 2011. *The Pleasure of Finding Things Out: The Best Short Works of Richard P. Feynman*. New York: Basic Books.

Feynman, R.P., Leighton, R.B. and Sands, M. 2011. *The Feynman Lectures on Physics, Volume 1: Mainly Mechanics, Radiation, and Heat*. New York: Basic Books.

Fiske, S.T., Gilbert, D.T. and Lindzey, G. 2010. *Handbook of Social Psychology*. Wiley.

Fogg, B.J. 2009. *Persuasive Technology: Using Computers to Change What We Think and Do*. San Francisco: Morgan Kaufmann.

Foucault, M. 1972. *The Archaeology of Knowledge*. Translated by A.M. Sheridan Smith. New York: Pantheon Books.

Foucault, M. 1978. *The History of Sexuality, Volume 1: An Introduction*. Translated by R. Hurley. New York: Pantheon Books.

Foucault, M. 1980. *Power/Knowledge: Selected Interviews and Other Writings, 1972-1977*. Edited by C. Gordon. New York: Pantheon Books.

Foucault, M. 1982. 'The Subject and Power', in Dreyfus, H.L. and Rabinow, P. (eds.) *Michel Foucault: Beyond Structuralism and Hermeneutics*. 2nd edn. Chicago: University of Chicago Press, pp. 208-226.

Foucault, M. 1995. *Discipline and Punish: The Birth of the Prison*. Translated by A. Sheridan. 2nd edn. New York: Vintage Books.

Frankl, V.E. 1959. *Man's Search for Meaning*, Boston: Beacon Press.

Fraser, N. 1981. 'Foucault on Modern Power: Empirical Insights and Normative Confusions', *Praxis International*, 1(3), pp. 272-287.

Frye, N. 1957. *Anatomy of Criticism: Four Essays*. Princeton: Princeton University Press.

Funtowicz, S.O. and Ravetz, J.R. 1993. 'Science for the post-normal age', *Futures*, 25(7), pp. 739-755. doi.org/10.1016/0016-3287(93)90022-L

Furman Shaharabani, Y., and Yarden, A. 2016. 'Toward narrowing the theory–practice gap: Characterizing evidence from in-service biology teachers' questions asked during an academic course', *International Journal of STEM Education*, 6(1), p. 20.

Gadamer, H.-G. 1976. *Philosophical Hermeneutics*. Translated and edited by D.E. Linge. Berkeley: University of California Press.

Gadamer, H.-G. 2004. *Truth and Method*. 2nd edn. Translated by J. Weinsheimer and D.G. Marshall. London: Continuum.

Gathorne-Hardy, J. 2000. *Sex the Measure of All Things: A Life of Alfred C. Kinsey*. Bloomington: Indiana University Press.

Gavin, F.P. 1991. 'Theory vs. practice in public personnel administration', *Journal of Public Administration Research and Theory*, 1(2), pp. 253-265.

Gerring, J. 2012. *Social Science Methodology: A Unified Framework*. 2nd edn. Cambridge: Cambridge University Press.

Gillings, M. 2017. 'Mathematics in the Time of COVID-19', *Plus Magazine*.

Gipps, R.G.T. 2013. 'Cognitive behavior therapy: A philosophical appraisal', in Fulford, K.W.M., Davies, M., Gipps, R.G.T., Graham, G., Sadler, J.Z., Stanghellini, G. and Thornton, T. (eds.) *The Oxford Handbook of Philosophy and Psychiatry*. Oxford: Oxford University Press, pp. 485-501.

Godfrey-Smith, P. 2003. *Theory and Reality: An Introduction to the Philosophy of Science*. University of Chicago Press.

Goldberg, L.R. 1993. 'The structure of phenotypic personality traits', *American Psychologist*, 48(1), pp. 26-34. doi. org/10.1037/0003-066X.48.1.26

Goleman, D. 1995. *Emotional Intelligence: Why It Can Matter More Than IQ*. New York: Bantam Books.

Greene, B. 2005. *The Fabric of the Cosmos: Space, Time, and the Texture of Reality*. New York: Vintage Books.

Gross, P.R. and Levitt, N. 1994. *Higher Superstition: The Academic Left and Its Quarrels with Science*. Baltimore: Johns Hopkins University Press.

Guba, E.G. and Lincoln, Y.S. 1994. 'Competing Paradigms in Qualitative Research', in Denzin, N.K. and Lincoln, Y.S. (eds.) *Handbook of Qualitative Research*. Thousand Oaks, CA: Sage Publications, pp. 105-117.

Gunaratana, B.H. 2011. *Mindfulness in Plain English*. 2nd edn. Boston: Wisdom Publications.

Gutting, G. 2005. *Foucault: A Very Short Introduction*. Oxford: Oxford University Press.

Haack, S. 2007. *Defending Science - Within Reason: Between Scientism and Cynicism*. Amherst, NY: Prometheus Books.

Hacking, I. 1999. *The Social Construction of What?*. Harvard University Press.

Hacking, I. 2012. 'Introductory Essay', in T.S. Kuhn, *The Structure of Scientific Revolutions*. 4th edn. University of Chicago Press.

Hare, R.M. 1979. 'Kinsey's Methods', *Philosophy of Science*, 46(4), pp. 588-595. doi.org/10.1086/288906

Harris, A. 2019. *Conscious: A Brief Guide to the Fundamental Mystery of the Mind*. New York: Harper.

Haslam, S.A., Reicher, S.D. and Platow, M.J. 2011. *The New Psychology of Leadership: Identity, Influence and Power*. Psychology Press.

Hawking, S. and Mlodinow, L. 2010. *The Grand Design*. Bantam Books.

Hegel, G.W.F. 1977. *Phenomenology of Spirit*. Translated by A.V. Miller. Oxford: Oxford University Press.

Heidegger, M. 1927. *Being and Time*. Translated by J. Macquarrie and E. Robinson. New York: Harper & Row, 1962.

Heidegger, M. 1971. *Poetry, Language, Thought*. Translated by A. Hofstadter. New York: Harper & Row.

Heidegger, M. 1999. *Ontologie: Hermeneutik der Faktizität (1923)*. Frankfurt am Main: Vittorio Klostermann.

Hirsch, E.D. 1967. *Validity in Interpretation*. New Haven: Yale University Press.

Hofstadter, D.R. 1979. *Gödel, Escher, Bach: An Eternal Golden Braid*. New York: Basic Books.

Hofstadter, D.R. 2007. *I Am a Strange Loop*. New York: Basic Books.

Husserl, E. 1913. 'Ideas Pertaining to a Pure Phenomenology and to a Phenomenological Philosophy', in *Book One: General Introduction to a Pure Phenomenology*. Dordrecht: Springer.

Huxley, A. 1945. *The Perennial Philosophy*. New York: Harper & Brothers.

James, W. 1902. *The Varieties of Religious Experience: A Study in Human Nature*. New York: Longmans, Green & Co.

Jones, J.H. 1997. *Alfred C. Kinsey: A Public/Private Life*. New York: W.W. Norton & Company.

Jung, C.G. 1959. *The Archetypes and the Collective Unconscious*. Translated by R.F.C. Hull. Princeton: Princeton University Press.

Jung, C.G. 1968. *Man and His Symbols*. London: Aldus Books.

Kabat-Zinn, J. 1990. *Full Catastrophe Living: Using the Wisdom of Your Body and Mind to Face Stress, Pain, and Illness*. New York: Delta.

Kant, I. 1998. *Critique of Pure Reason*. Translated by P. Guyer and A.W. Wood. Cambridge: Cambridge University Press.

Kinsey, A.C., Pomeroy, W.B., Martin, C.E. and Gebhard, P.H. 1953. *Sexual Behavior in the Human Female*. Philadelphia: W.B. Saunders Company.

Kipnis, K. and Diamond, M. 1998. 'Pediatric Ethics and the Surgical Assignment of Sex', *Journal of Clinical Ethics*, 9(4), pp. 398-410.

Knauff, M. and Spohn, W. 2021. 'Psychological and Philosophical Frameworks of Rationality - A Systematic Introduction', in Knauff, M. and Spohn, W. (eds.) *The Handbook of Rationality*. MIT Press.

Koch, C. 2004. *The Quest for Consciousness: A Neurobiological Approach*. Englewood, CO: Roberts & Company Publishers.

Koch, C. 2019. *The Feeling of Life Itself*. MIT Press.

Kuhn, D. 1991. *The Skills of Argument*. Cambridge University Press.

Kuhn, T.S. 2012. *The Structure of Scientific Revolutions*. 4th edn. Chicago: University of Chicago Press.

Kurtz, C.F. and Snowden, D.J. 2003. 'The new dynamics of strategy: Sense-making in a complex and complicated world', *IBM Systems Journal*, 42(3), pp. 462-483.

Latour, B. 1987. *Science in Action: How to Follow Scientists and Engineers Through Society*. Cambridge, MA: Harvard University Press.

Leahey, T.H. 2000. *A History of Psychology: Main Currents in Psychological Thought*. Prentice-Hall.

Lewis, C.S. 1940. *The Problem of Pain*. New York: HarperOne.

Lewis, D. 1986. *On the Plurality of Worlds*. Oxford: Blackwell.

Ling, S.J., Sanny, J., and Moebs, W. 2023. 'The Heisenberg Uncertainty Principle', in *University Physics Volume 3*. Pressbooks.

Logan, D. and Fisher-Wright, H. 2007. 'Rhetoric Unlobotomised: Transformation of Terministic Screens', *Barbados Group Working Paper No. 06-06*. doi.org/10.2139/ssrn.915321

Longino, H.E. 1990. *Science as Social Knowledge: Values and Objectivity in Scientific Inquiry*. Princeton, NJ: Princeton University Press.

Macionis, J.J. and Plummer, K. 2017. *Sociology: A Global Introduction*. 6th edn. London: Pearson.

Marcuse, H. 1960. *Reason and Revolution: Hegel and the Rise of Social Theory*. Boston: Beacon Press.

McInerny, D.Q. 2005. *Being Logical: A Guide to Good Thinking*. Penguin Random House: Canada.

Mele, A. R. and Rawling, P. (Eds.). 2004. *The Oxford Handbook of Rationality* (online edn., Oxford Academic, 2 Sept. 2009). doi.org/10.1093/oxfordhb/9780195145397.001.0001

Merleau-Ponty, M. 2012. *Phenomenology of Perception*. Translated by D.A. Landes. Abingdon: Routledge.

Merritt, D. 2020. *A Philosophical Approach to MOND: Assessing the Milgromian Research Program in Cosmology*. Cambridge University Press.

Midgley, M. 1992. *Science as Salvation: A Modern Myth and Its Meaning*. London: Routledge.

Money, J. 1992. *Gendermaps: Social Constructionism, Feminism, and Sexosophical History*. New York: Continuum Publishing.

Money, J. and Ehrhardt, A.A. 1972. *Man & Woman, Boy & Girl: Gender Identity from Conception to Maturity*. Baltimore: Johns Hopkins University Press.

Moreland, J.P. 2008. *Consciousness and the Existence of God: A Theistic Argument*. New York: Routledge.

Nagel, T. 1974. 'What Is it Like to Be a Bat?', *The Philosophical Review*, 83(4), pp. 435-450. doi.org/10.2307/2183914

Nagel, T. 1986. *The View from Nowhere*. New York: Oxford University Press.

Nanda, M. 2003. *Prophets Facing Backward: Postmodern Critiques of Science and Hindu Nationalism in India*. New Brunswick, NJ: Rutgers University Press.

National Institutes of Health. (no date) 'Ethics in Clinical Research'. NIH. Available at: www.nih.gov/health-information/nih-clinical-research-trials-you/ethics

Nietzsche, F. 1974. *The Gay Science*. Translated by W. Kaufmann. New York: Vintage Books.

Nolfi, K. 2015. 'Which mental states are rationally evaluable, and why?' *Philosophical Issues, 25*, 41-63. doi.org/10.1111/phis.12051

Norcross, J.C. 2011. *Changeology: 5 Steps to Realizing Your Goals and Resolutions*. New York: Simon & Schuster.

Nussbaum, M.C. 1997. *Cultivating Humanity: A Classical Defense of Reform in Liberal Education*. Cambridge, MA: Harvard University Press.

Okasha, S. 2002. *Philosophy of Science: A Very Short Introduction*. Oxford University Press.

Pavot, W. and Diener, E. 1993. 'Review of the Satisfaction with Life Scale', *Psychological Assessment*, 5(2), pp. 164-172. doi.org/10.1037/1040-3590.5.2.164

Penrose, R. 1994. *Shadows of the Mind: A Search for the Missing Science of Consciousness*. Oxford: Oxford University Press.

Peterson, J.B. 2018. *12 Rules for Life: An Antidote to Chaos*. Random House Canada.

Pinker, S. 2021. *Rationality: What It Is, Why It Seems Scarce, Why It Matters*. Viking.

Plato. 1966. *Apology 22d*. Translated by Harold North Fowler.

Plato. 2007. *The Republic*. Translated by Desmond Lee. Penguin Classics.

Plato. 1994. *The Symposium*. Translated by C. Gill. London: Penguin Classics.

Popper, K. 2002. *The Logic of Scientific Discovery*. London: Routledge.

Prochaska, J.O. and DiClemente, C.C. 1983. 'Stages and processes of self-change of smoking: Toward an integrative model of change', *Journal of Consulting and Clinical Psychology*, 51(3), pp. 390-395.

Putnam, H. 1967. 'Psychological Predicates', in Capitan, W.H. and Merrill, D.D. (eds.) *Art, Mind, and Religion*. Pittsburgh: University of Pittsburgh Press, pp. 37-48.

Pybis, J., Saxon, D., Hill, A. & Barkham, M. 2017. 'The comparative effectiveness and efficiency of cognitive behaviour therapy and generic counselling in the treatment of depression: Evidence from the 2nd UK National Audit of psychological therapies', *BMC Psychiatry*, 17(1), 215. doi. org/10.1186/s12888-017-1370-7

Regan, T. 1983. *The Case for Animal Rights*. Berkeley: University of California Press.

Reisman, J. 1990. *Kinsey, Sex and Fraud: The Indoctrination of a People*. Lafayette: Huntington House Publishers.

Reisman, J.A. 1998. 'Kinsey and the Homosexual Revolution', *The Journal of Human Sexuality*, 1(2), pp. 1-10.

Rescher, N. 1969. *Introduction to Value Theory*. Englewood Cliffs, NJ: Prentice-Hall.

Resnik, D.B. 2005. *The Ethics of Science: An Introduction*. London: Routledge.

Ricard, M. and Thuan, T.X. 2001. *The Quantum and the Lotus: A Journey to the Frontiers Where Science and Buddhism Meet.* New York: Crown Publishing Group.

Richardson, W.J. 1967. *Heidegger: Through Phenomenology to Thought*. New York: Fordham University Press.

Ricoeur, P. 1984. *Time and Narrative, Volume 1*. Translated by K. McLaughlin and D. Pellauer. Chicago: University of Chicago Press.

Ricoeur, P. 1991. *From Text to Action: Essays in Hermeneutics, II*. Translated by K. Blamey and J.B. Thompson. Evanston, IL: Northwestern University Press.

Rosenthal, D.M. 2005. *Consciousness and Mind*. Oxford: Clarendon Press.

Russell, B. 1945. *A History of Western Philosophy*. Simon & Schuster, p. 254.

Sacks, O. 2017. *The River of Consciousness*. New York: Knopf.

Saliba, G. 1994. *A History of Arabic Astronomy: Planetary Theories During the Golden Age of Islam*. New York: New York University Press.

Sartre, J.-P. 1943. *Being and Nothingness*. Translated by H.E. Barnes. New York: Washington Square Press, 1956.

Sauer, P. 2014. 'High levels of cynicism associated with lower income levels later in life, study says', PsyPost. Available at: www.psypost.org/high-levels-of-cynicism-associated-with-lower-income-levels-later-in-life-study-says/

Saussure, F. de 1983. *Course in General Linguistics*. Edited by C. Bally and A. Sechehaye, Translated by R. Harris. London: Duckworth.

Schleiermacher, F. 1998. *Hermeneutics and Criticism and Other Writings*. Edited and translated by A. Bowie. Cambridge: Cambridge University Press.

Schuetz, A. 1943. 'The Problem of Rationality in the Social World', *Economica New Series*, Vol. 10, No. 38. Available at: www.jstor.org/stable/2549460

Searle, J.R. 1992. *The Rediscovery of the Mind*. Cambridge, MA: MIT Press.

Seligman, M.E.P. 2002. *Authentic Happiness: Using the New Positive Psychology to Realize Your Potential for Lasting Fulfillment*. New York: Free Press.

Senge, P.M., Cambron-McCabe, N., Lucas, T., Smith, B., Dutton, J. & Kleiner, A. 2000. *Schools That Learn: A Fifth Discipline Fieldbook for Educators, Parents, and Everyone Who Cares About Education*. New York: Doubleday.

Seppala, E. 2017. 'Is Cynicism Ruining Your Love Life?', Psychology Today. Available at: www.psychologytoday.com/intl/blog/compassion-matters/201705/is-cynicism-ruining-your-love-life

Science Council. Available at: sciencecouncil.org

Singer, P. 1975. *Animal Liberation*. New York: Random House.

Skinner, B.F. 1953. *Science and Human Behavior*. New York: Macmillan.

Slaby, J. 2021. 'Ontic (Ontisch)', in Wrathall, M.A. (ed.) *The Cambridge Heidegger Lexicon*. Cambridge: Cambridge University Press, pp. 542-546.

Smith, J.K. and Jones, L.M. 2022. 'Beyond Mechanistic Approaches: Embracing Subjectivity in Understanding Disease Origins', *Journal of Holistic Health*, 47(3), pp. 215-230.

Snowden, D.J. 2002. 'Complex acts of knowing: Paradox and descriptive self-awareness', *Journal of Knowledge Management*, 6(2), pp. 100-111.

Snowden, D.J. 2005. 'Multi-ontology sense making: A new simplicity in decision making', *Informatics in Primary Care*, 13(1), pp. 45-53.

Snowden, D.J. and Boone, M.E. 2007. 'A leader's framework for decision making', *Harvard Business Review*, 85(11), pp. 69-76.

Snowden, D.J. and Stanbridge, P. 2004. 'The landscape of management: Creating the context for understanding social complexity', *Emergence: Complexity and Organization*, 6(1-2), pp. 140-148.

Sorell, T. 1991. *Scientism: Philosophy and the Infatuation with Science*. London: Routledge.

Tashvir, A. 2021. *BEING – The source of power*. Engenesis Publications: Sydney.

Tashvir, A. 2022. *Human Being – Illuminating the reality beneath the facade*. Engenesis Publications: Sydney.

Taylor, C. 1989. *Sources of the Self: The Making of the Modern Identity*. Cambridge, MA: Harvard University Press.

Tegmark, M. 2015. 'Consciousness as a state of matter', *Chaos, Solitons & Fractals*, 76, pp. 238-270. doi.org/10.1016/j.chaos.2015.03.014

Thompson, E. 2007. *Mind in Life: Biology, Phenomenology, and the Sciences of Mind*. Cambridge, MA: Harvard University Press.

Thompson, E. 2015. *Waking, Dreaming, Being: Self and Consciousness in Neuroscience, Meditation, and Philosophy*. New York: Columbia University Press.

Tillich, P. 1951. *Systematic Theology*. Chicago: University of Chicago Press.

Tononi, G. 2004. 'An Information Integration Theory of Consciousness', BMC Neuroscience, 5(1), p. 42. Available at: bmcneurosci.biomedcentral. com/articles/10.1186/1471-2202-5-42

Tye, M. 1995. *Ten Problems of Consciousness: A Representational Theory of the Phenomenal Mind*. Cambridge, MA: MIT Press.

Understanding Science Team. (no date) 'The Philosophy of Science', Understanding Science. Available at: undsci.berkeley.edu/ the-philosophy-of-science/

United Nations. 2015. *Transforming our world: the 2030 Agenda for Sustainable Development*. Available at: sdgs.un.org/2030agenda

Van der Kolk, B. 2014. *The Body Keeps the Score: Brain, Mind, and Body in the Healing of Trauma*. New York: Viking.

Varela, F.J., Thompson, E. and Rosch, E. 1991. *The Embodied Mind: Cognitive Science and Human Experience*. Cambridge, MA: MIT Press.

Visser, F. 2003. *Ken Wilber: Thought as Passion*. Albany, NY: State University of New York Press.

Wall, P.D. 2000. *Pain: The Science of Suffering.* London: Weidenfeld & Nicolson.

Walton, D. 1995. *A Pragmatic Theory of Fallacy.* University of Alabama Press.

Watson, D., Clark, L.A. and Tellegen, A. 1988. 'Development and validation of brief measures of positive and negative affect: The PANAS scales', *Journal of Personality and Social Psychology*, 54(6), pp. 1063-1070. doi. org/10.1037/0022-3514.54.6.1063

Watson, J. B. 1913. 'Psychology as the behaviorist views it', *Psychological Review*, 20(2), pp. 158-177.

Wheeler, M. 2013. 'Martin Heidegger', in Zalta, E.N. (ed.) *The Stanford Encyclopedia of Philosophy* (Spring 2013 Edition). Available at: plato. stanford.edu/archives/spr2013/entries/heidegger/

Wilber, K. 1984. *Quantum Questions: Mystical Writings of the World's Great Physicists.* Boston: Shambhala Publications.

Wilber, K. 1990. *Kosmic Consciousness* [Audio series]. Louisville, CO: Sounds True.

Wilber, K. 1995. *Sex, Ecology, Spirituality: The Spirit of Evolution.* Boston: Shambhala Publications.

Wilber, K. 1996. *A Brief History of Everything.* Boston: Shambhala Publications.

Wilber, K. 1997. *The Eye of Spirit: An Integral Vision for a World Gone Slightly Mad.* Boston: Shambhala Publications.

Wilber, K. 2000. *A Theory of Everything: An Integral Vision for Business, Politics, Science, and Spirituality.* Boston: Shambhala Publications.

Wilber, K. 2000. *Integral Psychology: Consciousness, Spirit, Psychology, Therapy.* Boston: Shambhala Publications.

Wilber, K. 2000. *The Collected Works of Ken Wilber, Volume 1.* Boston: Shambhala Publications.

Wilber, K. 2001. *A Theory of Everything: An Integral Vision for Business, Politics, Science, and Spirituality.* Boston: Shambhala Publications.

Wilber, K. 2001. *Eye to Eye: The Quest for the New Paradigm.* Boston: Shambhala Publications.

Wilber, K. 2006. *Integral Spirituality: A Startling New Role for Religion in the Modern and Postmodern World.* Boston: Integral Books.

Wilber, K. 2007. *Integral Vision: A Very Short Introduction to the Revolutionary Integral Approach to Life, God, the Universe, and Everything.* Boston: Shambhala Publications.

Wilber, K. 2014. *The Fourth Turning: Imagining the Evolution of an Integral Buddhism.* Boston: Shambhala Publications.

Wrathall, M.A. (ed.) 2021. *The Cambridge Heidegger Lexicon.* Cambridge: Cambridge University Press.

Yalom, I.D. 1980. *Existential Psychotherapy.* New York: Basic Books.

Young, J. 2001. *Heidegger's Philosophy of Art.* Cambridge: Cambridge University Press.

Young, R.M. 1985. 'Darwin's Metaphor: Nature's Place in Victorian Culture', *Science as Culture*, 1(1), pp. 60-83.

About the Author

A shkan Tashvir is a multi-disciplinary best-selling author and philosopher who has achieved significant attention for his ever-evolving body of work bridging the worlds of philosophy, business, technology and human potential. His frameworks, theories and books support individuals and organisations in comprehending and navigating complex concepts. Best known for developing The Being Framework, an ontological paradigm for leadership, performance and effectiveness adopted by thousands of leaders in over 53 countries to date, Ashkan continues to expand his work, which combines deep philosophical insights with practical guidance on the most effective ways to achieve sustainable personal growth and organisational excellence.

Having experienced intense challenges many can't fathom, Ashkan is committed to empowering others and serving humanity to help make the world a better place. Instead of being permanently scarred by life's brutality, he gained a unique perspective and learned the importance of being responsible for one's own choices and actions.

Through his scholarly pursuits, Ashkan has developed a deep respect for and knowledge of the works of philosophers and thinkers from Eastern, Western, Persian and faith-based traditions throughout the ages. His radical analyses of contemporary and existing approaches to understanding the world, existence, how we make sense of our lives and leadership have established him as a thought-provoking and original thinker. He links philosophical principles with practical applications and emphasises uniting different viewpoints and recognising their commonalities, a unique approach that resonates with a diverse audience and has established him as a significant voice in contemporary intellectual and philosophical discourse. In recognition of his frameworks, theories, vision and overall contribution to humanity, Ashkan was awarded an honorary doctorate in Business Administration from the College de Paris in 2024.

In addition to his intellectual and philosophical pursuits, Ashkan applies his body of work across a range of real-world and current contexts with a key focus on the economy. Here, he not only builds frameworks and models but also leverages entrepreneurship and investment to address critical areas that need attention in the world. In this capacity, his work has led to the creation of Engenesis, a global platform for human transformation, and Engenesis Ventures, a venture-building organisation that leads an international portfolio of startup companies. Beyond his business, writing pursuits and studies, Ashkan enjoys spending time with his family and their much-loved dogs. He is also an avid collector, a proficient cook and musician and relishes quality time in nature.

Connect with the Author and Explore Related Resources

Connect with Ashkan

Engenesis Platform: ashkan.engenesis.com

Youtube: https://www.youtube.com/@AshkanTashvir

LinkedIn: https://www.linkedin.com/in/tashvir/

Access Metacontent-related resources

Information and ordering details: https://ashkantashvir.com/metacontent

Diagrams: https://ashkantashvir.com/metacontent/diagrams

References: https://ashkantashvir.com/metacontent/resources

Explore Ashkan's other books

BEING: https://ashkantashvir.com/being

Human Being: https://ashkantashvir.com/human-being

Becoming – The Emergence of Being:
https://ashkantashvir.com/becoming/the-emergence-of-being

Find articles, events, courses, programs and communities

https://www.engenesis.com

Learn more about the Being Framework

Why being matters: https://engenesis.com/a/why-being-matters

How your way of being determines the results in your life –
An introduction to the Being Framework:
https://engenesis.com/a/how-your-way-of-being-determines-the-results-in-your-life

How the integrity of our Being is critical to an organisation's
performance – The application of the Being Framework in the
workplace (includes five workplace case studies):
https://engenesis.com/a/how-the-integrity-of-our-being-is-critical-to-an-organisations-performance-the-application-of-the-being-framework-in-the-workplace

The Being Profile: https://www.beingprofile.com

www.ingramcontent.com/pod-product-compliance
Lightning Source LLC
Chambersburg PA
CBHW052014030426
42335CB00026B/3141